The Science and Practice of Cheese-Making

by

Lucius Lincoln Van Slyke
Charles Albert Publow

APPLEWOOD BOOKS
Bedford, Massachusetts

The Science and Practice of Cheese-Making

was originally published in

1913

ISBN: 978-1-4290-1073-3

Thank you for purchasing an Applewood book.
Applewood reprints America's lively classics—
books from the past that are still of interest
to the modern reader.
For a free copy of
a catalog of our
bestselling
books,
write
to us at:
Applewood Books
Box 365
Bedford, MA 01730
or visit us on the web at:
For cookbooks: foodsville.com
For our complete catalog: awb.com

Prepared for publishing by HP

AMERICAN CHEDDAR CHEESE

The Science *and* Practice *of* Cheese-Making

A Treatise on the Manufacture *of* American Cheddar Cheese and other varieties
intended as a text-book for the use of dairy teachers and
students in classroom and workroom; prepared also
as a handbook and work of reference for the
daily use of practical cheese-makers
in cheese-factory operations

By

Lucius L. Van Slyke, Ph.D.

*Chemist of the New York Agricultural
Experiment Station*

and

Charles A. Publow, A.B., M.D., C.M.

*Associate Professor of Dairy Industry in the New York State
College of Agriculture at Cornell University*

Illustrated

New York
Orange Judd Company
1910

PREFACE

This book has been prepared to supply a need definitely expressed by dairy teachers, dairy students and cheese-makers. To meet the requirements of to-day, a book on cheese-making must be something more than a mere description, in a recipe-like form, of certain operations to be performed; it must also make prominent the reasons for each step in every operation and present as clearly as possible the facts and principles underlying the methods; in other words, it must present the science as well as the practice of cheese-making.

Knowledge of cheese-making, as of any art, is two-sided, practical and scientific. Practical knowledge tells us *what to do;* scientific knowledge gives us the *reasons for what is done.* Practice consists in *doing* things; science, in *knowing* things. Knowledge, to be complete, must be both practical and scientific; we must know not only *what* particular things to do but *why* we do them. Just in proportion as the practical and the scientific sides of knowledge advance together, does the practice become more nearly perfect. The more one knows, the more and better can one do.

The *practice* of cheese-making embraces a systematic series of mechanical operations, which have been gradually developed by experience and observation. In its widest application, it includes (1) the production and care of milk; (2) the conversion of milk into cheese; and (3) the care of the manufactured product until it is ready to be used as food.

The *science* of cheese-making embraces a collection of the underlying facts and principles relating to the practice, arranged in systematic form so as to show their relations. For example, it includes, among other lines: (1) A knowledge of the constituents of milk—what each has to do in the making of cheese and how each is related to the yield, composition and quality of the product; (2) the changes which each constituent of milk may undergo and the effect of such changes upon the yield, composition and quality of cheese; (3) the action of micro-organisms upon the constituents of milk and of cheese; (4) the effect of unorganized ferments upon milk and cheese; (5) the effect of temperature, humidity and other conditions upon the chemical changes that take place during the operations of cheese-ripening.

While cheese has been made for thousands of years, the growth of accurate, systematic knowledge regarding its inner details has been extremely slow; but within the past twenty years there has been an era of unprecedented activity in the investigation of the chemical, biological and other problems connected with milk and cheese. As the result of the application of new knowledge thus gained, the practice of cheese-making has undergone marked improvements. The problems that are peculiar to the manufacture of American cheddar cheese have been studied extensively in the United States and Canada, mainly under government direction in some form, and more especially at agricultural experiment stations. Two institutions have been prominent for the extent and thoroughness of their investigations and for the far-reaching influence of the results of their work—the agricultural experiment stations of the states of Wisconsin and of New York (Geneva). The results of these and of other useful investigations are not now easily available, being scattered through many reports and bulletins, most of which can be found only in large libraries. One of the tasks proposed at the outset in the preparation of this book was to digest this large mass of valuable material and present the results in systematic form, thus making it for the first time readily available to all dairy students. An exhaustive, detailed history of these investigations would compel one to present some results and interpretations which more accurate work has later shown to be erroneous. Those for whose use this book has been prepared are more interested in knowing what the status of our present knowledge is than in studying the various details which have preceded. The chief aim, therefore, has been to digest and summarize the results of investigation in such a way as to give what, in the light of our present knowledge, we may now regard as the probable facts and their proper interpretation. This task is a somewhat discouraging one, because new facts are being rapidly added to our knowledge and, in consequence, what we may now hold as true is quite likely to need modification in the near future.

The main portion of this book is devoted to cheddar cheese for the obvious reason that this is the kind most extensively made in America. A few other kinds of cheese are briefly discussed, so far as the assigned limits permit. Even in relation to cheddar cheese, the book is not intended as an encyclopedia, but an effort has been made to have it reasonably complete.

The language used by the practical cheese-maker in describing the operations of cheese-making has inevitably expressed his theories or explanations of observed facts. Many expressions have persisted even after they were known not to be in accordance with facts. It has seemed highly desirable that such inaccuracies should be corrected and the language made to correspond with our advanced knowledge. In addition, there have been many inaccurate and loose expressions in common use which have come simply from carelessness and lack of precision. Such expressions have been carefully revised in the preparation of this book.

A few words in regard to the general plan of the book will not be out of place here. The subject matter is divided into five parts. The first part is devoted mainly to a description of the operations employed in making American cheddar cheese under normal conditions, including the care of cheese, factory construction, equipment, etc. This portion of the subject is placed first in order in the book, as a matter of convenience, because it is the portion which will be most commonly referred to in connection with practical work. In order to avoid overloading the description of methods of cheese-making with too many details in the way of explanations, precautions, etc., many of these points are discussed with fullness in later portions of the book, appropriate references being given in part first. The second part is devoted to a study of the various defects that may occur in cheese as the result of abnormal conditions in the process of cheese-making. The third part, which comprises more than one-half of the book, is devoted to the science of cheese-making. This is the first attempt to treat the subject in a comprehensive, systematic manner. It is realized that not all of the chapters will appeal equally to those who use the book. For a satisfactory understanding of Chapter XXIV, some knowledge of chemistry is required. The fourth part of the book contains a description of methods of making some other varieties of cheese than American cheddar. In the fifth and last part are given a description of the tests used in cheese-making, an indexed bibliography of the subject, and other matter of a miscellaneous character.

Each illustration has been carefully selected with reference to giving supplementary, helpful, and specific information. The use of illustrations as a means of padding the book, or as a source of entertainment without reference to the subject-matter, has been carefully avoided.

In using this book, teachers will adapt it to the special conditions under which they work or to the special purpose they have in mind. For example, the amount and kind of matter studied will differ in the case of short-course and of long-course students. Material will be found for those most advanced, as well as for beginners. Good judgment will need to be exercised in respect to the combination of the different parts, but assistance in this respect is given by means of specific references. It is not expected that any book, however complete and clear, will enable one to make cheddar cheese successfully without the help of a competent teacher.

It is appreciated that, in the preparation of a work on new lines, the results are inevitably far from perfect. Those who have occasion to use this book will confer a favor if they will be free to call the attention of the authors to any defects which they find, whether in the line of omissions, incomplete treatment or inaccuracy of statement.

As to the respective shares of the work for which the authors are severally responsible, Chapters II, III, IV, V and XXVII represent combined work; Mr. Van Slyke has written, for the most part, Chapters I, VI and VIII; Mr. Publow, except for some minor changes and additions, has written Chapters VII and IX to XIII inclusive; Mr. Van Slyke has written Chapters XIV to XXVI inclusive, and also Chapters XXVIII to XXX.

We desire here to express our appreciation of valuable assistance received in various ways from the following persons: Mr. G. G. Publow, Kingston, Ontario, Canada, Chief Dairy Instructor in cheese-making; Mr. George A. Smith, Geneva, N. Y., Dairy Expert at the New York Agricultural Experiment Station; Mr. Alfred W. Bosworth, Geneva, N. Y., Associate Chemist at the New York Agricultural Experiment Station; and Dr. Donald D. Van Slyke, New York City, Assistant Chemist at the Rockefeller Institute for Medical Research.

September, 1908.

CONTENTS

PART I.

The Manufacture of American Cheddar Cheese.

Page

PART II.

Defects of American Cheddar Cheese: Causes, Remedies and Means of Prevention.

PART III.

The Science of Cheese-Making: The Chemical, Biological and Other Relations of Milk and Cheese.

PART IV.

PART V.

Methods of Testing, Factory Organization and Literature.

ILLUSTRATIONS

Part I

The Manufacture of American Cheddar Cheese

Details of cheese-making operations from care of milk to sale of cheese.

Commercial qualities and methods of judging.

Cheese - factory construction and equipment.

The Science and Practice of Cheese-Making

CHAPTER I

The Care of Milk for Cheese-Making

ONE of the fundamental requisites of successful cheese-making is clean milk. The cheese-making process begins in reality on the premises of the milk producer; and, of all the details of the process, the one that is, and has always been, productive of most trouble is the improper handling of milk by patrons. There has usually been complete absence of any adequate method in caring for milk. The occasional skimming or watering of milk always calls forth the severest condemnation, and properly; but actual losses caused dairymen in this way are insignificant in comparison with the losses caused by carelessness and neglect in properly caring for milk. It is to be hoped that the time may come when deliberate carelessness and indifference in the production and care of milk will be regarded as little short of criminal. The value of milk in cheese-making depends, in no small degree, on the care it receives from the time it is drawn from the udder until it is delivered at the factory. The quality of milk in respect to its cleanliness determines, to a great extent, the quality of cheese that can be made from it.

When milk is not properly cared for by patrons, it may acquire undesirable characteristics, which injure its usefulness in cheese-making, such, for example, as high acidity, offensive odors and tastes, formation of gases, etc.

The causes of these defects will be briefly considered under four headings: (1) Bacterial infection, (2) absorption of flavors, (3) food eaten, (4) physiological or disease processes in cows.

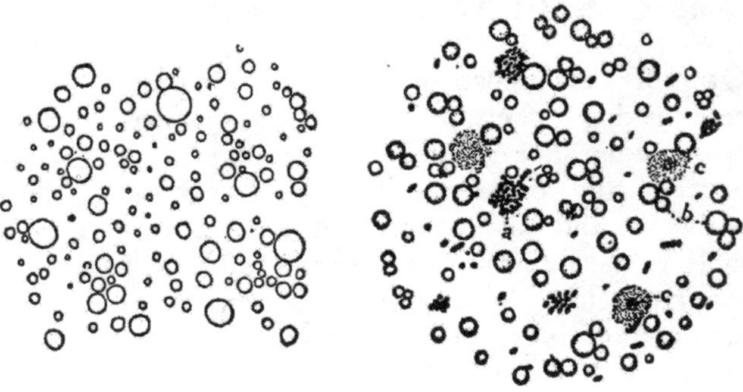

FIG. 1

Appearance of clean milk under the microscope. Only fat-globules are seen.

FIG. 2

Appearance of unclean milk under the microscope. The light, round bodies are fat-globules; the dark masses are groups of bacteria and cellular matter.

SOURCES OF BACTERIAL INFECTION

Milk, when drawn with careful precautions from the udder of a cow, contains comparatively few bacteria; but milk obtained and handled under ordinary conditions is found to contain large numbers, often several hundred thousand, in one cubic centimeter (somewhat less than one-quarter of an ordinary teaspoonful). The more dirt there is in milk, the more bacteria there will be. Bacteria and dirt always go together in dairy matters. The relations of bacteria to milk are considered in greater detail in Chapter XXII, p. 285.

The most common sources of bacterial infection are the following: (1) Unclean or unhealthy condition of cows; (2) unclean condition of stables or places of milking; (3) unclean condition of persons milking cows; (4) unclean condition of utensils used; (5) keeping milk in unclean surroundings, and especially at temperatures above 60° F. after milking.

Unclean condition of cows.—The hair on cows favors the accumulation of dirt and dust. The condition is worse in proportion as cows are not regularly and thoroughly cleaned. Dust particles and hairs, laden with bacteria, are in position to drop into the milk-pail. While the hairs and coarse chunks of dirt may be removed from milk by straining, the bacteria are, in large part, washed off into the milk and cannot be removed by any ordinary process of straining.

Unclean condition of stable.—A dirty condition of the floors, walls and ceilings of a stable tends to contaminate milk. Any condition in the stable that affords a supply of floating dust at the time of milking furnishes additional bacteria for milk

Unclean condition of milker.—The hands and clothing of a milker may easily be loaded with bacteria and thus become a source of infection. Particularly objectionable is the filthy practice of moistening the hands with milk when milking.

Unclean utensils, especially the milk-pails, strainers and milk-cans. The cracks and joints of **all**

utensils made of tin, unless great care in cleaning is used, contain dirt that holds large numbers of bacteria. Rust and imperfect soldering of joints furnish places for dirt to get out of easy reach. Without prompt and extreme care, strainers easily become filthy and are then simply breeding places for bacteria. When milk cans are used for carrying back whey to the farm from the cheese-factory, the cans often are not cleaned promptly, and, when finally attended to, are not treated with proper thoroughness. Through the medium of a dirty whey-vat, filth, as well as disease, germs may be distributed throughout the whole neighborhood. Even epidemics of typhoid fever have been traced to this source of infection; certain diseases have been similarly distributed among farm animals, as, for example, tuberculosis in calves and hogs.

Unclean surroundings after milking.—Milk, even when drawn under the cleanest possible conditions, very easily becomes contaminated by being kept, even for a short time, in any place that is not clean.

Keeping milk cool.—At temperatures above 60° F., milk more rapidly undergoes fermentation changes than at lower temperatures (p. 290).

ABSORPTION OF FLAVORS

Milk, particularly when warm, possesses remarkable ability to absorb and retain odors present in the surrounding air. The most common sources of such odors are the manure in unclean stables and any strong-smelling food present in the stable during milking-time. Among the most common conditions under which undesirable flavors are absorbed are the keeping of milk in or near cellars, silos, stables, pig-pens, or any place where strong-smelling substances of any kind are present.

FLAVORS FROM FOOD EATEN

Certain foods that have strong taste and odor impart to milk their characteristic flavors when eaten within a few hours before milking. Most common among these are onions, garlic, rape, turnips, leeks, cabbages, ragweed and decayed ensilage. Experiments have shown that with most of these the effects are largely, if not entirely, avoided when milk is not drawn for 8 to 12 hours after such food is eaten, provided an abnormal amount has not been taken. Similar results, but in milder form, may come from the feeding of excessive quantities of such materials as swill, brewers' grains and distillery slops. It is a safe rule, in the case of milk to be used for cheese, not to use at all such foods as are in danger of tainting milk, such as turnips, cabbages, rape, etc., and to keep cows where they cannot get at anything that may endanger the quality of the milk for cheese-making. Some green fodders, like second-growth clover, rye, etc., have been found to produce gassy and tainted milk and cheese. Such a condition is more likely due to bacteria on these foods than to any peculiar property in the foods themselves.

There is one marked point of difference between bad flavors of bacterial origin and those coming from absorbed flavors and strong-smelling food. The latter manifest their presence in the milk clearly when the milk is delivered at the factory and may be largely removed by proper aeration and care in the cheese-making operations; but those of bacterial origin do not usually reveal their presence until the cheese-making process is well along, or not even until the cheese has been made and acquired some age.

PHYSIOLOGICAL OR DISEASE PROCESSES IN COWS

It is well known that if a cow is abnormally heated or excited just before milking, tainted milk and cheese may result. Such a condition may be brought about by dogging cows or any form of ill treatment. Many diseases directly affect cow's milk and render it unfit for use in making cheese.

HOW TO OBTAIN CLEAN MILK

We have seen that the one chief source of bacteria is dirt. Hence, the one thing needful to prevent bacteria getting into milk is extreme cleanliness at every point of contact with the milk. The following suggestions are given to indicate what is meant by cleanliness in connection with milking and caring for milk.

Cows should be clean and healthy.—Too much pains cannot be taken to keep cows clean. In addition to regular currying and brushing all over, the udder and adjacent portions of the body should be carefully brushed before milking and also wiped with a damp, clean cloth. The udder should also be wiped after milking. . The best way to clean the parts is by using warm water and a cloth. The cleaning is made easier by clipping the hair close to the abdomen, udder and flanks. Dry-brushing of the udder before milking should not be practiced, as it makes conditions worse by stirring up dust which settles into the milk-pail.

The stable.—Every condition about the stable should be regulated with reference to absence of dirt, an abundant supply of pure air, and a direct exposure to sunlight. The floors should be tight and of a material not readily absorbing liquids. An abundance of clean bedding should be used, and the manure should be removed more frequently than once a day, and, in any case, not immediately before milking. The walls and ceiling should be swept often enough to prevent the accumulation of dust, but never just before milking-time. Once a year, at least, it is wise to clean the entire stable with extreme care and then go over the whole with a generous coat of whitewash. At such a time the stable should be thoroughly disinfected if there has been any contagious disease in the stable. The surroundings outside of the stable should be kept in a clean condition, so as not to interfere with the supply of pure air. Where water pressure can be had, as in case of a windmill, storage tank, etc., hose should be used in cleaning.

Milking.—The milker should wash his hands carefully before milking and have them perfectly dry while milking. It is also desirable to have a special coat or jacket for milking, made of some material that will not catch or hold dust easily. Only small-top milking-pails should be used. (Fig. 3.)

Cleaning dairy utensils.—All utensils that come in contact with the milk, such as milk-pails, milk-cans, aerators, etc., should be made of metal, preferably of pressed tin, with smooth, well-flushed joints and perfect seams. They should be kept entirely free from rust. Such vessels should never be allowed to dry when dirty, as dried particles of milk are particularly difficult to remove. In cleaning dairy utensils, rinse them first with cold or lukewarm water; and then scrub with a brush, using water containing some good washing-powder that will remove grease. Then scald

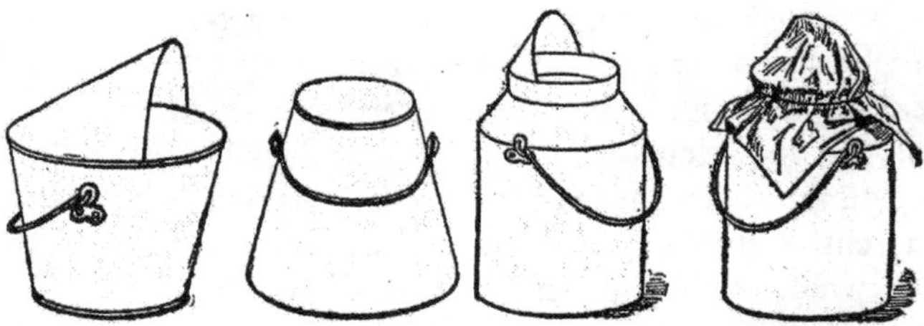

FIG. 3—DIFFERENT STYLES OF SANITARY MILKING-PAILS

with boiling water and complete the cleansing, if possible, by exposing to a jet of live steam for three to five minutes. Never dry with a cloth, but, when practicable, expose the utensils finally to direct sunlight for a few hours. Dust and flies should be prevented from entering the cans after washing. Strainers should be washed immediately after using, cleaning first in tepid water, following with hot water and soap or washing-powder and finally with hot water and then with steaming or boiling.

Treatment of milk after milking.—As soon as each cow is milked, the milk should be removed from the stable to some room free from all odors and with cleanly surroundings. The milk should be at once strained through a brass-wire strainer, having not less than fifty meshes to the inch, and also through three or four thicknesses of cheese-cloth. Still

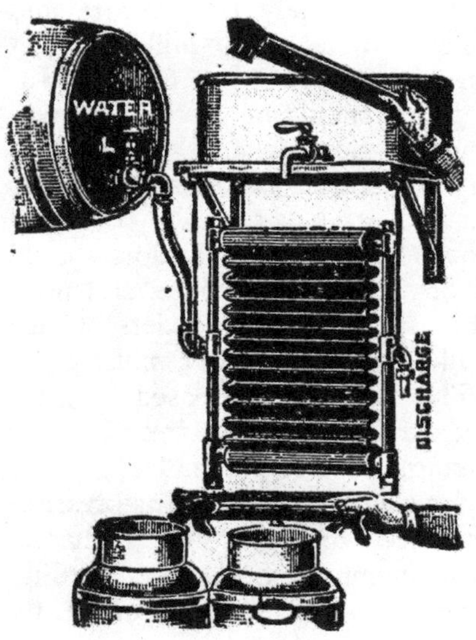

FIG. 4

A quick way of cooling milk. The milk in a thin layer runs over a surface made cold by running ice-water. The same water can be used repeatedly by adding ice each time. This method should be used only when the surrounding air is pure.

FIG. 5

The milk contained in these long "shot-gun" pails or cans, placed in ice-water, is stirred occasionally to insure even cooling.

more effective results in straining can be secured by the use of absorbent cotton, though its expense may make its use impracticable under ordinary conditions. After straining, cool at once to 60° F., or better to 50° F., by ice or cold water. (Figs. 4 and 5.)

Under usual conditions, it is best to cool the milk with as little exposure to air as possible and then cover it when milking is completed.

Aeration, if needed (p. 120), should be carefully performed as follows for the best results: (1) Aeration should take place only in a pure atmosphere. (2) Aeration should be performed at body temperature and therefore is best done immediately after milking. (3) Aeration should *precede* cooling and not be simultaneous with it. (4) Aeration should be carried out over the most extensive surface possible and as slowly as possible. Under ordinary farm conditions aeration is better not attempted.

Feeding-time.—Foods having marked odors should be fed only after milking and then at once, and none should be left in the stable. Dry fodders, which furnish dust, should likewise be fed after milking.

Diseased milk.—The milk of diseased animals should not be used nor that of animals fresh in milk before the ninth milking. Colostrum milk (p. 158) should never be used for cheese-making. The presence of such milk seriously affects the operations of cheese-making in the following manner: Soon after cutting, the curd becomes softer and will not firm sufficiently to make good cheese.

Contagious diseases.—No person suffering from, or recovering from, a contagious disease, nor any person that has anything to do in caring for such a person, should be allowed to have any contact with the dairy.

JUDGING MILK FOR CHEESE-MAKING

The only solution of the problem of obtaining clean milk for cheese-making lies in the education of the milk producer. It is necessary to do more than distribute printed instructions. Personal inspection of individual farm premises is also necessary. But it is essential, in addition to these methods of education, to give some additional specific inducement which will impress each patron as nothing else will and lead him to recognize not only the general importance of producing clean milk, but the application to him personally. The most effective means of making a deep impression is to give each one an opportunity to see how far his milk departs from the recognized standard of milk that is clean enough for making good cheese. These results can be realized by the introduction of a system of judging milk; and if the results of each judging can be made to affect the dividends, the patron soon realizes how near or how far from the proper standard his milk is.

The following method is suggested as an effective one in judging cheese-factory milk: Examine the milk for (1) acidity, (p. 426); (2) dirt in suspension, (p. 434); (3) micro-organisms by the fermentation test, (p. 434); and (4) flavor. Use the following scale of points for scoring milk:

When perfect

Acidity	15
(Acidity not over 0.18 per cent.)	
Dirt	15
(No dirt in suspension.)	
Fermentation test	45
(No signs of abnormal ferments.)	
Flavor	25
(Entire freedom from abnormal odor and taste.)	

In each milk, the score is diminished in the case of each quality if the milk shows any imperfections. This system will be found effective in application, if the judging is done carefully and the results made known to the patrons. If patrons can be persuaded to apply the results of such judging to the distribution of dividends, the work would be more effective, of course. For example, a patron's dividend could be marked down one cent per 100 pounds of milk for each ten points his milk scored below 100 on the above system. Of course, this method does not apply to cases in which the milk is obviously bad when brought to the factory. The only remedy in such cases is to refuse the milk altogether.

This is a matter which should be discussed at the annual meeting of patrons, in case of co-operative factories, when some definite policy should be adopted and intelligently enforced. For a more complete treatment of the subject of judging and scoring milk, see Modern Methods of Testing Milk and Milk Products, pp. 182-192 (published by the Orange Judd Co.).

CHAPTER II

Preliminary Steps in Making
- Cheddar Cheese

In entering upon the detailed study of the methods of cheese-making, we shall present the subject in accordance with the following outline of the different steps in the various operations that are performed:

    (1)   System of keeping records of the operations of cheese-making.

    (2)   First care of milk at the factory.
    (3)   Ripening the milk.
    (4)   Adding color.
    (5)   Coagulating the milk by rennet.
    (6)   Cutting the curd.
    (7)   Heating the curd.
    (8)   Removing the whey from the curd.
    (9)   Cheddaring the curd.
  (10)   Milling the curd.
  (11)   Salting and pressing curd and dressing cheese.
  (12)   Care, shipment and sale of cheese.

In describing the details of the methods of making American cheddar cheese, we shall limit our treatment largely to normal conditions, reserving for separate treatment abnormal conditions (p. 115). An effort is made not to overload the description with unnecessary details. The explanation of many details is given in other chapters, to which reference will be made as needed, instead of incorporating them with the description of the cheese-making operations.

SYSTEM OF KEEPING RECORD OF THE OPERATIONS OF CHEESE-MAKING

Few manufacturing processes require more careful and more skilled mechanical manipulation than does cheese-making; none demands more responsibility and intelligence. A successful cheese-maker must be quick to think and to act; he must know the details of his process and the principles underlying these details, and be able to apply his knowledge in controlling variations caused by climatic, biological and chemical conditions. In beginning his daily work, a maker should have clearly in mind the ideal he wishes to realize in the finished cheese, and should conduct his work with this end in view. It is absolutely essential to the highest success to keep daily records of the details of the work for constant reference. Below, we give a detailed blank form, and advise all cheese-makers and students of cheese-making to make constant and faithful use of it in their daily work:

1. Vat used (number of vat).
2. Condition of milk (flavor, temperature, acidity).
3. Amount of milk in vat .... pounds.
4. Fat in milk..........per cent.   Casein in milk...........per cent.
5. Ripeness of milk by—
   1. Acidity-test.................................,per cent of acidity.
   2. Marschall rennet-test...................................spaces.
   3. Monrad rennet-test ....seconds.
6. Kind of starter used..............Acidity..................per cent.
7. Amount of starter used.....................................pounds.
8. Time when starter was added.........................a. m.   p. m.
9. Amount of color added.
10. Kind of color used.
11. Temperature of milk when rennet was added..............degrees F.
12. Ripeness of milk when rennet was added—
   1. By rennet-test.............................seconds or   spaces
   2. By acidity-test..per cent.
13. Time when rennet was added........................a. m.   p. m.
14. Amount of rennet (or pepsin) used..............ounces or   grams.
15. Amount of rennet (or pepsin) used per 1,000 pounds of
   milk ....ounces or   grams.
16. Time when curd was cut.............................a. m.   p. m.
17. Time in coagulating.......................................minutes.

18. Condition of curd when cut (hard, soft, etc.).
19. Time when heating began.............................a. m.   p. m.
20. Acidity-test of whey when heating began....................per cent.
21. Temperature to which milk was heated after cutting, etc......degrees F.
22. Time at which temperature was reached...............a. m.   p. m.
23. Test when whey was removed—
       1. By hot-iron test.. inches.
       2. By acidity-test.................................... per cent.
24. Time at which whey was removed....................a. m.   p. m.
25. Time from cutting curd to removal of whey..........hours   minutes
26. Amount of fat in whey..per cent.
27. Condition of curd (sweet, tainted, solid, gassy, floating, etc.).
28. Time when curd was milled.........................a. m.   p. m.
29. Length of string on hot iron when curd was milled.............inches.
30. Acidity-test of whey-drippings when curd was milled..........per cent.
31. Time when curd was salted.........................a. m.   p. m.
32. Acidity-test of whey running from curd just before salting.....per cent.
33. Amount of salt used for 1,000 pounds of milk.................pounds.
34. Kind of salt used.
35. Time when curd was put in press....................a. m.   p. m.
36. Temperature of curd when put in press....................degrees F.
37. Condition of curd when put in press.
38. Kind of cheese made.
39. Number of cheeses made.
40. Time when cheese was dressed.......................a. m.   p. m.
41. Time when cheese was pressed.......................a. m.   p. m.
42. Time when cheese was taken from press..............a. m.   p. m.
43. Weight of green cheese...pounds.
44. Average amount of milk per pound of cheese..................pounds.
45. Amount of cheese from 100 pounds of milk....................pounds.
46. Amount of cheese made for 1 pound of milk-fat..............pounds.
47. Weather conditions (temperature, humidity etc.).
48. Amount of cheese from 100 pounds of milk calculated by
    formula 6 (p. 225).

    Special remarks.—(Include here any deviations from the usual modes of procedure not included in the foregoing list.)

FIRST CARE OF MILK AT THE FACTORY

Each can of milk, on arriving at the factory, should be carefully examined for acidity, cleanliness and abnormal flavors (p. 426). If any is sour or of bad flavor it should not be accepted. When any patron's milk is suspected, from the results of these tests, of containing ferments that work harm in cheese-making, the milk should be subjected to the fermentation test (p. 434). At any time when abnormal fermentations make trouble, each patron's milk should be thus treated until the source of trouble is located. For a quick test for acidity, see p. 428. When weighed, the milk should be strained through two layers of clean cheese-cloth to remove all insoluble dirt (p. 434). While the milk is accumulating in the vat, it should be stirred frequently up to the time of coagulating with rennet in order to keep the cream from separating. When the vat is full enough, the amount of milk present is figured, and the acidity of the milk is determined or a rennet-test made.

RIPENING MILK

This consists in the formation of a certain amount of lactic acid (p. 292). Its object is to control more completely the various operations of cheese-making; this is accomplished especially (1) by the repression of abnormal ferments; (2) by assistance in shrinking curd, expelling whey, and maturing the curd in body and texture. Lactic acid may be formed by allowing milk to stand a while at a temperature of about 86° F. When lactic acid bacteria are not present in abundance or are kept back in growth by injurious organisms, it is necessary to use a starter or culture.

Preparation of starter.—A starter is a material (usually milk), containing large numbers of lactic acid organisms, which is added to milk or cream for the purpose of causing lactic fermentation. Starters are of two kinds: (1) Natural and (2) commercial. (1) *Natural starters.*—A natural starter may be prepared as follows: Milk of the best possible character, taken under precautions necessary to insure cleanliness, is heated to 90° F. for one hour, aerated in a pure atmosphere, and immediately cooled to 65° F. In 24 hours the milk should be sufficiently sour to be ready for use. Some of this starter may be used in preparing a starter for the following day, putting a little into some skim-milk that has been heated to 180° F. for 30 minutes, cooled to 70° F., and then allowed to stand 18 to 24 hours. The starter may thus be propagated from day to day. Occasionally, almost pure cultures of lactic acid bacteria can be obtained in this way, but this is an exceptional experience. Results much more reliable come from the use of commercial starters. (2) *Commercial starters.*—Commercial starters are special preparations consisting of certain organisms that produce lactic acid. These are carefully prepared under the supervision of trained bacteriologists and sold to cheese-makers. They are usually known as cultures or pure cultures. The medium in which these organisms are sent out may be milk, broths, milk-sugar or porous paper. Proper directions, with necessary precautions, usually accompany these commercial preparations. Below is given a satisfactory method for the use of a commercial preparation in making a starter for cheese-making.

Inoculation of the culture.—In a can or glass vessel that has been thoroughly cleaned and sterilized with boiling water, place one quart of clean, sweet milk. Heat the milk to at least 185° F. for one hour by placing the can or vessel in boiling water. At the end of an hour cool the milk rapidly to 95° F. by setting the can or vessel in cold water. Then add the contents of the small bottle of a prepared culture to the milk, stirring it in with a sterilized spoon. Allow the milk to cool gradually to 70° F. and hold at this temperature for 24 hours. At the end of this time the milk should be sour and coagulated.

Propagation of starter.—In a can that has been thoroughly cleaned and sterilized, place two gallons of clean, fresh skim-milk. Heat the milk to 185° F. for one hour by setting the can in boiling water. Stir the milk frequently to insure even heating. After the milk has been held at this temperature for one hour, it may be cooled immediately to 70° F. by placing the can in cold water. Then add the contents of the small vessel that was prepared on the previous day, stirring it in with a sterilized spoon. Hold the tem-

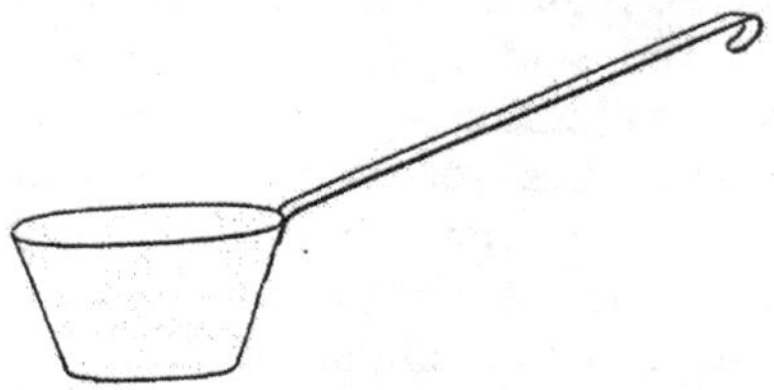

FIG. 6—THIS STYLE OF DIPPER HAS A SOLID HANDLE
AND IS EASY TO KEEP CLEAN IN EVERY PART

perature at 70° F. for 18 hours. At the end of this period the milk should be sour and firmly coagulated. A uniform starter can thus be prepared from day to day, always adding enough of the coagulated starter to the amount of pasteurized skim-milk necessary for the cheese-making process.

Precautions.—All vessels, pails, dippers, thermometers and everything with which the starter-milk comes in contact should be sterilized before being used. Starters should not be prepared from the milk mixed in the vat or from whey. A good starter is an invaluable aid in cheese-making, while a bad one is a sure source of trouble. As soon as the starter loses its clean, nutty, mild aroma and sharp taste, it should be replaced by a new one.

Use of starter in cheese-making.—The amount of starter that can safely be used will depend on the amount of acidity or ripeness of the milk at the start. Generally, from 0.5 to 2 per cent is sufficient, but, if the milk is very sweet, as much as 5 per cent can be used. In using a starter, reject the upper portion and pass the rest into the milk through a fine strainer. If colored cheese is being made, add the starter before the color; otherwise white spots in the curd may be produced.

Finding proper degree of ripeness.—The proper degree of ripeness can be ascertained by the following methods:

(1) By the use of the test for acidity (p. 426); (2) by the use of the Marschall rennet-test (p. 429); (3) by the use of the Monrad rennet-test (p. 431).

The general aim of ripening is to have such a degree of acidity when the rennet is added that the curd will remain in the whey not more than 2¾ to 3 hours. This time will vary with the seasons of the year, the important point being to have the curd firmed in the whey before too much acidity has developed. Usually when the acid test shows 0.19 to 0.21 per cent of acidity, or when the milk coagulates at 2½ spaces in the Marschall rennet-test, or in 45 to 60 seconds by the Monrad test, the proper degree of ripeness has been reached. Milk testing over 0.21 per cent acidity when delivered at the factory is generally overripe and liable to cause trouble; therefore, it should not be accepted, unless most of the other milk delivered at the time has considerably less acidity.

ADDING COLOR

When coloring-matter is used, it should be added just before the rennet, being diluted before addition and thoroughly mixed through the mass of milk. The amount used depends on the demands of different markets. About 1 ounce for 1,000 pounds of milk is generally sufficient, but the amount may vary from ½ ounce to 3 ounces.

PREPARATION AND ADDITION OF RENNET-EXTRACT

Adding rennet-extract is commonly known as "setting" milk with rennet. As soon as the milk is ripe enough the rennet-extract should be added. In the use of rennet, three points must be kept in mind: (1) Temperature of milk; (2) amount of rennet-extract to use; (3) method of adding rennet-extract and thorough stirring after addition.

(1) Temperature of the milk.—The ideal temperature, under normal conditions, is 86° F., although many successful cheese-makers prefer a temperature of 84° F. At higher temperatures the curd hardens too quickly to handle conveniently, and there is danger of loss of fat later in the cutting. Lower temperatures require a longer time for a proper degree of hardness, and, if the extra time is not allowed, give too soft a curd, which results in loss in cheese yield. The temperature should be uniform throughout the milk.

(2) Amount of rennet-extract to use.—This will depend on (1) the strength of the extract, (2) the temperature of the milk, (3) the acidity of the milk, (4) the composition of the milk, (5) the kind of cheese to be made, and (6) the temperature of curing (p. 61). In general, an amount sufficient to coagulate the milk fit for cutting in 25 to 35 minutes should- be used. Generally from 2½ to 4 ounces for 1,000 pounds of milk will suffice.

(3) Method of adding rennet-extract and subsequent treatment.—Before being added to milk, the rennet should be diluted with 40 times its volume of pure, cold water. The object of this is to enable one to distribute the rennet solution thoroughly and uniformly throughout the mass of milk before the rennet begins to coagulate the casein. Rennet acts more slowly when diluted with cold water (p. 307). The milk should be thoroughly stirred before the rennet is added. The diluted rennet should be gradually poured the whole length of the vat, and the milk at once stirred again for 3 to 5 minutes. A rake may be used to advantage for stirring. Then the surface is stirred gently to keep the cream from rising. All motion of the milk should be stopped as soon as, or before, coagulation starts. The vat should be covered to prevent cooling at the surface and to keep out flies and dust, and then left undisturbed until ready for cutting.

Causes of imperfect coagulation.—By imperfect coagulation, we mean (1) incomplete or delayed coagulation of casein, shown by slimy or gelatinous appearance of the coagulated milk and a curd containing too much whey; or (2) variation in degree of hardness in different portions of the mass of milk, some portions being too hard and others too soft. Imperfect coagulation results (1) in excessive loss of fat and of casein from the soft curd and (2) in imperfect texture and body in cheese, due to the hard pieces of curd.

The causes of imperfect coagulation may be:

(1)   For incomplete or delayed coagulation:
    (a)   Jarring of milk after coagulation starts.
    (b)   Weak rennet-extract or too small an amount.
    (c)   Low temperature, due to inaccurate thermometer (p. 309).
    (d)   The presence of formalin (p. 308).
    (e)   Abnormal milk, containing small percentage of casein or small percentage of calcium salts (p. 164).
    (f)   Pasteurized milk (p. 310).
    (g)   Presence of abnormal bacterial ferments.
    (h)   Heavily watered milk (p. 307).
    (i)   Use of badly rusted milk-cans (p. 309).

(2)   For uneven coagulation:
    (a)   Uneven temperature of milk in vat, due to lack of thorough agitation.
    (b)   Adding rennet to milk too soon after heating, while the sides and bottom of the vat are still hot. The curd sticks to the sides of the vat and makes cutting difficult.
    (c)   Agitation of milk after coagulation begins.
    (d)   Uneven distribution of rennet-extract.

CHAPTER III

Operations from Cutting Curd to Salting

CUTTING THE CURD

Purpose of cutting curd.—The object of cutting curd is to allow the whey to escape from it. The rapidity of the escape of whey increases with the smallness of the pieces of curd.

When to cut curd.—Curd must be cut at the right stage of hardness. The stage for cutting is ascertained in several ways. We give three of them. (1) The end of the index finger is inserted obliquely into curd half an inch or more and then slowly raised to surface. If the curd breaks apart with a clean fracture without leaving small bits of curd on the finger, and if the whey in the broken surface is clean and not milky, the curd is ready to cut. (2) Lay the back of the hand, including the fingers, on the surface of the curd near the edge of the vat and press it gently away from the side of the vat. As soon as it will separate from the side of the vat in a clean way, leaving no particles of curd on the side of the vat, it is ready to cut. (3) The following is probably the most accurate rule for determining when the curd should be cut: *Two and one-half times the period from adding rennet till the first thickening appears gives the time for cutting.*

25

Example:

Time when rennet was added, 7:30 A. M..

Time of first thickening, 7:40 A. M.

From adding rennet till first thickening=10 minutes.

2½ times 10 minutes=25 minutes.

7:30+25=7:55.

Time of cutting is 7:55 A. M.

When curd is cut too soon, the loss of fat, and probably of casein, is increased and there is a smaller yield of cheese. If the curd becomes too hard, it cannot be cut uniformly; if a wire knife is then used, the wires may break.

How to cut curd.—Uniformity in the size of pieces is the aim of good cutting. This can be most easily accomplished by cutting slowly lengthwise of the vat with a ⅜-inch steel horizontal knife having sharp edges. Then cut crosswise with a 5-16-inch perpendicular, wire knife. Finally, cut lengthwise with the same wire knife. Care should be taken not to smash the curd when inserting the knives or when turning them at the ends of the vat. The resulting cubes should be of uniform size to insure an even escape of whey, a well-regulated development of acidity in curd and a uniform color in the cheese. Extra losses of cheese constituents (p. 193) in the whey are due to carelessness or lack of skill in the cutting or in the subsequent stirring. The knives should be drawn straight and even and should not overlap the portions previously cut. The faster the cutting, the smaller and more uneven the cubes will be.

Effect of cutting curd fine or coarse.—The effect of cutting curd fine is to release the whey more rapidly and completely and to produce a cheese containing less moisture. This fact is made use of in the handling of overripe milk (p. 122); the quick escape of whey enables one to control better the acidity in the curd. Curd must be heated to a certain temperature for a certain length of time before it becomes firm enough to insure good body in the cheese. If the pieces of curd are larger, it takes longer for the whey to escape and longer for the pieces to contract and become firm. Consequently, if knives that cut coarser are used, the rennet must be added when the milk shows less acidity, in order to allow the curd to remain in the whey a longer time.

Behavior of curd after being cut.—After the curd is cut into small cubes, a slight coating or film begins to form on the outer surface of each cube. The existence of this film can be shown by breaking one of the curd cubes; the film can then be seen. The inner portion of the curd is observed to be softer, due to the larger amount of whey present. It is important that this film should not thicken or harden too rapidly and thus prevent the escape of whey in desired amount. The subsequent operations have for one of their important objects control of the expulsion of whey and simultaneous hardening or contracting of the pieces of curd. The contraction or hardening of the pieces of curd is known as "firming." It is probably due primarily to escape of whey. What share temperature, rennet and acidity each has in the process cannot now be stated definitely.

STIRRING CURD AFTER CUTTING

If the curd is not stirred immediately after cut-ting, it soon masses together or becomes lumpy. To prevent this, the curd must be kept in motion till the pieces become properly firmed. The stir-ring of the soft, tender curd should be very gentle at first and should be done with an agitator (Fig. 7). In large factories, steam-power agitators are used. After the pieces of curd become healed over on the surface by the formation of the film de-

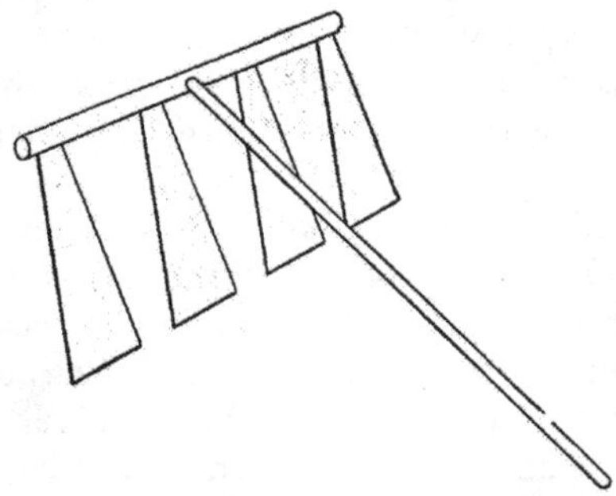

FIG. 7—McPHERSON HAND-AGITATOR FOR STIRRING
CURD IMMEDIATELY AFTER CUTTING

scribed above and start to contract, they can be stirred and kept separated more easily by using a wooden rake (Fig. 8). The curd should be pre-vented from collecting in the corners of the vat and from sticking to the sides. Rough handling of the soft curd crushes it and causes a severe decrease in the yield of cheese, as the result of increased loss of cheese-solids in the whey.

HEATING THE CURD

When to apply heat.—The rapidity with which the pieces of curd contract and the rapidity with which the lactic acid is being formed determine the time at which the heat should be applied. In any. case, the curd should be stirred gently for some time after cutting, until the small pieces have healed over, or formed a film, and have contracted slightly. Heat alone does not firm the curd. It is probably due to the combined action of heat, ren-

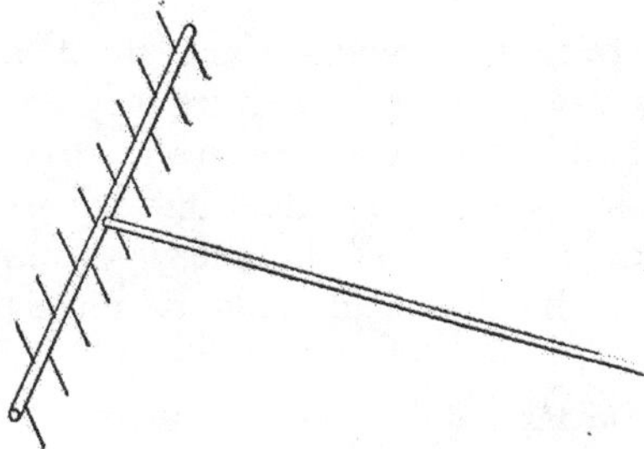

FIG. 8—DOUBLE-TOOTHED CURD-RAKE USED FOR
STIRRING CURD AFTER CUTTING

net and acidity. The firming and contraction of curd and expulsion of whey go on together. The faster the acidity is increased, the quicker will the curd contract. The action of heat in the process of contraction enables the curd to retain its firmness and also prevents the reabsorption of whey.

How high to heat curd.—The lower the temperature used for heating curd, provided the curd be properly firmed, the smoother will be the body of the cheese. As a rule, 98° to 100° F. will be high enough, but this can be varied from 96° F. in the springtime to 102° F. in the fall. Curd from milk rich in fat is harder to firm than curd from poor milk, owing generally to the smaller proportion of casein relative to fat. Thus, milk containing 3 to 3.6 per cent of fat ordinarily behaves at 94° to 96° F. the same as milk with 4 to 5 per cent of fat does at 98° to 102° F. In extreme cases, the temperature may have to be raised even higher to firm successfully the curd from overripe milk. High heating generally causes a corky or rubbery-bodied cheese.

How to regulate heat.—Care must always be taken not to raise the temperature of the curd too rapidly. Usually the temperature can be raised about 2° F. in every 5 minutes, but when the lactic acid formation is slow, 1° F. every 5 minutes may be sufficient. The following rule is a reliable guide in heating:

Rule for heating.—If, after cutting, the whey around the curd shows 0.12 per cent acidity, allow 60 minutes for heating; 0.13 per cent acidity, allow 40 minutes for heating; 0.14 per cent acidity, allow 30 minutes for heating; 0.145 per cent acidity, allow 25 minutes for heating; 0.15 per cent acidity, allow 20 minutes for heating.

It is noticeable that the whey at this stage contains 0.05 to 0.08 per cent less of acidity than the milk does when the rennet is added. This is due to the fact that the whey contains no casein and the casein in the milk has the power of acting like an acid in neutralizing alkali.

Applying heat too fast hardens the outside of the curd and prevents the escape of whey. The acid in the curd develops from the sugar present in the whey within the curd and not from the whey outside of the curd, so that, if too much whey is retained in the curd, too much acidity develops and an acid or sour cheese results.

WHEN TO REMOVE WHEY FROM CURD

How to ascertain.—Several indications show when the whey should be removed from the curd. (1) The pieces of curd should be contracted to less than one-half their original size. (2) They should be firm and rubber-like, or springy, so that when a mass of curd is pressed between the hands and then suddenly freed from pressure, the pieces should fall apart at once and show no tendency to stick together. (3) When firm, the curds should show fine threads $\frac{1}{8}$ inch long when rubbed on a clean, hot iron (p. 438). (4) The whey around the curd should have 0.16 to 0.18 per cent of acidity, as shown by the acid test. This will vary slightly, depending on the time required for removing the whey. The quantity of milk in the vat, the size of the outlet of the vat, and the condition of the curd should govern the amount of acidity developed at the time of starting to remove the whey. It is a good practice to draw off the whey down to the level of the curd in the vat a few minutes before sufficient acidity has developed. This gives a better chance to control the remainder. The most accurate rule to follow is to have 0.24

to 0.30 per cent of acidity in the whey running from the curd after it has been stirred dry enough and piled up for cheddaring. The amount of acidity developed will depend on the character of cheese desired and upon the amount of moisture left in the curd. A firm export cheese requires more acidity and less moisture than a quick-ripening cheese for home trade.

STIRRING CURD TO DRY IT

The proper place to stir and to dry the curd is in the whey, from the time the whey has reached the curd level until it is all removed. This gives a brighter and better color to the curd and requires less labor than when stirring is delayed until all whey has been removed. If the curd is not properly firmed, vigorous hand-stirring may cause serious loss of fat here. Too much free whey should not be left around or in the pieces of curd at this time, as it enables lactic acid to develop too fast, owing to the presence of the milk-sugar in the whey (p. 45).

CHEDDARING THE CURD

This operation is the main distinctive feature of the cheddar method of cheese-making. It consists essentially of two operations or a continuation of one operation in two stages: (1) *Piling* or *matting* of curd and (2) cutting curd into strips and continuing the operation of piling and repiling.

Piling or matting curd.—As soon as the curd has been stirred enough to become sufficiently dry, it should be piled evenly along the two sides of the vat, with an open channel 4 to 6 inches wide between the piles, to facilitate the ready drainage of the whey that comes from the curd. The vat should have dip enough to enable the escaping whey to pass away rapidly and keep it from lying in pools' around the curd. Up to this time the curd should not have been allowed to become lumpy, but, as far as possible, the small pieces should be kept separated. This results in a more uniform expulsion of whey, a more uniform development of acid and a more uniform color in the curd. Some cheese-makers use curd-sinks to dry the curd in during this stage. Others use strainer-racks on the bottom of the vats. In using these, the curd and whey are dipped in pails on to the racks, which are covered with cheese-cloth. The whey drains through the racks and the curd is easy to stir. The curd-sinks and vat-racks are of some aid in handling curd from overripe milk, but under normal conditions they have no particular advantage over the vat.

Cutting and repiling curd.—As soon as the curd has become matted together sufficiently, forming a solid mass about 6 inches deep, it should be cut into blocks or strips 6 to 8 inches wide and turned over, the top going on the bottom. This takes 15 to 20 minutes from the time of piling. If the curd contains excessive amounts of visible or free whey, the blocks should be cut very narrow and turned as soon as matted. After draining about 15 minutes, the strips are piled in layers two deep, each time the upper part being turned down. The blocks are then turned every 15 minutes until the operation is completed. After a while the strips may be piled in deeper layers. The repiling is performed again and again, always exposing to the air the portions that were turned inside on the previous piling, in order to keep the temperature uniform through the mass. The operation is hastened by piling the strips two or three layers deep. If the curd is very moist and the formation of acid goes on quickly, it is not advisable to pile the blocks in deep layers. It is better to separate them so that they will dry out as soon as possible.

Object of cheddaring operation.—The object of the cheddaring operation is to accomplish two results: (1) The formation of a curd containing less water by the removal of whey; and (2) the formation of a characteristic body and texture in the curd. The physical condition of the curd changes from a tough, rubber-like consistency with a high water content to a mass having a smooth, velvety appearance and feeling, and a softer, somewhat plastic consistency. The texture also changes so that the curd acquires a peculiar fibrous condition or grain, tearing off somewhat like the cooked meat of a chicken's breast. Along with these changes the curd forms longer strings on a hot iron, usually an inch or more after the cheddaring has continued for some time. Some chemical changes appear to take place in the proteins. The changes noted above are due to the formation of a substance in the curd which is dissolved in warm, 5 per cent brine (p. 147). This substance in pure condition forms very long strings when warm. (Figs. 32 and 33, p. 148.)

Completion of the cheddaring process.—The cheddaring process is regarded as complete when we have the following conditions: (1) The curd forms strings on a hot iron an inch to an inch and a half in length. (2) The whey running from the curd shows an acidity of 0.65 to 0.90 per cent, depending on the whey content of the curd and the manner in which it is cheddared. (3) The curd should be velvety in appearance and feeling, and tear apart like the breast-meat of a chicken.

MILLING CURD

When the cheddaring process is complete, as determined by the tests given, the curd is ready to mill. The objects of milling are to cut the curd into small pieces of uniform size, in order that the curd may be salted more evenly and handled more easily in salting during the rest of the cheese-making process; and also to permit the escape of more whey. In cheddaring the curd, it should be piled so that, when ready, the strips will be in convenient shape and size for milling. The mill should cut the curd into small pieces of uniform size, and should do it without crushing or squeezing the milk-fat from the curd. If a steam-power curd-mill is used, it should not be run too rapidly, for it will cut the curd unevenly and the texture of the cheese will be poor. After milling, the pieces of curd should be well stirred, kept apart, and freely exposed to fresh air. At this stage the freshly cut surfaces afford an excellent channel for the escape of gases and undesirable flavors. The airing and stirring are made easy by the use of forks.

After milling, the curd is piled up in order to flatten out pin-holes, if any, and stirred enough to keep it from matting together. The softening of the curd continues after milling, along with the further formation of lactic acid. The curd should be kept warm all the time.

If the operations up to this time have been properly managed, the whey remaining in the curd has become a part of it to such an extent that not a drop can be squeezed by pressure of the curd in the hand. If, however, the whey has not become perfectly incorporated with the curd-solids, more or less free or unassimilated whey is found inside the original, small pieces of curd; and, when these are broken in the milling, white whey runs out of the curd, involving considerable loss of fat.

CHAPTER IV

Operations from Salting Curd to Removal from Press

SALTING CURD

When to apply salt.—After the pieces of curd have become well contracted and feel silky and mellow, they are ready to be salted. The curd at this stage should show by the hot-iron test strings 1½ inches long, but this test cannot be relied upon, as most curds become more or less greasy after milling, and do not so easily stick to a hot surface. A test of the whey exuding from the curd is much more reliable. It should have 0.90 to 1.2 per cent of acidity, as shown by the acid test. This is the most reliable test for indicating when curd is ready for salting, and it is equally useful at other stages; but students and cheese-makers should be familiar with the use of all tests.

It is often a difficult matter to tell just when a curd is in the best condition for salting, and this knowledge comes only as the result of long experience. Generally, the curd smells like toasted cheese when rubbed on a hot iron; and, when squeezed between the hands, a certain amount of fat may start, but these tests are not reliable. The per cent of acidity allowed to develop before salting depends on the condition of the curd and also the conditions of temperature and moisture under which the cheese is to be stored and ripened. If the cheese is to be kept for any length of time in a warm room, the development of acidity should be greater and the curd matured more. This is especially true if the curd is gassy or weak-bodied. If the curd is free from gas, and the cheese is to be kept in cold storage till ready for consumption, the acidity need not be so great; but, in any case, it should be sufficient to insure a mellow body in the cheese.

Amount and kind of salt to use.—The amount of salt used depends on (1) the amount of whey in the curd, (2) its acidity, and (3) the type of cheese desired. For ordinary factory milk, from 1½ to 2½ pounds of salt for 1,000 pounds of milk used will be sufficient, but in extreme cases these limits may be exceeded. A moist curd is usually salted more. The weight of milk, however, is not an accurate basis for determining the amount of salt to use. It is much better to use the weight of curd or the percentage of fat in milk as indicated below. Assuming that curd ready for salting contains

Per cent of fat in milk	From 1,000 pounds of milk Pounds of milled curd containing 40 per cent of water	Amount of salt to use Lbs. Ozs.
3.0	87.4	1 12
3.1	89.8	1 13½
3.2	92.2	1 15
3.3	94.6	2 ½
3.4	97.0	2 2
3.5	99.4	2 3½
3.6	101.8	2 5
3.7	104.2	2 6½
3.8	106.6	2 8
3.9	109.0	2 9½
4.0	111.4	2 11
4.1	113.8	2 12½
4.2	116.2	2 14
4.3	118.6	2 15½
4.4	121.0	3 2
4.5	123.4	3 3½

about 40 per cent of water, 1,000 pounds of milk would furnish about the amounts of curd for the different percentages of fat in milk shown on page 38.

Salt of fairly coarse grain is preferable, because it dissolves more slowly and penetrates the curd more thoroughly. Special brands of cheese salt are prepared by manufacturers and are generally shipped in paper-lined barrels.

How to apply salt.—The curd should be spread out thinly over the bottom of the vat, and, if necessary, cooled to 90° F. Both curd and salt should be free from lumps. The salt should be put on in at least three applications, and each time should be evenly distributed over the surface. After each sprinkling of salt, the curd should be well stirred with forks. Applying salt too rapidly or all at once hardens the outside of the small pieces of curd and hinders its absorption. A fine hair or copper sieve is of considerable aid in regulating the application of salt. Salt in cheese affects flavor, body, texture and keeping quality (p. 343).

Effects of salting.—While salt is added mainly for the sake of the taste it gives to cheese, it produces other effects, such as (1) aiding in removal of whey; (2) hardening and contracting the curd; (3) checking or retarding the formation of lactic acid; and (4) checking undesirable forms of fermentation. An unsalted cheese cures more rapidly and is apt to develop a bitter flavor, the intensity increasing with increase of ripening temperature. Excessive salting makes a cheese mealy, because too dry, and it cures slowly. Much of the salt added passes into the whey. Green cheese normally salted contains 0.6 to 1 per cent of salt, and this increases somewhat in the ripened cheese, through loss of moisture (p. 344).

An increased quantity of salt is of advantage in correcting such defects as gassy, highly acid, or very soft cheese. Excessive loss of fat may often be avoided by the early addition of salt, which hardens the surface of the pieces of curd and prevents further exudation of fat.

PRESSING CURD AND DRESSING CHEESE

Condition and temperature of curd when ready for press.—Before the curd is placed in the hoops, the salt should be completely dissolved; the curd should feel mellow and silky. No fixed pressing temperature can be prescribed even for normal curd, since there are several variable factors which we must take into consideration. We can say that, in general, under ordinary, normal conditions, the temperature should be not much above 80° F., with a range of variation from 78° to 85° F., according to certain conditions, among the most important of which are the following: (1) Size of cheese made; (2) temperature of room; (3) condition of curd; and (4) rate at which pressure is applied. Small-sized cheese, such as Young Americas, Prints and Picnics, should be put in press warmer than larger-sized cheese, since they cool more rapidly. During early spring, late fall, and winter months, the pressing temperature should be higher than during the summer months. During the hot weather of summer, it may be necessary to cool the curd before pressing, which can be done by running cold water around the outside of the vat, or by placing the curd ·in a cold room for a short time. One can usually allow a somewhat wider range in the pressing temperature when handling a normal curd than in the case of one which is noticeably defective, such as a greasy or a harsh curd. The faster a curd is put into the hoop and pressed, the lower the temperature it may be permitted to have.

The effects of pressing at too high a temperature are the following: (1) Excessive loss of fat and consequent loss of yield; (2) the pieces of curd become greasy on the outside and do not stick together perfectly, which results in producing cheese of less close texture on account of the increased number and size of the mechanical-holes; (3) greasy curd prevents bandage sticking to cheese; (4) high temperature favors development of gas and consequent huffing; (5) the loss of fat has the same effect as skimming milk, as it makes the cheese too dry.

The effects of pressing at too low temperature are the following: (1) The pieces of curd do not stick together perfectly, resulting in cheese of open texture and imperfect rind formation, which affords an opportunity for entrance of mold and skippers; (2) it may sometimes cause a mottled appearance when a sample is drawn by a cheese-trier; (3) the cheese retains more whey.

Object of pressing curd.—The object of pressing curd is to give the cheese a convenient form for handling and a definite, characteristic shape for market, and not alone to squeeze out whey, which should be removed mostly while the curd is in the vat. Pressing will not make a close-textured cheese, if the curd is gassy or too sweet. If the cheese is to be close in texture, the curd must be full matured before salting.

Preparing hoop for receiving curd.—A round cotton cap-cloth of the size of the hoop is wrung out of hot water and placed in the bottom of the hoop. The bandage is then placed in the hoop, with the edge turned in evenly about one inch on the bottom. The curd is weighed in order to insure a uniform size of cheese and is then put into the hoop. The hoops should not be filled too full, since the curd will be squeezed out around the top when pressed. A cotton cap-cloth is then placed over the top of the curd, and then the ring and follower. Steel rings and followers are preferable to fibrous rings and wooden followers. They are more sanitary, easier to clean, are not absorbent, and do not contract or expand easily..

Applying pressure.—When the curd is put in press in normal condition, a moderate pressure will cause the pieces of curd to cement together in a smooth, solid mass. The pressure should be uniform and continuous for 24 hours. With a screw-press, the pressure is applied lightly and gradually at first, full pressure being reached in about 15 minutes, and the press is tightened as fast as the screws become loose, especially during the first hour. After the curd has been in the press 45 to 60 minutes, it should be firmly cemented and ready for dressing.

Dressing cheese.—Too much care cannot be taken in finishing a cheese for market. The appearance greatly influences an intending purchaser. As soon as the cheese is sufficiently pressed, it is taken from the hoop and placed on a dressing-bench. The bandage is pulled up, made free from wrinkles, and trimmed to about one inch on each end with a sharp knife. A starched cap-cloth is placed on each end, outside the bandage. Over these, the cotton cloths are placed, and the cheese is then returned to the hoop, where it is left until the following morning. The cheese should then be taken from the press and examined for imperfections in finish; if any are present, they should be remedied and the cheese then returned to the press until the hoops are required for use again. It is better to have the cheese in the hoops under pressure for 48 hours than for only 24.

Plenty of hot water and clean, soft press-cloths should be used to insure a good rind on the cheese. Some cheese-makers place a cotton cloth around the entire side of the cheese. This improves the rind and protects the surface from any dirt or rust marks that may be on the hoops. Others do not take the cheese from the hoops to dress them, but place a starched cap-cloth in the hoop before adding the curd. Then, in dressing, the bandage is pulled up from the top and, after being trimmed, a starched cloth is placed on the upper end. This method causes a greater waste of bandage, but otherwise is satisfactory. The mechanical manipulations involved in preparing the hoops and dressing the cheese can be properly learned only from actual practice.

SIZES OR STYLES OF AMERICAN CHEDDAR CHEESE

American cheddar cheese has come to be put upon the market in an increasing number of varieties or styles in respect to size. The main difference in most cases is simply one of shape or size. The following list includes the most common varieties that appear in trade:

Name	Shape	Approximate Size	Approximate Weight
		In. diam.	Pounds
1. Cheddar or Export	Cylindrical	14-15	60-70
2. Flats or twins	"	14-15	30-35
3. Home-trade	"	11-13	20-25
4. Daisies	"	12-13	20
5. Young America	"	7-8	8-12
6. Longhorn	"	5	12
7. Picnic	"	4-5	1-2
8. Square	Rectangular	Various sizes	—— (3-4 in. thick)
9. Print	"	10 x 10 x 2$\frac{5}{8}$	10 (marked in blocks or prints)

CHAPTER V

Moisture and Acidity in Curd and Cheese: Conditions, Effects and Control

The detailed operations of cheese-making have for their primary object, in large measure, regulation of the amount of water and degree of acidity in the curd. So important is the control of these factors in relation to the quality of cheese, that sometimes, under abnormal conditions, as, for example, in case of overripe milk, they can be regulated only by sacrifice of some of the fat, and the question of saving fat then becomes a matter of secondary importance. Of such importance is a knowledge of these factors and their relations to the detailed operations of cheese-making that a special chapter seems desirable, even though the treatment involves some repetitions.

To a considerable extent, moisture and acidity are closely associated. Water means whey, of course, and the most important constituent of whey is milk-sugar, the raw material used in making lactic acid. The larger the percentage of water or whey in curd or fresh cheese, the larger is the amount of milk-sugar, and, therefore, the greater is the degree of acidity that can be developed. The relations of moisture can be better understood if we keep in mind the connection between (1) *moisture*, (2) *whey*, (3) *milk-sugar* and (4) *acidity*.

CAUSES OF EXCESSIVE MOISTURE

Among the most common causes of excessive water in curd and cheese are the following: (1) Cutting curd coarse or when too hard; (2) insufficient heating of curd in whey; (3) heating too rapidly, thus hardening the outside of the pieces of curd and preventing escape of whey; (4) low degree of acidity before removing whey, usually associated with, or caused by, insufficient heating; (5) allowing curd to lie in whey too long and reabsorb whey; (6) insufficient stirring of curd after removal or partial removal of whey; (7) high piling of curd; (8) prolonged maturing in cheddaring operation and postponement of milling in case of soft curd; (9) insufficient amount of salt; (10) soaking curd in water previous to salting (p. 57).

CAUSES OF INSUFFICIENT MOISTURE

The following are common causes of insufficient moisture in curd: (1) Cutting curd very fine; (2) heating curd too long or at too high a temperature; (3) excessive stirring of curd when the whey is removed; (4) too much salt; (5) excessive loss of fat may cause curd or cheese to appear too dry; (6) high temperature and low humidity in curing-room.

EFFECTS OF EXCESSIVE AND OF DEFI-CIENT MOISTURE

Among the more prominent effects to be noticed in relation to water in cheese-curd and cheese, we mention the following: (1) Development of acidity; (2) influence on body; (3) relation to texture; (4) effect on flavor; (5) influence on keeping quality; and (6) relation to finish.

Moisture and acidity.—The introduction to this chapter gives the cause for the close relation of moisture in curd to the formation of acid.   In case of a *wet* curd, characterized by much water (whey), we have a greater amount of milk-sugar ready to form an additional amount of acid; and, if the temperature and other conditions are favorable, acidity increases rapidly. In the case of a *dry* curd, the acidity increases more slowly, because there is less whey, which means less milk-sugar with which to make acid.

Moisture and body.—Curd containing too much moisture (whey) becomes soft and produces a soft, weak-bodied cheese (p. 87), which in extreme cases is sticky and pasty (p. 63). The soaking of curd in water after milling causes the absorption of 5 per cent of water, more or less, and usually results in a poor body. Cheese containing too little moisture becomes dry, mealy, crumbly, more or less rubbery, tough and hard. Such cheese is in no way attractive. When curd is too dry, the maturing process takes place with some degree of difficulty and the curd is slow to change into the characteristic, mellow, smooth, meaty body that is desired. This is due to the presence of too little whey in the curd, that is, too little milk-sugar with which to form acid.

Moisture and texture.—Excessive whey in curd and cheese is apt to favor the production of holes, especially when exposed to high temperatures. Under the combined conditions of such defects of texture and the soft, pasty body characteristic of such cheese, the cheese easily loses its shape, bulging more or less; this sometimes goes so far as to cause the cheese to roll off the shelf.

Moisture and flavor.—Cheese made from curd containing a large percentage of water (whey) is apt to develop offensive flavors in ripening, especially when kept at temperatures above 65° F. In some cases, excessive moisture results in sour or acid cheese. Dry cheese develops flavor slowly and can stand a higher ripening temperature.

Moisture and keeping quality.—Cheese containing a large amount of moisture has poor keeping quality, as already indicated above in connection with flavor and texture, while the reverse is true of dry cheese.

Moisture and finish.—Cheese containing too much moisture loses its shape easily in hot weather, when the temperature of the curing-room can not be controlled. In such cheese, the rind formation is usually poor and cap-cloths do not stick well.

CONTROL OF MOISTURE IN CHEESE-MAKING

We now give briefly the means to be used in controlling moisture at different stages of cheese-making.

(1) **Cutting curd.**—The finer the pieces into which the curd is cut, the more easily does the

whey escape; the larger the pieces of curd, the less rapid the escape of whey. Under the same conditions of treatment, a coarse-cut curd retains more whey than one fine-cut. When curd is cut before it becomes hard the whey escapes more easily than in the case of curd cut after it becomes hard.

(2) **Heating curd in whey.**—When the temperature of curd in whey is raised too rapidly, the film on the outside of the pieces of curd is harder and more impervious, which seriously interferes with the escape of whey. If the temperature is not raised sufficiently high, the whey does not escape as completely as it should; this is especially the case when an insufficient degree of acidity is developed. Therefore the curd in the whey should be heated gradually (p. 30) and the temperature raised to the degree called for by the existing conditions (p. 29). For method of avoiding dry curd see p. 121.

(3) **Removal of whey.**—The whey should be removed promptly when the curd is properly firmed. When allowed to lie in whey after reaching the right condition, the curd may reabsorb whey, which can be removed only with extreme difficulty and usually with considerable loss of fat.

(4) **Stirring of curd.**—Curd should be freed from whey and made properly dry by sufficient stirring after removal of whey (p. 32).

(5) **Cheddaring curd.**—In case of wet curd, it should not be piled too high in the operation of cheddaring, since this results in retention of more whey than when curd is cut fine and not piled

at all. In the case of dry curds, pile higher, etc., (p. 121).

(6) Milling curd.—Early milling of curd favors the escape of whey and may be resorted to when too much whey is present at this stage, especially in the case of a soft curd. Dry curds should not be milled early.

(7) Salting curd.—The amount of whey in cheese can be controlled, to some extent, by the amount of salt used. In case of excessive moisture in curd at the time of salting, this may be reduced by using an increased amount of salt. In case of a dry curd, less salt should be used (p. 121).

(8) Ripening process.—The amount of moisture in cheese can be regulated to a considerable extent by control of temperature and humidity in the curing-room (p. 317). Covering cheese with a layer of paraffin goes far in retaining water in cheese (p. 319).

CAUSES OF EXCESSIVE ACIDITY

Among the common causes of excessive acidity in curd and cheese are the following: (1) Taking too much overripe milk from patrons; (2) ripening milk too much in vat before adding rennet; (3) use of too much starter; (4) too long contact of curd with whey or too high temperature; (5) any condition which favors the retention of too much whey in curd and cheese (p. 116).

CAUSES OF INSUFFICIENT ACIDITY

The following are common causes of too low a degree of acidity: (1) Insufficient ripening of milk before adding rennet; (2) low degree of temperature in heating curd in whey; (3) removal of whey too soon; (4) any condition that favors the rapid removal of whey and the formation of an excessively dry curd (p. 121).

EFFECTS OF EXCESSIVE AND DEFICIENT ACIDITY

Among the more prominent effects to be noticed in relation to acidity in curd and cheese, we mention the following: (1) Influence on rennet action; (2) relation to shrinking of curd; (3) effect on expulsion of whey; (4) influence on color of cheese; (5) relation to body of cheese; (6) effect on texture of cheese; (7) influence on flavor of cheese; (8) relation to keeping quality of cheese; and (9) effect on finish or general appearance.

Acidity and rennet action.—At the temperature used in cheese-making, rennet-extract coagulates milk-casein only when acids or acid salts are present (p. 306). The greater the percentage of acidity, up to certain limits, the more rapid is rennet coagulation, other conditions being uniform (p. 307).

Acidity and contraction of curd.—The greater the acidity of milk, the more rapid is the contraction of the curd, other conditions being uniform. This is not the same as saying that the contraction is caused by acidity; acidity is probably one of two or more causes, or it may be simply a necessary condition for the continued action of rennet, temperature being another important condition for the shrinking of curd. The knowledge of the relation of acidity and temperature to contraction of curd enables the cheese-maker to heat the curd in the whey more rapidly, since, in the case of excessive acidity at the start, he can increase with comparative rapidity the temperature, without danger of hardening the external film of the small pieces of curd and so preventing further expulsion of whey.

Acidity and expulsion of whey.—The contraction of curd is closely associated with expulsion of whey and the relation of acidity to the two actions is practically the same.

Acidity and color of cheese.—Formation of too great a degree of acidity bleaches the color in the curd, making it pale when the action is even, and mottled when the acidity is different in different portions. This condition is generally caused by the retention of too much milk-sugar (whey) in curd and cheese.

Acidity and body of cheese.—Excessive acidity produces imperfect body in cheese, making it harsh, corky and mealy. A certain degree of acidity is an essential condition, if not one of the causes, of the formation of a smooth, firm, silky body. Insufficient acidity may cause cheese to be weak-bodied.

Acidity and texture.—Cheese made from curd containing a small amount of acidity is often faulty in texture. Among such defects are holes, usually called "sweet holes." Excessive acidity and cracks in cheese are often associated.

Acidity and flavor.—The characteristic flavor of cheddar cheese is not developed without a certain degree of acidity. Excessive acidity (whey) gives the cheese a sour flavor. Insufficient acidity is apt to be accompanied by a sickish flavor, unless the cheese is ripened with care at sufficiently low temperature.

Acidity and keeping quality.—It has been already stated (p. 18) that the presence of lactic acid bacteria in milk and curd is essential to prevent the development of undesirable forms of fermentation, which may be present in the early stages of cheese-making. The lactic acid thus formed is the active material employed in doing this sanitary work. Cheese with too little acidity usually becomes defective in flavor in a comparatively short time.

Acidity and finish.—Excessive acidity (whey) causes formation of poor rind; frequently the rind cracks and leaks whey.

CONTROL OF ACIDITY IN CHEESE-MAKING

Below we give in brief form the means to be used in controlling acidity in the operations of cheese-making.

(1) **Producer's care of milk.**—In order to retard the too rapid growth of lactic acid bacteria before milk is delivered at the cheese-factory, the milk should be cooled at once after milking to 60° F., or better to 50° F., and not allowed to get above this temperature.

(2) **Ripening milk.**—In making sweet-curd cheese, care must be taken not to ripen the milk

too much, a mistake too often made by cheese-makers. Milk which is overripe, whether at the time of delivery or as the result of ripening after delivery, is difficult to handle (p. 122). In the methods often employed, much loss of fat is often experienced in order not to sacrifice quality in cheese. The use of commercial starters (p. 19) gives the most reliable results in ripening milk.

(3) **Control of whey.**—The degree of acidity in curd and cheese is primarily dependent upon the amount of whey retained, and control of the amount of whey really means control of acidity. The methods for this have been given (p. 48).

(4) **Amount of acid at different stages.**—The degree of acidity should be kept under careful control at each stage of the operations of cheese-making, which is done by careful regulation of temperature and the different prescribed manipulations of the curd. There must be a careful adjustment of conditions in respect to (1) the rapidity of formation and thickening of the film around the pieces of curd, (2) the contraction of the curd, (3) the expulsion of whey, and (4) the degree of acidity.

CHAPTER VI

Modifications of Cheddar Process and Miscellaneous Subjects

In describing and discussing in detail the various operations involved in making American cheddar cheese, it has seemed best to reserve for a special chapter several subjects which are more or less closely related to this method of cheese-making, but which do not form an essential part of it. Of the many topics which might come in this chapter, the following have been selected for consideration: (1) "Stirred-curd" method; (2) "soaked-curd" method; (3) pasteurized milk in cheese-making; (4) slow-ripening and quick-ripening cheese; (5) home-trade cheese; (6) use of artificial acids in cheddar cheese-making; (7) the use of pepsin in cheddar cheese-making; (8) whey butter; (9) distribution and value of whey; (10) cheese poison; (11) starters in relation to yield of cheese; (12) making butter and cheese.

THE "STIRRED-CURD" OR "GRANULAR" PROCESS OF CHEESE-MAKING

This process was exclusively used in America for many years and is still in operation in some cheese-factories. While it is not our purpose to present a detailed description of this method, it is desirable, as a matter of information, to state its most essential points, especially those in which it differs from the cheddar method. The cheddar and stirred-curd methods are identical until the time comes for the removal of the whey from the curd, when they differ in the following respects: (1) In the cheddar process the whey is removed from the curd when the hot-iron test shows strings ⅛ to ¼ inch long; in the stirred-curd process, the curd remains longer in the whey, until the hot-iron test shows strings ½ to 1 inch long. (2) After the removal of whey, the curd, in the cheddar process, is packed and then cheddared; while, in the stirred-curd process, the curd is transferred to a curd-sink and is more or less frequently stirred, so that the small pieces are kept separate; and at no time is the curd permitted to pack in a solid mass. The main object of keeping the curd longer in the whey is to firm the curd to such an extent that it can be kept in the "granular" form more easily. (3) In the cheddar process, the time between the removal of whey and salting is much longer than in the stirred-curd method; while (4) the time between salting and pressing curd is much longer in the stirred-curd process. These general differences are well

Method used	Time from reaching 98° F. to removing whey from curd	Time from removing whey to salting curd	Time from salting to pressing curd
	Minutes	Minutes	Minutes
Cheddar............	90	200	30
Stirred-curd......	175	25	95
Cheddar..........	62	133	10
Stirred-curd	100	15	100
Cheddar..........	90	230	30
Stirred-curd	164	25	140

illustrated by the foregoing data, which were obtained at the New York experiment station in making different portions of the same milk into cheese by these two methods.

It will be noticed that, in general, the total amount of time consumed is about the same by either method. The time is simply distributed differently at certain stages of the work.

It is much more difficult with this method to make cheese of perfect texture, at least considered from the standpoint of the type of cheese intended for export. It was the influence of the demands of the English market which caused American cheese-makers to change from the stirred-curd to the cheddar method. The cheddar process has the marked advantage of enabling the cheese-maker to control his operations more completely and produce cheese of close texture. Greater skill is required to produce results by the stirred-curd method equal to those obtained with the cheddar method. Under ordinary conditions, the stirred-curd method produces cheese with a little higher content of moisture, but not necessarily so. The loss of fat is the same by either method.

THE "SOAKED-CURD" METHOD

This is a modification of the cheddar method, which has for its object an increase of water other than that derived from the whey. It is to be distinguished from the advantageous practice of washing curd in the case of abnormal flavor, excessive acidity, etc. It is applied to both skim-milk and

normal-milk cheese.   The process is simply this:
When the curd has matured ready for salting, it is
covered with cold water and allowed to soak 10 to
15 minutes.   In this way the amount of water in
100 pounds of cheese can be increased ordinarily
4 or 5 pounds, producing a cheese with 41 to 44
per cent of water.   The soaking of curd by this

FIG. 9

Showing the effect of excessive moisture in a soaked-curd cheese upon the
body.   The cheese with normal moisture keeps its shape perfectly.   The soaked-
curd cheese bulges at the sides and flattens down if kept at temperatures 65 or 70
degrees F.

process not only increases the yield of cheese by
the incorporation of water other than what was a
part of the original milk from which the cheese was
made, but it also dissolves from the curd (1) milk-
sugar; and (2) the soluble calcium salts, especially
acid calcium phosphate.   These normal cheese constituents, which are thus removed from the curd,
are essential to the normal ripening process of the

cheese and, in their absence, cheese undergoes abnormal fermentations as the result of the action of putrefactive bacteria. These facts have been established by work done at the Cornell University experiment station. This practice has been defended on the ground of removing undesirable "impurities" carried into the cheese by the whey. This is a pure assumption which has no foundation in

FIG. 10

Showing the difference between the close texture of normal cheese and the loose, spongy texture of a soaked-curd cheese.

fact. The whey-solids, thus miscalled "impurities," are normal constituents of cheese and are necessary to the completion of the ripening process when present in normal amount. Cheese made by the soaked-curd process is very properly not permitted the use of the brand designed for whole-milk cheese in New York state, on the following grounds: (1) Water other than that present in the original milk from which the cheese was made is incorporated with the cheese for the purpose of increasing its

weight without improving its quality; and (2) the
soaking process removes normal constituents that are
essential to the ripening of the cheese.   These grounds
are based upon established facts.

Cheese produced by the soaked-curd process
usually exhibits the defects characteristic of cheese
containing an excessive amount of moisture; these
are weak body and loose texture (pp. 86-87).   When
kept at temperatures above 65° or 70° F., such
cheese fails to stand up like normal cheese and it
also suffers in texture from the effects of gassy fermentations.   Figs. 9 and 10 well illustrate the truth
of these statements.   They represent work done at
the Cornell University experiment station with
cheese made according to the soaked-curd method.

CHEDDAR CHEESE FROM PASTEURIZED MILK

Many attempts have been made to manufacture
cheddar cheese from pasteurized milk.   The results
in America have not been wholly encouraging up to
the present time.   The cheese is generally imperfect
in body, lacking in flavor and slow in ripening.   We
do not, therefore, think it desirable to devote further attention to the various modifications of details
required in its manufacture.   It is said that much
skim-milk cheese is successfully made in Denmark
from pasteurized milk.

CONDITIONS OF CHEESE-MAKING PROCESS FOR QUICK-RIPENING AND SLOW-RIPENING CHEESE

Certain conditions of the cheese-making process
promote, while others retard, the rapidity of ripen-

ing. The general relation of different conditions to the rapid or slow rate of cheese-ripening may be shown by the following form of statement:

Conditions that may promote ripening:	Conditions that may retard ripening:
(1) Increase of ripening temperature.	(1) Decrease of ripening temperature.
(2) Larger amount of rennet.	(2) Smaller amount of rennet.
(3) More moisture in cheese.	(3) Less moisture in cheese.
(4) Less salt.	(4) More salt.
(5) Large size of cheese.	(5) Small size of cheese.
(6) Moderate amount of acid.	(6) Deficient acidity or excess of acidity.

If a cheese is desired that ripens quickly, it should contain more than the usual amount of rennet, a moisture content of about 40 per cent or more, and about 1 to 1½ pounds of salt for 1,000 pounds of milk. Then it should be kept at a temperature between 60° F. and 70° F., if it is to be placed in the hands of consumers in one month or six weeks, and the atmosphere of the curing-room should have a humidity of 75 to 85 per cent of saturation. However, it should be stated that cheese made to ripen quickly gives better results in commercial quality when ripened at a lower temperature than 60° F. and held a longer time.

For a slow-ripening cheese, not more than 2½ ounces of rennet-extract, such as Hansen's, should be used for 1,000 pounds of milk, and about 2 to 2½ pounds of salt. The other conditions that influence the moisture content of cheese, such as the temperature of heating the curd, the fineness of cutting curd, the amount of acid developed in the curd, cheddaring, etc. (p. 45), should be well under control, so as to produce a cheese containing, when fresh from the press, about 37 per cent of water. For ripening, it should be kept at a temperature below 50° F. in a fairly moist atmosphere for a period of 3 to 6 months or more.

HOME-TRADE CHEESE

The majority of cheese consumers desire a cheese soft in body and with a mild, clean flavor. Softness is synonymous with richness in cheese to most people. While it is true that cheese rich in fat possesses a characteristic softness, it is not true that all soft cheese is rich in fat. The desire for a mild-flavored cheese is a reaction from the taste for a cheese of strong, pungent flavor. To meet in the easiest way the demand for soft-bodied, mild-flavored cheese, there has arisen quite an extensive manufacture of what is known as "home-trade" cheese. The method of making this kind of cheese varies in its details in different localities, but the general object is the production of a quick-curing cheese which will be ready for consumption in four to six weeks. The distinctive characteristics of such cheese are its high water content, a consequent softness of body and open texture, a mild flavor when a few weeks old, and a poor-keeping quality. These results are attained, in general, by using large amounts of rennet-extract, developing less acidity, heating the curd in the whey to 103° to 110° F. and ripening at 60° to 70° F. In many cases, where the conditions of ripening are not under control, home-trade cheese is made only in the fall, since there is less risk in handling the ripening process at a time when the temperature is not high. Home-trade cheese, when green, usually contains 38 to 40 per cent of water, but the percentage may run up to 43 or even 45. The fact that this soft cheese is more extensively made in the fall has led cheese-makers to believe that. "milk very rich in fat, such as strippers' milk, is liable to cause a pasty cheese." Such a belief could hardly be further from the truth, as shown by the facts given in Chapter XV, pp. 164-167, where the influence of advancing lactation on the composition of milk is discussed.

It should be stated in this connection that, in New York state, a large proportion of the cheese made under the name of home-trade is of a type quite different from that described above. In the process of making, the temperature is not allowed to go above 98° F. and the percentage of moisture is kept at 38 to 40. The resulting cheese is firm-bodied, close-textured and of good-keeping quality. It is the best type of home-trade cheese and is in large demand.

USE OF ARTIFICIAL ACIDS IN CHEDDAR CHEESE-MAKING

Attempts have been made to use artificial lactic and other acids in making cheddar cheese, in order to hasten the cheese-making operations. Theoretically, the addition of small amounts of dilute acid can take the place of starters in hastening the action of rennet, and, to some extent, in the subsequent stages. While it is possible to assist the lactic acid bacteria in this way, great caution is required. The addition of too much acid results in the production of cheese that does not ripen. So far as we know, the application of artificial acids in cheddar cheese-making has never been worked out to such an extent that all details are under control. While cheese of good quality can be made in this way, there is probably no advantage, even when the process is under absolute control; and, in the absence of such control, no one should ever attempt to employ such a method in practical work.

USE OF PEPSIN IN CHEDDAR CHEESE-MAKING

Commercial pepsin prepared from the stomachs of sheep has been successfully used in place of rennet-extract in making cheddar cheese. The special pepsin most used in this way is a scale-pepsin known as 1-3000 strength. Five grams of this pepsin equal the coagulating power of 3 ounces of Hansen's rennet-extract. The pepsin is dissolved in cold water for use. In using pepsin, one should make a solution and test it in comparison with rennet-extract on the same milk. (Modern Methods of Testing Milk, etc., pp. 125-126.) Pepsin has the following advantages over rennet-extract: (1) It is more concentrated and, therefore, more convenient and less expensive to ship. (2) If kept dry, pepsin retains its strength indefinitely, while rennet-extract does not. These advantages of pepsin over rennet-extract do not, of course, apply to rennet *powders*. The quality of cheese made by use of pepsin does not appear to be inferior to that made by the use of rennet. Commercial pepsin is probably more expensive to use than rennet-extract and is not uniform in strength.

MANUFACTURE OF WHEY-BUTTER

The fat in whey can be readily removed, in large part, by means of a centrifugal separator, and the resulting cream can be made into butter in much the same manner as cream separated directly from milk. The butter thus made is apt to be somewhat softer than in case of normal butter; the flavor is fair to good. From the whey produced in making 10,000 pounds of milk into cheese under normal conditions, about 25 to 30 pounds of whey-butter can be made under favorable conditions. This yield is based upon an average loss of 0.3 pound of fat in whey for 100 pounds of milk (p. 189). The removal of milk-fat from whey does not greatly reduce its feeding value.

The question of making whey-butter is largely a matter of cost of production. In the case of small cheese-factories, the yield of butter would not repay the labor. In larger factories, it would become, to some extent, a question of the amount of fat in the whey. In general, it may be said that the manufacture of whey-butter will be usually found profitable under the following conditions:

(1) When the daily average milk supply is not less than 10,000 pounds and the amount of fat in

whey averages 0.25 pound or more for 100 pounds of milk.

(2) When the average cost of making whey-butter can be kept sufficiently low. The usual cost is 5 to 8 cents a pound, including cost of fuel, labor, coloring-matter, salt, etc. Among the conditions that favor economy of production are the following: (a) A building so located and constructed that gravity can be used to carry whey to and from the separator at minimum cost; (b) a cheap supply of pure ice and cold water; (c) the possession of a centrifugal separator and a butter-making equipment as a part of the factory plant; (d) reasonable cost of fuel and labor.

(3) When a good quality of butter is made. This, of course, requires pasteurization of cream, the use of a good commercial starter, extreme cleanliness at every stage of the butter-making process and proper sanitary surroundings.

In St. Lawrence County, New York, several factories have formed a combination for the successful manufacture of whey-butter.   The separated cream is sent by each to a central butter-making station.   When all conditions are favorable, a cheese-factory receiving 10,000 pounds of milk a day on the average, could with profit install the equipment necessary for making whey-butter.

DISTRIBUTION AND VALUE OF WHEY

The theoretical yield of whey for 100 pounds of milk averages about 90 pounds, with a variation between 87 and 91.5 pounds, according to the yield of cheese for 100 pounds of milk. The theoretical yield is reduced by the losses in the cheese-making operations, due (1) to evaporation of water and (2) to mechanical losses. The yield of whey varies with the composition of the milk and, therefore, with the time of season and other conditions that affect the composition of milk (p. 204). In general, it is safe to say that the yield of whey is about 88 pounds for 100 pounds of milk, taking the season as a whole; but this yield is considerably reduced by losses in handling. In allowing each patron to take the portion of whey coming to him, the usual amount is 80 to 85 pounds for 100 pounds of milk delivered. Where the whey is valued by every patron, it is essential that each one be assigned his just portion; otherwise some will always take more than belongs to them. There are various satisfactory devices for controlling the amount of whey each patron can take.

The chief value of whey to patrons is as material for feeding pigs and calves in connection with other foods. The feeding value of sweet whey may be conservatively placed at 8 to 10 cents for 100 pounds. For the composition of whey, see p. 197. Whey sours rapidly and loses a considerable amount of its milk-sugar under ordinary conditions. In order that its highest food value may be realized, it is essential that it should be pasteurized promptly at 155° to 158° F. and the whey-vat always kept in clean condition (p. 127). It is not practicable to sterilize whey, because the heat needed for sterilization coagulates the albumin. Whey that is decidedly sour often has an injurious effect on the animals to which it is fed, especially when fed alone and in excess. There is another even more important reason why whey should be pasteurized. The whey-vat has been known to become a distributing source of disease among calves and pigs and of abnormal fermentations that injure the quality of cheese. Sweet whey has a value of 6 or 7 cents per 100 pounds when sold for the manufacture of milk-sugar, but comparatively little whey can be actually disposed of in this way.

CHEESE POISON

For a long time it was known that cheese sometimes acts as a violent poison, but it was not until about 25 years ago that a specific poisonous compound was isolated from cheese. Many cases of cheese poisoning had occurred in Michigan at the time and the matter was investigated by Dr. V. C. Vaughan, professor of physiological chemistry at the University of Michigan, who succeeded in separating from some of the poisonous cheese an intensely poisonous compound, which he called tyrotoxicon (cheese poison). The poison is present in cheese in only very minute amounts, but is intensely powerful. A drop of a highly dilute solution of this poison placed on the tongue produces a characteristic benumbing sensation. This poison is the result of bacterial action and is produced only by those bacteria which are associated with conditions of filth. There are sometimes also other poisons in cheese, less well known.

STARTERS IN RELATION TO YIELD OF CHEESE

When a cheese-maker uses comparatively large amounts of starter, as 5 pounds for 100 pounds of milk, the question arises as to whether this does not increase the yield of cheese and is not practically equivalent to adding the same amount of skim-milk. The amount of added casein thus introduced is about 2 ounces and is equivalent to an increased yield of cheese amounting to about 5 ounces for 100 pounds of milk. Theoretically, the practice of adding large amounts of starter might lead to abuse; but rennet-extract does not act upon the coagulated casein of sour milk or of buttermilk. The casein contained in the starter, although held fast in the coagulum at first, separates to a large extent during the cheese-making in the form of fine particles. When a large amount of starter is used, these small particles are very noticeable in the whey. The fact that the addition of a starter to milk does not increase the yield of cheese has been brought out by work done in the dairy department at the Cornell University experiment station.

MAKING BUTTER AND CHEESE

The question is often raised as to whether or not it pays to remove a part of the fat from milk and make butter and part-skim cheese. As a rule, it does not pay, unless one sells the part-skim cheese for whole-milk cheese, and this is very difficult to do now under our pure-food laws. The best advice that can be given is to make either butter or cheese, but not to mix the manufacture of the two products. Some cheese-factories drop cheese-making in the fall and make butter during the winter. The relative price of cheese and butter will determine which pays better. In general, it can be said that butter-making pays better than cheese-making whenever the price of butter is greater than two and one-third times the price of cheese per pound. For example, when cheese sells at 10 cents a pound, butter-making will pay better, if the price of butter is above 23 1-3 cents a pound.

CHAPTER VII

Care, Shipment and Sale of Cheese

It has been said that a cheese is really only half made when it is taken from the press. This is, in a great measure, true, because the conditions of temperature and humidity to which a cheese is subjected during the process of ripening or curing largely determine its quality. An excellent cheese may be absolutely spoiled by unfavorable ripening conditions, while a cheese of inferior quality may be much improved by being kept under favorable conditions. The subject of cheese-ripening in its practical relations is discussed in Chapter XXVI, pp. 379-394.

CLEANING THE SURFACE

When each cheese is taken from the press, it should be wiped off with a dry cloth, and any rust-spots or finger-marks removed. Deep-seated spots of dirt can be more easily removed by the use of a brush and hot water.

PLACING CHEESE IN CURING-ROOM

No cheese should be placed in the curing-room until it is clean and well finished. A badly finished or dirty cheese never attracts a cheese buyer, inspector or consumer. Imperfections in quality are

often overlooked if the finish and general appearance
are good.

When cheese is placed in the curing-room, it
should be arranged in a neat manner upon clean
shelves or tables. Too many cheese-makers allow
the cheese-shelves to become moldy and dirty; consequently, when a clean cheese is placed on them the
end surfaces soon become stained and dirty. The
shelves should be thoroughly cleaned after each shipment of cheese leaves the factory.

TURNING CHEESE DURING RIPENING PROCESS

Each cheese should be turned on the shelf every
morning until ready for shipment. At the time of
turning, if an excess of moisture or any mold is
present, it should be wiped off with a dry cloth, or
with a damp one wrung out of a 10 per cent solution
of formaldehyd.

MARKING DATE OF MANUFACTURE

When cheese is placed in the curing-room, the
date of its manufacture should be stamped on each,
so as to correspond with the number of the manufacturing record of the same date and thus avoid errors
in shipment.

USE OF CHEESE BRANDS

Many states have statutes providing for the
branding of cheese. The brand usually indicates
whether the cheese has been made from whole

milk or skimmed milk. Brass stencils for this purpose are usually sent to factories by the state departments of agriculture, which keep a record of the number of each factory, and this particular number appears as part of the brand. This is to protect the manufacturers of whole-milk cheese from dishonest competition with those who remove part or all of the fat from the milk before making it into cheese. In Canada many factories stamp the name of the factory on the cheese. In many instances, this is a good plan, if the quality of the cheese is good, but disastrous if the cheese is defective in quality.

WHEN CHEESE SHOULD BE SHIPPED

The age at which cheese should be shipped from the factory depends on several conditions. If the curing-room is one in which the temperature and humidity cannot be controlled at all, the cheese should be shipped within a few days to some place where it can be kept under proper conditions. In some places, central cold storages are located where cheese, either before or after selling, is sent to ripen. If the temperature in the cheese-factory can be controlled, the cheese should not be shipped so soon. Cheese 10 days old is young enough, and, if for export, two weeks will be much better. An export cheese is not very palatable in less than one month. A home-trade cheese containing a high percentage of moisture may be ready at an earlier date (p. 62)

During the past few years, complaints, in increasing number, have been made by foreign cheese merchants, who say that cheese is shipped to them before it is old enough.   The Canadian. government has lately been making vigorous efforts to overcome this practice, which has become too common.   The important point to be kept in mind is that the cheese should be in an edible condition when it reaches the consumer.

FIG. 11—DAIRY STUDENTS WEIGHING, PARAFFINING AND BOXING CHEESE

COVERING CHEESE WITH PARAFFIN

Loss of moisture in cheese can be largely prevented by coating the cheese with a thin layer of paraffin, and this can be done without injuring the quality.   The higher the temperature, the greater is the prevention of loss.   Another distinct advantage in using paraffin is that it prevents cheese becoming moldy. The cheese is allowed to dry well on the surface and is then dipped for 8 to 15 seconds, according to the size and temperature of the cheese, in melted paraffin at a temperature of at

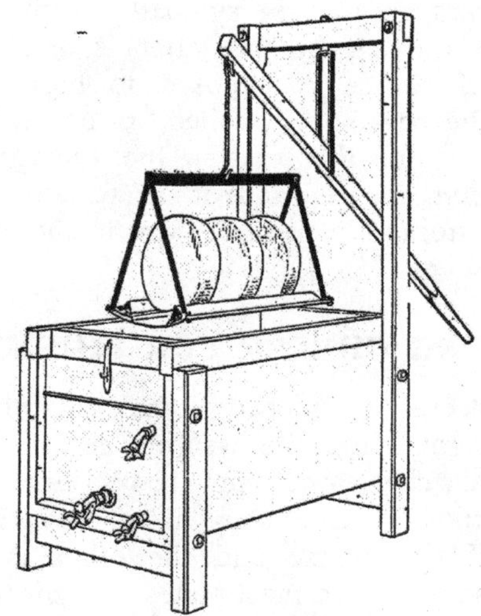

FIG. 12—APPARATUS FOR PARAFFINING CHEESE

least 220° F. Care must be taken to keep the paraffin from acquiring a disagreeable odor as a result of overheating. Cheese should be dry enough in three to seven days to be ready for paraffining, but the time will depend, of course, on the amount of moisture in the cheese and in the curing-room. The application of paraffin at a high temperature gives a thin coating that adheres tenaciously and destroys mold formation. If the temperature is too low, the coating will be too thick and will crack or break away from the cheese more easily. About 5 or 6 ounces of paraffin will cover an 80-pound cheese, and the cost is about 2½ to 3 cents. Most retail merchants are now in favor of having cheese coated with paraffin; but in England many of the large exporters are not in sympathy with the idea, although the number of the latter is gradually decreasing. If cheese is exposed to high temperatures after the paraffin is applied, its beneficial effect will be lost. For this reason, the average factory cannot paraffin cheese, and it is usually done at central cold-storage places, to which the cheese is shipped.

WEIGHING CHEESE FOR SHIPMENT

Before cheese is shipped, each one should be carefully weighed and the weights copied in duplicate. Special cheese-shipping books are available for this purpose. One copy is forwarded to the purchaser of the cheese and the other is kept at the cheese-factory. In most states, the cheese is sold according to the exact weight of each, "balanced beam." In Canada the factorymen are forced to allow the buyers "up-beam," plus ¼ pound. This means that, for every cheese sold, the factoryman gives away at least ¼ pound. In many cases it is more, because it is difficult for the cheese-maker to have the cheese always weigh so near the pound mark. Unfortunately, this has become an almost uncriticised practice and it is hoped that cheese-makers in Canada will soon awaken to a better method of selling cheese.

BOXING CHEESE FOR SHIPMENT

After cheese is weighed, each is placed in a box for shipment. A thin scale-board should be placed between the cheese and each end of the box to prevent the cheese sticking to the box. The box should fit the cheese closely and should be strong enough to stand shipment without breaking. If the box is too high, it should be pared down with a draw-knife. The lid of the box should just press lightly on the top of the cheese. Some shipping companies demand that the lids be securely fastened on every box. If the lids fit snugly, they will not come off easily in handling; but if nails are used, they should not be so long as to penetrate the cheese.

STENCILING THE BOXES

The weight of the cheese should be neatly stenciled on the side of the box in large figures and, if the cheese is for export, the name of the factory should also be stenciled on the side. It is bad practice to mark the weights with a lead pencil. Such marks do not look well and are often very indistinct, since all cheese-makers cannot make neat, plain figures. A rubber stamp is, perhaps, the quickest and neatest way. If a brass stencil is used, a mixture of coal-oil and lamp-black makes a very suitable blacking. Shoe-black-ing should not be used, because it easily becomes smeared and then makes the package appear untidy.

DRAWING CHEESE TO SHIPPING POINT

Most cheese-factories are located in country places some distance from railway and steamboat facilities. The cheese is usually drawn to shipping places by patrons of the factory. In many instances the wagons used are not fit for carrying cheese, and the boxes that were clean and neat become dirty or broken by the time they reach the

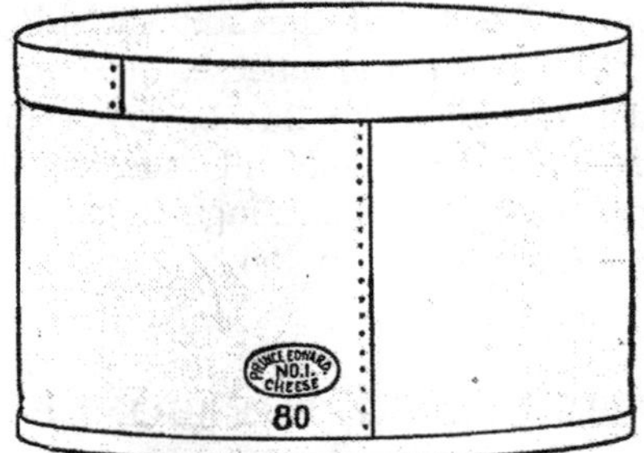

FIG. 13—A CHEESE-BOX, AS IT SHOULD APPEAR
WHEN READY FOR SHIPMENT

station. The cheese should be drawn in clean, spring wagons and should be placed so that the boxes do not roll around and break. Clean straw placed on the bottom of the wagon-box improves the conditions of transportation. A covering of oiled canvas placed over the load of boxes will protect them from dust, rain and the heat of the sun.

HOW TO SELL CHEESE

When cheese-factories were first operated, the cheese was purchased by buyers, who visited the factories and bought the cheese on its merits. Now most cheese is sold on the dairy boards of trade. Large dealers send representatives to each cheese board with instructions to buy cheese at a certain price. Usually there is enough competition between buyers to insure the full market prices. Buyers are allowed by their employer one-sixteenth to one-eighth cent per pound for buying cheese, and very often, in the heat of competition, they pay the cheese seller this commission in order to secure the cheese. This is not objectionable, if it does not continue too long. If the buyer receives no pay for his work, he frequently finds fault with or rejects the cheese and asks for a reclaim of a few dollars from the cheese-maker, when otherwise the cheese would pass inspection. In sections where cheese is inspected in the factories, the cheese-board method is fairly satisfactory, but when the cheese has to be sent to a distant center of inspection, there is continual complaining by either buyer or seller.

METHOD OF PAYING FOR CHEESE

With few exceptions, cheese is now shipped to the order of some bank. After the buyer has inspected and accepted the cheese, he gives the seller a draft of his firm on the local bank for the value of the cheese. The bank then draws on the firm and the cheese belongs to the bank till the draft is honored. This method is a real cash business and protects the factoryman from losses caused by fraudulent practices of dishonest cheese merchants.

Commercial Qualities of Cheddar Cheese and Methods of Judging

In commercial transactions in cheese, certain points or qualities have been adopted as a basis or standard in judging the commercial value of this product. The terms used in expressing the different qualities vary considerably in different market centers, and the same expression is used with different meanings by different persons. Frequently individuals use terms that are strictly local or personal. It is desirable that there should be a uniform usage and a common understanding in respect to the terms used in judging cheese. The attempt is made here to discuss the terms in common use and to define them as well as may be, in the hope that it may serve as an aid in bringing about a general agreement in respect to the use and understanding of the expressions employed in judging and scoring cheese. The definitions here given can hardly be expected to be in full agreement with the usage of everyone, since individuals differ from one another so much in their use of these terms.

SAMPLING AND TESTING CHEESE

In testing its commercial qualities, a sample of the cheese to be examined is obtained by means of a cheese-trier. This is inserted nearly its whole length, if possible, into the cheese, turned around once and then drawn out, bringing with it, as the sample, a long, round cylinder, commonly called "plug."

The plug should always be drawn from the top and not from the side, in order to avoid injuring the protective power of the bandage. The plug drawn is examined by smelling, feeling, appearance, etc., in reference to the various qualities mentioned below.

TERMS USED IN DESCRIBING QUALITIES OF CHEESE

The following qualities have been selected to serve as a basis in the commercial testing and scoring of cheese: (1) Flavor, (2) texture, (3) body, (4) color, (5) salt, and (6) appearance.

Flavor.—By flavor is meant the quality that is perceptible to the smell and taste. The sense of smell is depended upon in testing flavor in cheese much more largely than is the sense of taste, because, in examining a large number of samples of cheese in succession, constant tasting soon dulls not only the sense of taste but also that of smell. Flavor in cheese is due to the formation of some unknown compound or compounds during the ripening process (p. 375).

Testing flavor in cheese.—The flavor is best obtained by direct smelling of the plug as soon as it is drawn and, in addition, by crushing and warming some of the cheese between the thumb and fingers and then smelling.

Terms used in describing cheese flavor.—From a great variety of names applied to various flavors found in cheese, the following terms are selected for consideration: (1) Perfect, (2) high or quick, (3) clean, (4) low or flat, (5) strong, (6) too much acid, (7) too little acid, (8) sour, (9) sweet or fruity, (10) rancid, (11) tallowy, (12) tainted, (13) stable, (14) weedy, (15) bitter, (16) cowy, (17) fishy, (18) hydrogen sulphid.

(1) *Perfect* flavor applies to cheese when it somewhat resembles that of first-class butter with an added quality of its own that is characteristic but cannot be described further than to call it cheese-like. It is sometimes described as "nutty." This flavor should be marked, but not strong. It should be free from all other flavors, particularly the more or less offensive products of undesirable fermentations. The taste should be mild and somewhat lasting, but should not be so sharp as to "bite" the tongue.

(2) *High* or *quick* flavor is a delicate flavor that disappears quickly.

(3) *Clean* flavor is free from every trace of unpleasant aroma or taste.

(4) *Low* or *flat* flavor applies to slight traces, or absence, of flavor; it is insipid.

(5) *Strong* flavor is a good flavor very pronounced but free from everything offensive; it is a good flavor strongly developed.

(6) *Too much acid* applies to flavor that smells somewhat sour, but does not taste sour.

(7) *Too little acid* applies to a mild flavor, lacking in character.

(8) *Sour* flavor is characterized by a sour taste when the cheese is fresh, owing to the presence of too much whey.

(9) *Sweet* or *fruity* flavor is suggestive of artificial pineapple odor and is somewhat "sickish" to taste.

(10) *Rancid* flavor is that of butyric acid, more common in old cheese than in young. When very strong, it affects a delicate throat with a slight sensation of choking or strangling.

(11) *Tallowy* flavor is like that of tallow.

(12) *Tainted* flavor includes a variety of odors, mildly to strongly offensive.

(13) *Stable* flavor suggests the smell of cow manure.

(14) *Weedy* flavor applies to such abnormal flavors as come from onions, leeks, cabbages, ragweed, etc.

(15) *Bitter* flavor is self-descriptive. It is often due to certain fermentations that develop when a cheese is undersalted.

(16) *Cowy* flavor is suggestive of the breath of a cow and may develop in cheese from some form of a fermentation.

(17) *Fishy* flavor is self-descriptive. It is caused by certain ferments that are present in milk.

(18) *Hydrogen sulphid* is a gas which gives the odor that is characteristic of the water of sulphur-springs. It is found in cheese ripened at high temperature. The odor is rarely, if ever, as strong as in the water of a sulphur-spring. A cheese with this flavor, or a fishy flavor, is technically known as a "stinker." The presence of this gas can be detected by holding a bright silver coin against the cheese-plug

FIG. 14—CHARACTERISTIC AP-
PEARANCE OF A CLOSE-TEX-
TURED CHEESE

for a moment; the silver tarnishes if any appreciable amount of hydrogen sulphid is present.

Texture. — Texture, as applied to cheese, refers chiefly to compactness or appearance of solidity. It is quite common, unfortunately, to regard the

"body" as a part of the texture, but the t w o qualities are clearly distinct and should not be confused.

Testing texture in cheese.—The texture of cheese is tested by an examination of the plug with reference to the presence of holes. The plug is broken in two and

FIG. 15—CHARACTERISTIC APPEAR-
ANCE OF A LOOSE OR POROUS.
TEXTURE

the broken ends examined for the c h a r a c t e r i s t i c flinty appearance.

Terms describing t e x t u r e.— T h e following terms are among

FIG. 16—TYPICAL TEXTURE OF SWEET-
CURD CHEESE

those most commonly used in describing texture:
(1) Perfect, (2) close, (3) loose, (4) mechanical
holes, (5) gas or pin-holes, (6) Swiss-holes.

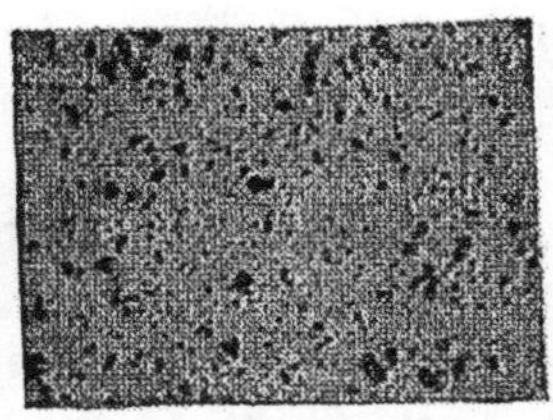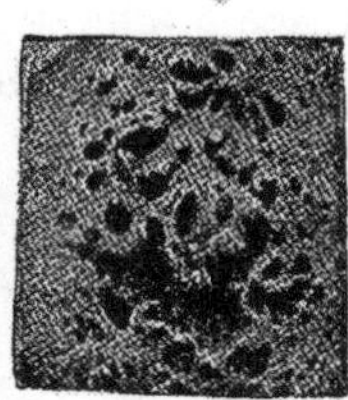

FIG. 17—EFFECTS OF GASSY FERMENTATION IN CHEESE

(1) *Perfect* texture in cheese is shown when a
plug or a cut surface of the inside of the cheese
presents to the eye a solid, compact, continuous
appearance, free from breaks, holes and chunks.

FIG. 18—MECHANICAL HOLES IN CHEESE NOT PERFECTLY
CEMENTED

When a plug is broken in two, it should show a flaky appearance, termed a "flinty" break, resembling the surface of broken flint or steel.

(2) *Close* texture describes the appearance of a cut surface of cheese when free from all kinds of holes. Such cheese is often described as "close-boring." (Fig. 14.)

(3) *Loose* or *porous* texture is indicated by lack of solid compactness, being more or less full of holes, which vary from a few (Figs. 15 and 16) to enough to make a spongy (Fig. 17) appearance. One variety is known as fish-eye, due to action of yeasts (p. 126).

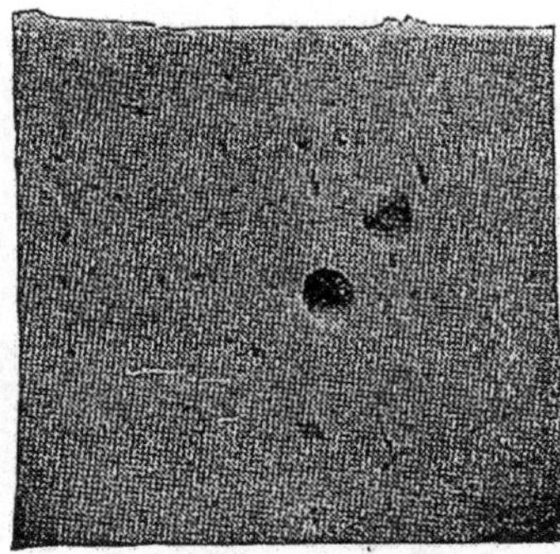

FIG. 19—SWISS-HOLES

(4) *Mechanical holes* in cheese are irregular, open spaces, caused by the incomplete cementing of the pieces of curd in the press. (Fig. 18.)

(5) *Gas-holes* or *pin-holes* are small holes, produced by gaseous products of fermentation.

(6) *Swiss-holes* are fairly large, round holes, such as are present in Emmenthaler cheese. (Fig. 19.)

Body.—This term, used in connection with cheese, refers to the consistency, firmness or substance of cheese. It is largely influenced by the amount of fat and moisture in cheese.

Testing body.—This quality is found by pressing a piece of cheese between the thumb and fingers.

Terms describing body.—The following terms are among those used in describing the body of cheese: (1) Perfect, (2) solid or firm, (3) smooth, (4) silky, (5) waxy, (6) pasty or salvy, (7) stiff, corky or curdy, (8) weak-bodied, (9) mealy, (10) gritty, (11) watery, (12) overdry.

(1) *Perfect* body in cheese is indicated when it feels solid, firm and smooth in its consistency or substance. It does not crumble under pressure. A plug drawn from a cheese of perfect body should be smooth in appearance and not "fuzzy."

(2) *Solid, firm* or *meaty body* is indicated when cheese offers a certain amount of resistance under pressure, somewhat like that shown by a piece of fat pork or cold butter. The term *meaty* is also used.

(3) *Smooth*-bodied cheese, when pressed between the thumb and fingers, feels smooth and velvet-like, as distinct from harsh, gritty or mealy.

(4) *Silky*-bodied cheese is smooth in feeling but not oversolid in consistency.

(5) *Waxy*-bodied cheese is much the same as silky, but possessing more firmness or solidity.

(6) *Pasty* or *salvy* cheese is very soft, usually from an excess of moisture. When pressed, it sticks to the fingers.

(7) *Stiff, corky* or *curdy* cheese is hard, tough, overfirm; it does not crush down readily when pressed in the hand.

(8) *Weak*-bodied cheese is very soft, lacking in firmness, but not necessarily sticky like pasty cheese.

(9) *Mealy* or *crumbly* cheese breaks down in fine crumbs when pressed.

(10) *Gritty*-bodied cheese feels harsh and gritty under pressure.

(11) *Watery*-bodied cheese is excessively soft, pasty and sticky.

(12) In an *overdry* cheese the body is very hard or mealy.

Color.—The color of cheese varies considerably, whether artificially colored or not. There appears to be an increasing demand for uncolored cheese. The coloring varies from a pale yellow to a reddish yellow, according to the demands of special markets.

Testing color.—The color is tested by inspection with the eye, the examiner noticing particularly unevenness and any extreme condition of color.

Terms describing color.—Color in cheese is described in the following terms: (1) Perfect, (2) straight, (3) translucent, (4) white specks, (5) streaked, (6) wavy, (7) mottled, (8) acid-cut, (9) high, (10) light, (11) uncolored.

(1) *Perfect* color in cheese is indicated by evenness of color throughout the mass. A plug held between the eye and light should appear somewhat translucent.

(2) *Straight* color is an even, uniform color through the whole cheese.

(3) *Translucent* applies to color in cheese which appears slightly translucent when the plug is held between the eye and the light.

(4) *White specks* is a term that describes itself. Such specks in cheese are a defect. They may

appear in cheese cured at low temperature (p. 332).

(5) *Streaked* color indicates that there are light-colored portions in the form of streaks.

(6) *Wavy* color applies to lighter portions appearing in the form of waves.

(7) *Mottled* color shows in cheese in lighter-colored spots.-of fairly large size, more or less irregular.

(8) *Seamy* color applies to the appearance of a pale rim surrounding each piece of curd and showing the outline of the pieces as they were before being pressed (p. 131).

(9) *Acid-cut* color is shown in cheese when considerable portions of the cheese have been made lighter in color by the presence of too much acid (whey).

(10) *High* color is indicated by a reddish color, caused by using too much coloring-matter. However, the question of color is a relative one, because the demand in different markets varies from uncolored to extremely high color.

(11) *Light* color is the term usually used in describing cheese that has been made uniformly dead white by the action of too much acid (whey).

(12) *Red spots* are places, usually small in area, having somewhat the appearance of iron-rust (p. 131).

(13) *Uncolored* cheddar cheese is not white, but of a light amber shade.

Salt.—The amount of salt in cheese varies somewhat with different markets. There is seldom experienced difficulty of uneven salting in cheese, because the salt slowly permeates the cheese in the ripening process. Little variations usually occur in different parts of the same cheese, but are so slight as to be incapable of being noticed by ordinary methods of examination.

Testing cheese for salt.—The quality of cheese as influenced by the salt is found simply by tasting.

Terms used in describing salt.—In describing the relation of salt to cheese, the following terms are used: (1) Perfect, (2) too much, (3) too little.

(1) *Perfect* applies to salt in cheese when just enough has been used to impart a sufficient taste of salt.

(2) *Too much* salt is indicated by salty taste. Too much salt in cheese causes a dry, mealy, overfirm body and imperfect flavor.

(3) *Too little* salt is shown by insipidity of taste. It is usually accompanied by bitter flavor and porous texture.

Appearance.—This term refers to the general appearance of the cheese to the eye in respect to uniformity, neatness and cleanliness. It may also include the boxing. One system, as in the case of butter, describes under "finish" the appearance of the cheese, and under "packages" the boxing; and we will follow this method here.

Testing appearance.—When the cover of the box is removed for sampling, in the case of boxed cheese, the appearance of the cheese is noticed and the box itself is examined. Cleanliness and neatness are the points to observe in judging appearance.

Terms describing appearance.—The general terms used in describing appearance are (1) finish and (2) package.

(1) *Finish* in appearance, in order to be *perfect*, must meet the following requirements: The rind must be smooth, even in color, free from cracks and fairly hard. The bandage must be without wrinkles and must be neatly rounded over the edges about an inch on each end of the cheese. The sides of the cheese should be straight and of uniform height all around.

The faults of appearance in finish are as follows, the terms being self-descriptive: (1) Cracks, (2) light spots, (3) roughness in rind, (4) uneven edges, (5) wrinkles in bandage, (6) lack of uniformity in ends and in height, (7) bulging out at sides or ends.

(2) *Package.*—The packages or boxes are regarded as perfect when of good material, well made, strong, clean, close-fitting, uniform in size and in undamaged condition.

JUDGING AND SCORING CHEESE

The qualities described in the preceding pages are used for judging and fixing the commercial value of cheese. Judging cheese consists in making an examination of a cheese with reference to the various points of quality, which have been described in the foregoing pages, as a basis for scoring cheese, which consists in assigning to each quality a definite value, corresponding to its character as found in the cheese examined. In judging cheese one must have in mind. (1) the perfection of quality in each case as a basis for comparison, and (2) the proper perspective of the different qualities in relation to each other.

Scale of points.—To each quality is assigned a definite numerical value and these numbers are called a *scale of points*. The different values assigned to the various qualities indicate perfection in each case and the totals aggregate 100. Slightly different values are assigned in different cheese markets and for cheese made by different variations in the process of manufacture. Below we present examples of different types of scale of points:

	Export cheese	Home-trade cheese	English market
Flavor	45	50	35
Texture........	15	{ 25	15
Body..........	15		25 (quality)
Color	15	15	15
Appearance..... (Finish)	10	10	10 (make)

In the case of home-trade cheese, a larger number of points is allowed for perfect flavor, because such cheese, on account of its high water-content, easily develops poor flavor and, consequently, flavor deserves more attention in judging and scoring than in case of export cheese, which, with smaller water-content, is more uniform in flavor. Then, again, in home-trade cheese, closeness of texture is not regarded as highly essential, the main emphasis being given to body.

In explanation of the English scale of points, it may be stated that the majority of Englishmen prefer cheese of considerable age, properly ripened and rather sharp in taste, and it is this character which they express by the word "quality."

Method of scoring.—In scoring a sample of cheese, an examination is made with reference to each of the qualities mentioned. In those qualities in which it is perfect, it is given the values or points assigned above. If the cheese is defective in any quality, that is, short of perfect, then a smaller value is given than the one indicated above in the scale of points; the more defective the cheese is in any quality, the lower is the value or number of points given it. When all the qualities have been scored, the numbers of points assigned to them are added and the total is the score of the cheese under examination.

It can readily be seen that judgment, trained by experience, is required to assign to each quality its proper number of points. The sense of smell and of taste must be highly developed by training in the field of experience. The eye and touch must also be trained by special experience in the actual work of sampling, studying and judging cheese.

Score-cards.—For convenience, score-cards are used in keeping records of the results of scoring where many samples are examined. The following form (see next page) illustrates a commercial score-card.

In commercial scoring, reasons for the number of points given are not stated; but in dairy schools and competitive public exhibitions, where educational purposes are in view, the reason for each

Name or number identifying sample.................................

Class or kind of cheese ....

Date.......................... Judge...........................

QUALITY	Score-points	Sample 1	Sample 2	Sample 3	Sample 4
Flavor.............	45	42	40	36	35
Texture.............	15	14	13	12	10
Body...............	15	14	15	12	10
Color...............	15	15	14	13	12
Appearance..........	10	10	8	10	8
		95	90	83	75

score should be given. The educational feature should be made especially prominent at country and state agricultural fairs, at conventions of dairymen's associations, etc. There is, and has been, altogether too little attention given to the educational feature; the main, and usually the sole, purpose has been to capture prizes. Such occasions can be made extremely valuable in an educational way by indicating in detail the defects and then indicating how these may be overcome. The following form of score-card for such purposes is a suggestion, which may be modified to suit any special conditions:

EDUCATIONAL CHEESE-SCORING CARD

Date...................... Judge..........................
Class ....
Name or number identifying cheese................................

NUMERICAL SCORE

Qualities:	Flavor	Texture	Body	Color	Appearance
Points for Perfection: }	45	15	15	15	10
Score given:	......	......	......	......	......
Total score:	......	......	......	......	......

DESCRIPTIVE SCORE (Check defects in list below)

Flavor	Texture	Body	Color	Appearance
Perfect	Perfect	Perfect	Perfect	Perfect
Clean Quick	Close	Firm	Straight	Finish: Perfect
Flat Strong	Porous	Smooth	Translucent	Cracks, Light spots
Too much acid	Mechanical-holes	Silky	Light	Rough rind
Too little acid	Pin-holes	Waxy	High	Uneven ends
Sour Bitter	Swiss-holes	Pasty	Mottled	Uneven edges
Cowy Stable	Fish-eye-holes	Weak-bodied	Streaked	Wrinkles
Sweet or fruity		Stiff or corky	Wavy	Bulging
Weedy Rancid		Crumbly	White specks	Packages:
Tallowy Fishy		Gritty	Seamy	Perfect
Tainted		Watery	Acid-cut	Clean Dirty
Hydrogen-sulphid		Overdry	Red spots	Neat Unif'm
			Uncolored	Loose Close

Remarks . . . .

Advice for overcoming defects. . . . .

Methods of grading cheese.—The classification of cheese according to the results of judging and scoring varies in different markets, the method in each case being arbitrary. For illustration, one classification is into (1) "fancy," (2) "firsts" and (3) "seconds." In the Canadian market, there are first, second and third grades.

CHEESE-MAKERS AND JUDGING CHEESE

It is a matter of regret that cheese-makers do not have more extended practical experience in judging cheese. Every cheese-maker who desires to acquire greater efficiency in his work should own a good cheese-trier and use it as often as practicable. It is well before shipment to examine one cheese from each day's make and then study the results in connection with the record of corresponding date, giving the details of the conditions of manufacture. This is frequently impracticable, because cheese is shipped before it can be properly judged. Then, again, cheese which appears well when shipped may develop imperfect qualities later; while some cheese, imperfect at the start, may improve later if kept under proper conditions.

CHAPTER IX

Cheese-Factory Construction

A cheese-factory should be a model of cleanliness in every dairy community. At the present time the word cheese-factory does not stand for any such ideal condition. In the construction or remodeling of factory buildings, attention should be given to the following points: (1) Location and site, (2) material to be used, (3) architecture, (4) water-supply, (5) drainage, and (6) curing-rooms.

LOCATION AND SITE

The selection of a suitable location and site is one of the most important factors in cheese-factory construction. The factory should be centrally located and, if possible, on a hillside where advantage may be taken of gravity and other natural conditions.

Before we were familiar with the importance of sanitation, cheese-factories were invariably erected on low, wet ground where a water-supply could easily be obtained. No attention was paid to the means of disposing of the excess of whey and of sewage from the building. The result was that in a short time the soil surrounding the factory became saturated with decayed waste products; the water-supply was made impure from the same source; in hot weather, flies gathered in large numbers, carrying bacteria and dirt from the stagnant surroundings into the vats containing milk and curd. As a result of these conditions, bad flavors appeared in the cheese, and cheese-makers experienced all sorts of difficulties in the factory operations. Most of these bad conditions have since been removed or remedied, but in many parts of the country they are still to be found. In Ontario, Canada, especially, great improvement has been made in the sanitation of cheese-factories since the passing of a special law and the appointing of special sanitary inspectors. Most factorymen now appreciate the **value** of cleanly conditions surrounding the entire manufacturing process, but many must be forced to put their buildings and equipment in proper condition.

MATERIAL TO BE USED

Appearance, cheapness, durability and efficiency should be kept in mind. Brick buildings are to be preferred, and, while their first cost is greater than wood, they are the most durable and cheapest in the end. Cement, when properly made and used, makes an efficient, fairly cheap and durable building. Stone and wood are commonly used. The relative economy with which the building material can be obtained will largely influence the character of buildings erected in different localities.

ARCHITECTURE

Plans and blue-prints of modern cheese-factories are always available, free of charge, from the agricultural departments of the different governments, so that it is unnecessary in this treatment of the subject to go into details. Suffice it to say that the architecture should be simple, attractive and convenient. The location and site will determine to a great extent the style of architecture.

WATER-SUPPLY

Nothing is of more importance in factory construction than the water-supply. The quality should be pure and an abundance of it should be assured. The purity of springs, deep wells, rivers, and lakes with a large outlet can usually be depended upon, but the character of the surrounding area drained must be considered. Surface water, by all means, should be kept out of the wells. If milk or whey enters a well accidentally or otherwise, the water soon becomes contaminated and unfit for use. When this occurs, the water should be pumped out and the well thoroughly cleaned.

DRAINAGE

Drainage is so closely related to the water-supply that they are naturally considered together. If possible in any way, natural drainage should be secured. In cheese-factory work there is usually a considerable volume of sewage, consisting of wash water and excess of whey. The best method for its disposal is now attracting the attention of factorymen and of those who enforce the laws of health and sanitation. The character of sewage at all cheese-factories is practically the same. The method of its disposal will depend on the water content, the character of the constituents, and slope of the surrounding soil. The waste or superfluous whey is the main cause for need of improved sanitation at cheese-factories. If it were not for this, the wash water could be more easily disposed of. However, the following methods have given excellent satisfaction when properly installed under suitable conditions.

Removal by cartage.—This system requires a storage-tank for wash water as well as for whey, although many factorymen allow the wash water to run into the whey-tank. Arrangements are made by which some person agrees to remove all sewage from the factory to some river, lake or satisfactory place of disposal and to clean the whey-vats at stated times in return for the superfluous whey he may receive to use for feeding purposes. As a rule, this method is satisfactory, and its use is advised when the others are not more practicable.

Direct disposal into large lakes and running streams of water.—Many factories are located on the banks of lakes and rivers, into which it is usually an easy matter to conduct the sewage by means of piping or tile. This makes an ideal method, if the body of water is large or has sufficient current to carry it to a suitable outlet.

Septic-tank system.—This consists of a series of tanks, in which the sewage is treated before being allowed to flow out into or on top of the surrounding ground. The number and size of tanks will depend on the size of the factory and the character of soil into which the treated sewage must pass. Fig. 20 illustrates a plan for a factory with a daily capacity for 10,000 pounds of milk, whose treated sewage passes out into heavy soil with little natural drainage.

The material used in tank construction can be iron, cement or wood. Each part should be large enough to hold the sewage of 24 hours. By this arrangement the sewage is in the tank for three days. At the end of this period it may be carried by piping or tile to its final place of deposit. The overflow-pipes should be ventilated to prevent siphoning of the contents after it starts to overflow. The tanks are

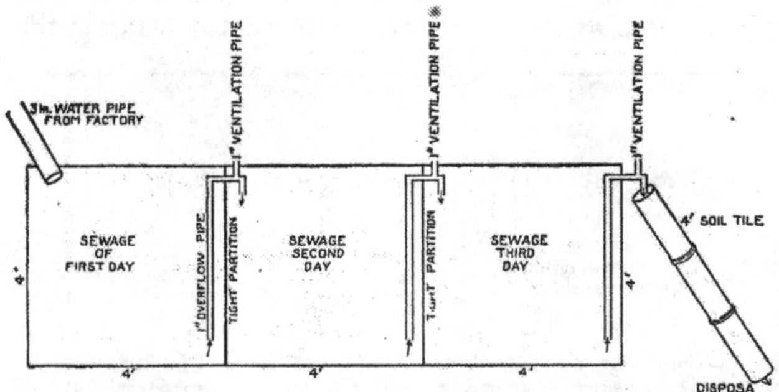

FIG. 20—SERIES OF SEPTIC TANKS CAPABLE OF HOLDING THREE DAYS' SEWAGE FROM A CHEESE-FACTORY HANDLING 10,000 POUNDS OF MILK A DAY

better placed under ground so that the top just reaches the surface. It should have a good top and may then be covered with earth. It is advisable to have a water-trap in the pipe delivering the sewage from the factory to the septic tank in order to prevent odors returning. This system is very efficient and may be used in almost any locality. In some places it is advisable to deposit the treated sewage on a prepared, gravel filter-bed.

Cesspools.—When the surrounding soil is of sand or gravel, the cesspool makes an efficient and cheap method for sewage disposal. For a factory with a daily capacity of 10,000 pounds of milk, a cesspool of the following dimensions and construction is advised: A hole 12 feet in diameter and 6 feet deep is excavated. This should be lined with loose stones up to within one foot of the ground surface. Over this, cedar logs, with good supports, are placed at intervals of 24 inches. A plank covering goes over the logs, and this again is covered with earth, making the

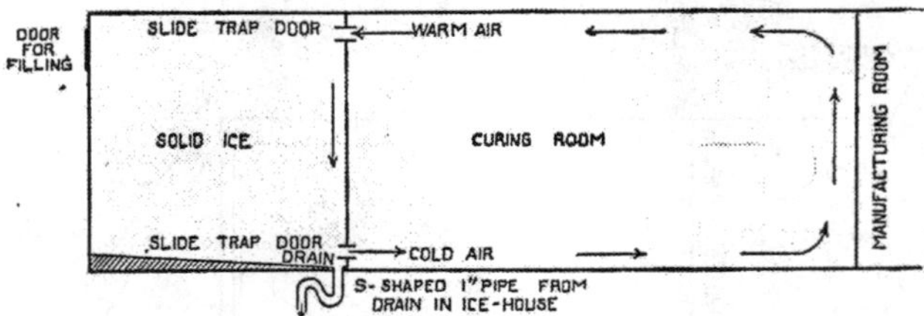

FIG. 21—PLAN SHOWING SATISFACTORY METHOD FOR SECURING CIRCULATION OF COLD AIR IN CHEESE-CURING ROOMS

spot unnoticeable. A cesspool should be located at least 20 feet away from the buildings, and on the lower side of the source of water-supply. The pipe leading from the factory floor to cesspool should have a water-trap to prevent returning odors. It is advisable to place on all whey-tanks an overflow pipe connected with the drainage deposit.

CURING-ROOMS

A curing-room should be so constructed that the temperature and humidity can be controlled. It should have good ventilation, insulation and circulation of pure air. Under ordinary conditions, ice provides the cheapest and most efficient method of maintaining a uniformly cool temperature in curing-rooms. In large cheese-making centers, artificial refrigerating machines are used, but they are too costly for ordinary cheese-factories. Sub-earth ducts have proved unsatisfactory, since they are too often least efficient when most needed.

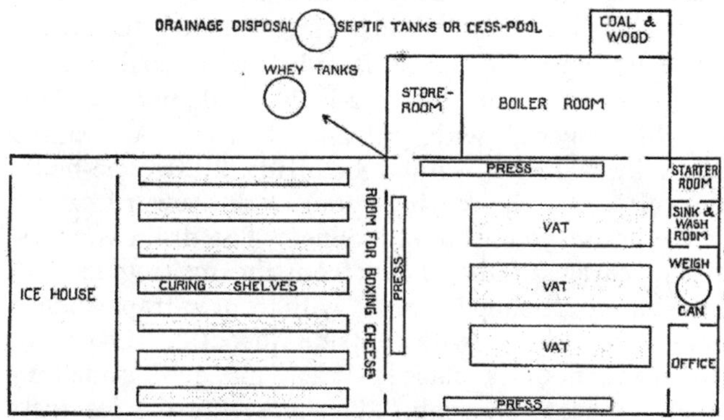

FIG. 22—MODERN PLAN SHOWING IDEAL ARRANGEMENT OF CHEESE-FACTORY ROOMS AND EQUIPMENT

The drawing on page 102 (Fig. 21) provides a scheme by which the air in the curing-room has a continuous circulation over a bed of solid ice

The curing-room and ice-house should have good insulation secured by the use of lumber, building-paper, air-spaces, shavings and cement floors. The ice-house should be one-third the size of the curing-room. Three thicknesses of lumber, one of damp-proof paper, and 6 inches of shavings provide sufficient insulation for the curing-room.   For the ice-house an extra thickness of lumber and damp-proof paper is advised in both ceiling and wall construction. The ice-house floor and walls halfway up are lined with galvanized iron.

The construction of the floor in the ice-house is important, as provision must be made for protecting the ice from the warm temperatures of the soil underneath.   A cement floor with gravel and stone support is first constructed.   Over this, 2-inch by 4-inch supports are placed on edge at intervals of 18 inches. Between these the space is filled with coal cinders or shavings.   Over this a 2-inch plank floor is laid, and this covered with galvanized iron.   A drain 2 inches by 2 inches should be made in the ice-house floor close to the curing-room wall, toward which the ice-house floor should incline.   The drain is necessary to carry off the water from the melting ice.   A close-fitting S-shaped pipe with water-trap should connect the drain with outside disposal.   Over the galvanized floor is placed a rack made of 2-inch by 4-inch supports on edge.   This prevents the ice from lying in water when it starts to melt.   During the winter months, the ice-house is packed full of ice. No sawdust is used, the insulation being sufficient to protect it

As Figure 21 shows, small trap-slides are placed near the ceiling and floor between ice-house and curing-room.   As soon as these are opened, the warm air in the curing-room enters the openings at the top, passes over the ice and out through the lower openings, thus creating a circulation of cold air through the curing-room.   A uniform temperature of from 52°

to 56° F. can be secured throughout the entire summer season in this way, and a uniform percentage of moisture is also assured

When this system is not used, the curing-room air may be cooled by hanging up large pans filled with ice, but the moisture from them generally stimulates mold formation. Where cold running water is available, it can be conducted through a system of coil-pipes around the walls of the curing-room and the temperature considerably lowered.

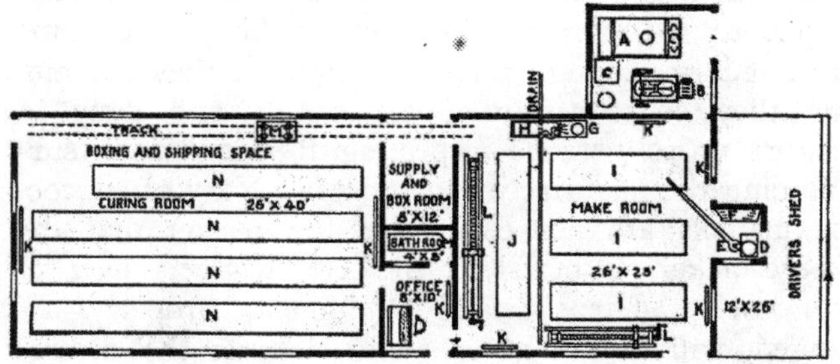

FIG. 23—PLAN FOR CHEESE-FACTORY HANDLING 12,000 TO 20,000 POUNDS OF MILK A DAY. (Baer)

A—Boiler; B—Engine; C—Sterilizing-oven; D—Weigh-can and scales; E—Conductor-spout; F—Bottle-rack; G—Milk-tester; H—Wash-sink; I—Cheese-vats; J—Curd-sink; K—Steam-radiators; L—Cheese-presses; M—Truck; N—Curing-shelves.

CHEESE-FACTORY PLANS

As a suggestion, we give the outline of a plan for cheese-factory construction with special reference to convenience of arrangement for equipment. (Fig. 22.)

We give also an outline plan published by U. S. Baer, of Wisconsin. (Fig. 23.)

CHAPTER X

Cheese-Factory Equipment

A cheese-factory should be so equipped that everything may be easily kept clean. The vats, presses, sinks and all utensils should be placed in positions that will insure convenience and a minimum amount of labor. Too many factories at the present time are not large enough for the equipment they contain, and they consequently appear untidy and dirty to visitors or to persons inspecting the conditions surrounding the manufacturing process. Very often, too, the utensils are not clean for the reason that the cheese-maker, being short of help, neglects part of the work. Utensils and equipment, properly arranged, will save a great many steps to the cheesemaker in a day. (Figs. 22 and 23.)

Advice, which is the result of varied experience and which is often of considerable help to persons in need of such assistance, can always be secured from experts employed by the different departments of agriculture.

The following apparatus is sufficient for a factory handling 10,000 pounds of milk daily.

(1) One 12-horse-power, return-flue, horizontal boiler with fixtures.

(2) Two steam-heating cheese-vats, with a capacity of 7,000 pounds each. In recent years, wood suitable for making cheese-vats has become expensive and hard to secure. Many manufacturers are using wood

of a poorer quality, and the vats are not durable. Steel vats have been placed on the market and are giving general satisfaction.   They are preferable to the average wooden vat now manufactured. (Fig. 24.)

(3)   Whey-tank, capacity of 12,000 pounds. If the factory is so located that its elevation permits the loading of whey without pumping, then one large tank can be used. However, two smaller tanks connected by an overflow-pipe are preferable, because, when one is empty, it can be cleaned while the other contains whey. Steel tanks are preferable to wooden or cement ones. They neither leak nor absorb, are easily cleaned, and are more durable.   Cement tanks are not durable,

FIG. 24—ONE TYPE OF STEEL CHEESE-VAT

because the acid and salt in the whey destroy the cement.

(4)   One 600-pound, double-beam scale.   Scales are in daily use at cheese-factories and it is advisable to purchase only those that are reliable and guaranteed, such as the "Fairbanks" and "Howe."

(5)   One 70-gallon weighing-can with a 3-inch gate.

(6)   One milk-conductor and head.

(7)   Apparatus and alkali for testing acidity.

(8) One Marschall or Monrad rennet-test.

(9) One 3-8-inch, horizontal, steel curd-knife.

(10) One 5-16-inch perpendicular, wire curd-knife.

(11) Two small solid-handle dippers.

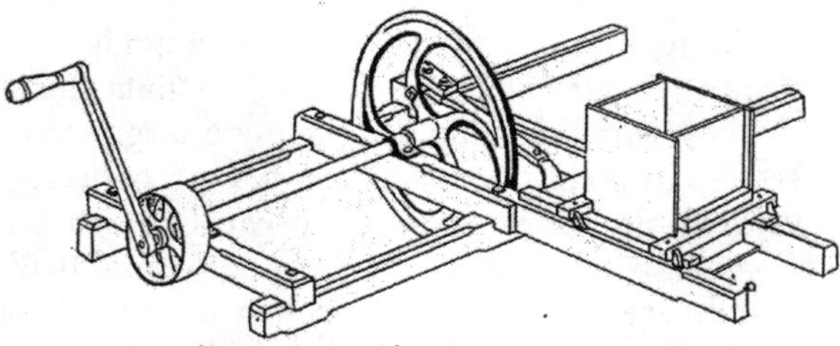

FIG. 25—BARNARD'S CURD-CUTTER

(12) One strainer-dipper.

(13) Two curd-agitators of McPherson type.

(14) Two curd-rakes.

(15) Two thermometers, strictly correct and reliable.

(16) One outfit for making commercial starters.

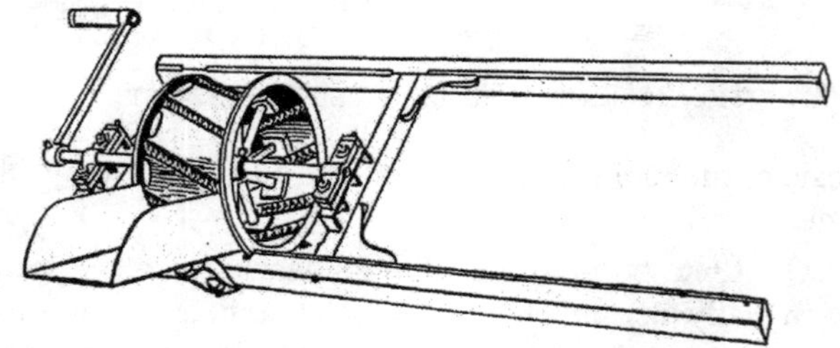

FIG. 26—GOSSELIN CURD-MILL

(17) Two whey-strainers for each vat.

(18) One large knife for cutting curd.

(19) One curd-mill. A curd-mill should be so constructed that its knives will go against the curd

in cutting. The curd should not be pushed against the knives. Such mills as the Barnard (Fig. 25), Beech and Gosselin (Fig. 26) are recommended. They can be had in hand or steam-power.

(20) Two curd-stirring forks of wood or steel, with points turned over so as not to puncture the tin vats during stirring.

(21) One curd-scoop.

(22) One flat-sided curd-pail.

(23) Two steel-frame, automatic, continuous-pressure gang-presses with hoops, followers, etc., com-

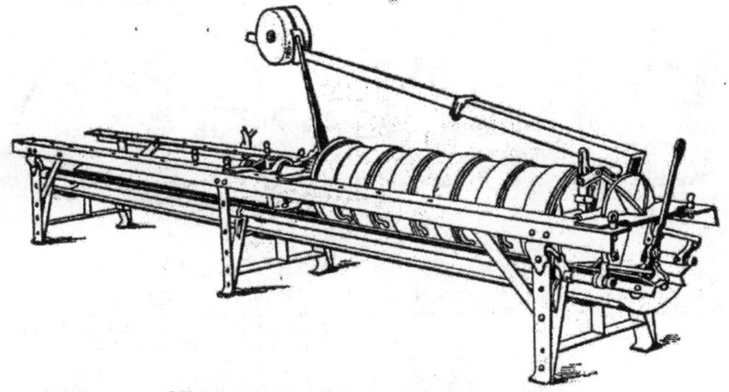

FIG. 27—CONTINUOUS-PRESSURE GANG-PRESS

plete. (Figs. 27 and 28.) Galvanized-steel followers are preferable to wooden ones, as they are more sanitary, are not absorbent, do not expand or contract readily, and are more durable. Galvanized rings are preferable to the fiber or rubber ones for the same reasons.

(24) One 240-pound cheese-scale.

(25) One 24-bottle Babcock milk-tester.

(26) Two composite-sample bottles for each patron.

(27) If the whey is to be separated and whey-butter made from the fat, a separator and machinery for butter-making will be necessary.

(28) An instrument for determining the amount of moisture in the air of the curing-room. (Fig. 29.)

(29) A sterilizing-oven for sterilizing milk to be used in the preparation of starters and also for the sterilization of the smaller utensils employed in the cheese-factory will be found convenient and highly useful. Home-made sterilizers can be used with good

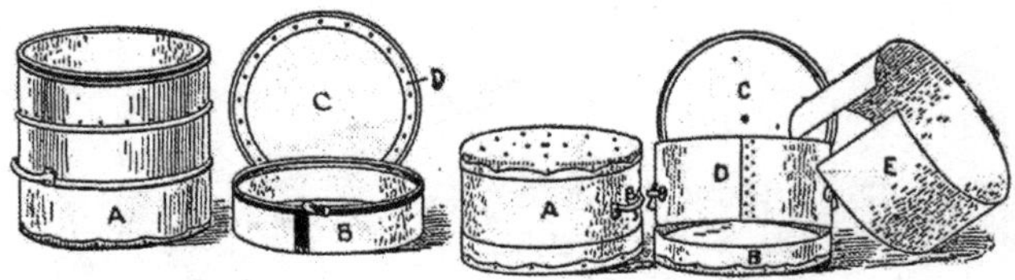

FIG. 28

FRASER HOOP
A—Complete hoop; B—Bandages; C—Follower; D—Fibrous press-ring.

WILSON HOOP
A—Complete hoop; B—Bottom cover with wide flange; C—Top cover with narrow flange; D—Closed or tight hoop or body; E—Open hoop or bandages.

results. A galvanized-iron box, double-jacketed, is arranged to admit steam between the walls. An opening in the top of the outside wall is arranged to regulate steam pressure and another at the bottom to carry off condensed water. The outside may be protected by a covering of asbestos or other boards.

(30) One Quevenne lactometer.

FACTORY FURNISHINGS

Fuel, coal or wood.

Rennet-extract (Hansen's is recommended).

Cheese color (Hansen's is recommended).
Commercial starter.
Vat-brooms.
Floor-brush.
Washing-powder.
Cotton for press-cloths.

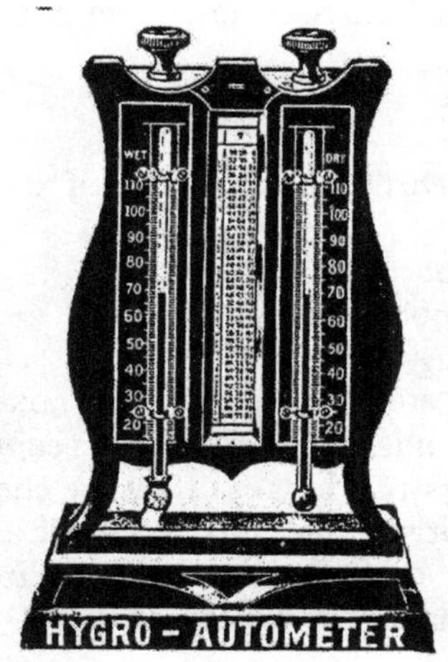

FIG. 29—APPARATUS FOR INDICATING
PERCENTAGE OF MOISTURE IN AIR
OF CURING-ROOM

Cheese-bandage. This should be seamless and the size ¼ inch smaller than the diameter of hoops; a cheese retains its shape better with such bandage.

Cheese-circles.

Cheese-salt. Paper-lined barrels are preferable. The salt should be regular cheese-salt. Fine butter-salt dissolves too rapidly and does not penetrate the curd so well. Such brands as Windsor, Diamond, Crystal, Genesee, LeRoy, Warsaw and Worcester are generally reliable.

Cheese-boxes. These are made of both wood and paper. If properly made, either material is satisfactory. The boxes should be strong enough to stand handling in shipping, and they should fit the cheese. One-quarter inch between the cheese and box is sufficient.

Scale-boards.

Milk-sheets.

Blanks for records of conditions of cheese-making (p. 16).

Blanks for reports to patrons.

Milk-record books.

Cheese-shipping books.

Materials and stencils for branding boxes.

It is a great mistake for factorymen to purchase cheap furnishings just because they are cheap. Cheese of the best quality is the most profitable to make, and no cheese-maker can afford to use poor furnishings if he expects to have his cheese of finest quality and appearance.

Part II

Defects of American Cheddar Cheese in Flavor, Body, Texture, Color and Finish:

Causes
Remedies
Means of Prevention

CHAPTER XI

Defects in Flavor

In this and several chapters following, an effort is made for the first time to present in systematic form a discussion of the imperfections that are most commonly found in our American cheddar cheese. The need of this requires no explanation, and the importance of the subject is only too obvious. The extent of defects in our cheese is well known and also their demoralizing effect upon the industry. In reality, the whole aim of the cheese-maker is, of course, to produce cheese free from imperfections. In discussing the subject, it is necessary to know (1) what the defects are, and (2) to what causes they are due. We are then in position to consider remedies and means of prevention. The subject will be presented under the following divisions:

Defects in
    (1) Flavor.
    (2) Body.
    (3) Texture
    (4) Color.
    (5) Finish.

In each division, the presentation will give (1) description of defect, (2) causes, (3) methods of prevention and (4) remedies. It is important to know how to prevent the recurrence of conditions that are responsible for cheese-making troubles, and also how to handle the details of the cheese-making process when the presence of the trouble is recognized. The facts will be presented more or less in outline form, in order to make reference to them more convenient.

ACID FLAVORS

These are indicated by a sour smell and taste.

Cause:

    (1)   Over-development of acidity during the process of cheese-making, which is commonly due to—

        (a)   Ripening the milk too much before adding the rennet.

        (b)   The use of too much starter.

        (c)   Failure to firm the curd sufficiently before removing the whey.

    (2)   Any condition that retains in the curd and cheese an excessive amount of whey (p. 46).

Prevention:

    (1)   Have less acidity in the milk before adding rennet-extract. Sour milk, or milk over 0.26 per cent in acidity, should not be accepted from any patron. High acidity can be overcome by patron, if he will cool milk to 60° F., or better 50° F., at once after milking.

    (2)   Use less starter. Generally $\frac{1}{2}$ to 2 per cent is sufficient.

    (3)   Add the rennet when such a degree of acidity is present that the curd will become firm in the whey before developing the desired amount of acid.

Remedy:

(See the treatment given under remedy for acid body (p. 122).

OFF FLAVORS

These are flavors that are not clean, such as rancid or butyric acid flavor, stable or cow-manure flavor, fishy flavor and hydrogen sulphid or sulphur-spring flavor. When these develop so as to become very strong, they are called *"stinkers."*

Cause:

Undesirable bacteria, which gain entrance to the milk or to the curd, commonly due to—

(1) Failure of patrons thoroughly to wash and scald all cans and utensils coming in contact with the milk. This is particularly true of cans in which whey is carried from the factory.

(2) Careless milking in unclean places.

(3) Allowing the milk to become exposed, after milking, in places where the air is impure.

(4) Keeping the milk at too high temperature.

(5) Using an unclean strainer at either the farm or cheese-factory.

(6) Using utensils in the factory that have not been thoroughly cleaned and scalded.

(7) Using badly-flavored starters.

(8) Using impure water for diluting rennet.

(9) Soaking curd in impure water after milling.

(10) Using tainted rennet or salt.

(11) Ripening cheese at temperatures above 65° F.

Prevention:

Strict cleanliness in the production and handling of milk and throughout the whole cheese-making process (pp. 8, 17).

(1) All utensils, especially the milk-strainer, should be thoroughly washed with warm water, using washing-powder, and then scalded with live steam.

(2) Milking should be done in clean places, where dust. cobwebs and flies are not present.

(3) Milk should be cooled to at least 60°, and better 50° F., immediately after being drawn from the cow.

(4) Tainted milk should not be received at the factory from any patron. If uncertain of the source of tainted milk or curd, use the fermentation test on each patron's milk (p. 434).

(5) A small amount of clean-flavored starter should be used.

(6) Impure or bad-smelling water should not be used.

(7) There should be screens on the doors and windows to prevent the entrance of flies.

(8) When curd is washed, only pure water should be used.

Remedy:

(1) Firm the curd a little more than usual in the whey by raising the temperature.

(2)   Develop a little more acidity before removing all the whey.

(3)   Mill the curd early and expose well to fresh air by stirring for some time immediately after. Excellent results can be secured at this time because each small piece of curd has six freshly cut surfaces which permit the gases and odors to escape.

(4)   Increase the amount of salt in curd in extremely bad cases.

(5)   Ripen the cheese at low temperature.

FRUITY FLAVORS

These are sweet flavors, having an odor like that of certain ripe fruits, such as pineapple, raspberry and strawberry. Such flavors are not pleasant to the taste and are rather sickish.

Cause:

(1)   Bacteria or yeasts carried into the milk by dirt.

(2)   Transporting both milk and whey in the same cans when not properly cleansed.

(3)   Exposing milk near hog-pens where whey is fed.

Prevention:

(1)   Cans used for delivering milk should not carry whey, unless they are emptied and thoroughly cleansed immediately after being brought from the factory.

(2)   All whey should be pasteurized at the factories. This would not only reduce greatly the source of badly flavored milk, but it would eliminate the danger of transmission of tuberculosis through the whey.

(3)   The whey-tanks should be cleaned and scalded at least twice a week. A steel tank has the following advantages: It is more durable than wood or cement, does not leak, does not absorb whey, is easily cleaned, and is cheaper in the end.

(4)   Use a clean-flavored commercial starter.

Remedy:

(1)   Firm the curd a little more in the whey by raising the temperature.

(2)   Develop a little more acidity before removing whey.

(3)   Air the curd well after milling.

(4)   In extreme cases use more salt in the curd.

BITTER FLAVORS

Indicated by a bitter taste and a weedy odor.

Cause:

(1) Bacteria and yeasts.
(2) Allowing cows to wade in and drink from stagnant pools.
(3) Using rusted milk-cans or other utensils.
(4) Using old starters that have developed too much acid.
(5) Using milk delivered in cans in which sour whey from dirty tanks is carried.
(6) Too little salt in curd.

Prevention:

(1) Milk should be cooled to at least 60° F., and better to 50° F., immediately after milking.
(2) Rusted cans or utensils of any kind should not carry milk.
(3) Cows should have only good water.
(4) Clean-flavored starters only should be used.
(5) Avoid the use of too little salt in the curd.

Remedy:

(1) Very little acidity should be developed before removing the whey.
(2) Firm the curd more than usual. Heat it higher in the whey and stir it drier when removing the whey.
(3) Mill early and expose well to fresh air by stirring.
(4) In extreme cases use more salt in the curd.

FOOD FLAVORS

These include flavors characteristic of the foods eaten by cows. A food flavor can be distinguished from one produced by bacteria in that a bacterial flavor usually gets worse as the cheese ages, while a food flavor generally passes off to some extent (p. 8).

Cause:

(1) Such foods as turnips, onions, leeks, weeds, garlic, rape, decayed ensilage and certain green fodders (p. 7).

(2) Exposing milk in an atmosphere where any of these are exposed.
(3) Storing milk in cellars where decayed vegetables are present.

Prevention:

(1) Foods that impart any objectionable flavor to milk should not be fed or made accessible to the cow.
(2) Use a good commercial starter.
(3) Careful and thorough aeration (p. 12) of milk is often helpful in removing odors derived from foods

Remedy:

(1) Heat the curd several degrees higher in the whey. The high temperature helps to drive off the volatile flavors.
(2) Air the curd well, especially after milling.
(3) Ripen the cheese at a low temperature.

CHAPTER XII

Defects in Body and in Texture

Dry Body

Shown in cheese that is too firm, mealy, rubbery or corky.

Cause:

Lack of moisture or milk-fat or both; produced by—
(1) Removing part of the fat from milk.
(2) Too high heating in the whey.
(3) Heating too long.
(4) Too much stirring at the time of removing the whey.
(5) Using too much salt.
(6) Curing cheese in an atmosphere that is too dry or too hot.
(7) A "high-cooked" cheese is rubbery or corky; one that has been stirred too dry is mealy or sandy; and one that is dry from excess of salt tastes salty. This is a convenient way of determining the cause of such defects.

Prevention:

(1) All the milk-fat should be retained in the cheese as far as possible.
(2) The lower the temperature used in properly firming the curd, the better will be the texture of the cheese.
(3) Be absolutely sure of the correctness of the thermometers used.
(4) Give attention to the moisture content of the curd; stir the curd as conditions require; and use the proper amount of salt.

Remedy:

(1) Pile dry curd higher.
(2) Keep the air moist by placing hot water in the vat.
(3) Do not mill the dry curd early.
(4) A dry curd can be made mellow by soaking in cold water after milling, but the cheese will not have good-keeping quality.
(5) Use less than the usual amount of salt.

(6)   Paraffin the cheese as soon as practicable.
(7)   Ripen the cheese in a cool room where the humidity
       of the atmosphere is at least 80 per cent.

ACID BODY

Cheese under this head may be either dry or moist, but in either case is of a mealy or sandy character. It has a sour taste.

Cause:

(1)   Overripe milk.
(2)   Ripening the milk too much before adding the rennet.
(3)   The development of too much acidity during the cheese-making process, especially before the whey is removed.
(4)   Acid or sour cheese is most frequently caused not by developing too much acidity, but by having the curd insufficiently firm in the whey when the acidity has developed.
(5)   Using large amounts of starter.

Prevention:

(1)   No sour milk, or milk containing more than 0.26 per cent of acidity, should be received from any patron.
(2)   The rennet should be added when the milk is at such a stage of ripeness that there will be time to firm the curd in the whey before too much acidity has developed.
(3)   Do not use too much starter.
(4)   Keep the development of acidity under control by controlling the amount of whey in the curd.

Remedy:

The method of handling overripe or sour milk, when it is absolutely necessary to make such milk into cheese, is as follows:

(1)   Heat the milk not above 84° F.
(2)   Use an extra amount of rennet.
(3)   Cut the curd into smaller pieces.
(4)   Heat higher. The degree of heat will depend on the rapidity with which the acidity is developing. Most fast-working curd contracts rapidly and therefore the raising of the temperature can be hurried.

(5) As soon as possible after heating, the whey should be run down to the level of the curd. This greatly facilitates stirring and firming the curd, and, if more than one vat is being used, time is saved when the remainder of the whey is to be removed. If by this time the curd is not firm and shows too much acidity, a sour cheese can be prevented by;

(6) Removing the whey and putting on water at a temperature of 102° F. The amount of water used and the time it is left on will depend on the amount of acidity in the curd. In extreme cases, it may be necessary to give a second treatment with water. As soon as the curd becomes firmed in the water and the acidity is reduced to a normal amount, the water should be removed. The curd should then be treated like a normal curd. This method is not to be confounded with the "soaked-curd" process, which is entirely different.

(7) If, after milling, the curd is sour, it can be improved by washing in pure water at 80° F. This resembles the "soaked-curd" process, and, as a rule, such cheese does not keep well. However, it is much better to do this than to allow the cheese to sour, and the process should be used in extreme cases.

(8) Use an extra amount of salt after washing.

LOOSE OR OPEN TEXTURE

Cheese with this texture is full of holes. Such cheese is generally soft in body. Such defects are more serious when found in export cheese, since a "close-boring" cheese is demanded for this trade.

Cause:

(1) Developing too little acid and retaining too much whey.
(2) Putting curd to press at too high a temperature.
(3) Lack of pressing.
(4) Soaking curd in water after milling.

Prevention:

(1) Have at least 0.24 per cent of acidity in whey running from curd after it is piled for cheddaring.
(2) The curd should be cooled to 80° F., at least, before pressing. This can be hastened by running cold water around the outside of the vat lining.

(3) Pressing for 48 hours is much better than for 24. A continuous pressure is of more value than a heavy pressure for a short time.
(4) Curd should not be soaked in water.

Remedy:

(1) Open-textured cheese can be closed up to some extent by pressing again.
(2) Ripen at lower temperatures.

GASSY CHEESE TEXTURE

Indicated by the presence of pin-holes. Such cheese usually has a bad flavor, is spongy, and the curd may float on the whey in the early stage of cheese-making.

Cause:

(1) Milk infected by gas-producing bacteria, which are carried in by dirt.
(2) Starters infected by gas-producing bacteria.

Prevention:

(1) Gassy milk should not be accepted from any patron.
(2) Gassy starters should not be used.

Remedy:

The method of handling gassy milk or curd is as follows:

(1) If it is known that the milk is gassy, use a safe amount of clean commercial starter.
(2) Ripen the milk a trifle more before adding the rennet.
(3) After cutting, stir the curd till the whey around it shows at least 0.15 per cent of acidity before heating.
(4) Heat slowly. Take 30 to 60 minutes.
(5) Care should be taken to have the curd not too firm in the whey before the acid begins to form. The acidity is a valuable guide at this time.
(6) A little more acidity should be allowed to develop before removing the whey. About 0.32 per cent after all the whey is off is sufficient.
(7) Should the curd float, remove the whey to such an extent that it can not float.
(8) Pile gassy curd before and after milling.
(9) After milling, the curd should be thoroughly stirred and aired before piling. The pressure causes the small pieces to become very thin. After the piling

and airing have been repeated a few times at inter
vals of 15 to 20 minutes, most of the gases should
have escaped. The pin-holes will then have become flattened and present a "dead" appearance.

(10) The whey running from the curd at this time should
show 1.2 per cent of acidity.
(11) Cool the curd well before putting in press.
(12) Press for 48 hours if possible
(13) Ripen in a cool place

GREASY TEXTURE

This is indicated by the presence of free fat in the
mechanical holes in the cheese. The surface of the
cheese is usually greasy. This condition is most
common in spring and in times of drouth.

Cause:

(1) Allowing separation and hardening or drying of cream
on milk before manufacturing. In factories that
do not take milk on Sunday, the trouble is always
greatest on Monday.
(2) Abnormal proportion of fat to casein in milk in times
of drouth (p. 164).
(3) Heating milk too high or too long before adding
rennet.
(4) Handling curd too roughly.
(5) Piling curd too much.
(6) Maturing curd at high temperature.
(7) Using a mill that bruises the curd.
(8) Ripening cheese at high temperatures.

Prevention:

(1) Make up the milk daily, or take pains to keep the
cream stirred in, to prevent formation of dry lumps
that cannot be worked back perfectly into the milk.
(2) Cut and stir the curd very carefully while soft.
(3) Do not pile the curd more than two layers deep.
(4) Do not heat the milk or curd too high. Be sure of the
accuracy of the thermometer used.
(5) Use a mill that cuts the curd without squeezing the
fat from it. The knives should go against the curd
and not the curd against the knives.
(6) Apply the salt soon after milling and mature the curd
after salting.
(7) Ripen the cheese in a cool room.

Remedy:

   (1) Rinse the curd with water at 90° F. before salting.
        Then use a trifle more salt.
   (2) Cool the curd before putting in press.
   (3) Use large, clean press-cloths to insure the formation
        of a good rind.
   (4) Use sufficient hot water at the time of dressing the
        cheese

FISH-EYE TEXTURE OR YEASTY CHEESE

This is indicated by holes or slits resembling the eye of a fish. (Fig. 30.) This is usually accompanied by a bitter flavor. The first indication of this texture is the formation in the cheese of a number of small pin-holes surrounded by white rings. These gradually enlarge until the characteristic slit-like

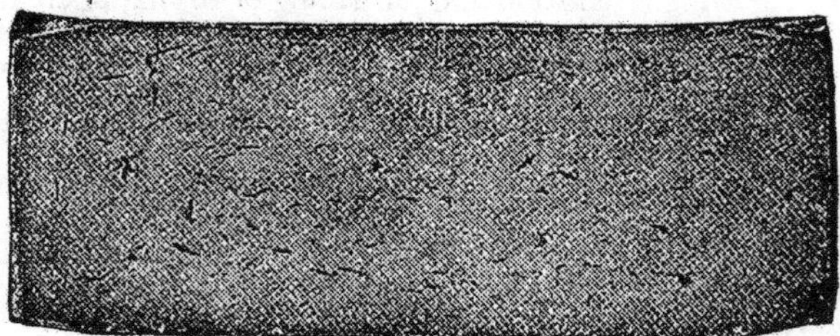

FIG. 30—TYPICAL ILLUSTRATION OF THE SLIT-LIKE HOLES
FORMED IN A "YEASTY" CHEESE

openings are formed. Usually they are most noticeable near the rind, but in advanced stages extend throughout the whole cheese. If present in colored cheese, the color may become badly mottled as the cheese ages. When the cause of this trouble is present in milk, there is a bitter taste, which becomes more pronounced as the acidity of the milk increases.

Acidity usually appears in the milk quite slowly, even after the curd has been first cut. When the formation of acid once starts, it increases very rapidly. This is usually during the interval when the whey is removed. The acid increases rapidly and the curd tends to become soft or mushy. In the cheddaring process the curd may become more or less filled with large, shining openings, resembling gas-holes. After milling, the curd is usually very slow to contract and, in severe cases, may soften and lose its body. Frequently yeasts are accompanied by gas-producing bacteria and, when this combination is encountered in cheese-making, it is very difficult to make cheese of passable quality. Whey from such cheese, when whey tanks are not frequently cleaned, may appear to boil, as though over a fire.

Cause:

Yeasts which gain entrance to milk. They have been found on hay-dust, leaves of trees, in unclean cellars, and in whey-tanks.

   (1) In cheese-factory work, the whey tank is the great source of germ contamination.
   (2) Allowing milk to be exposed to the dust of stables after milking (p. 6).
   (3) Keeping milk too warm after placing it in the cans.

Prevention:

   (1) After milk is drawn, it should immediately be taken into a clean atmosphere and cooled to 60° F., and better to 50° F.
   (2) Whey-tanks should be cleaned and scalded twice a week, at least, and, better still, every day.
   (3) All the whey should be pasteurized.
   (4) All cans and utensils used in carrying milk should be thoroughly cleaned and scalded.

Remedy:

When it is known that yeast-infected milk has been received, it should be treated in the following way:

(1) A good commercial starter should be used.
(2) The rennet should be added when the milk is at such a stage of ripeness that there will be time to firm the curd in the whey before too much acidity has developed.
(3) Use a higher temperature for heating. Generally about 2° F. higher is sufficient.
(4) Remove the whey with as little acidity as is necessary to mature the curd properly in cheddaring. If a good starter has been used, an acidity of 0.24 per cent, after the whey is all removed and the curd packed, should be sufficient.
(5) Stir the curd well at the time of removing the whey.
(6) Do not pile the curd high in cheddaring unless gas is present.
(7) Mill the curd early and air well immediately after.
(8) Should the curd become mushy after milling, apply one-half the amount of salt to be used. Then in about an hour, or as soon as the curd has shrunken and the holes have closed, apply the balance of the salt.
(9) Curing at low temperature helps to check the slit formation and the bitter flavor.

CHAPTER XIII

Defects in Color and in Finish

PALE OR ACID-CUT COLOR

This term refers to the lighter color of portions of cheese (p. 89).

Cause:

(1) The development of too much acid, which bleaches or renders paler the color of the curd.
(2) Failure to firm the curd in the whey early enough.
(3) Using large amounts of starter.
(4) Using poor cheese-coloring.

Prevention:

(1) Have the curd firmed in the whey before the acidity has developed to more than 0.18 per cent.
(2) Cheese should be colored to suit the market for which it is intended.

Remedy:

(1) The best place and time to produce a bright, even color in the curd is in the whey, while the whey is being removed. From the time the whey has reached the level of the curd till it is all removed, the curd should be well stirred. By watching the curd during this handling, the color can be seen to develop rapidly. This is due to the breaking of the film of moisture which surrounds each piece of curd.
(2) Allow the curd to stand some time after salting before putting in press.

MOTTLED COLOR

This means an uneven color, most noticeable in colored cheese.

Cause:

   (1) An uneven development of acid and moisture in the curd.

   (2) Uneven cutting, leading to an uneven contraction of the curd when heated in the whey.

   (3) Neglecting to strain the starter when lumpy.

   (4) Adding the starter after adding the cheese-color.

   (5) Uneven piling and maturing of the curd

   (6) Use of poor cheese-color.

   (7) Mixing the curd from different vats.

   (8) Lumpy condition of the curd at the time of removing the whey, or when salt is applied.

   (9) Adding old curd to fresh curd without proper precautions.

  (10) Yeasts. When due to these, the mottling increases with the age of the cheese.

Prevention:

   (1) By uniform cutting, heating and stirring. This is facilitated by the use of a 5-16-inch, perpendicular, wire knife; and a 5-8-inch, horizontal, steel knife.

   (2) Each small piece of curd should be kept separated from the others while being heated.

   (3) The starter should always be strained.

   (4) The starter should be added before the cheese-color is added.

   (5) The curd from different vats should not be mixed.

   (6) In using old curd, it should be placed in the vat about 15 minutes before the whey is removed.

   (7) Curd should always be firmed in the whey before too much acid has developed.

Remedy:

When the curd is badly mottled, there is no remedy that will make the color uniform. In some instances the color will become more even as the cheese ages. Prevention is the best remedy.

SEAMY COLOR

This is a condition in which the outline of each piece of curd can be easily seen in the cheese. The uniting surfaces are marked by a pale line. (Fig. 31.)

Cause:
- (1) Greasy curds, preventing even absorption of salt
- (2) Impure salt.

Prevention:
- (1) If curds are very greasy, they should be rinsed off with water at 90° F. just before salting
- (2) Only high-grade salt should be used.

Remedy:

There is no satisfactory remedy. Prevention is the only sure way of overcoming the trouble.

FIG. 31—ILLUSTRATION OF SEAMY COLOR AND ALSO OF LACK OF PRESSING

RUSTY SPOTS

These are red spots resembling rust, and usually located in the little pockets of fat that are found where two pieces of curd come together in pressing. This is most noticeable in white cheese.

Cause:
- (1) *Bacillus rudensis*, gaining entrance to milk or curd.
- (2) Unsanitary buildings and surroundings. When whey leaks through the factory floor, the red material

formed by these bacteria may develop. The infectious material may then be carried into the factory by wind or flies. Once in the factory, every utensil used in cheese-making soon becomes infected and the trouble constantly increases.

Prevention:

(1)   Keep everything used in the factory absolutely clean.
(2)   Do not allow the factory floor to leak. Cement floors are the most sanitary.
(3)   Keep the drain and drain-pipes clean.
(4)   Use screen-doors and windows during fly time.

Remedy:

(1)   The only way to get rid of this trouble is by a thorough cleaning and disinfection of the factory surroundings and of all utensils.
(2)   The starter, if one is used, should be renewed.

METHOD OF CLEANING AND DISINFECTION

(1)   Wash all utensils with a brush, hot water, and washing-powder, and put them into the large milk-vat.
(2)   Put a cover over the vat and turn live steam into it.
(3)   Steam the utensils for at least one-half hour.
(4)   If the drains are dirty, clean them with hot water and washing-powder. Then steam them for at least 20 minutes.
(5)   If the ground, surrounding or under the factory, is infected, have it covered with lime or fresh earth.
(6)   The inside walls, cheese-shelves, and all wood-work should be washed with a hot solution of bichlorid of mercury (corrosive sublimate). This is made by dissolving $7\frac{1}{2}$ grains of bichlorid of mercury in one pint of water. Handle this substance with care and apply this solution with a brush or broom, since it is a powerful poison.

DEFECTS IN FINISH

This includes anything that detracts from the appearance of a cheese. As a rule, such defects are due to carelessness on the part of the cheese-maker.

UNCLEAN SURFACES

Cause:
  (1) Placing cheese on unclean or moldy shelves in the curing-room.
  (2) Using dirty hoops or handling the cheese with dirty hands.

Prevention:
  (1) Wash the shelves after each shipment of cheese leaves the factory. Use a brush, hot water, and some good washing-powder that will remove grease. Place the shelves in the sunlight to dry.
  (2) Cheese-hoops should be clean. So should the hands of the maker.

CRACKED RINDS

These are openings in the side or ends of the cheese. They are unsightly and allow cheese-flies and molds to enter.

Cause:
  (1) Too much acid.
  (2) Greasy curd.
  (3) Use of hard press-cloths.
  (4) Lack of pressing.
  (5) Wrinkled bandages.
  (6) Too dry an atmosphere in curing-room.

Prevention:
  (1) Avoid excess of acid in making cheese (p. 53).
  (2) Rinse greasy curd with water at 90° F. before salting.
  (3) Press-cloths can be softened by soaking in a weak solution of sulphuric acid.
  (4) Press the cheese longer before dressing and have the bandages well pulled up.
  (5) The curing-room atmosphere should show 80 per cent humidity.

Remedy:
  (1) Press the cheese again after washing with warm water. If this fails,
  (2) Paraffin the cheese.

MOLDY SURFACES

This condition is familiar. The formation may be of several colors.

Cause:

The growth of molds is due to
(1) Too much moisture in the air.
(2) Too high temperature.
(3) Insufficient circulation of air.
(4) Lack of cleanliness in curing-room.

Prevention:

(1) Curing-rooms should be so equipped that the temperature and moisture can be controlled.
(2) Good circulation of air should be provided.
(3) Curing-rooms should be kept clean.

Remedy:

(1) By spraying cheese with formalin, containing 10 per cent of formaldehyd.
(2) By burning sulphur, 3 pounds to 1,000 cubic feet of air.
(3) By washing the ceilings, walls, shelves and all woodwork with a hot solution of bichlorid of mercury, made by dissolving $7\frac{1}{2}$ grains in a pint of water (p. 132).
(4) By whitewashing the walls and ceilings

UNEVEN SIZES
CROOKED SIDES
WRINKLED BANDAGES
COLLARS ON PRESS ENDS

All these are common defects in the finish of cheese. They are found in almost every factory.

Cause:

Such defects are nearly always due to carelessness on the part of the cheese-maker. The presses may be worn out or broken, the followers may not fit the hoops, or too heavy pressure may be applied immediately after dressing.

Remedy:

The only way by which defects in finish may be overcome is by proper care on the part of the cheese-maker. Very often cheese buyers pay less money for cheese of a good quality when it is poorly finished. If the cheese-maker has to pay the reclaim, he generally becomes more careful. There is no excuse for badly finished cheese, because it is within the power of every cheese-maker to make cheese with good finish. A poorly finished cheese is a disgrace to the man who made it.

Part III

The
Science of Cheese-Making:

*The Chemical,
Biological and Other Relations
of Milk and Cheese*

Relations of the Constituents of Milk to Cheese.

Relations of Micro-Organisms and En-zyms to Milk and Cheese.

Changes in Cheese During tne Ripening Process.

CHAPTER XIV

The Constituents of Milk

The following constituents of cow's milk **are of** special importance in cheese-making:

(1) Fat
(2) Casein
(3) Milk-sugar
(4) Salts
(5) Enzyms

If this list of milk constituents is compared with a complete statement of the composition of milk, it is noticeable that water and albumin are omitted. There are good reasons for such omission.

So far as the process of cheese-making and the character of the product are concerned, the amount of water in normal milks requires no special consideration. Slight variations in conditions of the operations of cheese-making affect the percentage of water in cheese much more than the variation of the percentage of water in normal milks. While dilution of milk by water beyond a certain proportion decreases the rapidity and completeness of rennet action (p. 307), the amount of water in different normal milks does not vary enough to exert any such retarding influence that is appreciable, so far as our observations go.

Milk-albumin calls for little or no study in cheese-making, since it remains in solution during the cheese-making process and passes out, for the most part, with the whey. Numerous attempts have been made to recover in cheese all or most of the albumin present in milk, but we know of no case which has resulted in making a product like normal cheddar cheese in its properties.

MILK-FAT

Milk-fat, also known as *butter-fat,* is not a single chemical compound, but is a somewhat variable mixture of several different compounds called glycerids. Each glycerid is formed by the chemical union of glycerin as a base with some organic acid or acids of a particular kind (butyric, palmitic, oleic, etc.). Under the action of certain kinds of micro-organisms, milk-fat undergoes decomposition, forming among other products free butyric acid, which is the compound responsible for the offensive flavor of rancid cheese and butter.

Fat-globules in milk.—Milk-fat is present in milk, not in solution, but suspended in the form of very small, transparent globules. The globules vary in size, the smaller being more numerous than the larger ones. The average size of fat-globules in milk is somewhat larger than one ten-thousandth of an inch in diameter. Contrary to what has been formerly taught, the fat-globules of milk have no special kind of covering, but are simply minute particles of fat, floating free in milk in the form of an emulsion. Skim-milk and whey contain few globules, as compared with normal milk, while cream, of course, contains many more than normal milk.   Even in butter and cheese, the fat-globules of the milk preserve their individuality to a large extent.

MILK-CASEIN

Milk-casein is of special importance in connection with cheese-making because the conversion of milk into cheese is dependent upon the peculiar properties of casein.   This constituent of milk, in an impure and changed form, is most commonly familiar as the solid, white substance, called curd, which forms in milk when it sours.   It is also familiar as a prominent constituent of separator-slime, and in this form is not materially changed from the condition in which it exists in milk.

Composition of milk-casein.—Casein, as it exists in milk, is a very complex chemical compound, belonging to a general class of nitrogen-containing compounds known as protein, and to a special subdivision called *phosphoproteins*.   Its elementary composition is about as follows.

Carbon	53.00 per cent
Oxygen	22.70 per cent
Nitrogen	15.70 per cent
Hydrogen	7.00 per cent
Phosphorus	0.85 per cent
Sulphur	0.75 per cent

The presence of phosphorus in casein is one of its distinguishing chemical features, but in what particular form of combination the phosphorus exists is not known at present.   Casein in milk does not exist as an uncombined protein, but is, according to the best evidence available, in combination with some form of calcium. Three general views have been held in regard to the relation of calcium (lime) compounds to milk-casein: (1) That milk-casein is in the form of calcium casein, being combined with about 1.50 per cent of calcium oxid; (2) that casein is combined directly with calcium phosphate; (3) that the compound calcium casein is also in combination with calcium phosphate. Some facts appear to indicate that the calcium casein of milk is a form containing 2.4 per cent of calcium oxid. It has been well established that casein forms compounds with calcium, but which particular form of combination exists in milk, as milk-casein, we cannot yet regard as settled beyond question.

Physical condition of casein in milk.—For a long time casein was believed to be in solution in milk and is still held to be so by those who have ignored the evidence to the contrary. Some have held that it was in a state of semi-solution. The view which must now be regarded as representing the truth beyond all doubt is that casein exists in milk in the form of extremely minute, gelatinous particles in suspension. The evidence which proves the correctness of this view is threefold: (1) While the solid particles of casein are so small that they easily pass through the pores of fine filter-paper, they do not go through the finer pores of unglazed porcelain (like the Chamberland filter) nor through animal membranes. It is thus possible to strain out casein from the soluble portions of the milk in quantities sufficient to see and examine. (2) Casein is separated from milk by centrifugal force, being deposited as a film on the surrounding walls of the centrifuge. By whirling milk for a number of hours, practically all of the casein can thus be separated from the milk. It is thus that it is deposited on the walls of the bowl of a centrifugal separator as separator-slime, in which the casein, in a gelatinous form, is mixed with dirt and other bodies. (3) These two preceding methods of proofs should be sufficiently convincing in regard to the insoluble condition of casein in milk; but the latest method removes all possibility of doubt. Within the past few months, an article has been published by Kreidl and Neumann, of Vienna, giving results of work done by them in studying milk by what is known as "ultramicroscopic" examination. This method enables one to see very much smaller objects than can be seen by the usual methods of microscopic work. These investigators were able to see the actual particles of casein swimming in milk, to treat them with reagents and to observe their various transformations. Their study included the milk not only of cows, but of other animals.

Action of acids upon milk-casein.—Milk-casein is made to appear in milk as a heavy, white solid or precipitate, in more or less flocculent form, by means of dilute acids, even by carbon dioxid under certain conditions, and also by acid salts. Treatment by acids changes the chemical and physical properties of milk-casein. The most obvious change is that of physical condition, the very minute, invisible particles of casein coming together into large, visible aggregations. The cause of this change cannot yet be fully explained. It has been usually explained by saying that acids unite with the calcium of the calcium casein, and the casein, thus deprived of its combined calcium, is changed from its condition of finely divided, gelatinous particles into larger masses and then appears as a solid, heavy precipitate. This explanation is not entirely satisfactory, since casein may be obtained in the form of a precipitate when little or no acid is present. The effect is probably to be ascribed rather to the formation of soluble calcium salts by the acid than entirely to the direct effect of acid upon the calcium of milk-casein.

When milk sours in the ordinary way, the lactic acid, thus formed, acts upon the calcium casein, two definite changes taking place when sufficient acid is present. First, the lactic acid combines with the calcium of the calcium casein, forming calcium lactate and calcium-free casein (casein set free from its combination with calcium). When more lactic acid forms than is sufficient to combine with the calcium, the second change takes place; the free casein or coagulum takes up the acid, forming a mixture which is familiar as the curd of sour milk. It was formerly believed that insoluble, precipitated casein combines with a definite quantity of acid, forming a definite compound; and that, under this supposition, the curd of sour milk is a compound known as casein lactate. But more extended, careful, and accurate work has shown that the evidence was misleading upon which was based the belief that casein unites with definite quantities of acids to form definite, insoluble compounds. Changes similar to those occurring when milk sours in the usual way take place when milk is treated with other acids, such as hydrochloric, acetic, sulphuric, etc.

Free casein is insoluble in water, and also in very dilute acids at ordinary temperatures. The action of acids on calcium casein and on free casein is hastened by increase of temperature. Less acid is required at higher temperature to precipitate casein. Casein dissolves easily even in quite dilute acids, more easily at higher temperatures, forming soluble compounds which are either combinations of acid with casein or decomposition products of casein, according to the concentration of the acid, the temperature and other conditions of treatment.

Action of alkalis on milk-casein.—Casein is acid in character in that it unites easily with fixed alkalis, ammonia and alkaline carbonates, forming salts easily soluble in water. Thus, the curd of sour milk or fresh cheese can be dissolved by treatment with dilute sodium carbonate or ammonia. This fact is made use of in cooking, when tough, insoluble cheese, such as that often made from skim-milk, is rendered more easily soluble by use of baking-soda. An interesting experiment in this connection is to rub in a mortar some pure casein, suspended in water, with some calcium carbonate. The calcium combines with the casein, and carbon dioxid gas is given off. The soluble compounds of casein with alkalis are not curdled by rennet, but are precipitated on treatment with acids.

Some of these salts formed by casein with alkalis are found in commerce in the form of dietetic and medicinal preparations.

Action of salts on milk-casein.—Milk-casein may be precipitated, apparently unchanged chemically, by saturating milk with common salt, magnesium sulphate, ammonium sulphate, etc., at ordinary temperatures. Milk-casein is also precipitated by small amounts of solution of alum, zinc sulphate and many other metallic salts. Calcium chlorid and some other salts coagulate casein in milk heated to 95°-113° F.

Action of heat on milk-casein.—Heat alone under ordinary conditions, even at the boiling point of water, does not coagulate the casein in milk. However, heated under pressure to 265°-285° F., casein salts are changed in their properties and casein itself is coagulated. The browning of milk heated under pressure is more or less due to changes in casein. The formation of a peculiar skin (haptogen membrane) on milk heated above 140° F. is largely due to the calcium casein of the milk and not, as was formerly supposed, to albumin. The skin itself contains practically all of the constitutents of the milk and may be regarded as a kind of evaporated milk. On removing the membrane, a new layer is formed and, by removing these one after another, practically all of the milk can be transformed into the membrane condition. It appears to be due to surface evaporation.

Action of rennet on milk-casein.—One of the most characteristic properties of milk-casein is its coagulation by the enzym or chemical ferment contained in rennet. This property makes possible the manufacture of cheddar and many other kinds of cheese from milk. The curd formed by the action of rennet is called *paracasein* or, more properly, *calcium paracasein*. The coagulation of milk-casein produced by rennet is quite different from that produced by acids. Calcium paracasein behaves, in general, much like casein toward acids and alkalis. The details of rennet action on milk-casein will be considered more fully in Chapter XXII (p. 299).

Other changes caused in milk-casein.—Under the action of chemical reagents, of enzyms and of various micro-organisms, calcium casein and paracasein may be changed into a large number of other substances. Among the compounds and classes of compounds thus formed are caseoses (albumoses), peptones, amino acids (crystallizable bodies) and ammonia. These products are never found in normal milk as it leaves the cow's udder, but may be present in milk that has stood exposed to air for some time.

Brine-soluble substance formed from casein.—When milk is treated with rennet and the curd is handled in the usual manner followed in cheese-making, a most interesting change begins to take place, which becomes especially prominent in the cheddaring operation (p. 32). The curd changes into a form which is soluble in a warm solution of 5 per cent brine (common salt); at the same time, the curd forms long strings on a hot iron and acquires the peculiar texture of the cooked meat of a chicken's breast, with a characteristic velvety mellowness of feeling and glistening, silky appearance. These changes are due, apparently, to the formation of this brine-soluble substance. More or less of this peculiar substance remains in the cheese indefinitely. For example, in a cheese two-and-one-half years old, the portion of the cheese insoluble in ether (fat) and in warm water consisted entirely of this brine-soluble substance. On being warmed, it could be drawn out in strings over a yard long. (Figs. 32 and 33.)

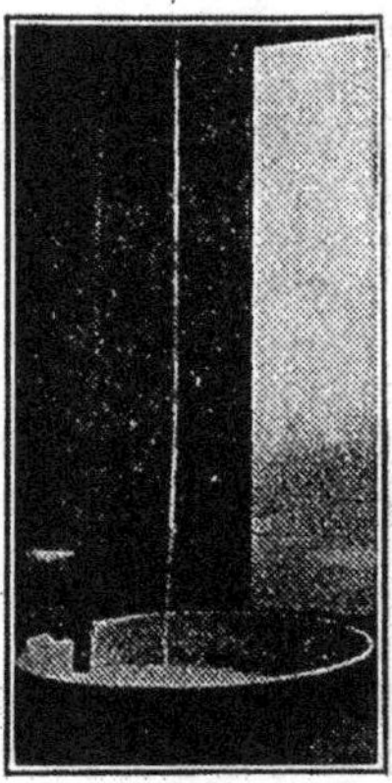

FIG. 32 — BRINE-SOLUBLE CHEESE PROTEIN WARMED AND FRESHLY DRAWN OUT IN A STRING SEVERAL FEET LONG

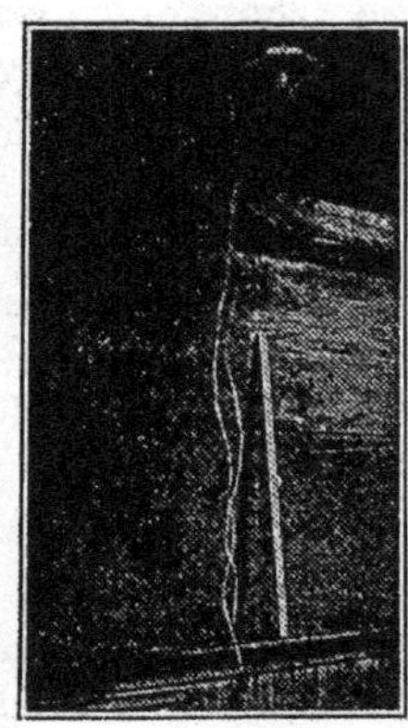

FIG. 33—STRINGS OF BRINE-SOLUBLE PROTEIN OF CHEESE SUSPENDED AND DRIED. STRINGS ABOUT FOUR FEET LONG

MILK-SUGAR

Milk-sugar, also called *lactose,* is present in cow's milk in solution. In general composition, it resembles ordinary sugar, but it is less sweet and less soluble in water; however, it differs much from ordinary sugar in its chemical behavior and especially in its relations to various ferments. The amount of sugar in milk varies from below 4 to over 6 per cent and averages about 5 per cent. Variation in the amount of sugar in different normal milks has little interest in connection with the operations of cheese-making for the reason that there is always an abundance for cheese-making purposes. The milk-sugar passes largely into the whey in the cheese-making process and forms a large percentage of the solids in whey. The milk-sugar of commerce is usually prepared by evaporating whey and purifying the impure product first obtained. The importance of milk-sugar in cheese-making depends on the fact that it is easily converted into lactic acid by certain forms of bacteria. In the making of cheddar cheese, only a small proportion of the sugar is changed into lactic acid during a considerable part of the process, but one per cent or more is so changed by the time the curd is salted. In cheese made from sour milk, such as cottage cheese, and in starters used in cheese-making, somewhat more than one-fourth of the milk-sugar is changed and there is formed in such cases about 0.7 or 0.8 per cent of lactic acid. When milk or whey is allowed to stand for some time at ordinary temperatures, over 1 per cent of lactic acid may be formed. Hence, sour milk or whey, when two or three days old, usually contains only 3.5 to 4 per cent of milk-sugar. In cheddar cheese made under normal conditions, we never find any uncombined or free lactic acid, since it combines with calcium of certain calcium salts in the milk to form calcium lactate, a compound which is neutral (neither acid nor alkaline), and which does not taste sour. Under the usual forms of fermentation, milk-sugar forms small amounts of other compounds in addition to lactic acid. The sour smell of whey and of sour milk is not due to free lactic acid, since pure lactic acid has practically no odor, but is caused by some of the other fermentation products formed, the exact nature of which is not fully known.

THE SALTS OF MILK

The salts of milk, commonly represented by the term "ash," are present in only small amounts, but they have extremely important relations to the process of cheese-making. Our knowledge of these compounds is very incomplete. The salts of milk are commonly spoken of as the ash or mineral constituents. This conception is somewhat misleading, because the materials appearing in the ash of milk are, to some considerable extent, combined in organic compounds, instead of existing in milk as separate inorganic bodies in the form in which they appear in the ash. The ash, therefore, represents in amount more than the so-called mineral constituents of milk and less than the salts of milk. While the average amount of ash in milk is about 0.7 per cent, the amount of salts is probably much nearer 0.9 per cent. To illustrate this point in more detail, the citric acid which is present in milk in the form of citrate salts does not appear at all in the ash, since it is destroyed in burning the milk to obtain the ash. In cheddar cheese the ash, not including the salt added in cheese-making, represents the salts of the milk even less accurately than in milk. In cheese, we have a considerable amount of calcium lactate, but, in obtaining the ash of cheese, the lactic acid portion is destroyed and so does not form a part of the ash. The percentage of ash in green cheese due to constituents obtained from the milk is usually between 2 and 3 per cent, varying, of course, with the amount of whey retained in the cheese.

In milk, a portion of the salts is present in soluble, and a portion in insoluble, form. The following portions of the salts of milk are present in solution: Sodium, potassium, chlorine, and citric acid compounds; amounts of phosphoric acid in the form of combined phosphates varying in different milks from 45 to 65 per cent of the total phosphoric acid present; 25 to 45 per cent of the calcium (lime); and over 50 per cent of the magnesium. In what specific forms of compounds these elements are present in milk is not known and the problem is a difficult one to solve. The suggestion has been made by Söldner that something like the following arrangement may be supposed to exist:

Compounds	Percentage of the total salts in milk
Calcium citrate	23.6
Mono-potassium phosphate	12.8
Sodium chlorid	10.6
Potassium chlorid	9.2
Di-potassium phosphate	9.2
Tri-calcium phosphate	8.9
Di-calcium phosphate	7.4
Potassium citrate	5.5
Calcium oxid in casein	5.1
Magnesium citrate	4.0
Di-magnesium phosphate	3.7

Whether this suggested distribution of compounds among the salts of milk is near the truth or not, it emphasizes the fact that the matter is one of no little complication. Some investigators believe that the calcium phosphate exists entirely as tri-calcium phosphate; others, as the di-calcium compound, probably on the basis of better evidence. The presence of soluble acid phosphate and, probably, of acid citrate also, accounts for a part of the acidity of fresh milk.

When milk is heated, the amount of soluble calcium salts is decreased as the result of being changed to insoluble forms.

The presence of soluble calcium salts in milk is essential to the coagulation of milk by rennet-extract (p. 306).

Acidity of milk.—In this connection, we will call attention to the acidity of fresh, normal milk. Milk in which lactic acid has had no chance to develop has the power of neutralizing alkalis and in that respect behaves like a solution containing acid.

The acidity of fresh milk varies with a number of conditions, such as (1) the milk of the same animal at different times, (2) the milk of different cows, and (3) with the stage of lactation, being highest at the beginning of lactation and gradually decreasing with the advance of the lactation period. The acidity of fresh normal milk is caused by no one substance, but is due to the presence of (1) acid phosphates, (2) citrates and (3) casein. It has been found to vary widely, from below 4 to over 10, expressed as cubic centimeters of one-tenth normal alkali, but in most cases it is between 7 and 9.

Lactic acid begins to be formed in milk soon after it is drawn, if the milk is not kept below 50° F. By the time milk reaches the factory, the normal acidity of the milk is usually increased about 0.05 to 0.10 per cent, corresponding to a total acidity of 0.12 to 0.18 per cent. In warm weather, the acidity often exceeds 0.20 per cent in the case of some herds. The increase of acidity over that existing in fresh normal milk is an indication of the temperature at which the milk is kept and also of the cleanliness observed in milking and in caring for the milk and the dairy utensils with which the milk comes in contact (see p. 4). An acidity equivalent to 0.20 per cent of lactic acid in milk when received at the factory is regarded as the danger line for cheddar cheese-making. Generally, only a part of the milk taken to a cheese-factory will exceed this limit, so that the average for the day may be considerably below the 0.20 per cent limit.

MILK-ENZYMS

Enzyms are chemical ferments; they have the power to produce changes in other substances without themselves undergoing change. Enzyms are the products of living cells. According to recent views, normal milk is not to be regarded as an inactive fluid, but possesses certain properties characteristic of living substances. Normal milk gives evidence of the presence of several different enzyms, among which are those called (1) diastase, (2) galactase, (3) lipase, (4) catalase, (5) peroxidase and (6) reductase. The subject has not been sufficiently studied to enable one to make anything like a clear or satisfactory presentation. It is quite probable that some of these enzyms, now described under different names, are the same or are mixtures. The quantity of these substances is so extremely small and the methods of separating them in pure form are so imperfect that their study presents peculiar difficulties. One of the main practical uses to which enzyms in milk have been put depends upon the fact that their presence serves to distinguish unheated from boiled milk, because the enzyms are all destroyed by heat. We shall not consider these substances in detail because, so far as we now know, most of them are not concerned in cheese-making. Galactase is the only one of special interest in this connection. This was discovered at the Wisconsin experiment station in 1897 and has received considerable attention in connection with studies of milk and cheese. We shall consider this enzym in more detail later (p. 297).

CHAPTER XV

Conditions Affecting Proportions of Constituents in Milk

In studying the composition of milk from different cows or herds, one of the first facts noticed is that the same constituents vary in amount more or less widely in different milks. This fact is of the highest importance in studying the relations of milk to cheese-making. As a foundation for a more detailed consideration of these relations of milk, it seems desirable that we should study with some degree of fullness the more important conditions which cause variation in the amounts of constituents of milk. Those constituents of greatest interest to us which vary most are fat and casein. Milk-sugar and salts vary only slightly as compared with the amount of variation in fat and casein. We shall find it to be a matter, not only of interest, but of practical importance, to study the extent of these variations and their causes, and also to learn to what extent different influences affect the relation of fat to casein. As we shall show later (p. 186), the percentages of fat and casein in milk largely determine the *yield* of cheese; while the proportion of these two constituents, relative to each other, determine the *composition* (p. 231) and to a considerable degree, the *quality* of cheese (p. 243).

AMOUNT OF FAT IN MILK

The percentage of fat in normal milk varies greatly, much more than any other constituent, especially if we consider single milkings of individual cows. In connection with the manufacture of cheese, we are more particularly interested in knowing the percentage of fat in the milk of different *herds* of cows rather than in that of single individuals. In the case of single herds of cows, such as are common in the dairy region of New York state, the lowest percentage of fat found on any one day, as the result of special investigations, was 2.90; the highest, 5.50, which occurred late in the season (October). Taking the average of different herds of cows for an entire cheese-factory season (April to November), the lowest percentage of fat was 3.31 and the highest, 4.31. In the case of cheese-factory milk, consisting of a mixture of the milk of different herds, the lowest percentage of fat found was 3.04 and the highest, 4.60. The average percentage of fat in mixed factory milk for an entire season is about 3.75; and this average has been found to vary only slightly in different factories and in different seasons. The Wisconsin experiment station reports 3.64 as the season's average percentage of fat in the milk of 347 factories. In the case of individual factories, a season's average as low as 3.20 per cent is given. The lowest percentage of fat in the milk of any single herd for a single day's milk is given as 2.30, while the highest reported is 5. Results reported in Canada appear to indicate a lower percentage of fat in milk than in the case of New York.

While many conditions cause the percentage of fat in milk to vary, we will notice only three as of special importance in connection with cheese-making: (1) Breed, (2) stage of lactation, and (3) change from barn to pasture.

Influence of breed of cows on fat content of milk. —The influence of what is known as breed upon the composition of cow's milk has been long recognized and extensively studied in a general way, but only in a comparatively limited way in its relation to cheese-making. It is largely owing to this influence that we find the milk of one country differing from that of another, or the milk of one section of a country differing from that of another section. For example, the average percentage of fat in milk in Germany and Holland is fully one-half per cent lower than in New York state, and probably in the United States at large, because the prevailing breeds of cows there are those producing milk comparatively low in fat. The results of recent tests go to show that in Canada the milk in Quebec province contains more fat than does that of Ontario, since in the former the native Jerseys are the predominant breed, while in the latter, Holstein-Friesians, Ayrshires and Short-

PERCENTAGE OF FAT IN MILK OF DIFFERENT BREEDS OF COWS

Name of breed	Per cent of fat in milk
Holstein-Friesian	3.26
Ayrshire	3.76
American Holderness	4.01
Shorthorn	4.28
Devon	4.89
Guernsey	5.38
Jersey	5.78

horns prevail. The foregoing table represents averages in the case of three to six individuals of each of seven different breeds for an aggregate of four to twenty lactation periods with each.

Influence of stage of lactation on fat content of milk.—From the time a cow "comes fresh in milk" up to the time she becomes "dry," the composition of the milk undergoes gradual changes, which are quite independent of other factors. The period of lactation varies in length with different individual cows, but, for practical purposes, lasts about 10 to 12 months. The changes observed in the percentage of fat during the progress of the lactation period are quite marked and fairly regular, without reference to individual or breed. The colostrum, which is the secretion produced by a cow soon after calving, is very different in composition from normal milk and is not considered at all in our discussion of the constituents of milk, because it has no interest for us in this connection. The

VARIATION OF PERCENTAGE OF FAT IN MILK WITH
ADVANCE OF LACTATION

Month of lactation	Per cent of fat in milk	Percentages in comparison with first month
1	4.30	100.0
2	4.11	95.6
3	4.21	97.9
4	4.25	98.8
5	4.38	101.9
6	4.53	105.3
7	4.57	106.3
8	4.59	106.8
9	4.67	108.6
10	4.90	114.0
11	5.07	118.0

figures presented in the table on page 158 represent the monthly averages of nearly 100 different lactation periods.

In studying this table, we notice that the percentage of fat decreases in the second month, as compared with the first, and then begins to increase, continuing to increase from month to month during the entire period of lactation. The rate of increase is more rapid during the last two or three months than previously. Such behavior appears to be the general rule. Variation from the comparative degree of regularity observed in the foregoing table may, of course, appear in the case of individuals.

It will be a matter of more immediate interest to consider the influence of advancing lactation upon the percentage of fat as observed in the case of milk used at cheese-factories. In general, dairymen have their cows begin the period of lactation in March and April, so that milk taken to a cheese-factory represents, during the season, stages of the lactation period extending from about the second

VARIATION OF FAT IN CHEESE-FACTORY MILK WITH ADVANCE OF LACTATION

Month	Per cent of fat in milk		Percentages in comparison with first month	
	New York	Wisconsin	New York	Wisconsin
April.................	3.43	3.48	100.0	100.0
May..................	3.58	3.49	104.4	100.3
June.................	3.64	3.50	106.1	100.6
July.................	3.62	3.55	105.5	102.0
August..............	3.84	3.63	112.0	104.3
September...........	3.98	3.84	116.0	110.3
October.............	4.23	4.08	123.3	117.2

to the eighth months. Cows kept under ordinary farm conditions are subject to greater variations of external influences than those used in the investigation represented by the figures in the preceding table. The figures in the table on page 159 represent results secured in New York and Wisconsin.

Influence of change from barn to pasture upon the percentage of fat in milk.—In the course of a study of cheese-factory milk in New York, it was noticed that, under certain conditions, a marked change in percentage of fat in milk took place. Each year while the study of factory milk was carried on, it was observed that about the middle of May there was a considerable increase in the percentage of milk-fat, accompanied by an increase of other solids and also by a larger yield of milk. Thus, during the first half of May, the milk contained 3.46 per cent of fat and, during the second half, 3.70 per cent. These results are in agreement with those reported by the Vermont and Wisconsin experiment stations and also by the Ontario agricultural college. This question has been more thoroughly studied at the Vermont experiment station than elsewhere and, according to the results obtained during a series of years, the general rule shows a change like that noticed above, but in some years little or no change could be observed. A careful study of all the available facts appears to justify the explanation that the increased percentage of fat in milk under the given circumstances was due to a marked change in the character of the food and environment of the cows, since they were turned out to pasture about the middle of May. Under the known existing conditions of the food and environment of cheese-factory cows, there was thus a change from dry food of an indifferent character, mainly straw or poor hay without grain, to a highly succulent food of a most palatable kind. It is probable also that the changes in the environment of the cows from confinement in barn and yard to the freedom of pasture exercised a beneficial, physiological influence.

AMOUNT OF CASEIN IN MILK

The percentage of casein in normal milk varies quite widely, though much less than in case of milk-fat. In the single milkings of individual cows, we have found casein as low as 1.59 per cent and as high as 4.49 per cent. The highest percentages were found in the case of cows far along in lactation and giving only small amounts of milk. In the case of individual herds of cows, the percentage of casein ranged from 1.79 to 3.02. In the case of milk consisting of a mixture of the milk of several different herds, the percentage of casein varied from 1.93 to 3.00.

The conditions which influence variation of casein in milk, so far as they are of special interest to us here, are (1) breed, (2) stage of lactation, (3) change from stable to pasture, and (4) effects of drouth.

Influence of breed of cows on percentage of casein in milk.—The following results illustrate, in general, the variation of casein in the milk of different breeds of cows:

PERCENTAGE OF CASEIN IN MILK OF DIFFERENT BREEDS OF COWS

Name of breed	Per cent of casein in milk
Holstein-Friesian	2.20
Ayrshire	2.46
American Holderness	2.63
Shorthorn	2.79
Devon	3.10
Guernsey	2.91
Jersey	3.03

Influence of stage of lactation on the percentage of casein in milk.—We will first present results representing the average of about 100 lactation periods of individual cows and then the results representing work done at the New York experiment station in connection with cheese-factories in New York state, already referred to:

VARIATION OF PERCENTAGE OF CASEIN IN MILK WITH ADVANCE OF LACTATION

Month of lactation	Per cent of casein in milk	Percentages in comparison with first month
1	2.54	100.0
2	2.42	95.3
3	2.46	96.8
4	2.52	99.2
5	2.61	102.8
6	2.68	105.8
7	2.74	108.0
8	2.80	110.2
9	2.90	114.2
10	3.01	118.5
11	3.13	123.2

According to these results, the percentage of casein decreases in the second month of lactation, as compared with the first, and then begins to increase, continuing to increase month by month to the end of the lactation period. The behavior very closely resembles that of fat.

Turning now to the results obtained at cheese-factories, we have the following data:

VARIATION OF CASEIN IN CHEESE-FACTORY MILK WITH ADVANCE OF LACTATION

Month	Per cent of casein in milk	Percentages in comparison with first month
April	2.29	100.0
May	2.34	102.2
June	2.47	108.0
July	2.43	106.1
August	2.39	104.3
September	2.55	111.3
October	2.81	122.7

In the foregoing figures, we see that the percentage of casein in milk increases in May and still more in June, after which a decrease takes place in July, followed by still further decrease in August. There is a rapid recovery and advance during September and October. The cause of these variations will be considered later.

Influence of change from barn to pasture upon the percentage of casein.—Attention has already been called to this subject in relation to fat. We now give corresponding figures for casein. During the first half of May, the milk contained 2.25 per cent of casein and during the second half of May, 2.45 per cent. The same explanation applies as in the case of increase of fat.

Influence of drouth upon the percentage of casein in milk.—During a time of severe drouth in New York, beginning in July and lasting through August, with infrequent and insufficient showers, a marked decrease was noticed in the casein of the milk, even when the fat was increasing. The analytical data are given later on p. 168. Under these conditions, the pasture grasses were badly burned, most of the dairymen were without supplementary supplies of food, and consequently the cows suffered a certain degree of starvation. The changes in composition of milk were accompanied by a severe shrinkage in yield of milk. Along with this impaired condition of food supply, the animals were subjected to the unfavorable effects coming from excessive heat combined with annoyance of flies. Cheese-makers often complain of the behavior of the cheese made at such times, without understanding the cause of their difficulty. The cheese leaks fat badly, does not press together well, and does not stand up perfectly, although behaving properly when first made. There is also noticed an excessive loss of fat in whey. This behavior is due to an abnormal decrease of casein in relation to fat, so that the milk and cheese contain an excess of fat. Cheese-makers at such times are really dealing with milk which is not normal factory milk, but which is like normal factory milk to which some cream has been added. The extreme heat of the weather, which causes the decrease of casein, also makes it more difficult to handle such milk in cheese-making. In the twelfth annual report of the Wisconsin experiment station, attention is called to a similar condition.

RELATION OF FAT AND CASEIN IN MILK

As we shall see later (p. 231), the relation of fat and casein in milk is an extremely important one in connection with cheese-making. At this point we shall call attention only to the general relation in different milks and to the conditions which influence this relation, leaving the various application of the facts to later chapters. We have already noticed the percentages of fat and of casein in milk and some of the conditions which cause variation. We now come to consider whether fat and casein vary alike; that is, whether fat and casein have the same relation to each other in milk under all conditions. We will consider this phase of the subject under the following divisions: (1) Individuality, (2) breed, (3) stage of lactation, and (4) fresh pastures and drouth.

Influence of individuality upon relation of fat and casein.—The results of the work done at the New York experiment station and elsewhere have shown that the relation of fat and casein varies greatly in the milk of different individuals, the variation being greatest, of course, in the case of single milkings. This fact has been well recognized for 15 years or more and is too familiar even to need illustration.

Influence of breed upon relation of fat and casein.—The following data are taken from those already given on preceding pages.

Name of breed	Per cent of fat	Per cent of casein	Parts of casein for one part of fat
			Fat: Casein
Holstein-Friesian	3.26	2.20	1: 0.67
Ayrshire	3.76	2.46	1: 0.65
American Holderness	4.01	2.63	1: 0.66
Shorthorn	4.28	2.79	1: 0.65
Devon	4.89	3.10	1: 0.63
Guernsey	5.38	2.91	1: 0.54
Jersey	5.78	3.03	1: 0.52

It is seen that the different breeds represented separate into two general groups in relation to the ratio of fat to casein. In the case of the first five breeds in the list, this ratio does not vary widely. The milk containing least fat contains the largest amount of casein in relation to fat; but, even though the percentage of fat in the case of this group increases to 4.89, as in the case of the Devon breed, the ratio of casein does not diminish greatly. The Guernsey and Jersey breeds constitute the second group, the fat being high in amount but the casein relatively low.

Influence of stage of lactation upon the relation of fat and casein.—We have already noticed that the percentage of fat and of casein increases gradually and quite regularly during the period of lactation. We will now consider the question as to whether these constituents increase in the same ratio.

RELATION OF FAT AND CASEIN DURING LACTATION PERIOD

Month of lactation	Per cent of fat	Per cent of casein	Parts of casein for one part of fat
			Fat : Casein
1	4.30	2.54	1 : 0.59
2	4.11	2.42	1 : 0.59
3	4.21	2.46	1 : 0.58
4	4.25	2.52	1 : 0.59
5	4.38	2.61	1 : 0.60
6	4.53	2.68	1 : 0.59
7	4.57	2.74	1 : 0.60
8	4.59	2.84	1 : 0.61
9	4.67	2.90	1 : 0.62
10	4.90	3.01	1 : 0.62
11	5.07	3.13	1 : 0.62

These results show a remarkable uniformity in the ratio of fat to casein throughout the lactation period. The ratio remains quite constant for seven or eight months and then increases slightly, remaining the same during the rest of the lactation period.

It will be of practical interest in this connection to observe what the relation of fat and casein is during the season in the case of the mixed milk of many herds of cows, as obtained at New York cheese factories

RELATION OF FAT AND CASEIN IN CHEESE-FACTORY MILK DURING SEASON

Month	Per cent of fat	Per cent of casein	Parts of casein for one part of fat
			Fat : Casein
April	3.43	2.29	1 : 0.67
May	3.58	2.34	1 : 0.65
June	3.64	2.47	1 : 0.68
July	3.62	2.43	1 : 0.67
August	3.84	2.39	1 : 0.62
September	3.92	2.55	1 : 0.65
October	4.23	2.81	1 : 0.66

The same fairly uniform relation holds except in the case of the month of August, when the casein decreased relative to fat. It is interesting to notice how closely the relation of fat and casein in cheese-factory milk agrees with that of the Holstein-Friesian and Ayrshire types as given in the table on p. 165. The cheese-factory cows were grade Holsteins and Ayrshires to a considerable extent

Influence of fresh pastures and of drouth upon the relation of fat and casein in milk.—Using the data already given, we have the following tabular statement in regard to the influence of turning cows from barn into pasture about the middle of May:

	Per cent of fat in milk	Per cent of casein in milk	Parts of casein for one part of fat
			Fat: Casein
First half of May..........	3.46	2.25	1: 0.65
Second half of May........	3.70	2.45	1: 0.66

It is seen that under the conditions indicated, the fat and casein maintain a relation that is very uniform.

Turning now to data obtained during a summer when extreme drouth prevailed during part of July and all of August, we have the following results:

EFFECT OF DROUTH UPON RELATION OF FAT TO CASEIN IN MILK

Month	Per cent of fat	Per cent of casein	Parts of casein for one part of fat
			Fat: Casein
May......................	3.58	2.40	1: 0.67
June.....................	3.59	2.33	1: 0.65
July.....................	3.71	2.20	1: 0.59
August...................	4.04	2.26	1: 0.56
September................	3.97	2.47	1: 0.62
October..................	4.20	2.69	1: 0.64

These results show, for cheese-factory milks, an abnormal ratio of fat and casein in July, which was still further from normal in August. In September, when abundant rains came and when, in addition, dairymen had fodder corn to supplement pastures with, the ratio became more nearly normal and still more so in October. From the standpoint of practical application, these facts indicate the necessity for dairymen to guard against the effects of drouth by making provision for furnishing some form of succulent food then. At such times, there is an enormous loss due to shrinkage in yield of milk; and, in cheese-making, there is an abnormal loss of fat in whey, resulting in decreased yield of cheese for 100 pounds of milk.

THE RELATION OF FAT AND CASEIN IN CHEESE-FACTORY MILK

We have seen that the relation of fat and casein is a variable one, the variations being less wide, of course, in the case of herd milk than in that of individual cows, and especially of single milkings of individuals. But, in the case of averages of several analyses of milk and in the case of milk of herds, especially when cows are of one general type in respect to breed, a certain degree of uniformity exists in the relation of fat to casein. In New York a careful study was made of the milk of each of 50 different herds of cheese-factory cows during one season (May to October), and, as one of the results, a general relation was noticed between the fat and casein. In general, it was found that when the fat in milk increases 1.0 per cent, there is an average increase of casein amounting to 0.4 per cent. This was found to hold quite satisfactorily when applied in case of ordinary herd milk varying in fat content from 3 to 4.5 per cent and, in many cases, outside of these limits. In milk containing less than 3 per cent of fat, the casein content is usually higher in relation to fat than in milk with more than 3 per cent of fat; while, in the case of milk containing more than 4.5 per cent of fat, the ratio of casein to fat is frequently less than in milk containing less than 4.5 per cent of fat. Starting with milk containing an average of 3 per cent of fat and a casein content of 2.1 per cent, milk with 4 per cent of fat was found to contain about 2.5 per cent of casein on an average.

RULE FOR CALCULATING AMOUNT OF CASEIN IN MILK

On the basis of the observed general relations stated above, the following formula was worked out for calculating the percentage of casein in milk when the per cent of fat is known:

$(F—3) \times 0.4 + 2.1 =$ per cent of casein.

F equals the number representing the per cent of fat in milk. Expressed as a rule, we have the following: From the number representing the per cent of fat in milk subtract 3; multiply the result by 0.4 and then add 2.1. The formula is apt to give results not quite up to the actual in case of milk produced after the eighth or ninth month of lactation period, when the casein is usually a little greater in relation to fat than during the previous stage of the lactation period. Applied separately to the milk of 50 herds of cows during the factory season, the average results for the season are summarized as follows: (1) In 4 cases, the results found by chemical determination were identical with those given by calculation; (2) in 36 cases, the results by calculation were within 0.1 per cent of those obtained by the chemical method; (3) in 8 cases the chemical method gave 0.1 to 0.2 per cent less than the calculated amount; (4) in 2 cases the calculated per cent exceeded that found by the chemical method to the extent of 0.23 and 0.25 per cent. It is thus seen that, taking the entire season's average, 80 per cent of the results by the method of calculation differed from those obtained with the chemical method by less than 0.1 per cent. The results given below represent the application of the formula in case of herd milk:

Per cent of fat in milk	Per cent of casein in milk, as found by	
	(1) Chemical method	(2) Calculation
3.25	2.38	2.20
3.31	2.19	2.22
3.42	2.27	2.27
3.52	2.30	2.30
3.55	2.34	2.32
3.55	2.18	2.32
3.63	2.45	2.35
3.63	2.33	2.35
3.71	2.29	2.38
3.71	2.48	2.38
3.71	2.35	2.38
3.84	2.44	2.44
3.84	2.37	2.44
3.92	2.42	2.47
4.00	2.53	2.50
4.14	2.50	2.56
4 25	2.51	2.60
4.31	2.37	2.62

For ordinary purposes, where the strictest accuracy is not required, the rule can be used with quite satisfactory results, when applied to herd milks within the limits specified, and most of our cheese-factory milks come within these limits. Of course, it is readily recognized that, when very accurate results are necessary, only a direct determination of casein by an accurate method can suffice for the purpose; and, by an accurate method, is meant one which can be relied upon to give results within one-tenth of one per cent of the truth.

AMOUNT OF FAT AND CASEIN IN ORDINARY FACTORY MILK

In the case of ordinary cheese-factory milk, we may expect to find the fat and casein run somewhat as follows:

Per cent of fat in milk	Per cent of casein in milk	Ratio of Fat: Casein
3.00	2.10	1: 0.70
3.25	2.20	1: 0.68
3.50	2.30	1: 0.66
3.75	2.40	1: 0.64
4.00	2.50	1: 0.62
4.25	2.60	1: 0.61
4.50	2.70	1: 0.60
5.00	2.90	1: 0.59

RELATION OF CASEIN AND ALBUMIN IN MILK

It is a matter of practical interest in connection with cheese-making to know whether, in milk with a high percentage of casein, there is also a proportionally high percentage of albumin. The higher the casein, relative to albumin, the greater is the proportion of cheese-producing constituents. We will study this question in relation to (1) breed and (2) stage of lactation. It should be stated that albumin, as here used, includes all the proteins of the milk other than casein.

In studying the results, it is noticeable that, in general, in the case of milk containing a low percentage of fat (p. 165), the albumin forms a larger proportion of the proteins than in case of milk containing a high percentage of fat, when we compare the milk of different breeds of cows under corresponding conditions. Also, in milks low in fat, the casein forms a smaller proportion of the proteins

INFLUENCE OF BREED UPON THE RELATION OF CASEIN
AND ALBUMIN

Name of breed	Per cent of proteins (casein and albumin)	Per cent of casein	Per cent of albumin	Parts of casein for one part of albumin	Per cent of total proteins in form of casein
				Albumin: Casein	
Holstein-Friesian....	2.84	2.20	0.64	1: 3.4	77.5
Ayrshire.............	3.07	2.46	0.61	1: 4.0	80.1
American Holderness	3.32	2.63	0.69	1: 3.8	79.2
Shorthorn..........	3.43	2.79	0.64	1: 4.5	81.3
Devon..............	3.93	3.10	0.83	1: 3.7	78.9
Guernsey...........	3.56	2.91	0.65	1: 4.5	81.7
Jersey..............	3.68	3.03	0.65	1: 4.7	82.3

than in ·case of milks higher in fat. ·Thus, in the
milk of Holstein-Friesian cows, we have the least
amount of fat (3.26 per cent), and the casein forms
a smaller part (77.5 per cent), and· the albumin a
larger part (22.5 per cent), of the proteins than in
case of any other breed under discussion. In the
case of Guernsey and Jersey milk, in which the fat
content is highest, the proportion of casein to proteins is greatest (about 82 per cent), while it is least
for· albumin (about 18 per cent). In its practical
application, these results mean that, in the case of
Jersey and Guernsey milk, a larger proportion of the
proteins ·is utilized in cheese-making and a smaller
proportion is lost in whey.

The relation of casein and albumin, as shown by
the following data, is ·remarkably uniform during
the first eight or nine months of lactation, varying
between 4.1 and 4.2 parts of casein for one of
albumin; or, stated in another way, the percentage
of total proteins in the form of casein varied from
80.3 to 80.9 and, in the form of albumin, from 19.1

INFLUENCE OF STAGE OF LACTATION UPON THE RELA-
TION OF CASEIN AND ALBUMIN

Month of lactation	Per cent of Proteins (casein and albumin)	Per cent of casein	Per cent of albumin	Parts of casein for one part of albumin Albumin: Casein	Per cent of total proteins in form of casein
1.........	3.16	2.54	0.62	1: 4.1	80.4
2.........	2.99	2.42	0.57	1: 4.2	80.9
3.........	3.04	2.46	0.58	1: 4.2	80.9
4.........	3.13	2.52	0.61	1: 4.1	80.5
5.........	3.25	2.61	0.64	1: 4.1	80.3
6.........	3.33	2.68	0.65	1: 4.1	80.5
7.........	3.40	2.74	0.66	1: 4.2	80.6
8.........	3.47	2.80	0.67	1: 4.2	80.7
9.........	3.57	2.90	0.67	1: 4.3	81.2
10.........	3.79	3.01	0.78	1: 3.9	79.4
11.........	4 04	3.13	0.91	1: 3.4	77.5

to 19.7. After the ninth month, the albumin increases relative to casein, the increase being very
marked in the two closing months of the lactation
periods studied.

In the case of the mixed milk of numerous herds
of cheese-factory cows, we have the following results:

Month.....	Per cent of protein (casein and albumin)	Per cent of casein	Per cent of albumin	Parts of casein for one part of albumin Albumin: Casein	Per cent of total proteins in form of casein
April.......	2.81	2.29	0.52	1: 4.4	81.5
May........	3.02	2.34	0.68	1: 3.4	77.5
June.......	3.24	2.47	0.77	1: 3.2	76.2
July........	3.07	2.43	0.64	1: 3.8	79.2
August.....	3.02	2.39	0.63	1: 3.8	79.1
September..	3.20	2.55	0.65	1: 3.9	79.7
October....	3.55	2.81	0.74	1: 3.8	79.2

The proportion of casein in relation to albumin
decreases until July, when a marked increase oc-

curs; and then the ratio remains uniform during the rest of the season, which extends approximately through the seventh or eighth month of lactation.

The general statement has been prominently current in literature to the effect that casein and albumin are present in cow's milk in very constant relative proportions, the amount of casein being five times that of albumin. In the case of herd milks, we have found casein varying all the way from 2.6 to 5.6 parts for one part of albumin. In single milkings of individual cows, the variations are considerably wider.

AVERAGE COMPOSITION FACTORY MILK

The following figures represent the average monthly composition of milk as obtained at cheese-factories in New York state. These data represent the work of several seasons and are taken from the records of the New York experiment station:

Month	Solids	Fat	Casein	Albumin	Sugar ash. etc.
April..........	11.98	3.43	2.29	0.52	5.74
May...........	12.43	3.58	2.34	C.68	5.83
June..........	12.64	3.64	2.47	0.77	5.76
July..........	12.52	3.62	2.43	0.64	5.83
August........	12.65	3.84	2.39	0.63	5.79
September.....	12.86	3.98	2.55	0.65	5.68
October.......	13.50	4.23	2.81	0.74	5.72
Average.......	12.67	3.75	2.46	0.68	5.78

The following figures show the extreme variations in composition of cheese-factory milk during the season:

	Lowest per cent	Highest per cent
Solids	11.47	13.91
Fat	3.04	4.60
Casein	1.93	3.00
Albumin	0.47	0.88
Sugar, ash, etc.	5.32	6.37

For a more general and, in some respects, more complete discussion of the chemistry of milk, the reader is referred to "Modern Methods of Testing Milk and Milk Products," published by Orange Judd Company.

CHAPTER XVI

Functions of Milk Constituents in Cheese-Making

Having considered the properties and amounts of different constituents in milk in connection with cheese-making, it is a matter of interest to notice what particular part each performs in the process or what particular contribution of value each makes to the finished product. It will be found that each constituent has a value peculiar to itself in relation to cheese and the process of cheese-making.

MILK-FAT

Milk-fat is the object of solicitous care on the part of the intelligent cheese-maker, and its peculiarities have much to do with certain details of the cheese-making process. Its part in the actual process of cheese-making is, however, a passive rather than an active one, since the details of the operations are governed, to a considerable extent, by the aim of retaining as much milk-fat as possible in the cheese and losing the smallest possible amount in whey. The reasons for keeping milk-fat in cheese are twofold, (1) on account of its influence on the yield of cheese and (2) on account of its effect upon the quality of the cheese.

So far as we know at present, milk-fat contributes little or nothing to the aroma of normal cheddar cheese; but its chief functions, in relation to quality of cheese, appear to be to give (1) a characteristic mellowness of body, (2) smoothness of feeling, (3) richness and delicacy of taste, apart from cheese flavor proper, and (4), in general, palatability. No other constituent can take its place satisfactorily in performing any of these offices. Of course, the high value of milk-fat as a food should not be lost sight of, but this does not necessarily enter into the question of quality of cheese as affected by the presence of fat. The peculiar and exclusive function of milk-fat in giving to cheese certain desirable qualities can be well appreciated by comparing different kinds of cheese, equally well made and differing only in the percentage of fat contained in them, as, for example, cheese made from normal milk containing added cream, cheese made from normal Jersey milk, cheese made from Holstein-Friesian milk, and cheese made from milk skimmed in varying degrees, down to separator skim-milk cheese.

The relation of fat to yield of cheese will be considered in detail in the next chapter.

MILK-CASEIN

Casein is the constituent of milk which, on account of its peculiar action toward rennet-extract solutions, makes possible the manufacture of cheddar and many other kinds of cheese. In the process of cheese-making, it performs two specific functions: (1) In its solidification, its first work is to imprison the fat-globules in the curd and then continue to hold them as firmly as possible throughout the manipulations of cheese-making. (2) Its second function is to retain whey in the curd in desired amounts, while, at the same time, permitting superfluous whey to escape from the mass of curd. The power of casein to hold moisture is somewhat like that of a sponge. Special experiments at the New York experiment station have shown that one pound of dry casein can easily absorb and hold about one pound and a quarter of water. Fat has, of course, comparatively little water-holding power, so that this function falls almost entirely on casein. It is obvious that this special work can be done by no other constituent of milk, and thus casein is recognized as the water-holder in cheese.

In the finished product, casein, or rather, the compound formed from it, performs two important and peculiar functions. (1) It gives to the cheese firmness and solidity of body under a wide range of temperature, conditions which are requisite for its keeping and convenient handling. The casein-derived product in reality constitutes the firm framework or skeleton which gives permanence to the form of the cheese. (2) It furnishes the protein material in which, it is believed, take place those changes that result in characteristic cheese flavors, while, at the same time, it is converted into soluble, nutritive compounds, which add largely to the value of the cheese as food. The peculiar properties of casein when made into cheese are such that its presence in excess in relation to fat or moisture causes serious deterioration in some of the properties of the cheese. For instance, when an excess of casein is used, as in the case of skim-milk cheese, the desirable firmness of body becomes objectionable hardness, unless the conditions of manufacture are so modified as to hold more whey in cheese, in which case objectionable properties of another kind are apt to result.

WATER

As we shall see later, when we come to study the composition of cheese, water is one of the most prominent constituents in amount. We have already indicated why the amount of water in normal milk has little interest in connection with cheese-making, but its presence in cheese is of great interest and the problem of its control in the cheese-making process is one of the highest importance. Water performs two chief functions in cheese: (1) Somewhat like fat, but in a much less satisfactory way, it influences the character of the body in cheese, imparting smoothness and a certain degree of mellowness, and (2) it furnishes suitable conditions for the work of those agents which change insoluble cheese proteins into soluble forms (p. 353).

In performing the first of these functions, water, therefore, supplements the work of fat, but cannot take its place in imparting richness and delicacy of taste. In the manufacture of skim-milk cheese, an effort is usually made to imitate the mellowness of body characteristic of a cheese made from normal milk, which is due to fat, by holding in the cheese a large amount of moisture. In illustration of this fact, we have examined cheese containing over 50 per cent of water, the cheese having been made from separator skim-milk. Unless this large amount of moisture is retained, the cheese is hard, tough and unpalatable. Even in cheese made from normal milk, the body becomes dry and mealy or crumbly, if the amount of moisture falls much below 30 per cent. The higher the fat content of the cheese, the lower can be the amount of water without impairing the body of the cheese. The temptation is often strong in making cheese to incorporate 5 per cent or more of moisture beyond the usual amount, because water is the only cheese constituent that can be had free of cost. The aim of cheese-makers should be so to control conditions of manufacture as to retain in cheese only the proper amount of moisture (p. 382).

We have already stated that another function of water in cheese is to furnish conditions suitable for the work of those agents which convert insoluble cheese proteins into soluble forms. If the amount of water is below a certain limit, 25 to 27 per cent, these changes do not take place and the cheese fails to become edible.

Some erroneously think that water in cheese is of a peculiar kind and possesses a special value as such,—that it is really different from water as we find it elsewhere. One writer goes so far as to speak of the water in cheese as "natural water," "natural moisture," as if it possessed some unusual virtue because it had gone through a cow and formed a part of milk before going into cheese as "natural" water. Such a belief is quite without foundation, because the water in cheese can be easily separated from the cheese and examined and is known to possess the usual composition of water wherever we find it. It is true, of course, that the presence of water in cheese is masked by the casein and fat and one of the aims of the cheese-maker is to conceal it thus as completely as possible; but this fact has no bearing on the composition or character of the water itself.

MILK-SUGAR

The only function milk-sugar appears to perform in the process of cheese-making is to furnish material for making lactic acid. Lactic acid does not remain in milk as free or uncombined acid, but, as fast as formed, it acts upon some of the salts of the milk, especially insoluble calcium phosphate, combining with a portion of the calcium and forming calcium lactate and soluble or acid calcium phosphate, an acid salt. There are probably other salts in milk acted upon, about the details of which we have not yet obtained complete knowledge. These soluble calcium salts (calcium lactate, and acid calcium phosphate, including probably also acid calcium citrate) resulting from the action of acid furnished by the fermentation of milk-sugar, perform several functions in the cheese-making process.

(1) These soluble calcium salts favor the rapidity and completeness of the action of rennet-extract in coagulating milk; in fact, their presence in certain amounts is essential to the action of the rennet-enzym. Now, while the immediate object of ripening milk in cheese-making is to convert milk-sugar into lactic acid, the real purpose is the formation of soluble calcium salts to hasten rennet coagulation.

(2) The soluble calcium salts probably perform some work in assisting in the contraction of the curd. After the curd is formed in the cheese-vat, the milk-sugar remains in the coagulated mass at first, but gradually passes out in solution as the whey exudes from the pieces of curd. The amount of sugar remaining in the curd is much reduced, but the formation of lactic acid continues, thus increasing the amount of calcium lactate, acid calcium phosphate, acid calcium citrate, etc. Cheese-makers speak of acid in curd frequently when they really mean whey or, more strictly, milk-sugar contained in whey within the pieces of curd and ready to form lactic acid sooner or later.

(3) The formation of soluble calcium salts is probably also more or less intimately connected with the changes in the curd during the cheddaring process, when the grain or texture rapidly changes, finally resembling the fiber of the cooked meat on a chicken's breast and when the curd develops the characteristic plastic properties exhibited by forming long, silky strings, when brought into contact with a hot iron. This change appears to depend upon the conversion of paracasein into a substance soluble in brine solution (p. 147).

The conversion of milk-sugar into lactic acid, with consequent formation of increasing quantities of soluble calcium salts, continues quite rapidly throughout the cheese-making process and also in the press and still later in the cheese. Under ordinary conditions, the last trace of milk-sugar disappears in about two weeks after the cheese is made. But, throughout the process of cheese-making, when the conditions are normal, there is never enough sugar converted into lactic acid to combine with all the available calcium in cheese and form free lactic acid; and there is never left in the cheese, under normal conditions, enough milk-sugar to form free acid. Therefore, in normal cheddar cheese, we never have free lactic acid.

When a large amount of whey is left in cheese, that means a corresponding amount of milk-sugar, a correspondingly large amount of acid, with formation of increased amounts of calcium salts, resulting in the production of what is known as "acid" or "sour" cheese.

(4) Another well-recognized function of milk-sugar, as a result of the formation of lactic acid and acid salts in milk, is the prevention of the growth of other micro-organisms which are often present in milk and give rise to forms of fermentation that interfere seriously with the production of good cheese, such as the micro-organisms that produce gases, ill-smelling compounds, etc. It is known that, if the acid salts and milk-sugar in cheese-curd are removed, as is done in the case of the "soaked-curd" process (p. 57), the resulting cheese undergoes abnormal changes in ripening, forming products that are putrefactive in character and which seriously impair or destroy the value of the cheese as food.

(5) It may be found that the fermentation products of milk-sugar are more intimately associated with the development of cheese flavor than has been previously thought.

SALTS OF MILK

The salts of milk appear, as already explained in connection with the functions of milk-sugar, to depend largely for the active part which they take in cheese-making upon the presence of lactic acid, by which insoluble calcium salts are converted into soluble forms, especially soluble calcium phosphate. When we determine the acidity of whey at various stages of the operations of cheese-making, we are really measuring directly the formation of acid compounds, which furnish, of course, a measure of the amount of lactic acid that has been formed.

It has been noticed that, when in the making of cheese a higher degree of acidity is produced, while the curd is still in the whey, that the amount of ash in the cheese is less than when so much acid is not formed. This is in accordance with what one would expect, since the more rapidly the insoluble calcium salts are dissolved while the curd is in the cheese-vat, the larger is the amount of soluble salts going into the whey.

CHAPTER XVII

Milk Constituents and Yield of Cheese

The relation of the composition of milk to yield of cheese is a subject of the highest practical interest and importance to cheese-makers. Comparatively little was known about it previous to 1892, because attention had been completely absorbed by the merely mechanical methods of cheese-making. We were completely in the dark in regard to such fundamental facts as the relation of fat and casein in milk to yield of cheese, the character and extent of losses of milk constituents in cheese-making, their causes and remedies, and, in general, the detailed relations existing between cheese and the material from which it is made. So profound was the ignorance regarding milk constituents and their relation to yield of cheese that it was very generally believed that the same amount of cheese was made from 100 pounds of milk in the case of the milks of different herds. We now have on hand an immense mass of data, the accumulated results of the investigation work of our American experiment stations, and these data enable us to reach very definite, positive and final conclusions.

The amount of fresh or green cheese produced by 100 pounds of milk depends upon three factors:

(1) The percentage of fat and of casein in milk.

(2) The percentage of fat and of casein lost in cheese-making.

(3) The amount of whey retained in cheese.

THE RELATION OF FAT AND OF CASEIN TO YIELD OF CHEESE

Those constituents of the milk that are insoluble and are present in suspension as solids or in emulsion, those that can be, for the most part, mechanically held by the coagulated casein, furnish the solid materials for cheese. They are: (1) Milk-fat; (2) milk-casein; and (3) insoluble phosphates. The fat and casein constitute so large a proportion of these cheese-producing solids of milk that we should not be far from the truth in saying that only these two constituents of normal milk are prominent in determining the yield of cheese. These two constituents of milk form over 90 per cent of the solid portion of cheese (cheese-solids); the only other solids in cheese are comparatively small in amount, consisting essentially (1) of the calcium salts of phosphoric, lactic and citric acids; (2) of the salt added in cheese-making; (3) of a small amount of milk-albumin; and (4) of some milk-sugar, which mostly disappears in a few days.

The yield of cheese from milk varies as the amount of fat and casein in milk vary, provided the conditions of cheese-making are the same, including under these conditions the quality of the milk with reference to cleanliness (bacterial content), (p. 4). As a rule, when the percentage of fat in milk increases, the percentage of casein also increases (p. 169) and the yield of cheese increases in proportion to the increase of fat and casein. At this point, the questions naturally arise: How much does milk-fat contribute to cheese yield? How much does milk-casein contribute to cheese yield? This at once brings us to a consideration of the losses of these constituents in the process of cheese-making.

THE LOSSES OF MILK CONSTITUENTS IN CHEESE-MAKING

In transferring fat and casein from milk into cheese through the operations of cheese-making, certain amounts of these constituents are unavoidably lost in the escaping whey and do not, consequently, contribute to the yield of cheese. It is obvious, therefore, that the cheese yield from a given amount of milk is dependent, to some extent, upon the degree of completeness with which the fat and casein of milk are worked into cheese; that is, upon the degree of success experienced in reducing these losses to a minimum. It is very important, then, that in studying the relation of milk constituents to yield of cheese, we learn something of the extent to which such losses are found in actual experience, the conditions responsible for these losses, and the means by which they can be made as small as possible.

The losses of milk-fat in cheese-making.—Less than 20 years ago cheese-makers almost universally believed that all fat in milk above 3.5 or 4.0 per cent must go into whey and not into cheese. Breeders of cows giving milk low in fat content openly declared, and without contradiction, that only cows of this type could be suitable for profitable cheese-making, because it was impossible to transfer the extra milk-fat into cheese when milk contained over

3.5 per cent. This question has been studied exhaustively at the New York experiment station under a great variety of conditions, including extended investigations in case of actual operations in many different cheese-factories. The following institutions have contributed additional, though less extensive, data, which fully confirm the results obtained in New York: The experiment stations of Wisconsin, Minnesota, Iowa, Vermont, Utah and the Ontario agricultural college. Probably much unpublished work has been done elsewhere.

Taking the results of extended study under cheese-factory conditions, we have found that the amount of fat lost for 100 pounds of milk varies from 0.20 to 0.50 pound (equivalent to 0.22 to 0.55 per cent of fat in whey), the average being 0.33 pound (equivalent to 0.36 per cent of fat in whey). This amounts to about 9 per cent of the fat in the milk. In one factory which was under observation for an entire season, the loss of fat for 100 pounds of milk varied from 0.20 to 0.36, and averaged 0.25, pound (equivalent to 0.22, 0.40 and 0.27 per cent of fat in whey). This average is equivalent to 7 per cent of the fat in the milk. In another factory, which was under observation at the same time, the amount of fat lost varied from 0.26 to 0.50, and averaged 0.37, pound (equivalent to 0.29, 0.55 and 0.42 per cent of fat in whey). The average loss in this case is nearly 10 per cent of the fat in the milk. In some cases, losses of fat under 0.20 pound have been reported, but such experience is not common in most cheese-factories. In general, it may be said that really efficient work is not being done by a cheese-maker when the percentage of fat in whey exceeds 0.30, if the milk furnished is in good condition in respect to cleanliness. An average loss of 0.25 pound (4 ounces) of fat for 100 pounds of milk indicates excellent work under factory conditions; this means that about 93 per cent of the fat in milk is recovered in cheese and not over 7 per cent lost in whey.

The data embodied in the following table include the results of several seasons' work in cheese-factories:

AMOUNT OF FAT IN WHEY AT CHEESE-FACTORIES DURING SEASON

Month	Average per cent of fat in milk	Pounds of fat lost in whey from 100 pounds of milk		
		Lowest	Highest	Average
April	3.43	0.29	0.42	0.36
May	3.58	0.20	0.50	0.35
June	3.64	0.20	0.36	0.28
July	3.62	0.21	0.45	0.32
August	3.84	0.22	0.40	0.34
September	3.98	0.22	0.46	0.37
October	4.23	0.26	0.44	0.33

The tabulated results on the next page show the relative amounts of fat lost in normal milks containing different percentages of fat. These results are in harmony with those of other investigators and the facts all go to show that *the loss of fat in cheese-making is quite independent of the amount of fat in milk*. The variations that occur in loss of fat are due either to the defective condition of the milk with reference to bacterial content, or to some special fault in the details of methods employed in cheese-making, or to both causes.

Even when cream is added to normal milk to an extent sufficient to raise the fat content to 7 or 8 per cent, the increased loss of fat, though considerable, is not necessarily greater in proportion to the increase of fat in milk.

AMOUNT OF FAT LOST IN CHEESE-MAKING IN CASE OF NORMAL MILKS

Group	Number of experiments	Per cent of fat in milk	Pounds of fat lost in whey for 100 pounds of milk			Percentage of fat in milk lost in whey	Percentage of fat in milk retained in cheese
			Lowest	Highest	Average		
I	22	3.0-3.5	0.21	0.39	0.32	9.55	90.45
II	112	3.5-4.0	0.21	0.50	0.33	8.33	91.67
III	78	4.0-4.5	0.20	0.46	0.32	7.70	92.30
IV	16	4.5-5.0	0.17	0.49	0.28	5.90	94.10
V	7	5.0-5.25	0.27	0.35	0.31	6.00	94.00

Why it is impossible to prevent loss of fat in cheese-making.—Attention has already been called (p. 140) to the fact that fat is present in milk in the form of very small globules, one cubic centimeter of ordinary milk containing between one and two billion globules. When the rennet-extract causes the casein throughout the mass of milk to solidify or coagulate, the fat-globules are retained or imprisoned in the solidified mass just where they are at the instant of coagulation. When the curd-knife passes through the solid mass, immense numbers of the fat-globules are exposed on every cut surface and billions of these are disengaged from the free surfaces of the small pieces of curd during its manipulation. The fat-globules, thus detached from the hold of the curd, float free in the whey and are consequently lost to the cheese.

Conditions favoring loss of fat in cheese-making. —Among the numerous conditions contributing to an increased loss of fat in cheese-making are the following:

(1) Any condition which interferes with complete coagulation of casein by rennet-extract, such as dilution with water, presence of preservatives, as salt, formalin, etc., necessarily causes extra loss of fat.

(2) There may occur cases of abnormal composition of milk, in which the casein is abnormally low in relation to fat. Attention has already (p. 164) been called to this condition as likely to occur in times of drouth. Cheese-makers do not realize the abnormal nature of the milk and so do not observe the precautions necessary in handling milk that is abnormally high in fat in relation to casein. But another condition usually prevails at such times, which makes the losses of fat unavoidable, and that is the presence of bacterial ferments, resulting from the accompanying effects of drouth such as contaminated water supply.

(3) Failure to keep the fat well distributed through the milk before and after adding rennet results in some accumulation of fat at the surface of the milk, most of which goes into the whey.

(4) In case of milk containing particles of dried cream or churned fat-granules, there is usually increased loss of fat, unless the particles are completely worked back into the form of emulsion by sufficient, but not rapid, warming and careful stirring.

(5) When milk is run through a separator and the cream and skim-milk then remixed, increased loss of fat occurs when such milk is made into cheese.

(6) Jarring or stirring milk after rennet coagulation has commenced and before it is completed may cause serious loss of fat.

(7) When curd is cut in too soft a condition, the loss of fat is greater.

(8) Added losses of fat in whey are caused by dull knives or by violent, careless and rapid motions of knife in cutting curd.

(9) Extra losses of fat occur when the curd in the soft stage is roughly or carelessly handled.

(10) Another cause of increased loss of fat in whey is heating the curd too rapidly or to too high a temperature.

(11) If the curd is not well firmed at the time the whey is removed, vigorous hand stirring causes large loss of fat.

(12) Excessive piling of curd, previous to cheddaring, causes unnecessary loss of fat.

(13) If the curd is salted at a temperature above 90° F., fat is apt to exude along with the whey and be lost.

(14) If curd is put in press too warm, the amount of fat lost in pressing increases on account of the greater softness of the warm curd.

(15) Too rapid application of pressure in the cheese-press increases loss of fat.

(16) Fermentations producing large amounts of gas and resulting in "floating" curds, also curd-dissolving fermentations, are attended with extra

losses of fat. The conditions of cheese-making have to be varied under such circumstances so as to make the best of a bad matter and obtain as good a product as possible in respect to texture, body and flavor. Such variations from the usual conditions of cheese-making cause extra losses of fat (p. 124).

(17) The making of cheese from milk containing too much acid results in unusual losses of fat, if the conditions are varied so as to obtain the best product possible from such milk (p. 122).

(18) Milling at too high a temperature, or too rapidly, or with dull knives, or feeding to mill too fast, or allowing the curd to become matted after milling,—any of these conditions increases loss of fat.

The losses of casein in cheese-making.—The larger portion of the casein lost in cheese-making appears to be in the form of fine particles of the coagulated casein (paracasein), which pass through the strainer when the whey is removed from the curd. These fine particles can readily be seen by letting a pail of freshly drawn whey stand until the curd particles settle. If the whey is then carefully poured from the pail, a noticeable quantity of finely divided curd can be seen at the bottom of the pail. This loss does not appear to be entirely avoidable. but is needlessly made greater (1) by carelessness or violence in cutting curd and in subsequent handling when the curd is still soft; (2) by agitation while removing the whey from the curd; (3) by imperfect strainers; and (4) by any condition that interferes with the complete coagulation of the milk-casein by rennet (p. 24). The amount of casein that thus passes into the whey averages about 0.10 pound for 100 pounds of milk.

In some cases of badly contaminated milk, casein-dissolving ferments may cause more or less loss of casein.

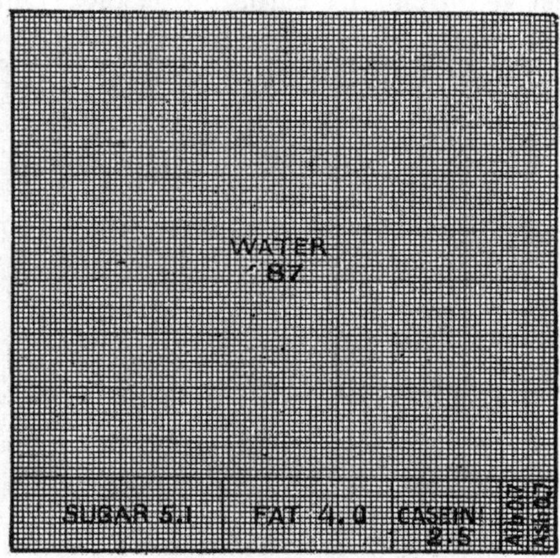

FIG. 34—COMPOSITION OF MILK, SHOWING PROPORTIONS OF WATER AND DIFFERENT SOLIDS. THE NUMBERS REPRESENT POUNDS IN 100 POUNDS OF MILK

COMPOSITION OF WHEY

The composition of whey (Fig. 35) varies according to (1) the composition of the milk from which it comes, and (2) the losses of milk constituents due to conditions attending the operations of cheese-making. It is obvious that the larger the percentage of sugar, albumin and soluble salts in milk, the larger will be their amount in whey. The matter of losses of fat and casein we have already treated.. The amount of acid in whey varies greatly, depending largely on the time when the determination of acidity is made. When the whey is removed from the curd, the acidity (equivalent

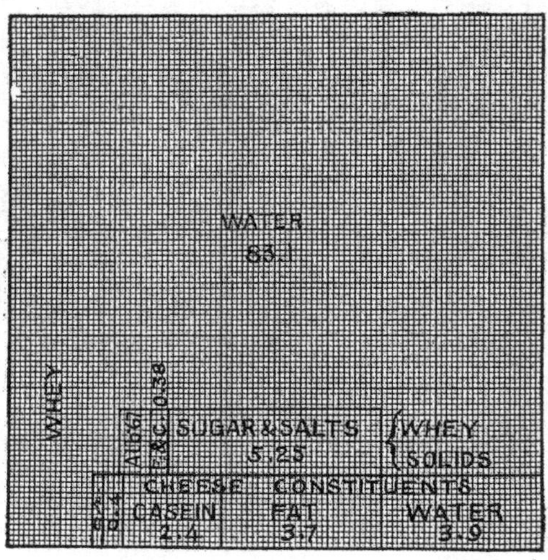

FIG. 35—DISTRIBUTION OF MILK CONSTITUENTS IN
CHEESE AND WHEY

From 100 pounds of milk, we obtain 10.6 pounds of cheese and 89.4 pounds of whey. The cheese contains 3.9 pounds of water, 3.7 fat, 2.4 casein, 0.4 salts and albumin and 0.2 sugar. The whey contains 83.1 pounds of water, 5.25 sugar and salts, 0.28 fat, 0.10 casein and 0.67 albumin. The lower part of the diagram shows amount and composition of cheese. The remainder is whey (water and whey-solids.)

to lactic acid) varies from 0.16 to 0.18 per cent, and this amount increases to the end of the cheese-making process. The whey, when it first separates from the curd, shows less acidity than the milk from which it comes, because the whey does not

.contain the milk-casein, which, as we have seen (p. 145), has the power of neutralizing considerable alkali, and of acting in this way like an acid. The percentage of sugar in whey depends upon the time when the whey is tested, the sugar decreasing in amount as it is changed into lactic acid.

In closing this discussion of the losses of milk constituents in cheese-making, we give below tabulated results of work showing the composition of whey as obtained at cheese-factories in New York through the work of the New York experiment station.

COMPOSITION OF CHEESE-FACTORY WHEY

Month	Per cent of water	Per cent of solids	Per cent of fat	Per cent of proteins (chiefly albumin)	Per cent of sugar, salts, etc.
April	93.17	6.83	0.40	0.73	5.70
May	92.98	7.02	0.38	0.81	5.83
June	92.99	7.01	0.31	0.88	5.82
July	93.05	6.95	0.35	0.83	5.77
August	93.08	6.92	0.38	0.80	5.74
September	93.18	6.82	0.41	0.85	5.56
October	93.04	6.96	0.38	0.98	5.60
Average	93.04	6.96	0.36	0.84	5.76

The following figures show the extreme variations in the constituents of whey during the period of investigation:

	Lowest per cent	Highest per cent
Solids	6.43	7.52
Fat	0.22	0.55
Proteins	0.65	1.07
Sugar, salts, etc.	5.39	6.43

THE RELATION OF WATER TO YIELD OF CHEESE

As we have seen, the amount of solids in cheese is determined by the amount of fat and casein in milk when the conditions of manufacture are normal. When we come to consider the amount of water held in cheese, we find that it bears no relation whatever to the amount of water in milk, but that it is dependent upon the conditions present in the operations of cheese-making, such as the degree of fineness or coarseness in cutting curd, temperature used in heating curd, degree of acidity, amount of salt, etc. (p. 45). The amount of water in cheese can easily be made to vary 10 per cent. Fresh cheese contains an average of 37 per cent of water, but in actual factory work the variations may be very wide, especially where cheese is manufactured for export trade at one part of the season and for home trade at another. Therefore, when we are discussing yields of cheese from milk, and especially in the case of comparison of different milks, it is absolutely necessary to know the percentage of water in the cheese. When we compare yields of cheese from different milks or under different conditions of manufacture, we should base our comparison on the yield of cheese which contains a uniform percentage of moisture, if the results are to have any definite relation to the milk constituents.

So important is it for us to appreciate the extent of variation of water in cheese, as made at cheese-factories, that we will present data obtained by the New York experiment station in 200 experiments carried on at cheese-factories under the usual conditions. In the table below, we present the results in groups, based on the percentage of fat in milk; in each group we give (1) the extreme variations in yield of cheese; (2) the percentage of moisture in the cheese; and (3) the corresponding yield of cheese based on a content of 37 per cent of water.

YIELD OF CHEESE AS AFFECTED BY MOISTURE

Number of experiments	Per cent of fat in milk	Pounds of cheese made for 100 pounds of milk	Per cent of water in cheese	Pounds of cheese (containing 37 per cent of water) made for 100 pounds of milk
22	3.00-3.49	Lowest - 8.47 / Highest- 9.68	34.77 / 39.09	8.43 / 9.46
59	3.50-3.74	Lowest - 9.25 / Highest-10.42	33.75 / 40.47	9.32 / 10.60
51	3.75-3.99	Lowest - 9.60 / Highest-11.00	32.69 / 40.17	9.76 / 10.76
43	4.00-4.19	Lowest -10.24 / Highest-12.44	34.15 / 42.90	10.38 / 10.93
25	4.20-4.40	Lowest -10.64 / Highest-13.17	33.53 / 43.89	11.03 / 12.03

In studying these results, we see that in the case of each group the cheese yield varies widely, as shown in the third column of the table; and also that the percentage of water varies widely, as shown in the fourth column. To illustrate, we will take the group representing milk containing 4 to 4.19 per cent of fat. The factory yield of cheese in this group varies from 10.24 to 12.44 pounds, a difference of 2 pounds, while the water in 100 pounds of cheese varies from 34.15 to 42.90 pounds. In the last column we see what the normal variation should be in the yield of cheese having the same percentage (37) of water; it goes from 10.38 to 10.93, a variation of 0.55 pound, as against an actual variation of 2 pounds. This difference, 1.45 pounds, is wholly due to difference of water in cheese. In the last group of the table, the factory yield of cheese varies 2.53 pounds, while the normal variation would be only 1.0 pound. We see at the same time that the amount of water in 100 pounds of cheese varies over 10 pounds.

These results might appear to indicate that cheese-makers have no control over the amount of water in cheese, but such a conclusion would not be justified, because it is well known that a skillful cheese-maker, under normal conditions, can control the amount of water in cheese within 3 or 4 per cent, so that the normal range of variation is usually between 35 and 38 per cent. The large amounts of water in the cases noted in the preceding table appeared there, not because the cheese-makers had no control of the process, but for the very opposite reason, that they did have such control and deliberately made the cheese to hold a high percentage of water

THE COMPARATIVE VALUE OF DIFFERENT MILKS IN RELATION TO CHEESE-PRODUCING SOLIDS

From what has preceded, it can be readily understood that we can divide the constituents of milk into two general classes, when considered with reference to their relations to cheese. The casein, fat and insoluble salts constitute one group, furnishing most of the solid matter in cheese, and we can call these constituents *cheese-producing solids*. On an average, milk contains about 0.90 per cent of salts, of which about 0.25 pound goes into cheese for each 100 pounds of milk and 0.65 pound into whey, varying, of course, with many conditions. The other constituents of the milk-solids,. the sugar, the albumin and the soluble salts, those constituents of the milk that exist in true solution, pass largely into the whey and are lost, except in so far as they are held by the water or whey in the cheese. Their amount in cheese will depend upon the amount of whey retained in the cheese. Those solid constituents existing in solution in the whey we may properly characterize as *whey-solids*. This division of milk constituents into cheese-producing solids and whey-solids is, of course, not strictly accurate, because small amounts of cheese-solids pass into whey and small amounts of whey-solids are retained in cheese. But, for the purpose of studying the general relations of milk-solids to cheese, the classification is close enough. The figures presented below are largely taken from work done at the New York experiment station, covering a period of four years and are largely derived from actual cheese-factory conditions.

The cheese-producing solids were found to average 6.50 pounds, varying in extreme cases from 5.25 to 7.75 pounds for 100 pounds of milk, but the greater . portion of factory milk comes within the narrower limits of 5.75 to 7.25 pounds. The whey-solids of milk varied from 5.75 to 6.75 pounds and averaged 6.25 pounds. Stated in another form, 49 per cent of the milk-solids goes into whey and 51 per cent into cheese as an average of factory milk.

The following arrangement shows the extent of average monthly variation during the factory season:

CHEESE-PRODUCING SOLIDS AND WHEY SOLIDS IN CHEESE-FACTORY MILK

Month	Percentage of cheese-producing solids in milk			Percentage of whey-solids in milk		
	Lowest	Highest	Average	Lowest	Highest	Average
April........	5.75	6.14	5.97	5.94	6.09	6.01
May.........	5.68	6.91	6.17	6.11	7.78	6.26
June........	6.06	6.61	6.36	6.17	6.44	6.28
July........	6.01	6.60	6.30	6.10	6.47	6.22
August......	6.09	6.76	6.48	6.06	6.35	6.17
September...	6.27	7.14	6.78	5.86	6.26	6.08
October.....	7.02	7.69	7.29	5.96	6.44	6.21

Expressing the relations of the general averages in the preceding table in the form of percentages of milk-solids, we have the following table:

Month	Pounds of milk-solids in 100 pounds of milk	Percentage of total solids of milk in form of cheese-producing solids	Percentage of total solids in milk in form of whey-solids
April.......	11.98	49.8	50.2
May........	12.43	49.6	50.4
June.......	12.64	50.3	49.7
July.......	12.52	50.3	49.7
August.....	12.65	51.2	48.8
September .	12.86	52.7	47.3
October....	13.50	54.0	46.0

We see a general tendency for the cheese-producing solids in milk to increase during the factory season, which is only another way of saying that the percentage of fat and of casein increases with advance of lactation. (p. 166).

Before leaving this phase of the subject, it will be found interesting to compare the ratio of cheese-producing solids and whey-solids in milk varying considerably in percentage of fat. From the figures in the following table, it is very strikingly shown that in normal milk rich in fat a very much larger proportion of the milk-solids goes into cheese and correspondingly less into whey, than in the case of milk poorer in fat.

CHEESE-PRODUCING SOLIDS AND WHEY SOLIDS IN RICH AND POOR MILK

Per cent of solids	Per cent of fat	Per cent of cheese-producing solids	Per cent of whey solids	Per cent of solids in form of cheese-solids	Per cent of solids in form of whey-solids
11.80	3.26	5.71	6.09	48.4	51.6
12.65	3.76	6.89	5.76	54.5	45.5
12.75	4.01	6.47	6.28	50.7	49.3
14.30	4.28	7.32	6.98	51.1	48.9
14.50	4.89	8.24	6.26	56.9	43.1
14.90	5.38	8.54	6.36	57.3	42.7
15.40	5.78	9.06	6.34	58.8	41.2

DISTRIBUTION OF MILK CONSTITUENTS IN WHEY AND CHEESE

Having learned what the principal losses of cheese-producing solids are, we will next show by illustrations in what amounts the different constituents of milk are divided between whey and cheese in cheese-making. The following results are based on average losses of milk constituents.

The cheese is assumed to contain 37 per cent of water, about 5 per cent of salts and no allowance is made for mechanical losses other than as indicated

		Water	Milk-solids	Fat	Casein	Albumin	Sugar, ash, etc.
I.	Pounds	Pounds	Pounds	Pounds	Pounds	Pounds	Pounds
Milk...	100.00	88.60	11.40	3.00	2.10	0.60	5.70
Whey..	91.70	85.55	6.15	0.21	0.10	0.57	5.27
Cheese	8.30	3.05	5.25	2.79	2.00	0.03	0.43
II.							
Milk...	100.00	87.00	13.00	4.00	2.50	0.70	5.80
Whey..	89.40	83.10	6.30	0.28	0.10	0.67	5.25
Cheese	10.60	3.90	6.70	3.72	2.40	0.03	0.55
III.							
Milk...	100.00	85.50	14.50	5.00	2.90	0.75	5.85
Whey..	87.10	80.75	6.35	0.35	0.10	0.72	5.18
Cheese	12.90	4.75	8.15	4.65	2.80	0.03	0.67

In connection with this table, study Figs. 34, 35 and 36.

RELATION OF MILK-FAT TO CHEESE YIELD

Much study has been given, especially in New York, to the quantitative relations existing between the percentage of fat in milk and the yield of cheese, or the amount of cheese corresponding to one pound of fat in milk. The relation is a very simple one to calculate and is found by dividing the number of pounds of cheese made from 100 pounds of milk by the number representing the per cent of fat in milk. For example, the yield of cheese from 100 pounds of milk containing 3 per cent of fat is 8.31 pounds;

the ratio of milk-fat to cheese yield is, therefore, 8.31÷3, which equals 2.77; that is, in this case, one pound of fat in milk is equivalent to 2.77 pounds of cheese. In the case of milk containing 4 per cent of fat and producing 10.60 pounds of cheese for 100 pounds of milk, each pound of fat in milk is equivalent to 2.65 pounds of cheese.

The study of this relation was first undertaken at the New York experiment station to ascertain whether a pound of fat in all normal milks is equivalent to the same amount of cheese. The bearing of this point upon the use of fat in milk as a basis of paying for milk at cheese-factories is obvious. If a pound of fat in milk were always equivalent to the same amount of cheese, then no question could arise as to the strict accuracy of a milk-fat basis in making dividends. If the amount of cheese made for a pound of fat in milk varies, then the fat could not be regarded as a strictly accurate measure of cheese yield, and other points than yield would need to be considered, such as the quality of the cheese, in measuring the value of milk for cheese-making. The details of the subject of methods of paying for milk at cheese-factories will be considered later (p. 253).

We have already seen that the yield of cheese is chiefly dependent upon two constituents of milk, casein as well as fat. It is obvious that if fat and casein were always present in milk in the same relative proportions, then the yield of cheese would always be in the same uniform ratio to milk-fat. But we have found (p. 164) that the ratio of fat and casein in milk varies considerably and, for this reason, the ratio of milk-fat to yield of cheese must also vary. It is a matter of practical interest and importance to know what the extent of such variations may be.

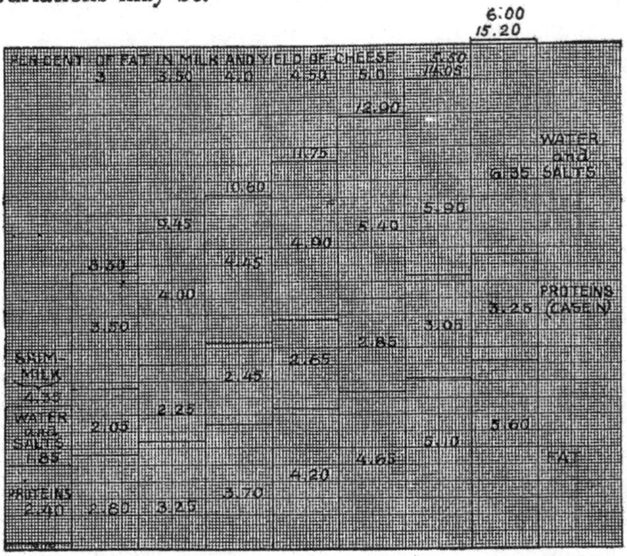

FIG. 36—YIELD AND CONSTITUENTS OF CHEESE FROM 100 POUNDS OF MILK CONTAINING AMOUNTS OF FAT VARYING FROM 0.10 PER CENT (SEPARATOR SKIM-MILK) UP TO 6.00 PER CENT.

The figures immediately above each column give the number of pounds of cheese (containing 37 per cent of water) made from 100 pounds of milk. The figures within the diagram give the pounds of each constituent in the cheese. The figures at the extreme top of the diagram indicate percentages of fat in milk.

Taking milk as it averages, we find the following variation of relation between fat and cheese yield in normal milks containing different amounts of fat. The cheese yield is based on a uniform percentage of water in the cheese, 37 per cent.

RATIO OF FAT TO CHEESE YIELD IN NORMAL MILK

Per cent of fat in milk	Per cent of casein in milk	Pounds of cheese made from 100 pounds of milk	Pounds of cheese made for each pound of fat in milk
3.00	2.10	8.30	2.77
3.25	2.20	8.88	2.73
3.50	2.30	9.45	2.70
3.75	2.40	10.03	2.67
4.00	2.50	10.60	2.65
4.25	2.60	11.17	2.63
4.50	2.70	11.74	2.61
4.75	2.80	12.31	2.59
5.00	2.90	12.90	2.58

In our study of the ratio of fat and casein in milk (p. 164), it was seen that the casein does not increase as rapidly as fat does, and that, therefore, milk richer in fat usually contains less casein in proportion to fat than does milk less rich in fat. In harmony with this condition, and as a result of it, the amount of cheese made for a pound of milk-fat decreases as the percentage of fat in milk increases. This is clearly shown in the preceding table.

An interesting fact shown in this table is that the rate of decrease of the ratio of fat to cheese yield is less rapid as the percentage of fat in milk increases. Thus, in the case of milks containing 3 and 3.25 per cent of fat, the decrease of cheese yield in relation to fat is from 2.77 to 2.73, a difference of 0.04 pound; between 3.25 and 3.50, and also between 3.50 and 3.75, the decrease is 0.03; for each 0.25 per cent of increase of milk-fat from 3.75 to 4.75 per cent, the decrease in the ratio is only 0.02; and between 4.75 and 5.00 per cent, the decrease is only 0.01. This is explained by the fact, already emphasized (p. 190), that in the case of milk rich in fat, a smaller proportion of the fat is lost in cheese-making than in the case of milk poorer in fat.

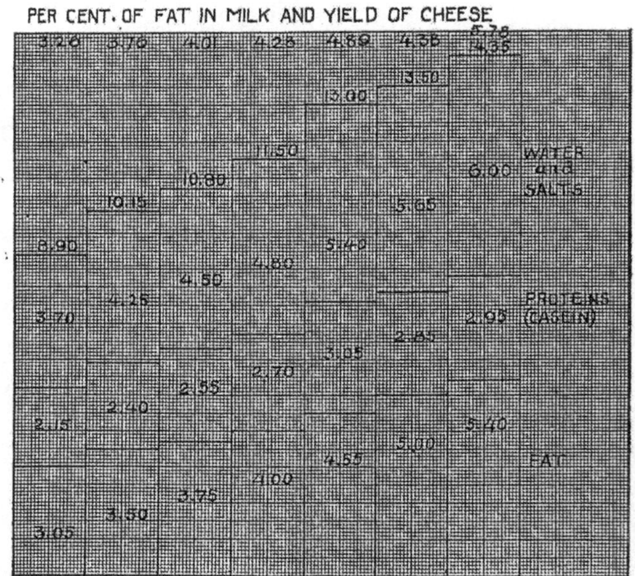

FIG. 37—DIAGRAM SHOWING YIELD AND CONSTITUENTS OF CHEESE FROM 100 POUNDS OF MILK OF DIFFERENT BREEDS OF DAIRY COWS

The figures immediately above each column give the number of pounds of cheese (containing 37 per cent of water) made from 100 pounds of milk. The figures in the diagram give the pounds of each constituent in the cheese. The figures at the top of the diagram indicate percentage of fat in milk.

·In this connection, it will be interesting to observe how the matter works out when applied in the case of the milk of different breeds of cows.

RATIO OF FAT TO CHEESE YIELD IN MILK OF DIFFERENT
BREEDS

Breed	Per cent of fat in milk	Per cent of casein in milk	Pounds of cheese made for 100 pounds of milk	Pounds of cheese made for each pound of fat in milk
Holstein-Friesian......	3.26	2.20	8.90	2.73
Ayrshire..............	3.76	2.46	10.14	2.70
American Holderness...	4.01	2.63	10.82	2.70
Shorthorn.............	4.28	2.79	11.52	2.70
Devon................	4.89	3.10	13.02	2.66
Guernsey.............	5.38	2.91	13.51	2.51
Jersey...............	5.78	3.03	14.36	2.49

Before closing our discussion of this subject, we
wish to call attention to the fallacy that may be
introduced by wide variations in the water content
of cheese, when we are making a comparison of the
yield of cheese with reference to the milk-fat. For
example, 100 pounds of milk containing 4 per cent
of fat may be made into cheese with a yield of 10.40
pounds in one case, and 11.00 pounds in another,
the difference being due wholly to water. In one
case the yield is 2.60 pounds for one pound of milk-
fat; in the other, it is 2.75 pounds. It is thus seen
that, when such comparisons are to be made with
reference to the relation of fat to yield of cheese,
the cheese should contain the same percentage of
water. The table on page 199 well illustrates the
variations of yield in relation to water. If we use
the results there given as a basis for calculating
the yield of cheese in relation to milk-fat, we find
that the amount of cheese made for one pound of
milk-fat varies from 2.51 to 3.11, when we take the
factory yield, with its great variation of water; but,

if the calculation is based on cheese containing a fixed percentage of water, the cheese yield varies in relation to fat only from 2.61 to 2.89. This is a much narrower range and represents such variations as are properly due to differences in composition of milk.

CHAPTER XVIII

Methods of Calculating Yield of Cheese

In the chapter preceding, we have seen that fat and casein in milk furnish most of the solid material which we find in cheese; we have also seen that certain amounts of fat and of casein are inevitably lost in whey during the operations of cheese-making; and we have further seen that the amount of water in cheese may be made to vary largely or may be held within comparatively narrow limits, being controlled by the conditions used in the process of cheese-making. From our preceding discussion, it might seem that the relations between composition of cheese and yield of milk were sufficiently understood to enable us to calculate the amount of cheese yield when the percentages of fat and of casein in milk are known, or even when the fat alone is given. As a matter of fact, several different methods have been proposed and have been employed in studying problems of cheese yield. There is an advantage in having some fairly reliable method for ascertaining the amount of cheese that can be made from 100 pounds of milk. Results thus obtained afford a basis of comparison with actual results. A cheese-maker can, by such means, ascertain if his losses in cheese-making are excessive or if he is retaining too much or too little water in cheese.

The different methods of calculating cheese yield which have been in use have never been carefully compared in such a way as to show their relative accuracy or value. It has seemed desirable that such a study should be made, and it is now our purpose to take up for consideration the various methods referred to. We shall discuss, in the case of each method, their underlying principles, indicate the points of fundamental weakness, and give the results of an exhaustive comparative study, based upon an application of each method to 200 experiments in cheese-making, using for this purpose the work done at the New York experiment station, which appears to offer the only material sufficiently complete to be available for such an investigation.

The methods which have been proposed for use in calculating the amount of green cheese are the following:

(1) The use of the percentage of fat in milk, which, expressed as a formula, is:

Yield of cheese=2.7 Fat.

(2) The use of the percentage of fat in milk and, in addition, a constant factor. This, expressed as a formula, is:

Yield of cheese=1.1 Fat+5.9.

(3) The use of the percentage of fat and of casein, which can be expressed in the following form:

Yield of cheese=1.1 Fat+2.5 Casein.

(4) The use of the percentage of fat in milk and of the solids-not-fat. This is somewhat more complicated and is expressed thus:

$$\text{Yield of cheese} = \left(\frac{\text{Solids-not-fat}}{3} + 0.91 \text{ Fat} \right) \times 1.58$$

(5)   A new method based on the use of the percentage of fat and the percentage of casein (either actual or calculated). The general formula for this method is as follows:

$$\text{Yield of cheese} = \frac{(\text{Fat} - 0.07 \text{ Fat} + \text{Casein} - 0.10) \times 1.09}{1.00 - \text{Water in cheese (expressed as hundredths)}}$$

As will be pointed out later, this can be much simplified, becoming

  Yield of cheese=(Fat+Casein)$\times$1.63

in the case of cheese containing a uniform amount of water (37 per cent). When only the fat is known and the casein is calculated from the formula on p. 170 the formula for both casein calculation and calculation of cheese yield is simplified into one:

(6)   Yield of cheese=2.3 Fat+1.4.

These last formulas, based upon results of New York experiment station work, are now published for the first time.

Before giving the detailed results of our comparative study of these different methods, we will discuss each one separately, explaining underlying principles and thus learning how the methods came to be suggested.

METHOD BASED ON RELATION OF FAT TO YIELD OF CHEESE (1)

The basis of this method has been discussed in the chapter preceding. In the investigations carried on at the New York experiment station, covering all varieties of factory conditions, it was found that when the yield of cheese for 100 pounds of milk was divided by the number representing the percentage of fat in milk, the averages, season by season, and factory by factory, were very uniform, being very close to 2.72 pounds of cheese for one pound of fat in milk. The individual results giving the average varied widely, from 2.51 to 3.11. These extreme variations were due to wide variations in the water content of the cheese rather than to variation in the real relation of fat to cheese yield proper, as we have pointed out in the chapter preceding. Based on a uniform percentage of water in cheese, the variations would be within much less wide limits, ranging from 2.61 to 2.89. This variation was due mainly to variation in the relation of the fat and casein in the milk and, in some cases, to excessive losses experienced in the process of cheese-making. The average result (2.7) is based upon milk containing 3.75 per cent of fat, 2.46 per cent of casein and upon cheese containing nearly 37 per cent of water. The ratio of milk-fat to casein is, therefore, 1 :0.665. When the ratio of fat and casein varies widely from this, we shall get more or less cheese than that called for by the rule. Thus, in milk in which the casein is high in relation to fat, as often happens in milk low in fat, the formula gives too low results (p. 207); while the reverse is true in case of milk high in fat in relation to casein, as often happens in milk rich in fat (p. 209). Therefore, as a result of the variations of the relation of fat and casein in cheese-factory milks, we may expect this method to give results varying from the actual yield of cheese, in extreme and uncommon cases, to an extent equal to 0.5 to 0.75 pound of cheese for 100 pounds of milk. When the variation is greater than this, it is usually due to excessive or deficient amounts of water in cheese.

METHOD BASED ON FAT IN MILK AND A FIXED NUMBER ADDED (2)

This method, stated in the form of a rule, is as follows: Multiply the number representing the per cent of fat in milk by 1.1 and to the result add 5.9. This formula was worked out at the Wisconsin experiment station and is based upon certain facts which will be briefly considered. One pound of milk-fat in butter can readily hold about 0.18 pound of water and it can just as readily hold the same amount in cheese. We multiply the per cent of fat in milk by 1.1 instead of 1.18, because not all of the milk-fat goes into the cheese. To illustrate, take milk containing 4 per cent of fat; in cheese-making, about 3.72 pounds of this fat in 100 pounds of milk goes into cheese. This figure, multiplied by 1.18, equals nearly 4.40, the same as 4 multiplied by 1.1. In other words, the amount of fat that actually goes into cheese multiplied by 1.18 gives about the same result as the amount (per cent) of fat in milk multiplied by 1.1.

The next question that presents itself is as to why we add the particular number 5.9 to the fat multiplied by 1.1. This figure is based upon the amount of cheese that can be made from 100 pounds of separator skim-milk of average composition, and is supposed to account for the milk-casein, the insoluble salts and the moisture not provided for in the milk-fat. It is in reality taking account of casein in milk, but only of the same amount for all milks.

The inherent weak points of this method are the following: (1) In the case of excessive losses of fat in cheese-making, the result found by multi-plying milk-fat by 1.1 is too high. (2) The estimate of 5.9 pounds as the measure of the cheese-making value of casein in skim-milk is based upon skim-milk of average composition. Therefore, in milk low in percentage of casein, 5.9 is too high, while in milk high in casein, the figure is too low. The method is faulty in that its accuracy depends upon a uniform percentage of casein in all milks, and we know that there are quite wide variations.

METHOD BASED ON FAT AND CASEIN IN MILK (3)

This method of finding the yield of cheese, stated in the form of a rule, is as follows: Multiply the number representing the per cent of fat in milk by 1.1, and to this add the result obtained in multi-plying by 2.5 the number representing the per cent of casein in milk. This formula was originally worked out at the Wisconsin experiment station and was first extensively applied and confirmed by the work of the New York experiment station.

This method is based upon the following facts: (1) Milk-fat is capable of holding mechanically one-tenth of its own weight of water. This has been already explained in detail in connection with the discussion of method 2. (2) The reason for mul-tiplying the amount of casein in milk by 2.5 is found in the yield of cheese from skim-milk and also in the results of some experimental work done at the New York experiment station. A prepara-tion of pure casein was made, dried, and then al-lowed to absorb as much water as it would be likely to hold in being made into green cheese. It was found that one pound of casein takes up water enough to increase its weight to 2.25 pounds. If to this is added the amount of ash constituents taken up in the same amount of cheese, the weight is increased to just about 2.5 pounds. This method has the following defects: (1) As already pointed out, the calculation of the amount of cheese yield coming from milk-fat is too high when there are abnormal losses of fat in cheese-making. (2) When the yield of cheese is calculated by this method, the percentage of water in cheese is not uniform, but varies with the percentage of casein in milk, because the water content of the cheese is made dependent largely upon the amount of casein. The inevitable result is that in case of milks containing high percentages of casein in relation to fat, the percentage of water is greater in the cheese calculated by this method than in case of cheese from milks in which the amount of casein is lower in relation to fat. When the ratio of fat and casein is fairly constant, the results are quite satisfactory. The manner in which this method of calculation favors the yield of cheese in case of milk low in fat and relatively high in casein as against the yield of cheese in case of milk high in fat and relatively low in casein can be illustrated by the data in the table on the next page.

Attention is called to the following facts in connection with the data contained in this table: (1) When the cheese made from the two different milks contains the same amount of water (37 per cent), the water in the cheese made from 100 pounds of milk amounts to 3.31 pounds in the case of the cheese made from the poorer milk and 5.31 pounds in the case of the cheese made from the richer milk. When the cheese from the two milks is made to contain the average amount of water (37 per cent) found in green cheese, there is a normal difference of 2 pounds of water in the cheese made from 100 pounds of milk. What do we find in regard to the yield of cheese and of water in the cheese, when the yield of cheese is calculated by method 3? The yield of cheese from 100 pounds of the poorer milk is increased 0.19 pound, from 8.90 to 9.09 pounds, an increase wholly

Per cent of fat in milk	Per cent of casein in milk	Pounds of cheese (containing 37 per cent of water) made for 100 pounds of milk	Pounds of water in cheese made from 100 pounds of milk	Pounds of cheese for 100 pounds of milk calculated by method 3	Pounds of water in cheese from 100 pounds of milk (method 3)	Per cent of water in cheese calculated by method 3
3.26	2.20	8.90	3.31	9.09	3.50	38.50
5.78	3.03	14.36	5.31	13.93	4.88	35.00

due to the greater amount of water contained in the cheese; the water increases from 3.31 to 3.50 pounds, and the percentage of water in the cheese, from 37 to 38.50. In the case of the cheese made from the richer milk, the reverse is found to be true. The yield of cheese containing 37 per cent of water is 14.36 pounds for 100 pounds of milk, and this is decreased 0.43 pound or from 14.36 to 13.93 pounds. This decrease is wholly due to the smaller amount of water in the cheese when the yield is calculated by method 3. Thus, the amount of water in the cheese containing 37 per cent of water is decreased from 5.31 to 4.88 pounds in the cheese calculated by method 3, and the percentage of water from 37 to 35 per cent. We see, therefore, that the difference of cheese yield in these two cases should be normally 5.46 pounds for the cheese made from 100 pounds of milk, but the difference is only 4.86 pounds, or 0.62 pound too small, when the yield is calculated by method 3. (3) Another objection raised to this method is that, under ordinary conditions, the percentage of casein in milk is not known and the method is consequently inapplicable. In reply to this, the percentage of casein in milk can be calculated from the percentage of milk-fat and the method carried out in the usual way. Even when the amount of casein in milk is calculated, the results are generally much more accurate than those given by method 2 (1.1 Fat+5.9).

METHOD BASED ON FAT AND SOLIDS-NOT-FAT IN MILK (4)

In the twelfth annual report of the Wisconsin experiment station there is a detailed discussion of the facts leading to the proposal of the following formula:

Yield of green cheese containing 37 per cent of water

$$= \left(\frac{\text{Solids-not-fat}}{3} + 0.91 \text{ Fat} \right) \times 1.58$$

This formula is based on the following details: (1) The amount of solids-not-fat in 100 pounds of milk, divided by 3, represents the amount of milk-solids, other than fat, available for cheese, including added salt in cheese; it therefore includes milk-casein and ash constituents. (2) The average amount of fat lost in cheese-making is taken as 9 per cent of the milk-fat and, consequently, 0.91 of the milk-fat is calculated as being in the cheese. (3) In using the factor 1.58, the cheese-solids are calculated to an equivalent amount of cheese containing 37 per cent of water. This method has been supposed to give more accurate results than any of the preceding methods.

The following objections to the method suggest themselves: (1) It involves the accurate determination of the specific gravity of milk in addition to the percentage of milk-fat. This ought not to be a serious objection, but is found to be so practically when cheese-makers try to find time to take the necessary lactometer readings. (2) The formula is, more complicated than any other, requiring more extended arithmetical work, although entirely of a simple kind. (3) The accuracy of calculating the non-fat cheese-solids as equal to one-third of the solids-not-fat of milk is not as close as is desirable, because, when applied in the case of different milks, the results are found to be quite irregular outside of certain limits, to which attention will be called later.

NEW METHOD BASED ON FAT AND CASEIN IN MILK (5)

On account of difficulties experienced in applying the methods under consideration with uniform and accurate results, an effort has been made, based on the results of the work done at the New York experiment station, to work out a method of determining cheese yield which should be simple and at the same time more accurate than the methods previously used. This method is based upon (1) the per cent of fat and of casein in milk; (2) a loss of fat proportional to the amount of fat in milk, based upon average results; (3) a uniform loss of casein; (4) an amount of salts and albumin in cheese proportional to the available fat and casein in the milk; and (5) a uniform percentage of water in cheese.

We will now briefly consider the details upon which the method is based, under the two following divisions: (1) Calculation of cheese-solids, and (2) calculation of water in cheese. The amount of solids in cheese is calculated by the formula, $(0.93\text{Fat}+\text{Casein}-0.10\times1.09$. This is based upon the following details: (1) Of the fat in milk, 7 per cent (0.07 pound for each pound of milk-fat) is lost in whey and 93 per cent (0.93 pound for each pound of milk-fat) remains in cheese (p. 190). (2) Of the milk-casein, about 0.10 pound for 100 pounds of milk is lost, the rest going into the cheese (p. 195). (3) The other constituents of cheese-solids, consisting mostly of salts (p. 187), form about 9 per cent (0.09) of the fat and casein present in cheese. Therefore, if we multiply the amount of fat and casein in cheese by 1.09 we obtain the total amount of cheese-solids (fat, casein, salts, etc.) in cheese. For example, suppose we have milk containing 4 per cent of fat and 2.5 per cent of casein, how many pounds of cheese-solids can be made from 100 pounds of such milk? Using the formula, we have [0.93×4 (fat)+2.5 (casein)—0.10]×1.09=(3.72+2.40)×1.09=6.67 pounds.

It remains now simply to calculate the cheese-solids into cheese with a given percentage of water. This can be done by subtracting from 1.00 the percentage of water desired in the cheese, expressed as hundredths, and then dividing by the result the solids in the cheese, as obtained above. The formula, thus amended, becomes:

$$\frac{(0.93 \text{ Fat} + \text{Casein} - 0.10) \times 1.09}{100 - W \text{ (water in cheese)}}$$

Continuing the illustration in which we have found 6.67 pounds of cheese-solids, we will suppose that we wish to know how much cheese, containing 37 per cent of water, can be made from this amount of cheese-solids. We simply divide 6.67 by 0.63 (1.00—0.37), which gives 10.6 pounds. To find the equivalent amount of cheese containing 35 per cent of water, divide by 65 (1.00—0.35); for cheese containing 40 per cent of water, divide cheese-solids by 0.60 (1.00—0.40).

If, then, we wish to have a method for calculating yield of cheese when the cheese contains a definite amount of water, say 37 per cent, which is the average amount in green cheddar cheese, we can use the formula:

$$\frac{(0.93 \text{ Fat} + \text{Casein} - 0.10) \times 1.09}{0.63}$$

This can be further simplified by dividing 1.09 by 0.63, when the formula becomes

(0.93 Fat+Casein—0.10)×1.73.

In other words, find, in the manner indicated, the

amount of fat and casein that go into the cheese and multiply by 1.73.

After satisfactorily applying the formula in this form to a large number of cases, it occurred that this might be used as a means of working out a still simpler relation between the fat and casein of milk and yield of cheese. Using the foregoing formula for calculating the cheese yield with milks covering quite a wide variation in percentages of fat and of casein, it was found that the formula could be simplified to the following form:

(5)   (Fat+casein)×1.63=yield of cheese
for 100 pounds of milk, the cheese containing 37 per cent of water. Stated in the form of a rule, this becomes: Add together the numbers representing the percentages of fat and of casein in milk and multiply the sum by 1.63.

From this formula, we can calculate in the following manner the equivalent amount of cheese containing any percentage of moisture. Multiply the cheese yield, calculated according to the last formula, by 0.37; subtract this amount from the weight of cheese and divide the remainder by 1.00 minus the number expressing the desired percentage of moisture. Expressed as a formula, this becomes:

$$\frac{P \text{ (Number of pounds of cheese)} - 0.37\ P}{100 - W \text{ (percentage of water desired)}}$$

For convenience, we have thus calculated a factor which can be used directly in determining cheese yield for each percentage of water from 30 to 50.

SIMPLE METHOD OF CALCULATING CHEESE YIELD FOR CHEESE CONTAINING DIFFERENT PERCENTAGES OF WATER

In order to obtain the amount of cheese yield containing a given percentage of water, substitute the number opposite the given percentage in the following list for 1.63 in the last formula above given, which would then become:

$$\text{Yield} = (\text{Fat} + \text{Casein}) \times N$$

(N being the number in the following list which corresponds to the percentage of water in cheese desired).

Per cent of water in cheese	Factor to be used as N in formula (Fat + casein) × N
30	1.47
31	1.49
32	1.51
33	1.53
34	1.555
35	1.58
36	1.605
37	1.63
38	1.655
39	1.68
40	1.71
41	1.74
42	1.77
43	1.80
44	1.835
45	1.87
46	1.90
47	1.94
48	1.98
49	2.015
50	2.05

SIMPLE METHOD FOR CALCULATING YIELD OF CHEESE FROM FAT AND CALCULATED CASEIN

In connection with the foregoing method, which is based in part upon the percentage of casein in milk, it may be objected that the method cannot be applied when we do not know the percentage of milk-casein. In reply to this, it can be stated that fairly accurate results' can be obtained by calculating the amount of casein in milk from the formula: Per cent of casein in milk=(Fat—3)$\times$0.4+2.1 (p. 170).

This formula can be combined with the following formula: Cheese yield=(Fat+Casein)$\times$1.63 and the two operations of calculating casein and cheese yield can be combined in one simple formula, as follows:

(6)   **Cheese yield=2.3F+1.4.**

Therefore, in multiplying the per cent of fat in milk by 2.3 and adding 1.4 to the result, we obtain directly the yield of cheese, containing 37 per cent of water, based on the percentage of milk-fat and the amount of casein corresponding to this percentage of fat, as found by the milk-casein formula.

The yield of cheese corresponding to any percentage of water from 30 to 50 can be similarly calculated. This is done by substituting for N in the following formula one of the numbers in the last table preceding, according to the desired percentage of water: (1.4 Fat+0.9)$\times$N.

METHOD OF CALCULATING YIELD OF RIPE CHEESE

The amount of moisture in cheese when it is sold for consumption necessarily varies with a number of different conditions (p. 315) and an effort to estimate the amount of cheese yield in marketable condition is, to some extent, a matter of guesswork, unless one knows something of the conditions of temperature, moisture, etc., under which the cheese has been kept. However, it is sometimes desired to know approximately the yield of ripened cheese. We can assume (1) that the green cheese contains an average percentage of water (37) and (2) that it loses 5 pounds of water for 100 pounds of cheese. This would have the effect of reducing the percentage of water in the ripe cheese to about 34. Therefore, the simplest way to calculate the amount of ripe cheese, if the composition of the milk is known, is to multiply the sum of the percentage of fat and casein in milk by 1.555; or, when only the per cent of fat in milk is known, to multiply the fat by 2.2 and then add 1.3.

COMPARISON OF ACCURACY OF DIFFERENT METHODS OF CALCULATING CHEESE YIELD

In making a comparative study of the accuracy of the different methods that have been used or proposed for calculating yield of cheese, the following procedure was adopted: As a basis upon which to work, there were taken 200 of the experiments contained in the records of the New York experiment station, which give full analyses of milk, whey and cheese, and yields of cheese. The yields of cheese as given were calculated to a uniform basis of cheese containing 37 per cent of water. The yield of cheese was then calculated according to each one of the formulas that have been discussed. In the case of the methods in which casein is a

factor, the yield of cheese was calculated both for the actual amount of casein in the milk as obtained by analysis and for the calculated amount of casein as obtained by the casein formula. There were thus compared, in reality, seven different methods. It is impracticable to give these results in detail, but it will be found sufficient to present them in the form of tabulated summaries. It has been found that the most effective means of comparison is to divide the experiments into several groups based on the percentage of fat in milk, and under each group to indicate the number of cases in which the results differ, within certain limits, from the actual yield of cheese. To illustrate, we will take Group I (p. 228), including 22 experiments, in which milk containing 3 to 3.49 per cent of fat was used. In the case of method 1 (Fat×2.7), there are 20 cases out of the 22 in which the calculated yield of cheese is within 0.25 pound (4 ounces) of the actual yield. There are 2 cases in which the calculated yield is within 0.26 to 0.35 pound of the actual yield. In the case of formula 2, there are only 5 cases in which the calculated yield is within a quarter of a pound of the actual yield, etc.

A study of the table on page 228 enables one to observe the truth of the following statements:

The different methods in some cases show great variation in respect to accuracy, according to the composition of the milk. Thus, method 1 (Fat× 2.7), which has usually been regarded as, perhaps, the least accurate of any method in use, is found to give most excellent results in the case of milks

COMPARISON OF DIFFERENT METHODS FOR CALCULATING
CHEESE YIELD

Group I 22 Exp'ts Fat 3-3.49% Variation from actual yield	1 Fat × 2.7	2 1.1 Fat + 5.9	3 1.1 Fat + 2.5 Casein Actual casein	Calculated casein	4 $\left(\dfrac{\text{Snf} + .91F}{3}\right) \times 1.58$	5 (Fat + Casein) × 1.63 (Actual casein)	6 2.3 F + 1.4 (Calculated casein)
0-0.25 lb.	20	5	10	11	5	19	21
0.26-0.35 lb.	2	2	4	9	10	2	1
0.36-0.50 lb.	..	7	7	2	5	1	..
0.51-0.75 lb.	..	7	1	0	2	..	..
0.76-1.00 lb.	..	1	..	..	..	..	..
Group II 59 Exp'ts Fat 3.50-3.74							
0-0.25 lb.	34	43	43	40	48	49	29
0.26-0.35 lb.	10	3	12	9	7	6	13
0.36-0.50 lb.	8	10	3	7	1	4	9
0.51-0.75 lb.	7	2	1	3	3	..	8
Group III 51 Exp'ts Fat 3.75-3.99							
0-0.25 lb.	33	29	35	32	38	37	31
0.26-0.35 lb.	8	6	3	12	7	7	10
0.36-0.50 lb.	9	12	6	7	5	5	9
0.51-0.75 lb.	1	3	6	..	1	2	1
0.75-0.99 lb.	..	..	1	..	..	..	..
Group IV 43 Exp'ts Fat 4.0-4.19							
0-0.25 lb.	20	8	29	27	20	35	29
0.26-0.35 lb.	9	13	5	3	8	4	1
0.36-0 50 lb.	9	9	6	4	5	3	3
0.51-0.75 lb.	4	4	2	6	4	1	6
0.75-0.99 lb.	0	5	1	3	6	..	4
1.00-1.50 lb.	..	7	..	..	..	..	..
Group V 25 Exp'ts Fat 4.2-4.4							
0-0.25 lb.	13	0	16	15	4	20	15
0.26-0.35 lb.	5	0	4	1	4	1	1
0.36-0.50 lb.	5	1	2	5	8	1	4
0.51-0.75 lb.	2	11	2	4	7	3	5
0.75-0.90 lb.	..	4	1	..	2	..	..
1.00-1.50 lb.	..	9	..	..	..	..	..

varying in fat from 3.0 to 3.50 per cent, and comparatively fair results in the case of milks containing fat up to 4.0 per cent. Method 2 (1.1 Fat+5.9) gives fairly good results in case of milks containing 3.50 to 3.75 per cent of fat, because the casein of such milks is near the average upon which this formula is really based (p. 215); but, outside of these narrow limits, it is the least accurate of all the methods that have been used or proposed. In case of milk containing 4.0 per cent of fat or more, the method is entirely useless, in some cases varying from the real yield of cheese 1 to 1.5 pounds. Method 3 (1.1 Fat+2.5 Casein), when the actual amount of casein is known, gives rather poor results in case of milk below 3.5 per cent in fat, excellent results when the per cent of fat in milk ranges from 3.5 to 4.0 per cent, fairly good results in case of milk containing as high as 4.2 per cent of fat, but less accurate with milks above this. Method 3, when the casein is calculated, gives results which are, in general, in very good agreement with those obtained when the amount of casein is determined by chemical analysis. Method 4

$$\left(\frac{\text{Solids-not-fat}}{3} + 0.91\ F\right) \times 1.58,$$

gives most excellent results when the milk contains 3.50 to 4.0 per cent of fat, but in other cases is, with the exception of method 2, the least accurate of any examined. This method has heretofore had the reputation of being, for all grades of milk, the most accurate method in use. Method 5, when the per cent of casein in milk is known, is seen to be the most accurate method of all. When the casein is calculated, method 6 gives excellent comparative results, the least satisfactory being in the case of milks containing 3.50 to 3.75 per cent of fat. In the case of milks containing 3 tu 3.50 per cent of fat the results are most excellent.

The following table gives a summary of the results, showing the percentage of cases in which the different methods are accurate within the limits designated, taking all the 200 results into consideration without reference to special groups in respect to percentage of milk-fat:

	1	2	3 Actual casein	Calculated casein	4	5 Actual casein	6 Calculated casein
0-0.25	60.	42.5	66.5	62.5	57.5	80	62.5
0.26-0.35	17.	12.	14.	17.	18.	10	13.
0.36-0.50	15.5	19.5	12.	12.5	12.	7	12.5
0.51-0.75	7.	13.5	6.	6.5	8.5	3	10.
0.76-0.99	0.5	4.5	1.5	1.5	4.	0	2.
1.00-1.50	0.	8.	0.	0.	0.	0	0.

From these results, the relative values of the different formulas can be judged in a general, comparative way. It is evident that method 2 (1.1 Fat+5.9) should not be used and that method 4,

$$\left(\frac{\text{Solids-not-fat}}{3} + .91 \text{ Fat} \right) \times 1.58$$

should, if employed at all, be used only in the case of milks containing 3.5 to 4.0 per cent of fat. When the percentage of casein in milk is known, only method 5 (Fat+Casein)×1.63 should be used. In case the casein has to be calculated from the percentage of fat in milk, then method 6 should be used. For ordinary purposes method 6 will probably be found to be the most useful, since the only factor needed is the percentage of milk-fat and the calculation is extremely simple (2.3 Fat+1.4).

CHAPTER XIX

Milk Constituents in Relation to Composition of Cheese

While the *yield* of cheese from 100 pounds of milk depends, as has been shown (p. 186), upon the amount of fat, casein and insoluble salts in milk, so far as the cheese-solids are concerned, the percentage *composition* of the *cheese-solids* depends practically upon the relation of fat and casein in milk.   Milk rich in fat, as compared with milk poor in fat, usually produces cheese containing more fat in proportion to other constituents.   The composition of cheese depends primarily upon the composition of the milk used, provided the process of cheese-making is performed in a normal manner, so as to avoid excessive loss of fat or casein.   In this connection we shall discuss the following points: (1) The relation of composition of milk to composition of cheese (a) in case of normal milk, (b) in case of skimmed milk, and (c) in case of milk containing added cream.   (2) The United States standard for cheese.

MILK CONSTITUENTS AND COMPOSITION OF CHEESE

Composition of cheese from normal milk.—The composition of green cheese, in case of normal factory milk, as made in New York state, shows the following range of variations and general average, as the result of the extended investigations carried on by the New York experiment station:

	Lowest	Highest	Average
Water..........................	32.69	43.89	36.84
Total solids......................	56.11	67.31	63.16
Fat..............................	30.00	36.79	33.83
Proteins.........................	20.80	26.11	23.72
Salts, etc. (represented in ash)	3.12	7.02	5.61
Percentage of solids in form of fat...	50.39	56.83	53.56
Ratio of fat to proteins.............	1:0.79	1:0.63	1:0.70

We can illustrate differences in composition of cheese made from normal milk by taking cheese made from the milk of different breeds of cows. For this purpose, we will use the composition of milk as given on p. 165 in case of four different breeds:

Breed	Solids in cheese	Fat in cheese	Proteins in cheese	Percentage of total solids in form of fat	Ratio of fat to proteins
	Per cent	Per cent	Per cent		Fat: Proteins
Holstein-Friesian	63.00	34.1	23.6	54.3	1: 0.69
Ayrshire.........	63.00	34.5	23.3	54.8	1: 0.67
Guernsey.........	63.00	37.0	20.8	58.7	1: 0.56
Jersey...........	63.00	37.5	20.4	60.0	1: 0.54

The difference in composition is very clearly seen, especially if we notice the percentage of the cheese-solids present in the form of fat and the ratio of fat to proteins as shown in the last two columns. In connection with this table, study Fig. 37 (p. 208).

The following table extends the illustration systematically to ordinary milks containing different percentages of fat.   We may regard these as representing milks of different herds.   See also Fig. 36.

Per cent of fat in milk	Cheese-solids	Fat in cheese	Proteins in cheese	Percentage of total solids in form of fat	Ratio of fat to proteins
	Per cent	Per cent	Per cent		Fat: Proteins
3.00	63.00	33.7	24.1	53.5	1 : 0.72
3.25	"	34.1	23.7	54.0	1 : 0.70
3.50	"	34.5	23.3	54.6	1 : 0.68
3.75	"	34.8	23.0	55.2	1 : 0.66
4.50	"	35.1	22.7	55.7	1 : 0.65
4.25	"	35.4	22.4	56.2	1 : 0.63
4.50	"	35.7	22.1	56.7	1 : 0.62

These tables strikingly indicate that, as milk increases in percentage of fat, the cheese made from such milk increases in percentage of fat and decreases in percentage of proteins.   The composition of the cheese-solids follows the composition of the milk as shown in the relation of fat and proteins.

Composition of cheese made from skimmed milk.—The removal of fat from milk reduces the amount of fat in relation to casein, because, in skimming milk, only a relatively small amount of casein is removed with the fat.   The remaining skim-milk is therefore richer in casein relative to fat, the ratio increasing with the amount of fat removed.   The effect of skimming milk upon its composition and upon the composition of cheese is illustrated in the two following tables.   The data are based upon (1) normal milk containing 4 per cent of fat, (2) removal of fat alone without other constituents, (3) a uniform percentage of casein in skim-milk, and (4) a uniform per cent (37) of water in cheese. While the data represent theoretical conditions, the results are not far from the truth in practical application and they serve satisfactorily to illustrate the point we desire to impress   In connection with this table, study Fig. 38.

EFFECT OF SKIMMING MILK ON COMPOSITION OF MILK AND YIELD OF CHEESE

Pounds of fat removed from 100 pounds of milk	Pounds of fat left in skimmed milk	Pounds of casein in skimmed milk	Ratio of fat to casein in milk	Pounds of cheese
			Fat: Casein	
(1)—0.00	4.00*	2.50	1: 0.63	10.60
(2)—0.50	3.50	2.50	1: 0.71	9.79
(3)—1.00	3.00	2.50	1: 0.83	8.98
(4)—2.00	2.00	2.50	1: 1.25	7.37
(5)—3.00	1.00	2.50	1: 2.50	5.71
(6)—3.90	0.10†	2.50	1: 25.0	4.33

*Normal milk.   †Separator skim-milk.

EFFECT OF SKIMMING MILK ON COMPOSITION OF CHEESE

Per cent of fat in cheese	Per cent of proteins in cheese	Percentage of cheese-solids in form of fat	Ratio of fat to proteins in cheese
			Fat: Proteins
(1)—35.1	22.7	55.7	1: 0.65
(2)—33.3	24.5	53.0	1: 0.74
(3)—31.1	26.7	49.4	1: 0.86
(4)—25.2	32.6	40.0	1: 1.30
(5)—16.1	41.7	25.5	1: 2.60
(6)— 2.3	55.5	3.7	1: 24.00

In making cheese from skim-milk, the yields given are lower than those obtained in commercial

work, because here we allow for only 37 per cent
of water, while commercial skim-milk cheese never
contains so little moisture, but usually from 40 to
55 per cent, the moisture held in cheese increasing

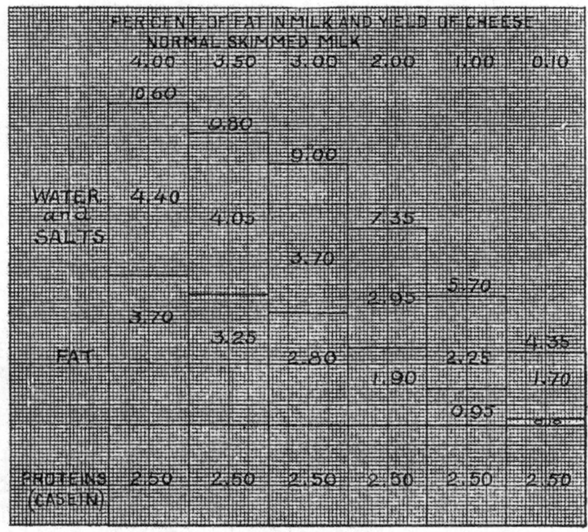

FIG. 38—DIAGRAM SHOWING EFFECT OF SKIMMING MILK
UPON THE YIELD AND COMPOSITION OF CHEESE

The figures immediately above each column give the number of pounds of
cheese (containing 37 per cent of water) made from 100 pounds of milk. The figures
within the diagram give the pounds of each constituent in cheese. The figures
at the top of the diagram give the percentage of fat in milk and skim-milk.

as the per cent of fat in skim-milk decreases. In comparing the results in this table with those in the
table on p. 232, in which the composition is shown
of cheese made from milk low and high in fat,
we see that the difference there is the same in

character as that brought about by partially skimming whole milk. For example, by skimming from
100 pounds of Jersey milk, containing 5.78 per cent
of fat, 1.25 pounds of fat, thus reducing the fat to
4.53 per cent, the resulting milk and cheese will then
be essentially the same in composition, in relation to
cheese-solids, as the normal Holstein-Friesian milk,
as shown by the following table:

	Per cent of fat	Per cent of casein	Ratio of fat to casein
			Fat: Casein
Holstein-Friesian milk.............	3.26	2.20	1: 0.67
Jersey milk (normal)...............	5.78	3.03	1: 0.52
Jersey milk (partially skimmed).....	4.53	3.03	1: 0.67

Of course, the same result could be accomplished
by adding skim-milk to milk rich in fat.

There is another way of comparing milks which,
like these, are poor and rich in fat. Thus, how
much fat would it be necessary to add to the Holstein-Friesian milk to have it make cheese like that
made from Jersey milk? Calculation shows that
nearly one pound of fat would need to be added
to 100 pounds of the Holstein milk, which is thus
shown:

Fat in milk	Fat added	Per cent of fat in enriched milk	Per cent of casein in milk	Ratio of fat to casein
				Fat : Casein
3.26	+ 0.94	= 4.20	2.20	1: 0.52

It can, therefore, be seen that the differences existing between rich and poor milk are, so far as
relates to the composition of the cheese made from
them, such as can be adjusted by removing fat

from the rich milk or adding skim-milk to it, or by adding fat to skim-milk. The difference in milk poor in fat which makes the fat go farther in making cheese is a difference which may be characterized, in a general way, as a skim-milk difference, because it depends upon a relatively high proportion of casein.

Composition of cheese made from milk containing added cream.—Addition of cream to normal milk affects the cheese made from such milk in a way directly opposite to that produced by skimming; that is, it increases the proportion of fat in cheese in relation to proteins. A single illustration will suffice. We give the composition of cheese made from normal milk containing 4 per cent of fat and also from the same milk after its fat content has been increased to 6 per cent by the addition of cream.

	Per cent of fat in milk	Pounds of cheese for 100 pounds of milk	Per cent of fat in cheese	Per cent of proteins in cheese	Per cent of cheese-solids in form of fat	Ratio of fat to proteins
						Fat: Proteins
Normal milk..	4.00	10.60	35.1	22.7	55.7	1: 0.65
Enriched milk	6.00	13.80	40.4	17.4	64.0	1: 0.43

THE UNITED STATES CHEESE STANDARD

At this point it seems desirable to call attention to the standard of purity adopted for cheese by the United States Department of Agriculture in connection with the national pure-food law. Its definition of cheese made from normal or whole-milk is as follows: "Standard whole-milk or full-cream cheese contains, in the water-free substance, not less than 50 per cent butter-fat." There has been widespread and needless misunderstanding in regard to the meaning of this standard. Many have interpreted it as meaning that normal or whole-milk cheese must contain 50 per cent of fat. The law does not say that at all, but that 50 per cent, not of the cheese, but of its *water-free substance* (cheesesolids) must consist of butter-fat. This can easily be made clear by giving a specific illustration of its application, and, for this purpose, we take a cheddar cheese of average composition, containing:

```
Water...................36.80 per cent.
Water-free substance      63.20      "
       Consisting of    (100.00)
       Fat........33.75             "
       Proteins....23.75            "
       Salts, etc... 5.70           "
                     ------         "
                      63.20         "
```

In order to apply the standard to any cheese, we need to know only the percentages of water and of fat. One then proceeds as follows: Subtract the percentage of water from 100, which gives the cheese-solids or water-free substance, and then divide the percentage of fat in cheese by the percentage of water-free substance. Expressed in outline, the statement becomes: (1) 100 minus per cent of water=per cent of water-free substance; (2) per cent of fat÷per cent of water-free substance= per cent of fat in water-free substance. Example: (1) 100—36.80 (per cent of water in cheese)= 63.20 (water-free substance in cheese). (2) 33.75 (per cent of fat in cheese)÷63.20=53.4, which is the per cent of fat in the water-free substance of the cheese. In order that a cheese be below standard, the fat must be less than one-half of the water-free substance. In this particular case, the cheese would be below standard if the fat were less than 31.60 per cent.

The question naturally arises as to what actual basis there is for such a specific standard. It is based upon very extensive studies of cheese made from normal milk. The work of the New York experiment station with cheese made in New York factories has shown that the fat is always more than one-half of the total solids or water-free substance of cheese. In the case of the lowest result, the percentage was 50.39; the highest, 56.83; and the average, 54. In very few cases was the percentage of fat in cheese-solids found below 51.0. These results are in agreement with those obtained in other states. For example, in the Wisconsin cheese-scoring contests for April, May, June and July (1908), results are given, showing that, even in the cheese poorest in fat, the fat was 51.35 per cent of the water-free substance. The percentage of fat in the water-free substance of the cheese varied from this figure to 56.4 as the highest.

In addition to the results of analysis of many samples of cheese made from normal milk, the composition of normal milk itself furnishes a good reason why the fat should amount to more than one-half of the water-free substance of cheese; since a study of normal milk, as it is found at cheese-factories in New York state, shows that such milk does not contain enough casein, relative to fat, to make cheese of composition such that its water-free substance contains less than 50 per cent of fat, provided, of course, there is no abnormal loss of fat in the process of cheese-making. For example, it can readily be seen from the table on p. 234 that normal milk containing 4 per cent of fat can suffer a loss of nearly one-fourth of its fat, before the composition of the cheese drops below standard. Normal milk containing 3.50 per cent of fat can be reduced to about 3 per cent of fat before the cheese made from it contains less than 50 per cent of fat in its water-free substance. Ordinary milk containing 3 per cent of fat could have its fat reduced nearly to 2.75 per cent before making cheese below standard. These facts go to show that the United States standard is well above the limits of danger for cheese properly made from normal milk.

Another question in connection with the cheese standard may be asked: Why not use as a standard the percentage of fat in the cheese itself instead of in the water-free substance? The present standard has for its purpose, the prevention of the use of skimmed milk for making cheese to be sold as normal or whole-milk cheese. It does not aim to control the amount of moisture in cheese. If the percentage of fat in cheese were used as a standard, then the amount of water in cheese would become an important factor; because the greater the moisture content of cheese, the less the percentage of fat in the case of cheese made from milk of the same composition. It is recognized that different markets call for different percentages of water in cheese and, by basing the cheese standard on the water-free substance of the cheese, this condition has not been interfered with.

Some of the state cheese standards.—In some states there are laws which aim to set up various standards according to the percentage of fat in cheese, having one percentage of fat for whole-milk cheese, another for partial-skim, another for half-skim and another for full-skim.   Such provisions are cumbersome in legal administration, as well as demoralizing to the best interests of the cheese industry and deserve only severe condemnation.

It is interesting to notice the legal provisions for cheese standards which are or have been in force in some states.   In California full-cream (whole-milk) cheese must contain 30 per cent of fat; half-skim 15 per cent of fat; while full-skim cheese is any cheese made from skim-milk.   Under these provisions it would be easily possible to make no normal-milk cheese, since all the cheese intended to comply with the requirements for so-called "full-cream" might be made from partially skimmed milk.   In Colorado 35 per cent of the cheese-solids (water-free substances) must be fat.   This is 15 per cent below the United States standard.   Under such a provision normal milk containing 4.0 per cent of fat could have one-half of its fat removed before the cheese would drop below the Colorado standard as given above.   Under such circumstances it would be a miracle if Colorado had an ounce of cheese made from normal milk except for the saving condition that the actual relation of such a standard is probably not clearly understood by Colorado cheese-makers and surely not by her legislators, it is to be hoped.   In Minnesota, the law has required that 45 per cent of the cheese-solids be fat, which is too low. In Missouri, the only provision has seemed to be that the cheese should be made from milk containing not less than 3 per cent of fat.   In Ohio, cheese containing less than 20 per cent of fat is skim-cheese. This is certainly a very generous allowance, since cheese made from normal milk rarely contains less than 32 per cent of fat even when green.   It is to be hoped that the provisions in these states for whole-milk cheese have been or will be changed to conform with the provisions of the United States pure-food law.

Misleading use of terms describing cheese.—The foregoing discussion impresses one with the unfortunate use of certain words in describing cheese made from normal milk or whole-milk.   The expressions, "full-cream," "factory-cream," etc., while in common commercial use, and clearly understood by those who use them, are misleading to one who interprets their meaning at their face value. Apparently, such terms imply normal milk containing added cream.   The use of the word cream in any form to describe normal milk is a relic of the inaccurate knowledge of former generations, and should be abandoned in the interests of clearness and precision. Whole-milk or normal milk is in every respect a much better expression to use in describing cheese made from milk that is normal.

CHAPTER XX

The Composition of Cheese in Relation to Quality

In the preceding chapter it has been demonstrated that cheese made from milk rich in fat contains relatively and actually more fat and less proteins than cheese made from milk poor in fat. Two such cheeses, made with equal skill, the milk being uniform in every way except in composition, show a marked difference in commercial quality (p. 244); and the one having the larger percentage of fat would be declared to be superior in quality. This has been demonstrated in practical ways by the experiment stations of Wisconsin, Iowa, Minnesota and New York; and their work, the first to be done along these lines, has been supplemented and confirmed by the work of others. It has been found generally true that cheese made from milk containing added cream is superior in flavor and texture to that made from ordinary normal milk; and that made from normal milk is superior in flavor, texture, body and keeping quality to cheese made from skim-milk.

Variation in quality in cheddar cheese follows more or less closely the relation of fat to proteins in cheese; the larger the proportion of fat, the better, in general, the quality of cheese and the higher the market value. This fact is, of course, associated with, and dependent upon, the function that milk-fat performs in cheese, that of imparting smoothness of feeling, mellowness of body, richness and delicacy of taste and palatability. Bearing on this particular point, the late Henry E. Alvord makes the following statement (Yearbook of U. S. Dept. of Agr., 1895, p. 471): "Other things being equal, a cheese containing a large percentage of fat is better, because, first, of finer flavor and taste; second, of its better consistency; third, of its improved aroma; fourth, of its increased digestibility; fifth, of its more perfectly answering the requirements of a complete food or 'balanced ration.'" In this connection, it is interesting to learn that in Germany the custom of selling cheese according to the percentage of fat contained in it is rapidly coming into use.

While the view expressed above is very generally held and is based upon experimental work, there have been no extensive commercial opportunities for demonstrating the matter in a systematic way. But some valuable facts bearing on this point in a most direct and practical form have just been developed in the four Wisconsin cheese-scoring contests held during April, May, June and July, (1908). The facts are all the more interesting because they are merely incidental to the general purpose of these contests. The method of conducting these competitive tests in Wisconsin cannot be too highly recommended to other states, especially because very full details are given, unusual under such circumstances, making the work of peculiar value in enabling one to study relations existing between the composition of cheese and its commercial value. In each of these monthly scorings, it is significant that the cheese scoring highest contained the largest amount of fat relative to proteins, while the cheese scoring lowest in every case contained the lowest amount of fat relative to proteins, as shown by the following data:

	Cheese scoring highest			Cheese scoring lowest		
	Per cent of fat	Per cent of proteins	Ratio of fat to proteins	Per cent of fat	Per cent of proteins	Ratio of fat to proteins
			Fat:prot'ns			Fat:prot'ns
April	36.	27.	1: 0.75	32.	29.2	1: 0.91
May	35.25	27.4	1: 0.78	35.	29.2	1: 0.83
June	35.	27.5	1: 0.79	34.5	29.8	1: 0.86
July	35.	29.46	1: 0.84	34.3	29.3	1: 0.86

The most striking difference is shown by the April results, the least by those of July. In studying all the available data, the only apparent cause that accounts for these differences is the difference in composition.   In the case of some of the cheeses that were scored second and third below the highest, as compared with others that were scored second and third from the lowest, the general relation of quality and composition was shown but not equally in every case. While these results do not in themselves absolutely prove the relation between composition and commercial quality, their special value is that they confirm, in a different way, the results of other work.

It cannot fail to be of value in the discussion of this subject to present the views of some of those who have been generally regarded as authorities in relation to the commercial as well as to the scientific aspects of cheese-making. For this purpose, we have chosen to give the views (1) of Dr. Robertson, so long Canada's most efficient leader in the progress of all branches of dairying and especially of cheese-making, and (2) of Dr. Babcock, who has been properly regarded as America's leading student of dairying in its scientific relations and who has given special attention to the question under discussion.

In the Report of the New York Dairymen's Association for 1891, we find the following statements in an address given by Dr. Robertson: "In every case there was a gradual reduction in the quantity of cheese when there was a less quantity of butter-fat in milk. . . . However, this is true also, that the increased yield of cheese is not in direct proportion to the increased percentage of butter-fat; that is, milk containing 3 per cent of butter-fat will yield a certain quantity of cheese, but if you take milk having one-third more fat (4 per cent) it will not yield one-third more cheese. *At the same time, such milk is worth one-third more for cheese-making, and thereby hangs a tale.* You see, if it does not yield so much cheese, it makes a *quality* of cheese so much better that the market value of the cheese from 100 pounds of milk is a third greater than the market value of the cheese in the other case" (pp. 198-199). "Every two-tenths of a pound of butter-fat will improve the quality of the cheese one-eighth cent per pound, as near as I can find out. Thus, you have a difference of about five-eighths of a cent per pound between cheese made from 3 per cent and 4 per cent milk" (p. 201).

Dr. Babcock approaches the question from quite another point of view (Report of New York Dairymen's Association for 1892, pp. 150, 153, etc.). After showing that fat is the constituent controlling the value of milk, cream and butter, he says: "It is evident that the market price of milk, of cream and of butter depends chiefly upon the price of butter-fat, and that other constituents have so little influence that they can practically be neglected.

"There is one other important dairy product to be considered, and that is cheese. Does the same principle hold with this? I believe it does, for on no other basis can I reconcile market prices all over the world."

He then goes on to show by actual market quotations that cheese varies in price according to its richness in fat, all the way from 11 cents per pound for whole-milk, fancy cheese down to 1 to 2½ cents a pound for full-skim cheese. Anticipating some objections raised to the method of reasoning as applied to the fat basis as a method of paying for milk at cheese-factories, he continues: "I cannot leave this subject without referring to some of the objections made to its use in cheese-factories. It is urged that because casein and fat are intimately mixed together in cheese, they bring the same price per pound when sold, and so should be given the same price in calculating the value of milk that is to be used for this purpose. If this is true, the water which comprises a larger proportion of cheese than the casein should be treated in the same way, and worthless constituents in any product should have the same value as the mixture in which they occur. It is absurd, on the face of it, as it gives entirely different values, to the same constituent according to the product considered. It makes the casein, water and fat worth each about one cent per pound in milk, the same constituent worth 30 cents per pound in butter and anywhere from 1 to 11 cents per pound in cheese, according to the proportions in which they are mixed. Whereas, the relative value plan gives consistent values in all.

"Again, it is said that the life-sustaining power of a pound of casein is about the same as a pound of fat, and that they should therefore have about the same value; but it must be borne in mind that the nutritive value and the market value of foods have no relation to each other. You can buy nutrients in corn meal cheaper than you can in wheat flour. Maple sugar costs you two or three times as much as beet sugar, although the two have identically the same effect. All of these things are controlled by the universal law of supply and demand, and have nothing to do with their relative food value.

"When any article has a high value for any special purpose, that fixes the price which must be paid for it for all other purposes. You cannot afford the use of rosewood or mahogany for fuel, not because they have less heat-producing power than maple or birch, but because they command a higher price for piano cases or other articles of furniture. The general public esteems butter-fat more highly than casein and are willing to pay a much higher price for it. It is folly to stand in your own light and argue that this is inconsistent."

These arguments of Dr. Babcock are based on general economic truths which hold good to-day as fully as when they were stated by him. They are facts which should be kept in mind when considering the relation of composition of cheese to commercial quality or market value. In the 12th annual report of the Wisconsin experiment station (p. 115), Dr. Babcock also says:

"It is a well-established fact that rich milk gives a better quality of cheese, which commands a higher price, than that from poor milk."

We add also the following quotation from an address given before the Wisconsin cheese-makers' convention at Milwaukee, in 1907, by Prof. E. H. Farrington, dairy husbandman at the Wisconsin experiment station: "It will be seen that the richer the milk, the better the price per pound of cheese made from it. I am occasionally asked if 100 pounds of milk testing 6 per cent of fat will make twice as much cheese as 100 pounds of milk testing 3 per cent of fat. The answer to this question is briefly that the cheese made from the richer milk is of much better quality and worth a higher price per pound than that made from the thinner milk, and this will help balance any difference in yield. The influence of the richness of milk on the quality of cheese is something that should not be lost sight of in considering the question of paying for milk at a cheese-factory by the Babcock test."

SKIM-MILK CHEESE

The manufacture of skim-milk cheese has been fostered and protected in some of our states. There are some considerations worthy of our attention in connection with the discussion of the composition of cheese in relation to quality.

(1) The removal of fat from ordinary normal milk, such as the mixed milk of our cheese-factories, results in producing cheese that differs in composition from whole-milk cheese. Such cheese, as we have seen, contains less fat and more casein than that made from normal milk having the same percentage of fat. Skim-milk cheese is an adulterated food product, according to the legal definition of adulteration.

(2) It is impossible to remove fat from ordinary normal milk without affecting the composition of the cheese unfavorably, and along with this, the quality as well. While skim-milk cheeses may differ from one another in composition and quality, they are all inferior to whole-milk cheese properly made from normal milk of good quality in all respects.

(3) Skim-milk cheese is not only deficient in fat, but it always contains an abnormally high percentage of water. This is absolutely necessary in order to make it edible and have it appear in body and general quality as a good imitation of whole-milk cheese. A skim-milk cheese containing

only the amount of water held by a whole-milk cheese would be practically unsalable on account of its hardness and toughness.   High percentages (50-55) of water are necessary in order to make the cheese appear to contain fat and have a smooth-feeling body.

(4)   Skim-milk cheese, on account of its high percentage of water, dries out very rapidly under ordinary conditions in the hands of the consumer and becomes inedible, though it can then be used by experts in some forms of cooking.

(5)   Skim-milk cheese, on account of its high percentage of water and of proteins, does not possess the keeping qualities of whole-milk cheese.   It develops undesirable flavors more easily and does not have the same length of life under the same conditions, especially when kept at temperatures above 60° F.

(6)   Skim-milk cheese generally becomes digestible less readily than whole-milk cheese kept under the same conditions; and when its proteins become rapidly soluble, offensive flavors usually develop, destroying its value.

(7)   The retail price of skim-milk cheese is always too high in comparison with whole-milk cheese. Separator skim-milk cheese usually sells at retail for 10 cents a pound, when whole-milk cheese sells for 16 cents.   Such skim-milk cheese sells for more than three times its real value.

(8)   The consumer is not really protected, even when an attempt is made by the state to do so. How many people want or even ask for skim-milk cheese?   The average consumer is ignorant of

systems of branding or other methods devised for his protection. He simply asks for cheese and takes what is offered. It should be made as dangerous for retailers to sell skim-milk cheese for whole-milk cheese as it is for them to sell imitation for pure butter.

(9) The indiscriminate sale of skim-milk cheese inevitably injures the sale of whole-milk cheese.

(10) Skim-milk, consumed as such or in the form of cottage-cheese, is a more economical and nutritious food than when used as skim-milk cheese.

(11) There is a strong inclination on the part of those interested in the cheese industry to believe that the real interests of dairymen and of the general public would be best protected and promoted by the absolute prohibition of skim-milk cheese, as demonstrated by Canada.

CHAPTER XXI

Methods of Paying for Milk for Cheese-Making

The subject relating to methods of paying for milk at cheese-factories has been one of more or less constant discussion for about twenty years. Shortly before the year 1890, some question was raised as to the fairness of paying for milk at cheese-factories by weight. Two factors worked against the realization of any practical results coming from such discussion: (1) Lack of knowledge regarding the relation of milk-constituents to yield and quality of cheese, and (2) the need of a practicable method for determining any of the cheese-making constituents of milk. In 1890 Dr. Babcock furnished his method of determining fat in milk, and then the discussion soon centered about the use of fat in milk as a basis for paying for milk used in cheese-making. The application of the test in the case of butter-making was at once understood and utilized; but, in connection with cheese-making, it was known that two constituents are concerned, fat and casein, and the question was therefore more complicated than in the case of butter-making, where only fat was concerned. During the years 1891 to 1895, a large amount of investigation was carried on, which resulted in giving us such a comprehensive and systematic knowledge of the relations of milk constituents to cheese as had not been possible previously. In general, it was shown that, while the amount of fat in milk is not an absolute guide in respect to the yield of cheese from milks containing different amounts of fat, it is a very much more accurate index than the mere weight of milk; and that, while, in case of milks containing higher percentages of fat, the yield of chéese is usually less for a pound of milk-fat than in the case of milk containing lower percentages of fat (p. 207), the cheese made from the richer milk is of more excellent quality and has a higher commercial value (pp. 243-249).

The fat basis began to be introduced into actual cheese-factory work about 1892, and its use spread quite rapidly during the next few years. This method was at first received with considerable enthusiasm. After a few years a reaction gradually took place and the system was abandoned in many factories, which went back to the old method of paying for milk by weight only. There are several reasons why the fat basis in paying for milk for cheese-making has experienced its ups and downs, like every other reform movement, and we will notice some of the most prominent of these.

(1) Wherever the fat basis replaced the weight-of-milk method, the change affected the dividends of different patrons in different ways. Those furnishing milk containing percentages of fat above the average received more money for their milk, while those furnishing milk containing percentages of

fat under the average found their dividends reduced. Therefore, the owners of cows giving milk low in fat were bitterly disappointed and exercised their ingenuity in discovering reasons why the fat basis was objectionable and unfair. This attitude of the producer of poor milk is, of course, the fundamental reason why the fat basis has been abandoned in some cases where it had been introduced. The other objections raised were subordinate to this one, though some of them had, perhaps, some real basis.

(2) The reliability of the Babcock test was attacked and the accuracy of its results called into question. The points of objection raised on this ground were, (a) that the Babcock method of testing milk for fat is unreliable under all circumstances; (b) that, while the method, when properly handled, is accurate, cheese-makers are careless or inefficient in operating the test, and their results are therefore inaccurate; (c) that the glassware was not always accurately graduated and consequently gave incorrect results; (d) that cheese-makers deliberately gave some patrons higher results than those indicated by the test. The general charge of inaccuracy of the test itself was, of course, prompted by ignorance or malice or both. There was probably once some justification for the charge of carelessness and inefficiency against operators of the Babcock test; for it was undoubtedly true to some extent that cheese-makers attempted to employ the method who had not been properly instructed in its use nor acquired the requisite accuracy of manipulation. There was at

one time a strong disposition to over-emphasize the extreme simplicity of the Babcock test and to lose sight of the fact that even so simple a method requires careful attention to every detail and that certain precautions must be strictly observed. It was also true that some manufacturers became careless and put on the market glassware that was inaccurate. This difficulty has been effectively overcome in most of the prominent dairy states by an official testing of all graduated glassware used in the Babcock test, before it is placed on sale.

(3) Many cheese-makers object to the added work involved, even when paid for it. An unwilling cheese-maker can easily influence patrons against the method.

(4) Another cause for the discarding of the fat basis in many cases was the confusion introduced by proposing some modification of the method in the interest of the producer of poorer milk, a point which we will consider more fully later.

In the history of the cheese-making industry, we can distinguish in the order of their appearance, five methods which have been proposed for the purpose of paying for milk at cheese-factories:

(1) Weight of milk.
(2) Amount of fat in milk.
(3) Relative values of fat and other cheese-solids based on yield and composition of cheese.
(4) Modification of fat basis to include part of the milk-casein.
(5) Amount of fat and casein in milk.

We will now consider each of these methods as to their comparative merits and defects.

PAYING FOR MILK ON BASIS OF WEIGHT

Under this system each patron receives the same amount of money for each 100 pounds of milk delivered at the factory. This method possesses the advantage of simplicity and economy of time, involving no additional work. Among the disadvantages of this method are the following: (1) It assumes, as a fundamental basis of its fairness, that all kinds of normal milk have the same cheese-producing value; that, from 100 pounds of any milk, we make the same amount of cheese. This assumption has been abundantly proved not to be true, since the yield of cheese from 100 pounds of milk may (p. 207) vary all the way from 8 to 13 pounds or more. The method is, therefore, unfair to the producers of milk containing higher percentages of fat. (2) This system discourages the production of milk of higher percentage in fat. When weight alone is considered in making payment, more money can be received by increasing the amount of milk produced, without regard to its composition; and it is thus found more profitable to produce milk as low in fat as legal requirements permit. (3) This system breeds criminality, because it encourages the addition of water, removal of cream and all similar forms of dishonesty. Some dairymen have regarded the direct addition of water to milk as the most economical way of increasing milk production for cheese-making purposes, but the experience is not usually attended with most economical results for any length of time.

However much difference of opinion there may exist in regard to the efficiency of different methods of paying for milk for cheese-making, all who are in position to give a reliable judgment in the matter agree on this one point, viz., among the various methods proposed, this one is farthest from doing justice to all producers of milk.

PAYING FOR MILK ON BASIS OF FAT

When milk is paid for on the basis of its fat content, each patron receives the same amount of money for each pound of fat in the milk delivered. For example, the patron whose milk contains 3 per cent of fat receives payment for 3 pounds of fat for each 100 pounds of milk delivered by him; while the patron whose milk contains 4 per cent of fat receives payment for 4 pounds of fat for each 100 pounds of milk furnished by him. The second patron receives one-third more per 100 pounds of milk than the first one, while, under the weight-of-milk method, each would receive an equal sum. This can be illustrated as follows:

For the sake of simplicity, we will compare the milks furnished by two patrons, one milk containing 3, and the other 4, per cent of fat. We will assume that the cheese sells for 10 cents a pound. We will make the comparison on the basis of 100 pounds of milk, allowing that the cheese yield from 100 pounds of milk containing 3 per cent of fat is 8.30 pounds, and from milk containing 4 per cent of fat, 10.60 pounds, a total of 18.90 pounds, bringing 189 cents. By the weight-of-milk method, this sum is divided equally between the two patrons, because each furnishes the same amount of milk. Hence, each receives 94.5 cents for the cheese made from his milk. On this basis the one furnishing milk containing 3 per cent of fat receives 11.4 cents a pound for each pound of cheese made from milk furnished by him; while the other receives 8.9 cents for each pound of cheese made from his milk.

Dividends based on the percentage of fat in milk are made as follows: One patron furnishes 3 pounds of fat and the other 4. There are, all told, 7 pounds of fat, the cheese corresponding to which sells for 189 cents. Therefore, each pound of fat is credited with 27 cents; one patron receives 81 (27×3) cents and the other, 108 (27×4) cents. In this case the one furnishing the poorer milk receives 9.76 cents a pound for the cheese made from his milk, and the other, 10.19 cents. The existing difference, 0.4 cent a pound, is generally held to represent an actual difference in the quality and value of the cheese (p. 246). These results can be very well shown in the following tabulated form:

		Weight-of-Milk Method			Milk-Fat Basis		
Pounds of fat in 100 pounds of milk	Pounds of cheese made from 100 pounds of milk	Dividend	Money rec'd for each pound of cheese	Money rec'd for each pound of milk-fat	Dividend	Money rec'd for each pound of cheese	Money rec'd for each pound of milk-fat
3	8.30	Cents 94.5	Cents 11.4	31.5	Cents 81	Cents 9.76	Cents 27
4	10.60	94.5	8.9	23.6	108	10.19	27

Of the various objections deserving any attention, which have not been already noticed, the following are the chief ones urged against this method:

(1) The percentage of fat in milk is not generally an accurate measure of the amount of cheese made from 100 pounds of milk. A pound of fat in milk containing 3 per cent of fat represents more cheese than does a pound of fat in milk containing 4 per cent of fat; in the former case, the cheese yield is 2.77 pounds for one pound of fat in milk, while in the latter it is 2.65 pounds. On this account, the milk containing least fat does not receive pay for all the cheese it makes.

(2) The cost of making the test is often raised as an objection. In actual practice, the difficulty has been satisfactorily overcome. The usual custom is to pay the cheese-maker at the rate of 20 to 25 cents a month for each patron.

The principal reasons given for favoring the fat basis are the following:

(1) This method recognizes the fundamental truth that normal milks varying in percentage of fat possess different values for cheese-making.

(2) The amount of fat in milk offers a practicable and just basis for determining the cheese-producing value of milk, when we consider both quality and quantity (p. 246).

(3) All temptation to adulterate milk by watering or skimming is absolutely removed, since a man receives pay for the number of pounds of fat that he furnishes and not merely for the number of pounds of liquid he carries to the factory. No other

method now in use so completely eliminates the temptation to adulterate milk.

(4) This method promotes improvement in the character of milk production. This is not merely a theoretical statement, but has been proved to be true in practice. It offers an inducement to each dairyman to improve the composition of his milk.

(5) Improvement in the character of dairy animals and in the consequent yield and composition of milk means economy of production and increase of profit. Cheese-solids in rich milk can be produced at less cost than in poor milk.

(6) This method awakens interest in the subject of milk production, stimulates a desire for further knowledge and tends to place the production of milk on a higher plane of intelligence.

PAYING FOR MILK ON THE BASIS OF YIELD AND RELATIVE VALUE OF CHEESE-SOLIDS

In the twelfth annual report of the Wisconsin experiment station (pp. 114-119), Dr. Babcock has worked out a system of payment by which the yield of cheese and composition are both taken into consideration. The principles embodied in this method have not received the general attention deserved. "It is not sufficient for a system to give the true yield from each patron's milk, for this makes skim-milk cheese equally valuable with that from the richest milk. The perfect system of making dividends in cheese-factories must include, not only the amount, but also the relative values of fat and the other cheese-producing solids; with such a system each patron will receive his just proportion whether he brings skim-milk, watered milk or cream." His proposed method gives to milk-fat a value of 6.6, as compared with a value of 1.0 for the cheese-solids not fat. The following table

Per cent of fat	Lactometer Degrees											Per cent of fat
	26	27	28	29	30	31	32	33	34	35	36	
2.0	2.86	2.88	2.89	2.91	2.93	2.94	2.96	2.98	3.00	3.01	3.03	2.0
2.1	2.98	3.00	3.01	3.03	3.05	3.06	3.08	3.10	3.12	3.13	3.15	2.1
2.2	3.10	3.12	3.13	3.15	3.17	3.18	3.20	3.22	3.24	3.25	3.27	2.2
2.3	[illegible]	3.24	3.25	3.27	3.29	3.30	3.32	3.34	3.36	3.37	3.39	2.3
2.4	3.34	3.36	3.37	3.39	3.41	3.42	3.44	3.46	3.48	3.49	3.51	2.4
2.5	3.47	3.49	3.50	3.52	3.53	3.54	3.56	3.58	3.60	3.61	3.63	2.5
2.6	3.59	3.61	3.62	3.64	3.65	3.67	3.69	3.71	3.73	3.74	3.76	2.6
2.7	3.71	3.73	3.74	3.76	3.77	3.79	3.81	3.83	3.85	3.86	3.88	2.7
2.8	3.83	3.85	3.86	3.88	3.90	3.91	3.93	3.95	3.97	3.98	4.00	2.8
2.9	3.95	3.97	3.98	4.00	4.02	4.03	4.05	4.07	4.09	4.10	4.12	2.9
3.0	4.07	4.09	4.10	4.12	4.14	4.15	4.17	4.19	4.21	4.22	4.24	3.0
3.1	4.19	4.21	4.22	4.24	4.26	4.27	4.29	4.31	4.33	4.34	4.36	3.1
3.2	4.31	4.33	4.34	4.36	4.38	4.39	4.41	4.43	4.45	4.46	4.48	3.2
3.3	4.43	4.45	4.46	4.48	4.50	4.51	4.53	4.55	4.57	4.58	4.60	3.3
3.4	4.55	4.57	4.58	4.60	4.62	4.63	4.65	4.67	4.69	4.71	4.72	3.4
3.5	4.68	4.70	4.71	4.73	4.75	4.76	4.78	4.80	4.82	4.83	4.85	3.5
3.6	4.80	4.82	4.83	4.85	4.87	4.88	4.90	4.92	4.94	4.95	4.97	3.6
3.7	4.92	4.94	4.95	4.97	4.99	5.00	5.02	5.04	5.06	5.07	5.09	3.7
3.8	5.04	5.06	5.07	5.09	5.11	5.12	5.14	5.16	5.18	5.19	5.21	3.8
3.9	5.16	5.18	5.19	5.21	5.23	5.24	5.26	5.28	5.30	5.31	5.33	3.9
4.0	5.29	5.31	5.32	5.34	5.36	5.37	5.39	5.41	5.43	5.44	5.46	4.0
4.1	5.41	5.43	5.44	5.46	5.48	5.49	5.51	5.53	5.55	5.56	5.58	4.1
4.2	5.53	5.55	5.56	5.58	5.60	5.61	5.63	5.65	5.67	5.68	5.70	4.2
4.3	5.65	5.67	5.68	5.70	5.72	5.73	5.75	5.77	5.79	5.80	5.82	4.3
4.4	5.77	5.79	5.80	5.82	5.84	5.85	5.87	5.89	5.91	5.92	5.94	4.4
4.5	5.89	5.91	5.92	5.94	5.96	5.97	5.99	6.01	6.03	6.04	6.06	4.5
4.6	6.02	6.04	6.05	6.07	6.09	6.10	6.12	6.14	6.16	6.17	6.19	4.6
4.7	6.14	6.16	6.17	6.19	6.21	6.22	6.24	6.26	6.28	6.29	6.31	4.7
4.8	6.26	6.28	6.29	6.31	6.33	6.34	6.36	6.38	6.40	6.41	6.43	4.8
4.9	6.38	6.40	6.41	6.43	6.45	6.46	6.48	6.50	6.52	6.53	6.55	4.9
5.0	6.50	6.52	6.53	6.55	6.57	6.58	6.60	6.62	6.64	6.65	6.67	5.0
5.1	6.62	6.64	6.65	6.67	6.69	6.70	6.72	6.74	6.76	6.77	6.79	5.1
5.2	6.74	6.76	6.77	6.79	6.81	6.82	6.84	6.86	6.88	6.89	6.91	5.2
5.3	6.86	6.88	6.89	6.91	6.93	6.94	6.96	6.98	7.00	7.01	7.03	5.3
5.4	6.98	7.00	7.01	7.03	7.05	7.06	7.08	7.10	7.12	7.13	7.15	5.4
5.5	7.10	7.12	7.13	7.15	7.17	7.18	7.20	7.22	7.24	7.25	7.27	5.5
5.6	7.23	7.25	7.26	7.28	7.30	7.31	7.33	7.35	7.37	7.38	7.40	5.6
5.7	7.35	7.37	7.38	7.40	7.42	7.43	7.45	7.47	7.49	7.50	7.52	5.7
5.8	7.47	7.49	7.50	7.52	7.54	7.55	7.57	7.59	7.61	7.62	7.64	5.8
5.9	7.59	7.61	7.62	7.64	7.66	7.67	7.69	7.71	7.73	7.74	7.76	5.9
6.0	7.71	7.73	7.74	7.76	7.78	7.79	7.81	7.83	7.85	7.86	7.88	6.0

is worked out, based on yield of cheese and relative value of cheese-solids for milks containing different percentages of fat from 2 to 6. Values are given which can be used directly in the same manner as the percentages of fat are used in case of the fat basis. These values appear to be quite accurate, especially for milks containing 3.5 to 4.0 per cent of fat. The only additional labor required is to apply the lactometer to a sample of each milk and take the reading. "This modification would give to each patron the same amount of money which he would obtain if his milk were manufactured by itself. In this respect it differs widely from those modifications of the relative-value plan which aim to make dividends in proportion to the pounds of cheese which each milk will produce, leaving out entirely the quality of the cheese." The following illustration shows the application of this method:

One patron furnishes milk showing by test 3 per cent of fat and a lactometer (Quevenne) reading of 28; another, milk with 4 per cent of fat and a lactometer reading of 34. Turning to the preceding table, it is found that milks corresponding to these percentages of fat and lactometer readings have relative values for cheese-making represented by the numbers 4.10 and 5.43. To find the dividend of each, we divide the amount of money (189 cents) received, by the sum (9.53) of these two numbers, which gives 19.83. This number multiplied by 4.10 and 5.43 gives the respective dividends of the two patrons.

Pounds of fat in 100 pounds of milk	Pounds of cheese made from 100 pounds of milk	Dividend	Money rec'd for each pound of cheese	Money rec'd for each pound of milk-fat
		Cents		Cents
3	8.30	81.3	9.80	27.10
4	10.60	107.7	10.16	26.92

By comparing these results with those given by the simple fat basis (p. 259), and other methods, we see that the values are much closer to the results of the fat basis than by any other method.

Application of principle to fat and casein.—This same principle could be readily applied when we know the percentages of fat and of casein in milk. We might be even more liberal and, instead of allowing only one-sixth for casein, allow as much as one-fourth. In this case, the dividends would be based on the fat plus one-fourth of the casein in each case. This is illustrated in connection with the fat and casein method of making dividends (p. 270).

MODIFICATION OF FAT BASIS KNOWN AS THE "FAT-PLUS-TWO" METHOD

By this method the percentage of fat in milk is increased by 2 and the results used as in making dividends on the fat basis. The method originated in Canada. The first suggestion was made about 1893, when at one of the cheese-factories the plan was adopted of adding 1 to the fat in making dividends, because it was noticed that this method more closely approximated the cheese yield than the use of fat alone. This method was made a subject of study at the Ontario Agricultural College and was modified by adding 2 to the fat in making dividends.

The dividends are made in the following manner under this method, using the illustration already given (p. 258) for milks containing 3 and 4 per cent of fat. The receipts from sale of cheese are 189 cents. Instead of one patron receiving three-sevenths and the other four-sevenths of this amount, one receives five-elevenths and the other six-elevenths, as shown thus:

$$3+2=5$$
$$4+2=6$$

—————

11

The results, compared with those of the fat basis, are as follows for this particular illustration:

Pounds of fat in 100 pounds of milk	Pounds of cheese made from 100 pounds of milk	Fat-Basis method			Fat-plus-2 method		
		Dividend	Money received for each pound of cheese	Money received for each pound of milk-fat	Dividend	Money received for each pound of cheese	Money received for each pound of milk-fat
		Cents	Cents			Cents	Cents
3	8.30	81	9.76	27	86	10.36	28.7
4	10.60	108	10.19	27	103	9.72	25.7

This method is based on an attempt to approximate yield of cheese as a basis to use in paying for milk. It is supposed that the addition of 2 to the per cent of fat makes allowance for the casein of the milk, and, therefore, that milks which are low in fat will get such a proportion of casein as will balance the difference existing between milk poor in fat and milk rich in fat in respect to yield of cheese per pound of fat; and that, therefore, taking the casein into consideration along with the fat will give us a more accurate relation in regard to yield of cheese and percentage of fat in milk. This ought to be true and is true to a certain degree. So far as we do take casein into consideration, we get just that much nearer to the average of cheese yield, speaking of *yield alone* and not considering *quality*.

The objections which have been brought against this method are the following:

(1) It does not recognize any casein in milk above 2 per cent; it would be a fair measure of yield of cheese if all milks contained 2 per cent of casein, no more and no less. This is, of course, not in accordance with the actual facts. The additional amount of casein above 2 per cent, which is usually found in richer milks, is wholly ignored by this method. For example, under this method, milk containing 4 per cent of fat would, after adding 2, be given a value of 6, whereas it should be given a value of 6.4 or 6.5 or more on the basis of its usual casein content.

(2) This method is, therefore, in the interest of milk low in fat. It gives undue advantage to poorer milk, and, to the same extent, works against the producer of richer milk. It has been generally held that too much encouragement cannot be given

to farmers to produce milk of richer composition. In the illustration given above, one fails to see the justice of a method which gives to the producer of poorer milk 10.36 cents a pound for his cheese and to the producer of richer milk, only 9.72 cents a pound for cheese that is better if the milk is made into cheese by itself.

(3) This method offers a premium on watering milk, because the percentage of fat in milk (high or low) is credited with only 2 per cent of casein; and, hence, the lower the percentage of fat, the larger will be the relative amount of casein and the greater the price received for each pound of fat. For example, a patron furnishing milk with 4 per cent of fat could add, say, 33 pounds of water to 100 pounds of milk, thus reducing the percentage of fat to 3.   He would then have the benefit of the added factor for 133 pounds of milk instead of 100 pounds.   He would thereby increase his dividend from 103 to 108 cents.

(4) This method also offers a premium on skimming as well as watering milk. This can best be made clear by illustration.   A patron who furnishes milk containing 4 per cent of fat skims it so as to make it contain 3 per cent and then adds enough water to make the weight of milk 100 pounds again.   The cheese made from 100 pounds of such milk would be about 8.9 pounds. The milk of the other patron, who furnishes 100 pounds of normal milk containing 3 pounds of fat, makes 8.3 pounds of cheese, a total of 17.2 pounds for the 200 pounds of mixed milk.   This, we assume, sells for 172 cents and is evenly divided between

the two patrons, because each furnishes milk containing 3 per cent of fat. Each, therefore, receives 86 cents. If the patron who produces milk with 4 per cent of fat takes the normal milk to the factory, he receives on the "fat-plus-two" basis 103 cents, as we have already seen. If he skims his milk as described above, he receives 86 cents, or 17 cents less; but he has, as an offset to this, one pound of milk-fat which he can sell for 25 cents to 30 cents. Therefore, he is the gainer by all that he can get for his pound of milk-fat over 17 cents.

(5) This method, in opposition to the teachings of Robertson, Babcock and many others, wholly ignores the fact that composition and quality vary with fat in milk and that cheese made from richer milk is of higher value.

While these objections hold good, still the "fat-plus-two" method is unquestionably a great advance over the old weight-of-milk method. The most unfortunate feature about this method is the confusion which its introduction has caused among dairymen. Instead of regarding it as a modification of the fat basis, dairymen have, in many cases, thought that the whole principle of paying for milk by any other method than the weight-of-milk system was under suspicion. Dairymen do not yet understand the details of different methods clearly enough to discriminate, and, when they are told that the fat basis is unreliable and inaccurate, they most naturally lose confidence in all methods based on the fat-test and go back to the weight-of-milk system. Those who produce poor milk take advantage of such an opportunity to upset the entire system based on the fat-test. Thus, the whole situation has been needlessly confused, rather than benefited, for the average cheese-factory patron.

PAYING FOR MILK ON BASIS OF FAT AND CASEIN

By this method the percentages of fat and casein in each patron's milk are added and the figures thus obtained are used in apportioning dividends, as in the fat basis.   This can be illustrated as follows:

We will make use of the figures already employed in illustrating the other methods.   One patron furnishes milk containing 3 per cent of fat and 2.1 per cent of casein; the other, milk with 4 per cent of fat and 2.5 per cent of casein.   Each furnishes 100 pounds of milk; the total amount of cheese made is 18.9 pounds, realizing 189 cents. We add together the amounts of fat and casein in the two milks, obtaining 11.6 as the total number of pounds of fat and casein in the 200 pounds of milk.   The total amount of money received for the cheese is divided by the total amount of casein and fat, which gives us 16.3 cents as the value of each pound of mixed fat and casein in milk.   The dividend of the patron furnishing the poorer milk is 16.3×5.1, which equals 83 cents; the dividend of the other is 16.3×6.5, which equals 106 cents.   In this case, each receives the same price for the cheese, 10 cents a pound, but not the same for milk-fat; the poorer milk receives 27.7 cents a pound for its fat; the richer milk, 26.5 cents. Below are given in tabulated form the results of this and other methods already considered, and also the modification of the fat-and-casein basis, in accordance with the relative-value suggestions of Dr. Babcock; that is, we allow full value for fat and one-fourth value for casein (p. 264).

Per cent of fat in milk	Per cent ot casein in milk	Pounds of cheese	Dividend by fat and casein	Dividend by fat method	Dividend by fat and one-fourth casein (P. 264)	Dividend by "fat+2" method
3	2.1	8.30	Cents 83	Cents 81	Cents 82	Cents 86
4	2.5	10.60	106	108	107	103

The fat-and-casein method has the following advantages:

(1) It is an accurate measure of the yield of cheese in the case of all kinds of milk when the losses of milk constituents are not excessive.

(2) The temptation to adulterate by watering is entirely removed.

The following disadvantages suggest themselves:

(1) Assuming that a test for casein gives results as accurate as the Babcock test for fat in the hands of ordinary cheese-makers, it is objected that the test involves extra labor on the part of the cheese-maker, for which he cannot well afford the time. The same objection is often made against the Babcock test, and it would, of course, be much more forceful in regard to a casein-test.

(2) An extra test involves additional cost, even in case a cheese-maker could find time to

make both fat and casein tests.   If a cheese-maker were paid on the basis of what is received for making fat-tests, it would amount to $50 or $60 a season for most cheese-factories.   To this must be added cost of materials and breakage of glassware, which might be conservatively placed at $10 to $15. There would thus be a total outlay on the part of the patrons amounting to $60 to $75 for the season in having the casein-test made.

(3)   The fat-and-casein method does not recognize any difference in the value of cheese made from milk high and low in percentage of fat.   It places the market value of casein on an absolute level with milk-fat, while Dr. Babcock gives milk-fat in cheese a value 6.6 times that of casein (p. 262).

(4)   The use of the fat-and-casein method offers a temptation to remove fat from milk or to add skim-milk, in case of milk to be used for cheese-making.   To illustrate, casein in skim-milk has a market value for the dairyman not to exceed 2 or 3 cents a pound, while milk-fat is worth about 30 cents a pound.   In good cheese, casein and fat together bring about 18 cents a pound.   If casein is paid for on a par with fat, then by adding skim-milk to normal milk, one can increase the price of his skim-milk casein about nine times.   The same would be true if fat were removed from milk and sold as butter or cream.   In whatever manner one increases the ratio of casein to fat in milk, he increases the dividend value of casein in cheese-making, when fat and casein are treated as of equal value in making dividends.

(5) The fat-and-casein method requires more time in calculating dividends.

(6) Some have expressed the fear that, under this system, the increased value of casein would lead dairymen to breed cows for milk high in casein, and that this would result in a poorer quality of cheese and general consequent danger to the cheese industry. In fact, the use of cows giving milk with a high casein content has been specifically emphasized by some as a desirable end to work for and it is urged that such an aim would be realized by the recognition of casein in cheese-making as of equal value with fat. Assuming that the percentage of casein in milk could be notably increased in an economical manner, what would be the result? By referring to pages 231-237, it can readily be seen that the process would be nothing more or less than a system of adding skim-milk to normal milk, thereby increasing the amount of casein in milk relative to fat. This fact is probably not fully appreciated by those who are advocating the process. We have probably reached the limits of safety, in more than one sense, in many strains of Holsteins and Ayrshires, as regards the high relation of casein to fat. We do not need to spend time and energy to breed cows for milk in the direction of skim-milk for cheese-making. Some progressive dairymen are, happily, still so old-fashioned in their ideas as to advocate the opposite process, viz., increasing the yield of fat in milk without paying any attention to its skim-milk constituent, casein. This is simply raising the old question that used to be discussed so much 20 years

and more ago regarding the "butter cow" and the "cheese cow." Thus, in the 1892 report of the Vermont experiment station (pp. 122, 123), this whole question is ably discussed, the article closing as follows: "The logical conclusion, then, is that the so-called 'cheese cow,' that is, the cow which is especially good for cheese rather than for butter, does not exist, and that whenever a cow is found that is good for cheese-making purposes, the milk of that cow is equally good for the manufacture of butter." The following statement is found on page 471 of the 1895 yearbook of the United States Department of Agriculture, in an article by the late Henry E. Alvord: "Cumulative evidence is unnecessary. These important truths are established, namely: The best milk makes the best cheese, and the most of it; the milk which is most profitable for butter is also the most profitable for cheese; the best butter cow is the best cheese cow." In a discussion of the same subject, Bulletin No. 9 of the New Hampshire station contains the following statements: "We are told that cows which are giving milk poor in fat and are therefore poor butter cows are great cheese cows. . . . A milk rich in fat is not only a good milk for butter but also a good milk for cheese, while the reverse is also true."

In harmony with the general tenor of the preceding statements, the investigation carried on with different breeds of cows at the New York experiment station appears to demonstrate clearly that a pound of cheese-solids can be produced at less cost in case of milk rich in fat than in case of milk poor in fat.

(7) Another highly important question has been raised in connection with the use of a casein-test in paying for milk at cheese-factories—Is it worth the time and trouble expended on it? It is not worth the time, if, with Dr. Robertson, Dr. Babcock and others, we believe that casein is not equal in value to fat for cheese production in relation to composition and quality of cheese. If, on the other hand, we believe that yield of cheese alone should be considered and that fat and casein are of equal value, pound for pound, in cheese production, even then we can ask the question—Are the differences caused by variation in casein worth the trouble and expense involved in making a casein-test in addition to fat? To what extent will dividends be readjusted among patrons and in what manner? While this question can not be answered finally until results have been secured in numerous factories, we have sufficient data on hand to give a definite answer in the case of one representative New York factory for one season. We have fat and casein determinations during one factory season for each of 50 different herds of cows whose milk was taken to one cheese-factory. The analyses of milk were made every other week for each herd separately from May to October inclusive. In 23 cases, the fat-and-casein method gave a larger dividend than did the fat alone by an average of 1.6 cents for each 100 pounds of milk, the greatest difference in the case of any one patron being 5.9 cents, and the least 0.1 cent. In one

case, both methods gave the same result. In 26 cases, the fat method gave higher results by an average of 1.4 cents for 100 pounds of milk, the difference varying in the case of different individuals from 5.1 cents to 0.1 cent.

The greatest difference found in favor of the fat and casein basis, 5.9 cents per 100 pounds of milk, would mean for an entire factory season nearly $20, assuming that this patron furnished 33,600 pounds of milk, an average of 224 pounds for 150 days, which was the actual average for each patron. Summarizing the results on this basis, we have 23 men receiving more money by the fat-and-casein method, amounting altogether, for the season, to $123.46, the increased dividends of each varying from 33.6 cents to $19.83, and averaging $5.39. As a matter of fact, about two-thirds of the money would go to 8 patrons. One patron receives the same amount either way. The remaining 26 patrons receive less by the fat-and-casein method than by the fat basis, amounting altogether to $123.46, varying from 33.6 cents to $17.13, and averaging $4.75 each.

On the basis of the estimated cost of $60 to $75 spent in paying for the test, more than half of the difference ($123.46) would be used up, so that, if those who benefited by the casein-test paid for it, there would be distributed not more than half of the amount above given. This would mean an expenditure of $60 to $75, in order to adjust a difference of $123 in the interest of 23 men who furnish milk which tests below the average in fat. The entire sum involved amounts to less than 0.4

per cent of the factory's receipts from cheese. Under such circumstances, it is not at all likely that the 27 patrons would vote to employ the fat-and-casein method in distributing dividends, nor is it likely that most of the 23 men benefited would ask it, when the high relative cost of making a redistribution was understood. While the results represent only one cheese-factory, the conditions are typical of those prevailing in New York state, and results that are strikingly different from these would probably be exceptional. If the dividends were made on the basis of allowing less for casein than fat, as recommended by Dr. Babcock (p. 264), the difference in favor of the patrons furnishing extra casein would be less than one-quarter what they are when we allow the same price for casein as for fat. On such a basis, the difference would be only about half the cost of making the casein-tests.

PAYMENT ON BASIS OF FAT AND CALCULATED CASEIN

In view of the fact that so many cheese-factories are still paying for milk on the basis of weight alone, as a result of the confusion that has been created in regard to the fairness of the fat basis, a method might be suggested which would find use in factories that are now using no test system, which would be far superior to the weight-of-milk method and at the same time possess certain advantages over other modifications of the fat basis. Such a method would be to pay on the basis of the fat and of the casein calculated according to the formula, $(Fat - 3) \times 0.4 + 2.1$. Such a method is not recommended where the fat basis is being used, but only as a compromise where it comes to a choice between some such basis and the weight-of-milk method; in other words, where the prejudice against the fat basis is too strong to be overcome. The amount of casein obtained thus is added to the fat and the dividends calculated in the manner given on p. 284. The use of a method basing dividends on the fat-test and the amount of calculated casein would possess the following advantages:

(1) It would be preferable to the fat-and-casein method, which requires two separate tests to be made, since no test would be needed for casein, but only for fat. It would, therefore, involve no additional expense of time, labor or money, as is the case with the casein-test.

(2) It would be more fair than the "fat-plus-two" method, because milk containing higher percentages of fat would receive payment for the increased amount of casein that goes with that increased percentage of fat, instead of receiving credit for only 2 per cent of casein, rich and poor milks alike. This method gives results that are in most cases much closer to the yield of cheese than the "fat-plus-two" method.

(3) The watering or skimming of milk could not affect the results, because the casein is made to depend on the fat content. In this respect the method is much superior to the fat-and-casein or the fat-plus-two method.

(4) No more labor need be involved than in the case of the fat basis, either in the matter of testing or in the matter of calculating dividends. The matter can be simplified by the consultation of a· table, which can be made out once for all. The following formula can be used in preparing such a table:

(Fat—3)×1.4+5.10=Amount of fat and casein in 100 pounds of milk.

Such a table, already prepared, is here given:

Per cent of fat in milk	Dividend number	Per cent of fat in milk	Dividend number
3.00	5.10	4.05	6.57
3.05	5.17	4.10	6.64
3.10	5.24	4.15	6.71
3.15	5.31	4.20	6.78
3.20	5.38	4.25	6.85
3.25	5.45	4.30	6.92
3.30	5.52	4.35	6.99
3.35	5.59	4.40	7.06
3.40	5.66	4.45	7.13
3.45	5.73	4.50	7.20
3.50	5.80	4.55	7.27
3.55	5.87	4.60	7.34
3.60	5.94	4.65	7.41
3.65	6.01	4.70	7.48
3.70	6.08	4.75	7.55
3.75	6.15	4.80	7.62
3.80	6.22	4.85	7.69
3.85	6.29	4.90	7.77
3.90	6.36	4.95	7.84
3.95	6.43	5.00	7.90
4.00	6.50		

(5) The introduction of the fat-test is called for by this method, and thus a great step in advance would be made in comparison with the weight-of-milk method. This might ultimately lead to the adoption of the simple fat basis.

The following objections to such a method may be suggested:

(1) It aims to pay for the amount of cheese produced without regard to composition or quality. Of course, this same objection applies to the fat-and-casein method and the fat-plus-two method.

(2) The method of calculation may give amounts of casein differing from those actually present in milk.   In individual cases and for single tests, this might be true, but, taking the average of a whole season, the differences would not usually be found great, and the season's average would be the factor on which to base a comparison as to accuracy.   As a matter of fact, in the case of the 50 herds already referred to, in no case was there a difference in the season's results greater than 0.25 per cent of casein between the calculated amount and that obtained by the chemical method; while in the case of 40 out of 50 patrons the results differed by less than 0.1 per cent, in several cases being identical.   The casein-test, even in skillful hands, may give results that differ as much as 0.2 per cent from the regular chemical method.

METHODS OF CALCULATING DIVIDENDS AT CHEESE-FACTORIES

In concluding this chapter, we will illustrate somewhat more in detail how dividends at cheese-factories are calculated according to the different methods that have been discussed.   For this purpose, we will make use of the following data which, for convenience, are given here in a body for reference.   In all cases, the following three items must be known: (1) The amount of milk delivered by each patron during the dividend period; (2) total or gross amount of money received for the cheese produced during the same period; and (3) the expenses to be deducted from gross receipts, such as cost of manufacture, cheese-boxes, cartage, selling, etc.

Name of patron	Pounds of milk delivered during dividend period	Pounds of cheese for 100 pounds of milk	Per cent of fat in milk	Per cent of casein in milk	Pounds of cheese made from milk delivered by each patron
A	350	10.6	4.0	2.50	37.1
B	650	9.7	3.6	2.34	63.0
C	835	13.3	5.2	2.98	111.0
D	965	11.5	4.4	2.68	111.0
E	1200	11.1	4.2	2.58	133.2
Totals	4000				455.3

From the stated amounts of milk there are made 455.3 pounds of cheese. We will suppose that this is sold at a price which realizes 10 cents a pound, or $45.53, after all expenses are deducted.

Calculating dividends on basis of weight of milk. —In the table preceding we have a total of 4,000 pounds of milk furnished in the dividend period and the cheese made from this nets $45.53. Dividing this sum of money by the number representing the pounds of milk delivered (4,000), we find the net receipts from 1.0 pound of milk to be 1.138 cents. This amount is multiplied by the number representing the pounds of milk furnished by each patron and the result gives the amount of the dividend of each. The results are given in the following table:

Name of patron	Pounds of milk delivered	Value of 1.0 pound of milk	Dividend of each for period	Pounds of cheese made from milk furnished by each	Money received for each pound of cheese	Money received for each pound of milk-fat furnished
		Cents			Cents	Cents
A	350	1.138	$3.98	37.1	10.73	28.4
B	650	"	7.40	63.0	11.75	31.1
C	835	"	9.51	111.0	8.57	21.9
D	965	"	10.98	111.0	9.90	25.9
E	1200	"	13.66	133.2	10.26	27.1

The figures in the last two columns emphasize the fact that this method of paying for milk gives results that have little or no relation to the cheese-producing values of the milk. It is fair to all only when the milk furnished by each patron is of the same composition and cheese-producing value as the milk of every other patron, a condition rarely, if ever, found to exist.

Calculating dividends on basis of fat in milk.— Having the data already given above in the table on p. 280 we multiply the amount of milk-fat delivered by each patron by the net price realized for one pound of fat. We will consider the method in three separate steps.

Step 1. To find the number of pounds of milk-fat furnished by each patron, multiply in each case the weight of milk by the number indicating the per cent of fat and divide the result by 100.

Step 2. Find the net value of one pound of milk-fat by dividing the total net receipts by the total number of pounds of fat delivered by all the patrons during the dividend period.

Step 3. Multiply the number of pounds of fat delivered by each patron by the net price received for one pound of fat.

Example: Step 1. The data and results are indicated in tabular form, as follows:

Name of patron	Pounds of milk delivered during dividend period	Per cent of fat in milk	Pounds of fat in milk delivered
A..............	350	× 4.0	= 14.00
B..............	650	× 3.6	= 23.40
C..............	835	× 5.2	= 43.42
D..............	965	× 4.4	= 42.46
E..............	1200	× 4.2	= 50.40
Total number of pounds of fat delivered by all patrons ..			173.68

Step 2. From the amount of milk indicated above, the amount of cheese made was 455.3 pounds, which realized 10 cents a pound after deducting all expenses, making a total of $45.53. This sum divided by 173.68, the total pounds of fat delivered, gives 26.2 cents as the net price received for each pound of fat.

Step 3. The data and results are indicated in tabular form, as follows:

Name of patron	Pounds of fat delivered	Net price received for fat per pound	Amount of dividend due each patron	Net price received for cheese per lb.
		Cents		Cents
A..........	14.00	× 26.2	= $ 3.67	9.90
B..........	23.40	× 26.2	= 6.14	9.75
C..........	43.42	× 26.2	= 11.38	10.25
D..........	42.46	× 26.2	= 11.13	10.03
E..........	50.40	× 26.2	= 13.21	9.92

Calculating dividends on basis of yield and relative value of cheese-solids.—By this method one proceeds exactly as in case of the fat-basis method, except that in place of the percentages of fat, one uses the number obtained from the table (p. 262) corresponding in each case to percentage of fat in milk and the lactometer reading.

Calculating dividends on basis of milk-fat plus two.—The following table indicates the general method of procedure:

Name of patron	Pounds of milk delivered during dividend period	Per cent of fat in milk + 2 (casein)	Pounds of fat and casein furnished corresponding to fat + 2	Price of each pound of fat and casein	Amount of dividend due each patron	Net price received for cheese per pound	Net price received for fat per pound
						Cents	Cents
A......	350	× (4.0×2=)6.0	= 21.0	× 17.95	= $3.77	10.16	27.0
B......	650	× (3.6×2=)5.6	= 36.4	× 17.95	= 6.54	10.40	28.0
C......	835	× (5.2×2=)7.2	= 60.1	× 17.95	= 10.78	9.71	24.8
D......	965	× (4.4×2=)6.4	= 61.8	× 17.95	= 11.10	10.00	26.1
E......	1200	× (4.2×2=)6.2	= 74.4	× 17.95	= 13.34	10.02	26.5

In explanation of the foregoing table, it is seen that the amount of milk furnished by each patron is multiplied by the per cent of fat plus two. These results are added and the sum (amounting to 253.7) divided into the amount of money received for the cheese ($45.53), giving 17.95 cents as the value of each pound of mixed fat and casein (represented by 2 pounds of casein in 100 pounds of milk). The number, obtained in each case by multiplying the number of pounds of milk furnished by the number representing the per cent of milk-fat+2, is then multiplied by 17.95, the result being the dividend in each case. It is noticed that this method makes a pound of cheese or of milk-fat yield larger money returns in case of poor than in case of rich milk.

Calculating dividends on basis of fat and casein. —The same process is followed as before, except that the yield of fat and casein, taken together, constitutes the basis of division. The percentages of fat and of casein in milk are added together, in each case, and the sum multiplied by the number of pounds of milk furnished, thus giving the number of pounds of fat and casein furnished by each patron. The total amount of fat and casein furnished by all the patrons for the dividend period (279.36 pounds) is divided into the net proceeds from the sale of cheese and the result is the net dividend value (16.3 cents) of one pound of mixed fat and casein. This figure is then multiplied by the amount of fat and casein furnished by each patron. The details are indicated below.

Name of patron	Pounds of milk delivered during dividend period	Per cent of fat and casein in milk	Pounds of fat and casein furnished	Amount of dividend due each patron	Net price received for cheese per pound	Net price received for fat per pound
					Cents	Cents
A.....	350	×(4.0×2.50=)6.50	=22.75×16.3 =	$3.71	10.00	26.5
B.....	650	×(3.6×2.34=)5.94	=38.61×16.3 =	6.29	10.00	26.8
C.....	835	×(5.2×2.98=)8.18	=68.30×16.3 =	11.13	10.00	25.6
D....	965	×(4.4×2.68=)7.08	=68.32×16.3 =	11.14	10.00	26.2
E.....	1200	×(4.2×2.58=)6.78	=81.38×16.3 =	13.26	10.00	26.3

CHAPTER XXII

The Relations of Micro-Organisms and Enzyms to Cheese-Making

Milk, on standing under ordinary conditions, undergoes a variety of changes sooner or later, many of which destroy its value for cheese-making purposes. The most common and extensive changes occurring in milk are due to fermentations. One result of some kinds of fermentation is the production of bad flavors, but these may be acquired also by direct absorption from the surrounding air or from the food consumed (p. 6). We shall see that certain kinds of fermentations are useful and necessary in cheese-making, while others make it difficult or impossible to prepare a good product.

FERMENTATIONS AND FERMENTS

The souring of milk is one of the most familiar cases of fermentation. The important change taking place is the formation of lactic acid from milk-sugar and the change is caused by certain living organisms. An equally familiar case of fermentation is the coagulation of milk by rennet-extract. In this case the change is produced, not by a living organism, but by a chemical substance. That which causes fermentation is called a *ferment*.

Fermentation may be defined as a chemical change of an organic compound through the action of living organisms or of chemical agents. We thus have two general kinds of ferments, (1) organized ferments and (2) unorganized ferments, known also as chemical ferments or enzyms. In the illustrations given above, the ferments are (1) lactic acid organisms and (2) rennet ferment; in one case the organic matter changed is milk-sugar; in the other, milk-casein. Organized ferments are living micro-organisms, capable, as a result of their growth, of causing fermentations. Unorganized ferments are chemical substances, or ferments without life, capable of causing marked changes in many complex organic compounds, the enzyms themselves undergoing little or no change.

General characteristics of ferments.—Ferments possess certain general characteristics in common, among which may be mentioned the following: (1) A very small amount of ferment is capable of producing very great changes. (2) They are all dependent upon temperature as a condition of activity. They cease to act at low and also at high temperatures. Most of them find the temperature that is best suited to their greatest activity between 80° and 100° F. (3) Ferments are destroyed by heat, the temperature of boiling water, in most cases, completely destroying their power to act. Their activity is checked by low temperatures, but, when again warmed, they renew their activity. (4) The action of ferments is checked or prevented by many substances. (5) When the products formed by ferments accumulate in certain amounts, the ferment action usually stops. (6) All ferments are closely connected with living processes.

Organized ferments, or living micro-organisms capable of causing fermentations, are divided into

several classes; but those of greatest interest in connection with cheddar cheese-making are called *bacteria.* These are the smallest conceivable forms of
plant life. Each individual consists of a single cell,
averaging in diameter one-thirty-thousandth of an
inch.

(1) *Kinds.*—Bacteria appear in three general
varieties of form: (a) Ball *(coccus),* (b) short rod
(bacillus), and (c) corkscrew *(spirillum).* (Figs.
39-42.)

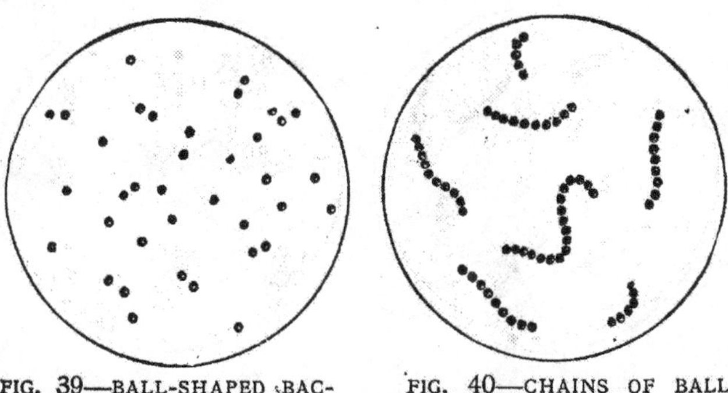

FIG. 39—BALL-SHAPED BAC-
TERIA (COCCUS).
(Rogers)

FIG. 40—CHAINS OF BALL-
SHAPED (COCCUS) BAC-
TERIA
(Rogers)

(2) *Method of growth and reproduction.*—They
multiply in number, or reproduce, by simple division;
that is, when a cell grows in size, it increases more
in one direction, so as to result in lengthening out
slightly, and a partition forms across the cell, thus
producing two new cells in place of the old one; and
then each of these subdivides again and so on continuously. Some kinds of bacteria form spores in
the cells; these are to bacteria what seeds are to

higher plants. Spores are not so easily killed by heat as are bacteria. Under favorable conditions, the rapidity of growth of bacteria is remarkable. Thus, in some cases, one cell divides into two cells in 20 minutes; if this rate were kept up for 24 hours, the one cell would multiply into several millions.

(3) *Food requirements of bacteria.*—Bacteria require as food for satisfactory growth compounds containing nitrogen, carbon, hydrogen and, in addition,

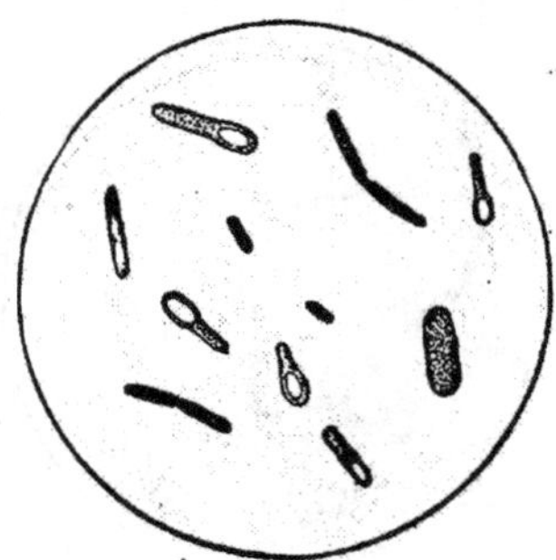

FIG. 41—ROD-SHAPED BAC-
TERIA (bacillus). CLEAR
AREAS IN SOME ARE
SPORES.   (Rogers)

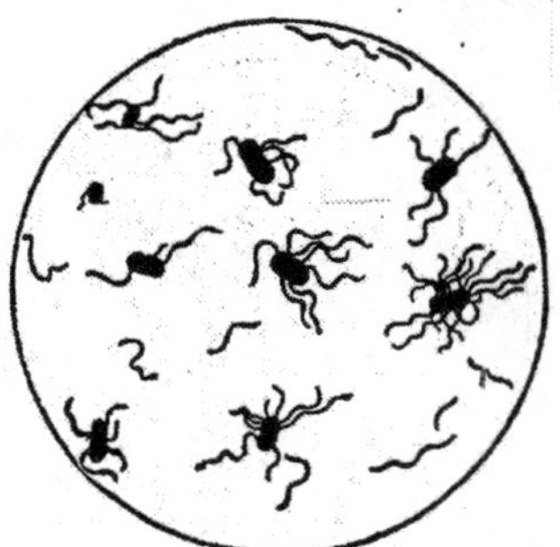

FIG. 42—B A C T E R I A WITH
HAIR-LIKE ORGANS, WHICH
THEY USE IN MOVING
THEMSELVES ABOUT IN
LIQUIDS   (Rogers)

small amounts of inorganic or mineral matter. The sugar, casein, albumin and salts in milk and its products furnish a supply of food very readily utilized by bacteria.

(4) *Temperature.*—The bacteria commonly present in milk grow between the limits of 40° and 110° F., the most favorable limits being between 80° and 95° F. Many bacteria are killed between 130° and

140° F., when exposed to this heat for ten minutes, and most of them are destroyed at 185° F. Many spores are killed at temperatures only above 212° F., and even then require heating one to three hours. (Fig. 43.) Dry heat is less effective than moist heat. Live steam, therefore, affords a most effective means of destroying bacteria. All bacteria are rendered inactive at low temperatures and some may be killed by intense cold. Many bacteria may retain life on being dried and become active again when placed under favorable conditions of moisture and temperature.

(5) *Action of sunlight, chemicals, etc.*—Sunlight kills many bacteria when they are exposed directly to the sun's rays for a few hours. Bacteria are either checked in growth or killed by many different chemical compounds. Those compounds that simply retard the rapidity of growth of bacteria are called *antiseptics,* among which are carbolic acid, salt, saltpeter, etc.; those that destroy bacterial life are called *disinfectants,* among which are mercuric chlorid (corrosive sublimate), formaldehyd (formalin), potassium bichromate, chloroform, etc. The activity of each kind of bacteria is stopped by an accumulation of products formed by it and, in some cases, by the products of activity of other bacteria. Thus, most kinds of lactic acid bacteria stop growing when about 0.9 per cent acid is formed, and much less than this amount of lactic acid also prevents the growth of many other bacteria.

(6) *Changes produced.*—In the course of their growth, bacteria produce great changes in the materials in which they grow; and the process by which these changes are brought about are known,

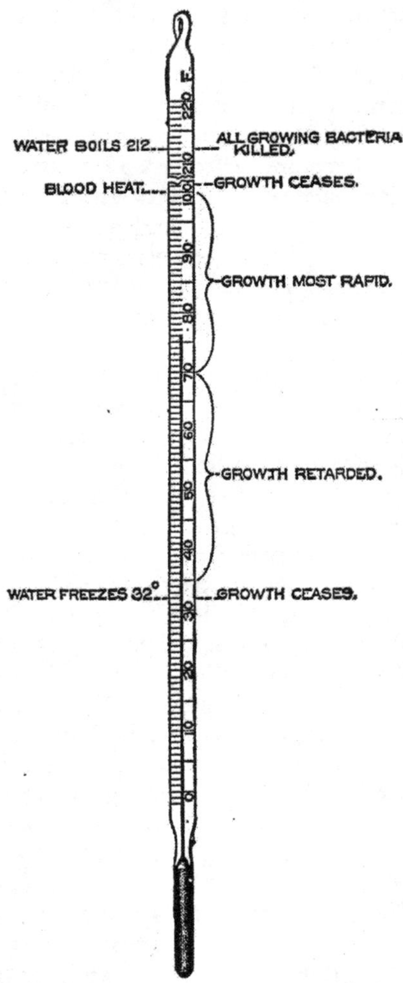

FIG. 43—INFLUENCE OF TEMPERATURE ON BACTERIA ORDINARILY
FOUND IN MILK   (Rogers).

as previously stated, under the general name of fermentation.

(7) *Distribution.*—Bacteria are found distributed nearly everywhere in the soil, in the air and in water. They are always present in large numbers wherever vegetable or animal matter is undergoing decay. They are, therefore, always closely associated with dirt and filth. While some are the causes of dreaded diseases and of serious troubles in cheese-making, most of them are either harmless or actively helpful in many ways.

Unorganized ferments or enzyms.—Many enzyms are produced directly by bacteria and are the direct agents producing the observed changes of bacterial activity, while many are formed in higher plants and in animals. Thus, the pepsin found in the human stomach is an enzym; its special power or form of activity enables it to change protein compounds from insoluble to soluble forms. The ptyalin contained in saliva is another enzym and is capable of changing starch into sugar. Enzyms are destroyed by high temperatures and by many disinfectants. Some substances, like ether, chloroform and formaldehyd, do not seriously interfere with the activity of enzyms, while they do destroy bacteria.

In connection with the subject of ferments, we shall consider the following ones as those of most importance in connection with cheese-making: (1) Lactic acid bacteria, (2) gas-producing bacteria, (3) digesting bacteria, (4) bacteria producing undesirable flavors, (5) yeasts, (6) milk-enzyms, (7) rennet-enzyms, and (8) pepsin. The ferments that are responsible for many of the defects found in American cheddar cheese will be discussed only briefly here, because their relations to cheese-making are fully treated from a practical standpoint in Part II, pp. 115-130.

LACTIC ACID FERMENTATION

The ordinary souring of milk is due to the formation of lactic acid, which is produced by the action of lactic acid bacteria *(Bacillus lactici acidi.* Fig. 44) upon the sugar in milk. A large number of different kinds or types of bacteria are able to produce lactic acid from milk-sugar. Some interesting work has been done recently (Bull. No. 42, Mich. Agr. Coll. Exp. Sta.) which shows that other micro-organisms are often associated with the micro-organisms of lactic fermentation and that these associate micro-organisms

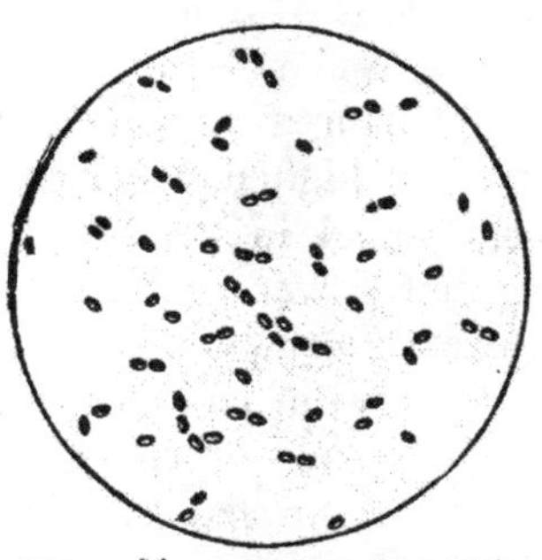

FIG. 44—TYPICAL LACTIC-ACID BACTERIA (Rogers)

often have the power of furnishing products that exert a decided influence upon the rapidity of the growth of the lactic micro-organisms.

We have already (p. 150) called attention to the fact that the sour taste of milk is not due to the presence of uncombined lactic acid, since little or no free lactic acid is present in sour milk until it has quite a high degree of acidity; but is due to acid phosphate of calcium, which is formed by the action of lactic acid upon the insoluble calcium compounds in the milk. Milk begins to taste sour when its acidity amounts to about 0.3 per cent; which really means when a little over 0.2 per cent of lactic acid has been formed from milk-sugar; because the milk-casein itself and the soluble phosphates have an acidity of nearly 0.10 per cent (p. 153) when the milk is freshly drawn and no milk-sugar has had a chance to be changed into lactic acid. According to recent work done at the New York experiment station, milk curdles on boiling when the acidity reaches 0.32 to 0.46 per cent, and at ordinary room temperature when it reaches 0.58 to 0.72 per cent. When artificial lactic acid is added directly to fresh milk, curdling takes place on boiling when the acidity reaches 0.36 per cent and at room temperature when the acidity reaches 0.57 per cent. Bacteria continue actively converting milk-sugar into lactic acid, until the amount of acid reaches 0.8 to 1.0 per cent of the milk; and then they greatly diminish or cease their activity, because they cannot thrive in a solution showing this amount of acidity. Their activity is thus stopped by the accumulation of the chief product of their own activity, and not because the supply of milk-sugar runs out; for, when their activity ceases, about three-quarters of the milk-sugar remains still unconsumed. Products besides lactic acid are formed, varying according to temperature and other conditions. In recent work at the New York experiment station, we have obtained, in the form of lactic acid, about 80 per cent of the milk-sugar that was decomposed. In connection with cheese-making, the total acidity of the whey may rise as high as 1.2 per cent. Under conditions, which are not present in cheddar cheese-making, some micro-organisms may produce as much as 3 per cent of lactic acid, decomposing a corresponding amount of milk-sugar.

The range of temperature most favorable to lactic acid organisms is 90° to 95° F. Below 80° F. their activity gradually decreases and practically ceases at 50° F. At 105° F., they are fairly inactive; many are killed at 135° to 140° F., and all at 150° to 160° F.

While the lactic acid fermentation spoils milk for the taste of most people, at least for ordinary uses, it is a very essential factor in the manufacture of cheese. Very few lactic acid bacteria are found in fresh milk, but they increase so rapidly at ordinary temperature (70° F.) that in 12 to 18 hours they generally exceed in number all other bacteria in milk. In summer weather, when the temperature is especially favorable to their rapid growth, the lactic acid bacteria usually constitute, at the time the milk sours, more than 95 per cent of all the micro-organisms in the milk.

While the growth of lactic acid organisms in milk is favored by the presence of a small amount of acid, most other organisms do not thrive so well in an acid environment. Therefore, as soon as enough milk-sugar has been converted into lactic acid to produce a slightly acid condition, other organisms decrease in activity, while the lactic acid organisms vigorously increase, unhindered. It is quite commonly thought that milk is peculiarly liable to sour during thunderstorms, as the result of some peculiar electrical condition or other mysterious influence. The hot weather preceding such storms favors the more rapid growth of the lactic acid bacteria and this is a sufficient explanation, and the proper one. Milk free from such micro-organisms never sours during thunderstorms.

The lactic acid fermentation we have been considering is what we may call the normal form, the particular form we desire to have present in milk in cheese-making. Their presence is insured by the use of good starters (p. 18). Milk in which this form of lactic fermentation has occurred produces, in souring, a firm curd free from gas bubbles and with only a little whey on the surface. When agitated, the curd breaks apart readily into small particles, which settle slowly and leave a clear whey. The milk should have a pleasant, clean, acid taste, entirely free from anything resembling a tainted flavor. So far as we know, the lactic acid bacteria belonging to this normal group never form products of a poisonous character.

GAS-PRODUCING BACTERIA

Some of the bacteria that decompose milk-sugar with formation of lactic acid are usually grouped with the lactic acid bacteria, though they possess distinguishing characteristics which mark them as abnormal, so far as their behavior in cheese-making is concerned. While they decompose milk-sugar and produce lactic acid, they produce other products besides, especially gases; they may also produce volatile products that are offensive. These bacteria are responsible for many of the defects in cheese (pp. 116-130). When gas-producing ferments are present in milk, they are usually responsible for increased losses of fat in the cheese-making process.

DIGESTING BACTERIA

A large group of bacteria curdle milk without souring it and then slowly digest or dissolve the curd;

therefore, they are often called "liquefiers." These effects are due to enzyms which are produced by the bacteria. Some of these bacteria form products that are offensive in flavor; some produce gases, and some, acid. They may be a source of serious trouble in cheese-making in the production of gassy curd and offensive flavors in cheese. They may also cause some dissolving of the curd, in which case the loss of fat is unusually large. These bacteria are widely distributed, being found in stable filth, in soil, water and floating dust. They are nearly always present to some extent in milk. Fortunately, their activity is checked by the presence of lactic acid, and the easiest method of controlling such ferments in cheese-making is to make conditions favorable for the rapid growth of normal lactic acid bacteria; this is usually accomplished by the use of a pure starter. The growth of digesting bacteria in milk is favored by high temperature; consequently, in hot weather, when the high temperature favors the growth of the digesting bacteria more than it does the lactic acid organisms, the undesirable forms get beyond control and seriously impair the operations and results of cheese-making.

BACTERIA PRODUCING UNDESIRABLE FLAVORS

Different bacteria are responsible for many different kinds of bad flavors in milk and cheese, among which are the following: Bitter (p. 119), fishy, rancid or butyric acid, hydrogen sulphid (p. 116).

YEASTS

Yeasts are micro-organisms resembling bacteria in some respects, but usually larger. They are very widely distributed and are common in milk. The conditions usually present in milk are not favorable to their growth and they are not, therefore, the source of trouble so often as are bacteria. Among the effects which can be attributed to the action of different yeasts are the formation of bitter and of fruity flavors (pp. 118, 126).

MILK-ENZYMS

Milk contains several different enzyms. Some of them, at least, are of bacterial origin. It would take us too far from the purpose of this discussion to go into details relating to milk-enzyms. We shall confine our attention to the one known as *galactase*. In 1897, Babcock and Russell announced the discovery of an unorganized ferment or enzym in milk to which they gave the name of galactase. They were led to this discovery by observing that fresh milk coagulates, even when obtained as free as possible from bacteria, and when all bacterial activity has been stopped by treatment with ether or chloroform. The milk first coagulates and then the curd gradually dissolves. Having excluded the seeming possibility of bacterial action in the milk after it was drawn, they concluded that the observed coagulating and dissolving action must be due to enzym action, probably two different enzyms. Galactase is probably a mixture of two or more different enzyms, since it has been shown that separator-slime, when treated according to Babcock and Russell's method in preparing galactase contains at least three distinct enzyms, galactase proper, peroxidase and catalase. The distinctive feature of the action of galactase is its power to change insoluble proteins like milk-casein into soluble forms.

The following have been given as some of the more prominent characteristics of galactase. (1) Galactase readily attaches itself to finely divided particles in suspension like milk-casein and fat-globules; hence, it is found in separator-slime and in cream to a greater extent than in milk or skim-milk. (2) The most favorable temperature for the action of galactase lies between 98° and 108° F. Heated for ten minutes above 168° F., its activity is destroyed, as shown by the following table:

EFFECT OF HEAT ON GALACTASE IN MILK

Temperature used in heating milks	Age of milks when analyzed	Soluble nitrogen expressed in percentage of nitrogen in milk
Degrees	Months	Per cent
90°C.(194°F.)	13	4.26
85°C.(185°F.)	8	10.8
85°C.(185°F.)	7	9.7
95°C.(203°F.)	15	5.52
95°C.(203°F.)	16	5.5
98°C.(208°F.)	14	11.5

(3) Free acids, especially hydrochloric acid, retard the activity of galactase. Neutral or alkaline reactions favor its action. (4) Many disinfectants, like mercuric chlorid, carbolic acid, formaldehyd, carbon disulphid, etc., retard or prevent the action of galactase. (5) Its activity is greater in the early stage of working, as measured by the rapidity with which casein is changed into soluble compounds.

As a result of their work, Babcock and Russell concluded that galactase is a trypsin-like ferment, except that one of its most distinctive characteristics is its ability to form, among other products, ammonia, and that, therefore, galactase plays a principal role in cheese-ripening. Their galactase work has been confirmed to the extent that there is in milk some enzym that causes more or less decomposition of milk-casein and of cheese paracasein in the presence of chloroform or ether. In work done at the New York experiment station, the ability of galactase to form ammonia was not confirmed either in case of milk or cheese. Cheese kept in an atmosphere of chloroform produced no ammonia or, at most, only slight traces even at the end of 15 to 24 months. Samples of the cheese were sent to the Wisconsin experiment station, and the absence of ammonia was there confirmed. The view previously held to the effect that galactase was able to account for most of the changes in cheese-ripening was then modified.

RENNET-ENZYMS

Rennet-extract contains one or two unorganized ferments or enzyms. There has long been a difference of opinion as to whether there is in rennet-extract one enzym which acts in two different ways or two different enzyms, each with its own characteristic action. So far as the essential facts are concerned, rennet-extracts possess the power of effecting two distinct kinds of changes: (1) coagulation of milk-casein and (2) dissolving or digesting the milk-casein coagulum. Those who regard these two actions as due to two different enzyms contained in rennet call the coagulating enzym *rennin* or *chymosin,* and the dissolving-enzym, *pepsin*. The best evidence at hand at present rather favors the existence of two enzyms. For our purpose, it is immaterial whether there is one enzym or more. Our chief interest in rennet, in connection with the cheese-making process, lies in its characteristic property of coagulating milk-casein. Whether the dissolving action of rennet-enzym plays any part in the operation of cheese-making, we do not know at present. We do know, however, that it has some action in the cheese-ripening process (p. 362).

Source of rennet-enzym.—The rennet-extract used in cheese-making is a dilute and impure form of rennet-enzym. The usual source of rennet-extract is the fourth stomach of a suckling calf. It is also prepared in more concentrated condition in the form of powders and of tablets. Enzyms having the same action as that of rennet are found also in plants and in other animals than calves. Some bacteria produce a coagulating enzym like that in rennet.

Home-made rennet-extract.—Formerly, cheese-makers purchased rennets from farmers and prepared the extract from time to time as needed. The stomach of a freshly slaughtered calf was cleaned, salted and dried by farmers and sold to the cheese-maker. In preparing the home-made extract, a number of rennets are cut in pieces and just covered with salt brine in a suitable vessel, about 3 or 4 pounds of salt being added to 100 pounds of water. The mixture is vigorously stirred and pounded. Once a week the rennets are removed from the brine and passed through a press or clothes-wringer and then placed in the brine again. It requires about four weeks to complete the extraction. The solution thus obtained is filtered through clean straw, sand, and charcoal and then treated with enough salt to prevent decomposition; a brine containing 6 or 7 pounds of salt to 100 pounds of solution is about the proper strength. Rennet-extract properly prepared is dark in color, but clear. The appearance of turbidity in the extract is an indication of the beginning of decomposition. It must be kept in a cool, dark place. In some cases, whey was once used as a medium for preparing rennet-extract, a practice that would insure a large number of objectionable micro-organisms in the extract. It can readily be seen how home-made rennet-extract may be a source of serious bacterial contamination in milk. The preparation of home-made extracts is, fortunately, much less common now. The serious objections to their use are (1) liability to bacterial contamination and (2) variation in strength of different lots, usually requiring the use of quite variable amounts of one preparation as compared with another.

Commercial rennet-extract.—The general substitution of commercial for home-made rennet-extracts is of distinct advantage in cheese-making, because the commercial forms are much more uniform in strength and less liable to bacterial contamination. Commercial rennet-extracts contain about 16 per cent of salt and a trace of boric acid. Some have expressed the fear that the boric acid used as a preservative in rennet-extract might injure the value of cheese as a pure food. There need be absolutely no alarm felt, when we consider the small amount of rennet-extract used in cheese-making and the very small proportion of this that goes into cheese. In fact, the amount of boric acid introduced into cheese through the rennet-extract is too small to identify by delicate chemical tests. Commercial rennet-extracts vary in strength and new lots always need testing before being used (p. 430).

Strength of rennet-enzym in coagulating milk-casein.—How powerful the action of rennet-enzym is in coagulating milk-casein can be seen in cheese-making, where we use only about one part of rennet-extract for 4,000 or 5,000 parts of milk, and it must be kept in mind that rennet-extract is only a dilute form of the rennet-enzym. It has been estimated that one part of pure rennet-enzym can coagulate three million parts of milk. Apparently, rennet-extract does not exhaust itself by its own action, a general characteristic of enzyms, but can be repeatedly used; at least this is theoretically true. For example, if we could recover from whey and curd the rennet used in coagulating milk, it would coagulate an equal quantity again. As stated already, one of the most characteristic properties of an enzym is that it can produce very powerful effects without itself being affected in any way.

Explanation of the coagulating action of rennet-enzym.—A large amount of effort has been devoted to the study of the coagulating effect of rennet-enzym in order to ascertain just what the rennet does to the milk-casein to make it coagulate. Many different explanations have been offered, but in the present state of our knowledge it is impossible to give an explanation of the process that can be regarded as satisfactory and conclusive. The most we can do here to advantage is to present the details of the process, so far as they appear to be worked out. The rennet coagulation of milk-casein is believed to take place in three quite distinct stages or phases, as follows: (1) Change of casein into paracasein; (2) change of the calcium salts of the milk into soluble form; and (3) precipitation of uncoagulated paracasein by the soluble calcium salts.

(1) *First stage of rennet action; change of casein into paracasein.*—The change of casein into paracasein is wholly dependent on the action of rennet-enzym. There is no change visible to the eye, neither increase of consistency (viscosity) nor any apparent coagulation. In the absence of soluble calcium salts, the paracasein that has been formed remains in this uncoagulated condition. The action in this stage of the process takes place as well in the cold as at higher temperatures. What evidence have we that casein is changed into paracasein before coagulation takes place? This is shown experimentally as follows: To a solution containing some salt of casein, free from soluble calcium salts, we add rennet-extract. No coagulation takes place. This solution is heated high enough to destroy the power of the rennet to act and then cooled, after which calcium chlorid or some other soluble calcium salt is added, when coagulation appears at once. It may be stated here that one of the most characteristic differences between milk-casein and paracasein is that soluble calcium salts do not coagulate milk-casein at ordinary temperatures, but they do cause coagulation of paracasein. In the foregoing experiment, rennet does something to the casein compound which causes the casein to do what it could not do before, that is, coagulate at ordinary temperatures by addition of soluble calcium salts, even

when the rennet-enzym itself had been removed from the field of action.

(2) *Second stage of rennet action; change in calcium salts of milk.*—In the second stage of rennet action, it is believed that the rennet-enzym acts upon the insoluble calcium salts of the milk, converting them into a form sufficiently soluble to enable them to coagulate the paracasein. This action appears to take place more slowly than does the conversion of casein into paracasein. This accounts for the period of time that elapses between addition of rennet and coagulation; this time can be shortened by addition of soluble calcium salts.

(3) *Third stage of rennet action; precipitation of uncoagulated paracasein.*—During this period, increased viscosity (thickening) and visible coagulation take place. This change, it is generally agreed, is caused by the action, either physical or chemical, of soluble calcium salts upon the uncoagulated paracasein formed during the first stage of the process. After the second stage is completed or nearly so, coagulation commences and proceeds rapidly. The paracasein coagulum (curd) formed in milk always contains insoluble calcium phosphate, which is probably held in a purely mechanical way, although some believe that it is in combination with paracasein.

What is the evidence leading us to believe that a soluble calcium salt is necessary for the coagulation of milk-casein? Two lines of experimental evidence have been furnished. (1st) If we prepare a pure solution of neutral calcium casein or sodium casein, containing no soluble calcium salts, rennet-extract will not coagulate such a solution, but, after the addition of some soluble calcium salt, as calcium chlorid, coagulation takes place promptly. (2nd) Milk from which the soluble calcium salts have been removed by precipitation with ammonium oxalate or by dialysis is not coagulated by rennet-enzym until a soluble calcium salt is added. We may, therefore, summarize as follows what appears to be fairly well established in explanation of the coagulating action of rennet: (1) That milk-casein is the only substance in milk involved in the rennet coagulation, excepting phosphates of calcium and other soluble salts of calcium. (2) That in rennet coagulation, no change of reaction or acidity occurs; the milk becomes neither acid nor alkaline through rennet action. (3) That the two active agents in the rennet coagulation of milk are rennet-enzym and soluble calcium salts.

Relation of casein and paracasein.—In the foregoing discussion of the process of rennet coagulation, there is nothing to indicate just what happens to milk-casein in being changed into paracasein, or, in other words, just how paracasein really differs from milk-casein. It must be confessed that we do not know at all clearly, although there are many suggestions. We know only this with certainty, that milk-casein does not readily coagulate in the presence of dilute calcium salts at ordinary temperatures, but paracasein does. Otherwise the general properties of casein and paracasein are very similar. Some hold that the difference is purely physical, the paracasein consisting of larger particles than the casein. While the ultramicroscopic study (p. 143) of rennet coagulation enabled the observers to see the minute particles of casein come together and form larger aggregations under the action of rennet, this does not show whether this physical change was accompanied by any chemical change in the milk-casein.

Dissolving or digesting action of rennet-enzym.—Rennet-extract has the power of dissolving paracasein, this peptic action being slow but continuing for a long time in cheese. Whether one enzym does both the coagulating and the digesting, or whether there are two specific enzyms (rennin and pepsin), each performing its special kind of work, is not fully settled, but, as already stated, the results of most recent investigations point to two distinct enzyms.

Conditions of action of rennet-enzym.—The conditions under which rennet-enzym coagulates milk-casein have been extensively studied and we will now consider some of the more important ones. The rapidity and completeness of coagulation of milk-casein by rennet-enzym are dependent upon the following conditions:

(1) *The presence of soluble calcium salts* appears to be necessary for the coagulation of milk-casein by rennet-enzym. This has been discussed already.

(2) *Effect of acids.*—Milk must be neutral or acid in reaction in order to be coagulated by rennet-enzym. Free acids or acid salts favor the action. All acids, whether organic or inorganic, show very marked effect upon the coagulation, though they differ from one another in respect to the extent of influence which they exert on rennet action. The more acid there is in the milk, up to a certain limit, the more quickly does coagulation by rennet-enzym take place. Milk sour enough to curdle is not coagulated by rennet; similarly, sour buttermilk is not coagulated. The following table shows the results of some work done at the

New York experiment station on this subject. The experiments were made by treating 350 cubic centimeters of fresh milk at 84° F. with 1.0 cubic centimeter of rennet solution, made by dissolving one of Hansen's rennet-tablets in 150 cubic centimeters of distilled water.

Acids used	Original milk coagulated in seconds	Strength of acid used				
		0.01 per cent	0.02 per cent	0.03 per cent	0.04 per cent	0.05 per cent
		Time of coagulation in seconds				
Acetic........	110	70	45	35	25	20
Sulphuric.....	105	70	50	30	25	20
Citric.........	105	80	60	45	40	35
Lactic........	110	80	65	45	35	30
Hydrochloric .	105	85	70	60	50	45
Phosphoric ..	135	110	90	80	75	60

This effect of acids upon rennet action is commonly explained by saying that the added acid dissolves the insoluble calcium phosphates of milk and thus increases the amount of soluble calcium salts. It is known that even carbon dioxid gas favors rennet coagulation, due to its dissolving action on insoluble calcium salts in milk.

(3) *Dilution* of milk by water both delays rennet action and renders coagulation less complete, because the proportion of soluble calcium salts is decreased. Addition of calcium chlorid or free acid to milk thus diluted not only hastens the time of coagulation, but makes more complete the amount of milk-casein coagulated. Apparently, milk may be diluted more than 10 per cent with water before the time of rennet

coagulation is greatly affected. The effect of water is illustrated in the following table:

Cubic centimeters of milk	Cubic centimeters of water added to milk	Percentage of added water in watered milk	Cubic centimeters of rennet solution used	Time of coagulation
				Minutes-Seconds
175	175	50	0.5	5 — 20
175	175	50	1.0	3 — 20
280	70	20	1.0	2 — 00
315	35	10	1.0	1 — 50
332½	17½	5	1.0	1 — 45
350	0	0	1.0	1 — 30

(4) *Different chemical compounds and metals* affect the rennet coagulation of milk in different ways. Acid salts, in general, like free acids, favor rapidity of coagulation. Alkalis and alkaline salts retard it. The following substances, if present in certain amounts, retard rennet coagulation of milk-casein: Sodium chlorid (common salt), sodium acetate, borax, chloroform, formalin and some other sub-

Compound used	Original milk	Strength of Compound Used					
		0.01 per cent	0.05 per cent	0.10 per cent	0.5 per cent	1.0 per cent	2.0 per cent
		Number of seconds required to coagulate milk					
Sodium chlorid	110	—	—	—	115	120	160
Sodium nitrate	—	—	—	—	—	150	225
Sodium bicarbonate......	115	115	170	265	—	—	—
Sodium acetate	115	120	180	280	—	—	—
Borax.........	100	120	270	600	—	—	—
Boracic acid...	100	100	100	90	—	—	—
Ammonium chlorid......	135	140	130	130	—	—	—
Ammonium carbonate...	135	150	195	300	—	—	—
Lime-water ...	—	—	—	—	(10cc.) 150	(20cc.) 165	(30cc.) 210

stances, which are used in milk as preservatives. The foregoing table shows the results of some work done at the New York experiment station on this point.

It has been shown at the Wisconsin experiment station that some metals exert a retarding effect on the coagulating action of rennet. As a practical application, it is pointed out that in rusty milk-cans enough iron may be dissolved by milk that is at all acid to interfere with the rennet coagulation.

(5) *Finely divided, inert matter,* like ˙starch or sawdust, added to milk, hastens the coagulation by rennet.

(6) *The temperature of the milk* affects (1) the time of coagulation, and (2) the character of the curd.

(a) For complete coagulation, the time decreases when the temperature increases.

Temperature, F..............	75°	80°	85°	90°	95°
Time, seconds..............	270	140	110	80	65

Stated in another way, the coagulation in a given time is most complete at 106° to 108° F. and less complete at temperatures above and below these limits. Fleischmann gives the following figures, indicating the proportion of milk-casein coagulated in the same period of time required to effect complete coagulation at 106° to 108° F.

Temperature	Proportion of milk-casein coagulated
68°	18 per cent
77°	44 per cent
86°	71 per cent
95°	86 per ecnt
104°	98 per cent
106°	100 per cent
113°	89 per cent
122°	50 per cent

(b) The character of the coagulation is affected by the temperature at which the rennet-enzym acts. Thus, at 60° F., the curd is flocculent, spongy and soft; at 77° to 113° F., it is more or less firm and solid; at 122° and above, it is very soft, loose and inclined to be gelatinous.

(c) Milk heated above 150° F. for a considerable length of time coagulates less rapidly than normal milk. The coagulum of such heated milk is highly flocculent, never a firm and solid mass, in the absence of soluble calcium salts or acids. Boiled milk fails to coagulate normally, if at all, by rennet-enzym, unless treated with some soluble calcium salt or some acid. The degree of heat used decreases the amount of soluble calcium salts in milk and also drives out any carbon dioxid present.

(7) *Exposure to sunlight* weakens the coagulating power of rennet-extract.

(8) *Solutions of rennet-extract are affected by heat.*—Rennet-extract heated for some time above 140° F. becomes permanently weaker, or inactive. Rennet-enzym begins to suffer injury at about 120° F. Weak solutions are injuriously affected at temperatures as low as 105° F. Strong solutions are weakened by heating at 150° F. for 15 minutes, but are not entirely destroyed. High temperatures destroy the activity of rennet-enzym gradually, not instantaneously.

(9) *Increase in amount of rennet-extract* or in strength of rennet-enzym hastens coagulating effect on milk.

(10) *Milk, freshly drawn,* curdles more completely than when allowed to cool, due to lowering of temperature and, perhaps, to the presence of more

carbon dioxid. In freshly drawn milk, the proportion of casein coagulated decreases until the temperature of the surrounding air is reached, when it becomes stationary, until the formation of lactic acid causes increase in activity of rennet-enzym. When fresh milk fails to coagulate with rennet-extract, it is probably slightly alkaline or contains no soluble calcium salts; that is, it is abnormal.

(11) *Different milks behave differently* toward rennet-enzym. This is true not only of milk from different cows, but also of milk from the same cow at different times. The following results of work done at the New York experiment station illustrate this statement:

	Time of coagulation and date of testing							
Number of cow	July 9	July 16	July 21	Aug. 10	Aug. 21	Sept. 15	Sept.25	Oct. 30
	M.—S.	M.—S.	M.—S.	M.—S.	M.—S.	M.—S.	M.—S.	M.—S.
1	6—15	5—00	5—20	4—20	6—45	8—30	7—00	6—00
2	3—45	3—45	3—45	4—20	3—40	3—30	5—00	4—15
3	2—15	2—50	2—50	3—00	2—45	2—00	2—00	2—00
4	2—50	2—50	2—30	2—25	1—50	3—30	.....	.....
5	2—10	2—15	2—05	2—05	2—00	1—25	2—00	2—30
6	2—00	2—00	2—05	2—05	2—50	2—45	2—40	2—15
7	2—05	1—55	2—00	2—05	1—55	1—50	1—55	1—40[2]
8	2—00	1—50	2—10	2—30	4—00[1]	.....	.....	3—10
9	4—15	4—20	3—00	2—40	3—30	3—00	3—45	2—00
10	1—35	1—50	2—10	1—45	1—25	1—40	1—45	.....
11	1—35	1—35	1—35	1—35	1—35	1—35	1—40	.....
12	2—10	2—00	2—20	1—50	1—55	1—45	2—30	.....
13	1—05	1—10	1—10	1—10	1—05	1—05	1—10	.....
14	23—00	16—20	10—00	10—00	29—00	4—45	50—00	7—00
15	0—50	0—45	0—50	0—45	1—00	0—50	0—40	0—45
16	2—05	2—30	2—00	1—55	3—00	3—00	3—10	.....
17	1—55	1—45	1—55	2—05	1—40	1—35	1—40	1—30

[1]Close of lactation period.　　[2]Fresh in milk.

These results show that in the individual milkings of these 17 cows the time of rennet coagulation of fresh milk varied from 40 seconds to 50 minutes. In the case of one individual (No. 14), the variations were from 4 minutes and 45 seconds to 50 minutes. A study of the ordinary composition of the milk gave no clue to the cause of such differences. The specific causes are not yet understood, but are probably related to the calcium salts in milk and their solubility.

PEPSIN-ENZYM

The chief enzym of the gastric juice in the stomach of man is known as pepsin. The same enzym is also present in the stomach of many animals. A preparation made from the stomachs of sheep is on the market, which may be successfully used as a substitute for rennet-extract in cheese-making. This has the property of both coagulating and digesting milk-casein. The pepsin most experimented with has been the scale pepsin of Armour & Co. This pepsin does not coagulate very sweet milk as readily as rennet-extract, but in milk having an acidity of 0.20 per cent, it acts just as well, when used in the proportion of 5 grams for 1,000 pounds of milk. The pepsin is dissolved in any convenient amount of water before addition to milk. The solution should be prepared fresh for each day's use. The complete identity of rennet-enzym and pepsin is not fully settled. Assuming that the coagulating effect of these preparations is due to one enzym (rennin) and the digesting effect to another (pepsin), the various preparations differ in respect to the amounts of these two enzyms which they contain. Rennet-extracts contain more rennin and less pepsin, while the commercial preparations made from the stomachs of pigs and sheep appear to contain more pepsin and less rennin.

CHAPTER XXIII

The Ripening of Cheese

It is well known that cheddar cheese must have age before it is edible. When taken from the press, cheese is said to be unripe, green, or uncured. At this time, it has no real cheese flavor, and little flavor of any kind. Its body is very firm, somewhat tough, rather elastic, and rubber-like. Its proteins are only slightly soluble in water. It is not palatable and requires much mastication before it can be swallowed comfortably. Green cheese gradually undergoes very marked changes in the course of some weeks or months, the time required depending upon a variety of conditions. The cheese finally becomes mellow in body and acquires richness of taste and a characteristic delicacy of flavor. It is highly palatable and, when a piece is held on the tongue a short time, the cheese dissolves, giving a sensation of smoothness and richness. The casein-derived proteins, which are insoluble as found in the curd and green cheese, become soluble to a large extent. The process, by which the qualities of the newly made cheese are so profoundly changed and as a result of which the product becomes edible, is known as *ripening* or, less aptly, as curing.

For a long time the importance of caring for cheese after it leaves the press was not appreciated, and not until within about 15 years has much attention been given to methods of cheese-ripening in this country. The rule has been and still is, in too many cases, to place the cheese in some room in the factory where are provided no means of controlling temperature and moisture and where the variations in these factors closely follow, up and down, the conditions existing out of doors. It has come to be realized that a cheese, perfect when it leaves the press, may easily be ruined for market by lack of care during the ripening process. It is appreciated now more than ever before that the ripening of cheese is a part of the manufacturing process, that it is the real finishing of the product, and must not be slighted any more than any other important step.

CHANGES RESULTING FROM RIPENING PROCESS

Several different changes take place in cheese during the ripening period. These may be divided into two general classes, (1) loss of weight and (2) chemical changes in the cheese constituents. We shall now take up for consideration a somewhat detailed study of (1) the extent to which these changes take place, (2) the various conditions under which they occur, (3) their relations to the character of the cheese and (4) the commercial relations of cheese-ripening.

LOSS OF WEIGHT IN CHEESE-RIPENING

The loss of weight in the cheese-ripening process, when the conditions are normal, may be regarded for practical purposes as being due entirely to the evaporation of water from the cheese. Of course, there is some mechanical loss of fat by exudation ("leaking") from cheese kept at high temperatures, but such conditions are abnormal. The small amount of loss due to the formation and escape of carbon dioxid (p. 334) and other gases can be neglected for practical purposes.

CONDITIONS AFFECTING LOSS OF WATER IN CHEESE-RIPENING

The rapidity and extent of loss of moisture in cheese during the process of ripening vary with several conditions, chief of which are the following: (1) The temperature of the room, (2) the proportion of water-vapor present in the air of the room, (3) protection of surface of cheese, (4) size and shape of the cheese, (5) the percentage of moisture originally present in the cheese, and (6) the texture of the cheese. The data used in illustrating these points are taken largely from the results of investigations carried on at the New York experiment station.

Temperature and loss of weight.—We present, first, data showing the influence of temperature upon the loss of moisture at six different temperatures, viz: 55°, 60°, 65°, 70°, 75° and 80° F.

The cheeses used in furnishing data in the table on page 316 were 15 inches in diameter and weighed about 65 pounds, the usual standard size of the most common type of American cheddar cheese intended for export trade.

These results show an increase in loss of weight with increase of temperature. As between 55° and 80° F., the loss increased on an average 1 ounce per 100 pounds of cheese for each additional degree of temperature during the first 4 weeks; 2 ounces per 100 pounds of cheese for each degree during the first 2 months; and 3½ ounces at the end of 3 months.

LOSS OF MOISTURE AT DIFFERENT TEMPERATURES

Temperature of curing-room	Water lost by 100 pounds of green cheese in									
	1 wk.	2 wks.	3 wks.	4 wks.	8 wks.	12 wks.	16 wks.	20 wks.	24 wks.	28 wks.
Degrees F.	Lbs.	Lbs.	Lbs.	Lbs.	Lbs.	Lbs.	Lbs.	Lbs.	Lbs.	Lbs.
55	1.6	2.6	3.2	3.7	5.2	6.1	6.8	7.5	8.1	8.6
60	1.7	2.8	3.4	3.9	5.5	6.5	7.5	8.5	9.3	9.9
65	1.9	3.0	3.6	4.1	5.8	7.0	8.2	9.2	10.1	10.5
70	2.0	3.1	3.7	4.3	6.0	7.8	9.0	10.1	11.1	12.0
75	2.2	3.3	4.0	4.7	7.2	9.7	11.4	——	——	——
80	2.4	3.7	4.5	5.2	8.3	11.6	15.5	——	——	——

The average weekly loss of weight increases with increase of temperature. In the following table, it is seen that the loss is greater the first week than in any succeeding week. The loss usually decreases gradually as the cheese grows older; but cheese kept at a temperature of 75° F. and above does not follow this general rule, since at the higher temperatures there is apt to be an increase of loss of weight due to leakage of fat after the first month. This is shown in the table below:

AVERAGE WEEKLY LOSS AT DIFFERENT TEMPERATURES

Temperature of curing-room	Average loss per week. Water lost by 100 pounds of green cheese.									lbs. total loss for six months
	1st wk.	2d wk.	3d wk.	4th wk.	2d mo.	3d mo.	4th mo.	5th mo.	6th mo.	
Deg. F.	Ozs.	Ozs.	Ozs.	Ozs.	Ozs.	Ozs.	Ozs.	Ozs.	Ozs.	Lbs.
55	25.6	16.0	9.6	8.0	6.0	3.6	2.8	2.8	2.4	8.1
60	27.2	17.6	9.6	8.0	6.4	4.0	4.0	4.0	3.2	9.3
65	30.4	17.6	9.6	8.0	6.8	4.8	4.8	4.0	3.6	10.1
70	32.0	17.6	9.6	9.6	6.8	4.8	4.8	4.4	4.0	11.1
75	35.2	17.6	10.2	10.2	10.0	10.0	6.8	——	——	——
80	38.4	20.8	12.8	10.2	12.4	13.2	15.6	——	——	——

The comparatively rapid loss of moisture during the early stage of ripening is due to the fact that the cheese contains its highest amount of moisture when new. In addition, the bandage is practically saturated with water, which quickly evaporates. Then, again, the outer surface of the cheese, in drying, begins to harden, the meshes of the cheese-cloth filling to some extent with dried matter, and this condition tends constantly more and more to diminish evaporation, provided cracking is prevented.

Moisture in air of curing-room and loss of weight.—The relative amount of moisture in air or, more properly, the degree of saturation, exercises a marked influence upon loss of water in cheese-ripening. To illustrate this influence, we give results of an experiment in which two cheeses made from the same milk were kept at 60° F. One cheese was kept on a shelf in the ordinary manner, the air of the room containing from 75 to 80 per cent of all the moisture it could hold at 60° F. The other cheese

LOSS OF MOISTURE IN CHEESE KEPT IN AIR COMPLETELY AND PARTIALLY SATURATED WITH MOISTURE

Age of cheese	In air partially saturated		In air completely saturated with moisture	
	Moisture in cheese	Water lost by 100 pounds of cheese	Moisture in cheese	Water gained by 100 pounds of cheese
	Per cent	Pounds	Per cent	Pounds
2 weeks....	35.99	———	35.93	———
1 month...	35.23	0.76	35.87	———
2 months..	34.86	1.13	36.01	0.08
6 months..	31.87	4.12	37.04	0.11
12 months..	26.30	9.69	37.63	1.70
15 months:.	24.85	11.14	37.85	1.92

was placed under a bell-jar and kept in an atmosphere completely saturated with moisture. The results secured by this treatment are presented in the table on the preceding page.

The results of this experiment are quite striking. In the cheese kept in air incompletely saturated with moisture, there was a steady loss, so that the cheese which contained 36 per cent of moisture at the start had its moisture content decreased to less than 25 per cent. On the other hand, the cheese kept in a saturated atmosphere not only lost no moisture, but actually gained water by absorption, so that its percentage of water was increased from about 36 per cent at the beginning to nearly 38 per cent at the close of the experiment. The two cheeses, which contained the same percentage of moisture at the beginning, were found to differ, at the end of 15 months, 13 per cent in moisture, solely as the result of being kept in air containing different degrees of moisture.

The same fact is well illustrated in experiments made at the Wisconsin experiment station. A comparison was made of the relative humidity of the air in a curing-room with that inside a closed cheese-box, in which a cheese was kept.

	Temperature	Relative humidity in room	Relative humidity inside cheese-box
		Per cent	Per cent
Room 1........	35°-40° F.	85-92	100
Room 2........	50°-55° F.	55-75	94
Room 3........	60°-69° F.	50-70	84-90

These results indicate that the storage of cheese in boxes in curing-rooms is one means of avoiding the results of too rapid loss of moisture. Of course, difficulty arises in the way of molds in the case of cheese so stored, unless they are properly fumigated (p. 134) or covered with paraffin, a point which will be considered next.

Protection of surface of cheese and loss of weight.—The covering of the outer surface of cheese with a layer of paraffin has been found to diminish greatly the loss of weight. The first suggestion of the practical use of paraffin in connection with covering cheese came, so far as we know, from the Standard Oil Company about 10 or 12 years ago, when it advertised a preparation of yellow-colored paraffin for use in protecting cheese from mold. Some experiments were made at the Wisconsin experiment station in 1899 to prevent mold by the use of paraffin, but the results were not regarded as sufficiently satisfactory in every way to justify its recommendation for general use. In experimental work at the New York experiment station, cheese was covered with paraffin in order to control moisture, without any reference to the thought of practical application. The matter was later taken up in a practical way here and in Canada. The results of co-operative work between the United States Department of Agriculture and the experiment stations of Wisconsin and New York, carried on in 1902-3, may be regarded as the first demonstration in the United States that attracted serious attention. Since then the practice has grown

rapidly, but the primary object is quite as much prevention of loss of weight as protection from mold.
The results of the work done at that time in New
York will suffice as a basis of discussion. Cheeses
weighing 70 pounds were used, some being covered
with paraffin, while others were left in the usual condition. The results are given as follows:

Cheese	Age	Pounds lost for 100 pounds of cheese		
		Kept at 40°F.	Kept at 50°F.	Kept at 60°F.
	Weeks			
Normal................	17	2.5	2.4	4.2
Paraffined.............	17	0.3	0.5	1.4
Normal................	25	3.1	4.0	—
Paraffined.............	25	0.6	0.9	—
Normal................	32	4.5	—	—
Paraffined.............	32	0.9	—	—

By covering cheese with paraffin, a saving in loss
of moisture can be effected, amounting to 5 or 6
pounds per 100 pounds of cheese at 60° F.; while at
50° F., and below, the total loss of moisture can be
reduced to less than 1 pound per 100 pounds of cheese.
In every case, cheeses covered with paraffin were
entirely clean, while the others were more or less
heavily coated with molds. The saving effected by
paraffining small-sized cheeses is even greater than
with those of larger size.

**Size and shape of cheese in relation to loss of
weight.**—The amount of external surface is greater
in relation to weight in the case of a small cheese than
of a larger cheese, and we should, therefore, expect
a larger loss of moisture.

The following table illustrates the losses of weight in the case of cheeses 7 inches in diameter; this is the type commonly known as "Young America." They were made from one vat of milk and kept at 65° F.

WEIGHT LOST BY CHEESES OF VARYING HEIGHT AND UNIFORM DIAMETER

Height of cheese	Weight of green cheese	Water lost by 100 pounds of green cheese in								
		1 wk.	2 wks.	3 wks.	4 wks.	8 wks.	12 wks.	16 wks.	20 wks.	24 wks.
Inches	Pounds	Lbs.	Lbs.	Lbs.	Lbs.	Lbs.	Lbs.	Lbs.	Lbs.	Lbs.
3	4.6	3.4	5.3	6.4	7.0	10.7	12.9	13.9	15.9	17.0
4	6.1	3.3	5.1	6.1	6.7	9.7	11.5	13.0	14.0	15.6
5	7.9	2.8	4.2	5.5	6.3	8.3	9.8	11.2	12.6	13.4
6	9.3	2.5	3.9	5.2	6 0	7.8	9.4	10.6	11.6	12.8
7	11.0	2.3	3.4	4.7	5.6	7.4	8.9	10.5	11.2	12.4

The loss of weight decreases with increase in height. Taking the total loss of weight for different periods of time, it is seen that an increase of one inch in height reduced the loss of weight per 100 pounds of cheese 5 ounces at the end of 4 weeks, 13 ounces at 8 weeks, 16 ounces at 12 weeks and 18 ounces at 20 weeks.

In the table on the next page we show the loss of weight in the case of cheeses having different diameters and kept at temperatures ranging from 55° to 80° F. It is seen that, in general, the loss of weight increases at all temperatures as the diameter increases, the difference being greater at higher temperatures.

Variation of loss of moisture with different kinds of cheese.—In making small cheeses like "Young Americas," and smaller sizes (p. 44) the proportion of loss is much greater, and hence the demand

WEIGHT LOST BY CHEESES OF VARYING DIAMETER AND
UNIFORM HEIGHT

Diameter of cheese	Weight of green cheese	Temperature of curing-rooms	Water lost by 100 pounds of cheese							
			1 wk.	2 wks.	4 wks.	8 wks.	12 wks.	16 wks.	20 wks.	24 wks.
Inches	Lbs.	Deg.F.	Lbs.	Lbs.	Lbs.	Lbs.	Lbs.	Lbs.	Lbs.	Lbs.
15	65	80	2.4	3.7	5.2	8.3	11.6	15.5	...	...
7	9	80	3.6	5.2	7.3	10.9	12.7	14.5	16.3	17.1
15	65	75	2.2	3.3	4.7	7.2	9.7	11.4	...	...
7	9	75	3.1	4.8	6.6	9.2	11.1	12.7	14.1	15.1
15	65	70	2.0	3.1	4.3	6.0	7.8	9.0	10.1	11.1
11	23	70	3.0	4.2	6.1	7.7	9.2	10.6	11.6	12.4
7	9	70	2.9	4.5	6.2	8.9	10.9	12.2	13.9	14.6
15	65	65	1.9	3.0	4.1	5.8	7.0	8.2	9.2	10.1
13	31	65	2.0	3.4	5.1	6.2	7.7	8.7	9.3	10.2
11	22	65	2.6	3.7	5.3	6.9	8.1	9.5	10.4	11.3
7	9	65	2.5	3.9	5.6	7.9	9.5	10.9	12.1	13.1
15	65	60	1.7	2.8	3.9	5.5	6.5	7.5	8.5	9.3
13	31	60	1.7	2.7	4.3	6.1	7.3	8.4	9.5	...
11	22	60	1.9	3.6	4.5	6.3	7.5	8.7	9.6	10.5
7	9	60	2.4	3.7	5.5	7.7	9.3	10.6	11.9	12.8
15	65	55	1.6	2.6	3.7	5.2	6.1	6.8	7.5	8.1
13	29	55	1.5	2.7	4.2	5.7	7.2	7.9	8.9	9.4
11	20	55	2.1	3.6	4.6	6.4	7.4	8.8	9.4	10.1
7	9	55	2.2	3.6	5.1	7.2	8.8	9.8	11.0	12.0

is still more imperative that these shall be cured
under conditions where the loss of moisture shall
be greatly reduced. This applies also to such
sizes as "Flats" and "Twins." It is not surprising
that the manufacture of small cheeses of the cheddar type has been discouraged. Even at the
higher prices they bring, the extra loss of moisture
and additional cost of manufacture are not satisfactorily covered. In the manufacture of small, fancy
kinds of soft cheese, these statements do not apply,
because an essential part of the equipment consists of

curing-cellars of fairly low temperature and high moisture content.

Percentage of moisture in cheese and loss of weight.—Below are given results obtained with cheese made so as to contain water varying from 35 to 55 per cent when taken from press.

LOSS OF MOISTURE IN CHEESES CONTAINING DIFFERENT PERCENTAGES OF WATER

Water in 100 pounds of green cheese	Water lost by 100 pounds of green cheese			
	In 1 week	In 2 weeks	In 3 weeks	In 4 weeks
Pounds	Pounds	Pounds	Pounds	Pounds
55	9.0	11.2	12.3	16.8
50	5.5	9.2	11.0	12.9
45	4.5	6.3	8.0	9.5
35	3.3	4.2	4.9	5.7

These results show that the more moist a cheese is when made, the greater is the proportion of water lost by evaporation; and, hence, the moisture in the different cheeses tends to become more nearly alike than at the start. Thus, cheese containing 55 per cent of moisture lost about three times as much weight as did the cheese containing 35 per cent of water and nearly twice as much as the one with 45 per cent. Even when cheeses do not differ so widely in water content as those above, the same general rule holds good, other conditions, of course, being the same.

Pounds of water in 100 pounds of green cheese..	41.7	38.7	37.6	35.4
Pounds of water lost by 100 pounds of green cheese in 6 weeks......................	5.3	4.6	4.5	4.2

Texture of cheese and loss of moisture.—Cheese filled with holes will occupy more volume than the same weight of cheese free from holes. Hence, cheese with such faulty texture has a larger surface exposed for evaporation relative to its weight and will lose

RIPENED AT 40°F

RIPENED AT 60°F

FIG. 45—SECTIONS OF TWO CHEESES RIPENED AT DIFFERENT TEMPERATURES. CLOSE-TEXTURED, CHEDDAR TYPE

more moisture. Then, in addition, the presence of numerous holes in cheese greatly facilitates the escape of moisture from the interior of the cheese to the surface. This is a partial explanation of the fact that cheese high in moisture loses water more rapidly than cheese containing less moisture. It is well known that cheese containing high percentages of water usually develops holes abundantly, especially when cured at or above ordinary temperatures.

These statements are effectively illustrated in the experiments carried on at the Wisconsin experiment station; results are given for two distinct types of cheese, which were used in studying the effects of temperature during ripening: (1) Close-textured,

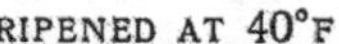

FIG. 46—SECTIONS OF TWO CHEESES RIPENED AT DIFFERENT TEMPERATURES. SWEET-CURD TYPE

firm-bodied, long-keeping type, suitable for export trade, typical Wisconsin cheddars. (2) Sweet-curd type, as represented by Iowa and Illinois methods of manufacture. In connection with the table below, study Figs. 45 and 46.

The following table gives the results in loss of moisture in the cases of these two types of cheese:

LOSS OF MOISTURE

Age when ex- amined	Type 1 (cheddar) 27 cheeses kept at 40°F.	Type 2 (sweet-curd) 9 cheeses kept at 40°F.	Type 1 (cheddar) 9 cheeses kept at 60°F.	Type 2 (sweet-curd) 5 cheeses kept at 60°F.
Days	Per cent	Per cent	Per cent	Per cent
10	0.38	0.69	0.96	1.05
20	0.44	0.82	1.74	1.77
30	0.58	0.96	2.05	2.29
60	0.83	1.15	2.95	3.67
90	1.00	1.42	3.57	4.47

CHAPTER XXIV

Chemical Changes in Cheese-Ripening

In studying the chemical changes which take place during the process of cheese-ripening, it will be an advantage to consider the subject under the following main lines of inquiry:

1. What chemical compounds are found in unripe cheese?

2. What chemical changes do the compounds of unripe cheese undergo as cheese ripens?

3. What conditions influence the character and extent of these chemical changes?

4. What causes the chemical changes of cheese-ripening?

The first three points will be considered in this chapter, the fourth being reserved for a separate chapter.

CHEMICAL COMPOUNDS IN UNRIPE CHEDDAR CHEESE

Starting with unripe cheese as it comes from the press, we find the same chemical compounds and groups of compounds mentioned in connection with the composition of milk, viz: (1) Water, (2) proteins, (3) fat, (4) sugar, (5) neutral and acid salts, (6) salt and (7) gases.

Water.—The functions, amounts and ripening losses of water in relation to cheese have already been considered.   We shall later consider its relation to the chemical changes in cheese-ripening.

Proteins.—In cheddar cheese fresh from press, there appear to be different protein compounds, the precise nature of which has not yet been determined.   There have been shown to be the following forms: (1) Protein soluble in warm (122°-131° F.), 5 per cent solution of sodium chlorid, which, for convenience, we shall speak of as brine-soluble protein, (2) protein insoluble in brine solution, and (3) proteins soluble in water.   The first constitutes the largest amount, often being 75 to 90 per cent of the total amount of proteins in cheddar cheese; the water-soluble protein is quite fairly constant, varying usually between 4 and 5 per cent of the total proteins, and a part of this is readily accounted for by the milk-albumin in the whey retained in the cheese.

Fat.—The fat present in unripe cheese is, in composition and physical condition, essentially milk-fat.

Milk-sugar.—The sugar in newly made cheese is simply milk-sugar in solution in the whey that is retained by the cheese.

Neutral salts and acid salts.—The most prominent neutral salt in unripe cheese is calcium lactate, formed as a result of the lactic acid (produced by the fermentation of milk-sugar) upon the insoluble calcium phosphate originally present in the milk, most of which is carried into the cheese-curd and held there.   The soluble acid salts present in largest amounts are calcium acid phosphate and, probably, citrate.

Salt.—The unripe cheese contains common salt which has been added to the curd in the operation of cheese-making.   This is held in solution, really constituting a weak brine containing about 3 per cent of salt.

Gases.—In normal, unripe cheese, gaseous products, except carbon dioxid, are present in only minute amounts, if at all.   In cheese made from milk containing abnormal micro-organisms, there may be present such gases as hydrogen, carbon dioxid, etc.

CHEMICAL CHANGES IN COMPOUNDS OF UNRIPE CHEESE

We will now take up each division of the compounds which we have considered briefly in the preceding section and notice some of the changes which they undergo.

Water.—So far as we know, the water in cheese undergoes no chemical change.   It gradually evaporates from the cheese in the form of water-vapor, the rate of evaporation varying with conditions studied in the preceding chapter.

Proteins.—Of all the compounds contained in unripe cheese, the proteins are the ones that are most extensively affected by the chemical changes of ripening, because these compounds are not only the seat of those changes but the material itself which undergoes chemical changes more profound and complex than any other constituent of the cheese.   There have been and still are many difficulties in carrying on a study of the chemical changes in cheese proteins during ripening, owing largely (1) to a lack of detailed knowledge of the compounds formed and (2) to need of more perfect methods for estimating the amounts of these compounds, many of which are formed only in very small quantities.

Beginning with the milk-casein in the cheese-vat at the time the rennet is added, we have, from that time on, a succession of changes in the curd and cheese, resulting sooner or later in the formation of a series of compounds, which, so far as our present knowledge goes, appears in something like the following consecutive order:

(1) Calcium paracasein (formed from the calcium casein of milk by action of rennet). Insoluble in water and in warm, 5 per cent salt-brine.

(2) Protein soluble in warm, 5 per cent salt-brine. (Figs. 30 and 31, p. 148.)

(3) Protein insoluble in salt-brine, water, etc.

(4) Proteins soluble in water:

(a) A protein which is precipitable by dilute hydrochloric acid, called *paranuclein*.

(b) A protein substance coagulated in neutral solution at the boiling point of water. This substance appears to occur only rarely, except in the case of cheese ripened near freezing point.

(c) *Proteoses* or *caseoses* (albumoses), which are proteins or protein derivatives soluble in water, not coagulated by heat, and usually precipitated by saturating their solutions with zinc sulphate or ammonium sulphate.

(d) *Peptones*, protein derivatives simpler than the proteoses, soluble in water, not coagulated by heat, and not precipitated by saturation with zinc sulphate or ammonium sulphate; precipitated by phosphotungstic acid, tannic acid and some other reagents.

(e) *Amino acids,* the simplest protein derivatives (except ammonia).

(f) *Ammonia.*

It would be beyond the scope of this book to go further into the details of the chemistry of these compounds, since they are very complex and require a special knowledge of organic chemistry to understand.

The amounts of these protein-derived products vary with many conditions, some of which will be considered later (p. 337).

Fat.—There have been numerous investigations made by different workers to ascertain whether the milk-fat in cheese decomposes during the ripening process. The general results of these investigations show that cheese-fat is unchanged milk-fat and that these glycerin-acid compounds (glycerids) (p. 140) do not share extensively in the ripening process, especially in the case of hard cheese, such as cheddar. In one case, it was found that from 1.0 to 7 per cent of the cheese-fat had undergone some decomposition, the higher amounts occurring in soft cheese. One of the early investigators (Blondeau) made several analyses of Roquefort cheese at various ages and reported that the proteins of the unripe cheese changed rapidly into fat. This statement, though frequently disproved later, has not even yet entirely disappeared from physiological literature. The conclusions were based upon

evident errors of analysis, which are readily apparent on careful examination. More recent work,
however, claims that some organisms can change
casein into fatty acids, while this is especially
denied by another investigator. So far as we now
know, the matter appears to be one mainly of
academic interest, since the change must be insignificant in amount, if it occurs at all. In all of
our extended work with cheese, we have found no
evidence of an increase of fat at the expense of
proteins. And no one has yet reported an accumulation of fat in a separator skim-milk cheese during
the ripening process, where the conditions surely
furnish enough protein material for such a trans-
formation.

There is, however, one interesting condition
under which some fat appears to be changed, and
that is in case of cheese cured at low temperatures,
when we should ordinarily least expect such
change. It has been observed that, in cheese cured
near the freezing point of water, small white specks
may appear. These have been noticed at both the
Wisconsin and New York experiment stations as
well as in Europe. They have been supposed by
some to be salts of the cheese crystallized out in
little white aggregations, due to the dryness of the
cheese and the low temperature. One investigator has reported the spots as due to the result of
bacterial action on the fat in cheese, some of which
was decomposed, the decomposed portions forming
the minute white spots. Recently some cheese
filled with these white specks has been examined
at the New York experiment station. The white

spots are about one-eighth the size of an ordinary
pin-head. They are more or less completely distributed through the mass of the cheese, appearing,
perhaps, more numerous or, at least, more prominent in the lines where the pieces of curd are
cemented together. Wherever there is a mechani-
cal-hole, its walls are well covered and here the
specks appear specially prominent because they
simply lie on the walls and are not imbedded in
the body of the cheese. They can be easily detached. When examined under a magnifying glass,
the small specks appear glistening white and also,
in some cases, the edges of the curd pieces, where
they are cemented together, have the same appearance, very closely resembling paraffin. The specks
crush easily, like fat. An examination showed them
to contain calcium, but no phosphoric acid or other
inorganic salt in appreciable amounts. Besides
calcium, there appears to be some fatty acid, so
that the substance appears to be a calcium soap.
Some of the fat in the cheese is probably decomposed by bacteria acting only at low temperatures
and a reaction takes place between the fatty acid
set free and the calcium salts of the cheese. The
flavor and other qualities of the cheese do not appear to be affected in any appreciable way.

Milk-sugar in cheese, under the action of acid
organisms, completely decomposes, forming lactic
acid chiefly, with small amounts of some other
products. The sugar in fresh cheese may amount to
1 or 2 per cent, but it seems to disappear from the
cheese, for the most part, in 48 hours and completely
within two weeks.

Neutral salts and acid salts.—As already stated, there rarely appears to be any free acid in normal cheese. The calcium compounds (mainly phosphates and citrates) are sufficient in amount to make use of the lactic acid which is formed, as previously explained (p. 149). The same process continues in the unripe cheese which previously begins in the milk and curd in the cheese-vat. It is probable that in ripened cheese the ammonia combines with the acid salts to neutralize their acidity more or less completely, because, in overripe cheese, we usually find the reaction alkaline instead of acid.

Salt.—So far as known, salt undergoes no chemical change in cheese-ripening. As the water decreases, the brine or whey of the cheese simply becomes stronger, as a matter of course.

Gases.—In ripened cheese, different gases in different relative proportions have been found, but little work has been done in connection with cheddar cheese. The amounts and kinds of gases undoubtedly vary according to various conditions, depending primarily (1) upon the kinds of microorganisms introduced into the cheese through the milk, and (2) upon the temperature at which the cheese is ripened. The gases usually found in largest amounts are carbon dioxid and hydrogen. We have found also hydrogen sulphid. The dry matter in cheese is slightly reduced, owing to the formation and escape of gases. In one experiment at the New York experiment station having for its object a determination of the rate and amount of carbon dioxid formed during ripening at 60° F. by cheddar cheese, it was found that, under normal conditions, the cheese began giving off carbon dioxid gas at the start and continued to do so in increasing amounts.   At the end of two months, the rate of formation was still near its highest and did not begin to drop markedly until after about 20 weeks. Measurable amounts of gas were still coming from the cheese at the end of 32 weeks, when the experiment was discontinued.   The total amount of carbon dioxid gas given off during the entire experiment was equal to 0.5 per cent of the fresh cheese, while, at the end of two months, it amounted to only 0.1 per cent of the original weight of the cheese.

CONDITIONS OF CHEESE-RIPENING AND CHEMICAL CHANGES

We have now considered the kinds of chemical compounds present in unripe cheese and some of the chemical changes which these compounds undergo.   It is known that many of these changes take place gradually, some very slowly, but there is a more or less definite progression of chemical changes.   The same cheese examined at intervals is found to show quite marked variations in the character of its proteins and protein-derived compounds.   Cheeses made from the same milk under the same conditions of manufacture and subjected to different conditions during the ripening process show a difference in chemical composition.   Also, cheeses manufactured under different conditions and ripened under uniform conditions may vary in the character of their nitrogen compounds.   It is, therefore, important to know something of the relation of various specific conditions to the formation of those products which are used as ·a measure of the rate and extent of cheese-ripening.

Method of measuring rate of cheese-ripening.— The development of flavor and the changes in body characteristic of ripening cheese may be used as indications of the rate and extent of the ripening process, but such a method is too crude for accurate work. Up to the present time, the most satisfactory method has been to determine the amount of different products derived from the proteins of the unripe cheese. From a chemical point of view, in which we consider solely the chemical changes occurring, without reference to their cause, cheese-ripening consists mainly of a change of insoluble proteins into water-soluble forms that consist of other and simpler protein-derived compounds, a list of which is given above (p. 330). Hence, in a ripening cheese, we have progressively increasing amounts of proteins or protein-derived substances, and decreasing amounts of insoluble proteins. Therefore, as a measure of the rate and extent of ripening in cheese, we ascertain the amounts of water-soluble proteins and protein-derived substances and, from these amounts, reach conclusions as to the degree of ripening that has taken place. In many cases, the determination of the amounts of water-soluble and water-insoluble substances alone is sufficient; while in others it is necessary to· know something in detail of the amounts of each of the protein-derived constituents. Stating the matter in a more comprehensive way, *the amount of water-soluble proteins and protein-derived substances is used as a measure of the extent of cheese-ripening, considered from a chemical standpoint.*

The special-conditions to be studied in relation to their influence upon the character and extent of chemical changes in cheese-ripening are the following: (1) Time, (2) temperature, (3) moisture, (4) size, (5) salt, and (6) rennet-enzym. From the large number of data accumulated, we can give only enough, in somewhat condensed form, to serve as illustrations of the general facts discussed.

Time and cheese-ripening.—Under all normal conditions that influence cheese-ripening, we find that, as cheese advances in age, there is a progressive change resulting in an increase of water-soluble proteins and protein-derived substances. The effect of time as a factor in cheese-ripening is modified by a variety of conditions, which will be considered later. For purpose of illustration, we give below averages of the results obtained under the

SHOWING EFFECT OF TIME ON CHEESE-RIPENING

	Nitrogen, expressed as percentage of nitrogen in cheese, in form of:						
Age of cheese	Brine-soluble protein	Water-soluble proteins and derivatives	Para-nuclein	Case-oses	Pep-tones	Amino acids	Ammonia
Months	Per cent	Per cent	Per cent	Per cent	Per cent	Per cent	Per cent
1½	20.18	21.44	2.06	3.15	3.84	9.88	1.56
3	27.26	30.98	4.45	4.56	4.65	14.36	2.45
6	27.55	36.15	3.57	4.92	4.22	19.96	3.52
9	24.14	43.45	4.02	4.59	3.56	26.53	4.74
12	19.04	44.75	3.52	4.16	3.95	28.38	5.41
18	12.65	47.25	3.40	3.88	2.57	30.46	6.62

various conditions employed. Each analysis represents the average of the results obtained with 24 different cheeses.

It is noticeable that all of the soluble forms of nitrogen compounds increase in amount; while some increase continuously, like amino acids and ammonia, others increase for some months and then decrease, as paranuclein, caseoses, and peptones. Taking the total water-soluble forms in the cheese at the end of 18 months, we see that, of the total amount (47.25 per cent), 45.4 per cent was formed in the first six weeks, 65.5 per cent in the first 3 months, 76.5 per cent in the first 6 months, and 92 per cent in the first 9 months, which is one-half the entire period covered by our study. In general, it is seen that, under uniform conditions, (1) the formation of water-soluble proteins and protein derivatives increases as cheese ages; (2) the rate of formation of such compounds is more rapid in the early stages of ripening, steadily diminishing with age; (3) about two-thirds of these compounds are formed in the first 3 months and over 90 per cent in the first 9 months.

Temperature and cheese-ripening.—In general, we find in every individual cheese that temperature exerts a marked influence upon the changes taking place in the proteins. The effect of temperature is, of course, modified by other conditions. As illustrative of the effect of temperature, we give in the table following averages in which each analysis embodies the analytical results furnished by four different cheeses ripened at the same temperatures.

We consider also the factor of time along with that of temperature.

SHOWING EFFECT OF TEMPERATURE ON CHEESE-RIPENING

Temperature of curing-room	Form of proteins and derivatives	Nitrogen expressed as percentage of nitrogen in cheese					
		1½ mos.	3 mos.	6 mos.	9 mos.	12 mos.	18 mos.
Deg.F.		Per cent	Per cent	Per cent	Per cent	Per cent	Per cent
32	Total water-soluble...	12.80	18.64	23.06	32.66	34.02	36.75
55	"	20.56	31.46	36.09	43.91	45.09	49.40
60	"	23.14	33.69	39.97	46.89	48.62	50.16
70	"	29.24	40.13	45.50	50.34	51.25	52.67
32	Brine-soluble	20.58	43.14	36.55	43.00	34.48	21.37
55	"	33.01	33.66	35.10	25.61	19.26	19.45
60	"	13.89	18.81	19.94	16.15	12.32	9.45
70	"	13.24	13.45	18.62	11.83	10.10	7.86
32	Paranuclein	1.27	4.05	3.44	4.47	4.15	4.12
55	"	2.39	5.34	4.25	4.27	3.64	3.68
60	"	2.54	2.71	3.90	4.23	3.59	4.73
70	"	2.03	3.71	2.68	3.13	2.45	2.60
32	Caseoses....	1.05	2.97	5.24	4.29	4.17	5.06
55	"	4.08	4.50	5.03	4.76	4.73	4.27
60	"	3.44	6.14	6.03	5.07	3.68	3.00
70	"	4.07	4.63	3.37	4.24	4.12	3.20
32	Peptones ..	1.30	2.23	4.53	4.36	4.53	4.17
55	" ..	3.90	4.95	3.99	3.10	3.72	2.84
60	" ..	3.33	5.99	4.70	3.44	4.03	1.80
70	" ..	6.81	5.45	3.67	3.33	3.51	1.50
32	Amino acids	4.82	6.36	8.70	17.55	18.73	19.44
55	"	8.69	14.33	19.55	27.05	29.00	31.66
60	"	12.16	14.55	21.39	28.84	31.14	33.54
70	"	13.86	22.20	30.80	32.68	34.65	37.19
32	Ammonia ..	0.61	0.61	1.21	1.91	2.14	3.98
55	" ..	1.50	2.42	3.30	4.69	5.57	6.95
60	" ..	1.67	2.54	3.89	5.43	6.12	7.35
70	" ..	2.47	4.22	5.71	6.91	7.49	8.19

Summarizing our results, we find that, other conditions being uniform, (1) the water-soluble proteins and derivatives in cheese increase, on an average, very closely in proportion to increase of temperature; (2) from the average of our results, there is an increase of 0.5 per cent of these water-soluble compounds for an increase of one degree of temperature between the limits of 32° and 70° F.; (3) the amino acids and ammonia are formed in the cheese more abundantly at higher temperatures and accumulate in the cheese, while the other water-soluble compounds do not appear to be regularly influenced by temperature in the early stages of ripening, but after some months they decrease in quantity with increase of temperature.

Moisture and cheese-ripening.—In order to study the effect of moisture in cheese upon the chemical changes taking place in the nitrogen compounds, two sets of cheeses were made for comparison, 4 different cheeses in each set being made under parallel conditions. One lot was covered with melted paraffin, in order to retard the evaporation of water from the cheese; the others were left in the usual condition. These cheeses were all kept in the same curing-room at a temperature of 55° F. In the tabulated results following, we give the averages obtained with the 4 different cheeses in each set of experiments, those that were covered with paraffin being indicated as 2, the others as 1.

The cheeses covered with paraffin had somewhat less water when made, but the others lost water more rapidly, so that at the end of 3 months their water content was about the same. After this the

SHOWING EFFECT OF MOISTURE IN CHEESE ON CHEESE-RIPENING

No. of cheese	Form of proteins, and derivatives	Nitrogen expressed as percentage of nitrogen in cheese					
		1½ mos.	3 mos.	6 mos.	9 mos.	12 mos.	18 mos.
		Per cent	Per cent	Per cent	Per cent	Per cent	Per cent
1	Total water-soluble...	17.32	27.09	31.76	39.09	39.80	42.77
2	"	17.14	27.40	36.41	46.59	54.52	56.76
1	Brine-soluble	24.89	41.59	35.43	28.81	21.70	13.72
2	"	21.17	30.42	49.29	20.16	9.81	5.30
1	Paranuclein	2.70	5.32	4.77	4.20	3.79	4.10
2	"	0.87	4.35	4.45	4.89	8.01	7.90
1	Caseoses ...	2.99	5.80	4.24	4.41	4.19	4.26
2	" ...	3.58	3.64	5.38	5.06	4.32	4.70
1	Peptones....	2.12	4.09	3.75	3.57	3.97	1.95
2	" ...	4.49	4.80	6.19	4.00	4.43	3.20
1	Amino acids	7.50	9.79	16.00	21.65	22.89	26.73
2	"	7.22	12.59	17.12	26.03	29.44	29.00
1	Ammonia ..	1.34	2.15	3.04	4.17	4.53	5.72
2	" ..	0.98	1.99	4.26	6.52	8.27	12.16
1	Water......	36.40	35.27	32.41	27.86	28.02	27.75
2	"	35.96	35.00	33.37	33.24	32.66	32.10

paraffined cheese contained considerably more water, the difference increasing with age, until at the end of 12 months it was over 4.5 pounds per 100 pounds of cheese.

A general review of these results indicates the formation of larger amounts of water-soluble nitrogen compounds in cheese containing more moisture, other conditions being uniform.

Size of cheese and ripening.—On page 320 we considered the influence of size of cheese upon the rapidity of evaporation of water from the cheese. Our results show that the percentage loss of moisture is always greater in smaller-sized cheeses. This is what might naturally be expected, since the amount of external surface exposed for evaporation is greater, relative to weight, in small than in large cheeses. Hence, difference in size of cheese practi-

SHOWING EFFECT OF SIZE OF CHEESE ON CHEESE-RIPENING

W'ght of cheese	Form of proteins and de-rivatives	Nitrogen expressed as percentage of nitrogen in cheese					
		1½ mos.	3 mos.	6 mos.	9 mos.	12 mos.	18 mos.
Lbs.		Per cent	Per cent	Per cent	Per cent	Per cent	Per cent
10	Total water-soluble...	17.32	27.09	31.76	39.09	39.80	42.77
30	"	20.56	31.46	36.09	43.91	45.09	49.40
10	Brine-solu-ble......	24.89	41.59	35.43	28.81	21.70	13.72
30	"	33.01	33.66	35.10	25.61	19.26	19.45
10	Paranuclein	2.70	5.32	4.77	4.20	3.79	4.10
30	"	2.39	5.34	4.25	4.27	3.64	3.68
10	Caseoses ...	2.99	5.80	4.24	4.41	4.19	4.26
30	" ...	4.08	4.50	5.03	4.76	4.73	4.27
10	Peptones ..	2.12	4.09	3.75	3.57	3.97	1.95
30	" ..	3.90	4.95	3.99	3.10	3.72	2.84
10	Amino acids	7.50	9.79	16.00	21.65	22.89	26.73
30	"	8.69	14.33	19.55	27.05	29.00	31.66
10	Ammonia ..	1.34	2.15	3.04	4.17	4.53	5.72
30	" ..	1.50	2.42	3.30	4.69	5.57	6.95
10	Water	36.40	35.27	32.41	27.86	28.02	27.75
30	"	36.31	35.11	33.46	32.29	31.54	28.56

cally means difference in rapidity of loss of moisture, the larger cheese retaining its moisture content longer. We should expect, then, to find essentially the same differences of ripening in cheeses of different size that we find in cheeses having a different moisture content. To make a study of this point, we present on page 342 some data showing, at different stages of ripening, the amounts of derived protein compounds found in cheeses weighing respectively 30 and 10 pounds, approximately. The data represent averages of 4 different lots of cheeses ripened at 55° F.

An examination of the table shows, in brief, that the larger cheeses contained more moisture after the early stages of ripening and that there was a more rapid increase in the formation of total water-soluble derived proteins, especially of amino acids and ammonia, than in the smaller cheeses.

Amount of salt and cheese-ripening.—It is a fact that has long been observed by cheese-makers that increase of salt in cheese delays the rapidity with which the cheese becomes marketable, but, until about five years ago, no detailed chemical results were published in relation to the subject. In order to study the influence of salt upon the ripening process in cheese properly made and kept, there were made, as nearly alike as possible, four different lots of cheese under normal conditions. In each lot there were 4 cheeses weighing 30 pounds each, and salt was added to these in proportions varying as follows: No salt, 1.5, 2.5, and 5 pounds of salt for 1,000 pounds of milk. During the ripening, one lot was kept at 32° F., one at 55° F., one at 60° F. and one at 70° F. On page 345 we give the averages of the 4 lots of cheese kept at the different temperatures. Whether we consider each lot of cheeses by itself or their averages, the results are strikingly concordant in respect to the effect of salt upon the formation of proteins and their derivatives in the ripening process.

We are to regard the salt in cheese as being in solution in the whey held by the cheese, practically forming a dilute brine. In common practice, cheese-makers add from 2 to 2½ pounds of salt to the curd made from 1,000 pounds of milk. Cheese thus salted contains about 1 per cent of salt. Such cheese usually contains about 35 to 37 per cent of water. Consequently, under such conditions we should have, approximately, a 3 per cent brine. It is evident that, in proportion as a cheese loses moisture by evaporation, the brine remaining becomes more concentrated with the advancing age of the cheese.

A study of the table leads to the following statements:

(1) The amount of salt retained in cheese is not proportional to the amount of salt added to the curd. While salt was added to the different cheeses in the ratio of 1: 1.67: 3.33, the salt retained in the cheese was in the ratio of 1 :1.40 :2.20. Of necessity, a considerable proportion of the salt added to the cheese-curd passes into the whey. Moreover, it has been found by examining different portions of the same cheese that the salt is not commonly distributed with perfect uniformity through the cheese mass.

SHOWING EFFECT OF SALT ON CHEESE-RIPENING

Am't of salt used for 1000 lbs. of milk	Form of proteins and derivatives, etc.	Nitrogen expressed as percentage of nitrogen in cheese					
		1½ mos.	3 mos.	6 mos.	9 mos.	12 mos.	18 mos.
Lbs.	Total water	Per cent	Per cent	Per cent	Per cent	Per cent	Per cent
0	soluble	23.42	34.26	40.52	49.10	51.38	53.96
1½	"	21.80	32.10	37.67	44.13	45.88	50.73
2½	"	21.67	29.92	34.73	42.93	43.52	44.65
5	"	18.84	27.70	31.70	37.64	38.19	39.62
0	Brine-soluble						
	ble	17.33	27.06	23.27	21.82	16.75	12.56
1½	"	20.86	28.43	26.16	22.38	17.98	12.61
2½	"	21.81	24.47	28.30	23.54	18.04	13.74
5	"	20.73	29.02	32.49	28.81	23.41	11.71
0	Paranuclein	1.85	4.44	3.80	4.66	3.83	3.44
1½	"	2.13	4.47	3.52	4.01	3.72	3.89
2½	"	2.27	4.55	3.51	3.80	3.30	3.34
5	"	1.98	4.35	3.42	3.63	3.23	2.96
0	Caseoses ...	3.41	4.94	4.94	5.60	4.95	3.87
1½	" ..	3.24	5.02	5.17	4.53	3.69	4.04
2½	" ...	3.21	4.14	4.98	4.16	3.97	3.84
5	" ...	2.75	4.14	4.58	4.08	4.05	3.77
0	Peptones ..	4.86	5.02	4.84	3.47	4.13	2.69
1½	" ..	3.50	5.16	4.29	3.54	4.87	3.40
2½	" ..	4.20	4.02	4.02	3.97	3.98	2.07
5	" ..	2.91	4.42	3.74	3.25	2.81	2.14
0	Amino acids	10.22	15.86	22.18	28.89	32.19	35.09
1½	"	10.46	14.77	20.13	27.31	29.33	32.36
2½	"	9.78	13.83	19.20	26.72	27.61	29.57
5	"	8.82	12.97	17.34	23.21	24.40	24.81
0	Ammonia ..	1.67	2.96	4.64	6.54	7.77	8.89
1½	" ..	1.67	2.53	3.69	4.69	5.36	7.04
2½	" ..	1.51	2.36	3.13	4.30	4.54	5.83
5	" ..	1.41	2.03	2.64	3.43	3.61	4.70
0	Per cent water in cheese	39.27	38.22	35.60	35.22	34.09	30.96
1½	"	36.66	35.60	33.50	32.62	31.61	28.80
2½	"	35.69	34.43	32.31	31.54	30.99	27.68
5	"	33.63	32.62	29.52	29.88	28.61	26.97
0	Per cent salt in cheese..	0	0	0	0	0	0
1½	"	0.59	0.70	0.84	0.94	0.92	....
2½	"	0.82	1.20	1.15	1.26	1.27	....
5	"	1.29	1.50	1.62	1.87	1.83	....

(2) An increase of salt in cheese-curd results in decreasing the amount of moisture held in cheese. This fact is very strikingly shown by the figures in the table. The cheese containing no salt retained most moisture, and increasing additions of salt decreased the amount of moisture held in the cheese. The same general relation held true throughout the whole period of investigation.

(3) An increase of salt in cheese was accompanied by a decrease in the amount of water-soluble protein-derived compounds and this was true through the whole 18 months of the investigation. While this influence of salt is more noticeable in the case of the amino acids and ammonia, it is clearly evident in the case of the paranuclein, caseoses, and peptones.

(4) It is readily seen from the results embodied in the table that the rapidity of formation of water-soluble protein-derived compounds is decreased in the presence of increased amounts of salt in cheese. This is due, in part, to the effect of salt in decreasing the amount of moisture held in cheese and, in part, to the direct retarding action of salt upon some of the agents that produce the changes of cheese-ripening.

Amount of rennet-enzym and cheese-ripening.— Before any careful studies were made of the effect of rennet-enzym upon the chemical changes of cheese-ripening, there was difference of opinion among cheese-makers as to whether the amount of rennet-extract used had any influence on the ripening of the cheese. The various studies made of the subject by different investigators agree in showing that rennet-enzym does influence the rapidity of the ripening process. In the results

SHOWING EFFECT OF DIFFERENT AMOUNTS OF RENNET
UPON CHEESE-RIPENING

Age of cheese	Amount of rennet-extract used for 1000 pounds of milk	Condition of cheese	Water in cheese	Nitrogen expressed as percentage of nitrogen in cheese in form of:			
				Water-soluble proteins and derivatives	Paranuclein, caseoses and peptones	Amino acids	Ammonia
Months	Ounces		Per ct.	Per ct.	Per ct.	Per ct.	Per ct.
1	3	Normal....	37.54	18.90	10.31	8.36	....
1	6	Normal....	38.06	23.40	13.37	9.47	....
1	3	Paraffined .	38.45	18.20	9.95	8.29	....
1	6	Paraffined..	38.56	24.90	15.30	9.63	....
3	3	Normal....	35.59	26.70	13.34	12.00	1.87
3	6	Normal....	36.25	29.70	15.40	12.50	1.86
3	3	Paraffined..	37.97	27.90	13.39	12.60	1.96
3	6	Paraffined..	37.61	33.20	16.35	14.70	2.18
6	3	Normal....	33.58	29.80	12.02	16.20	2.09
6	6	Normal....	33.51	35.40	15.11	18.20	2.60
6	3	Paraffined..	37.59	31.80	12.84	17.30	2.23
6	6	Paraffined..	36.79	36.80	16.76	17.30	2.70
9	3	Normal....	31.84	37.30	13.47	21.20	2.59
9	6	Normal....	30.63	35.50	13.00	20.00	2.50
9	3	Paraffined..	36.81	38.90	14.93	20.30	3.73
9	6	Paraffined..	35.40	45.20	14.36	26.60	4.26
12	3	Normal,...	28.13	38.00	12.05	22.10	4.10
12	6	Normal....	29.98	42.40	14.38	24.00	3.60
12	3	Paraffined..	36.07	40.40	14.10	23.60	2 93
12	6	Paraffined..	34.51	48.10	15.34	27.50	4.60
15	3	Normal....	26.73	39.10	12.05	22.90	4.53
15	6	Normal....	25.97	43.60	13.19	25.50	4.31
15	3	Paraffined..	34.35	41.20	12.96	23.80	4.92
15	6	Parafined...	33.21	49.90	16.87	28.00	5.54
24	3	Normal....	24.76	42.70	12.30	25.10	5.06
24	6	Normal....	23.33	48.50	14.54	28.50	5.84
24	3	Paraffined..	30.93	46.40	11.34	28.70	6.52
24	6	Paraffined..	28.22	50.20	11.75	30.80	7.92

given on page 347, the study was made with the use of 3 to 6 ounces of Hansen's rennet-extract in 1,000 pounds of milk. The cheeses were made to contain about the same amount of moisture. In each case, one cheese was covered with paraffin in order to delay the evaporation of moisture, while the other was kept in the usual condition.

The data in the preceding table show quite generally a greater increase of water-soluble protein-derived compounds in the cheese containing the larger amount of rennet, other conditions being the same. The cheeses covered with paraffin contain more moisture than those not so covered and, as we should expect, show a larger increase of soluble compounds than do the other cheeses; but here, also, the cheese containing the larger amount of rennet ripens more rapidly than the one containing less rennet.

If we examine the different classes of the water-soluble protein and protein-derived compounds, we notice that the increase caused by the increased use of rennet is more noticeable in the case of the paranuclein, caseoses and peptones than in the case of the amino acids and ammonia, especially during the first 6 or 9 months.

GENERAL SUMMARY OF RESULTS RELATING TO CONDITIONS OF CHEESE-RIPENING AND CHEMICAL CHANGES

Reviewing briefly the results that have been presented in the preceding pages, we have found that different conditions affect the chemical changes in the protein compounds of cheese as follows:

(1) **Time.**—The formation of water-soluble protein-derived compounds increases as cheese ages, other conditions being uniform. The rate of increase is, however, not uniform, since it is much more rapid in the early than in the succeeding stages of ripening.

(2) **Temperature.**—The amount of soluble protein-derived compounds increases, on an average, quite closely in proportion to increase of temperature, when other conditions are uniform.

(3) **Moisture.**—Other conditions being alike, there is formed a larger amount of water-soluble protein-derived compounds in cheese containing more moisture than in cheese containing less moisture.

(4) **Size.**—Cheeses of large size usually form water-soluble compounds more rapidly than smaller cheeses under the same conditions, because large cheeses lose their moisture less rapidly and after the early period of ripening have a higher water content.

(5) **Salt.**—Cheese containing more salt forms water-soluble compounds more slowly than cheese containing less salt. This appears to be due, in part, to the direct action of salt in retarding the activity of one or more of the ripening agents and, in part, to the tendency of the salt to reduce the moisture content of the cheese.

(6) **Rennet.**—The use of increased amounts of rennet-extract in cheese-making, other conditions being uniform, results in producing increased

quantities of water-soluble protein-derived compounds in a given period of time, especially such compounds as paranuclein, caseoses and peptones.

TRANSIENT AND CUMULATIVE PRODUCTS IN CHEESE-RIPENING

In studying the influence of various conditions upon the chemical changes of the protein compounds in the normal cheese-ripening process, we have noticed that the compounds which are grouped under the names, paracasein, caseoses and peptones usually vary within comparatively narrow limits and do not appear to accumulate in the cheese in constantly increasing quantities. These compounds do not appear to show much definite regularity in the amounts formed under different conditions. On the other hand, amino acids and ammonia accumulate in increasing amounts from the early age of the cheese during the whole process of normal ripening. The difference in the apparent behavior of these different classes of compounds is most readily explained by regarding the compounds first formed in cheese-ripening as intermediate or transient products. Thus, we find paranuclein, caseoses and peptones present in the earliest stage of cheese-ripening, and they show a tendency to increase somewhat for a period of time and then decrease. Whatever may be the precise chemical relation and order of formation, the point we wish to keep in mind is that the amounts of these compounds do not increase regularly or accumulate continuously in the cheese. The extent to which any accumulation occurs in these transient stages depends upon the conditions of ripening. For example, at low temperatures, the transient protein products formed appear to pass into other forms less rapidly than at higher temperatures, and they tend to accumulate to some extent. This can be shown by comparing the results secured with cheeses ripened at 32° F. and at 70° F.

Age of cheese	Percentage of nitrogen in form of paranuclein in cheese at		Percentage of nitrogen in form of caseoses in cheese at		Percentage of nitrogen in form of peptones in cheese at	
	32°F.	70°F.	32°F.	70°F.	32°F.	70°F.
Months	Per cent	Per cent	Per cent	Per cent	Per cent	Per cent
1½	1.27	2.03	1.05	4.07	1.30	6.81
3	4.05	3.71	2.97	4.63	2.23	5.45
6	3.44	2.68	5.24	3.37	4.53	3.67
9	4.47	3.13	4.29	4.24	4.36	3.33
12	4.15	2.45	4.17	4.12	4.53	3.51
18	4.12	2.60	5.06	3.20	4.17	1.50

Now, quite different from the behavior of these compounds is that of amino acids, which appear beyond question to be formed from the peptones, and of ammonia, which is formed from the decomposition of amino acids. Ammonia is an end-product and the amino acids are end-products to a considerable extent in cheese normally ripened. They therefore accumulate in increasing quantities under all conditions that favor their formation.

INFLUENCE OF PRODUCTS OF CHEMICAL CHANGE IN THE CHEESE-RIPENING PROCESS

Attention has been called to the fact that chemical changes in the proteins of cheese take place much more rapidly in the early stages of ripening than later.   It is shown that, in the first 3 months of the 18-month period of study, over 65 per cent of the nitrogen was changed into the form of water-soluble compounds.   How can we explain this observed fact that the rate of chemical change, as measured by the formation of water-soluble nitrogen compounds, decreases as the age of cheese increases?   The most obvious explanation is associated with the generally observed fact that in fermentation changes the products of the process weaken the action of the ferment, often inhibiting it altogether (p. 286).   In cheese, we have an accumulation of fermentation products in the form of water-soluble protein and protein-derived compounds and, apparently, they serve to diminish the action of the agents that cause the changes.

In this connection, it is interesting to notice that the end-products, the amino acids and ammonia, appear to exert a stronger influence than do the other soluble protein compounds in decreasing the action of the ripening agents.   This is indicated by the following data:

Age of cheese	Percentage of nitrogen in form of paranuclein, caseoses and peptones	Percentage of nitrogen in form of amino acids and ammonia	Monthly average rate of increase of soluble nitrogen compounds for 100 pounds of nitrogen in cheese
Months			Pounds
1½	9.05	11.44	15.0
3	13.66	16.81	6.3
6	12.71	23.48	2.1
9	12.17	31.27	2.4
12	11.63	33.79	0.4
18	....	37.00	0.4

Thus, it is seen that the first-formed products of cheese-ripening, paranuclein, caseoses and peptones, remain fairly uniform, while the amino acids and ammonia continuously increase.

WHY MOISTURE INFLUENCES THE CHEESE-RIPENING PROCESS

We have seen that an increased moisture content in cheese favors more active chemical changes in the process of ripening. This may be due to one or both of two effects. First, moisture in itself may favor the activity of the ripening ferments. It is well known that moisture is necessary for the action of ferments and that increase of moisture above a certain amount increases their action. Second, the presence of increased amounts of moisture serves to dilute the fermentation products and, to that extent, to counteract their unfavorable effect.

In ordinary cheese-ripening, there is a constant loss of moisture and this serves to make more concentrated the fermentation products, which are increasing at the same time the moisture is decreasing. Accordingly, after 3 to 6 months, difference in moisture appears to exert a more marked influence upon the increased formation of soluble nitrogen compounds than in the early stages of ripening.

CHAPTER XXV

Causes of Chemical Changes in Cheese-Ripening

A large amount of work has been done during the past 30 years in connection with different varieties of cheese, in an effort to ascertain what agents cause the changes taking place in cheese during the ripening process. Many of the results have been peculiarly confusing and progress has been slow. Much of this work has been done with the hard types of cheese, the Emmenthaler in Europe and the cheddar in England and America. The scope of this book does not permit an historical review of these investigations, and the most we can hope to do, within the assigned limits of treatment, is to give a brief summary of what may be regarded as the present state of knowledge in respect to the causes of cheese-ripening in the case of cheddar cheese. It is well to preface our discussion with the statement that the amount we actually know at present is disappointingly small, and how much of what we think we know now will be modified by further investigation no one can confidently say. In our treatment of the causes of cheese-ripening, we confine our attention mainly to the changes that take place in the protein compounds, which come originally, as we know, from milk-casein; because, in this portion of the cheese substance, the most profound and extensive changes occur, changes which are most intimately connected with the changing qualities that appear in the process. As previously stated, the cheese-ripening process, considered from a chemical standpoint, consists mainly in the change of the complex protein, paracasein, as it exists in cheese-curd, into a number of less complex compounds.

Many difficulties beset the experimental study of cheese-ripening, some of which will be briefly noticed later. One of the great difficulties in the past has been a failure to recognize that there was more than one agent at work in the process of cheese-ripening. The investigator is always at a disadvantage when his point of view is too narrow, since he inevitably overlooks essential details, and interprets his results within the narrow range of his vision. This truth has been amply illustrated in the history of the investigation of the causes of cheese-ripening, since many investigations were based upon the conception that only one agent was the cause; and the object of the investigator was, unconsciously, not so much to find out what the real cause might be as to show that the one particular agency he had in mind was the actual and sole cause.

We shall not attempt to treat the subject in the order of its historical development, but rather in the order in which the different agencies become most active in the ripening process. So far as our present knowledge goes, the different agents taking part in the change of the protein, paracasein, into simpler proteins and protein-derived compounds are the following:

1. Some acid, usually lactic.

2. Rennet-enzym.
3. Galactase.
4. Micro-organisms, commonly bacteria.

Just what part is played by each agent in the formation of water-soluble proteins and derived proteins, or what interdependence there may be of the work of one agent upon the products of the work of another, we are at present able to say only in part, and not very definitely at that. We will now present an outline of what we may conceive as the distribution of work among these different agents in the light of the experimental results that are now available. We are conscious of the possibility, or rather probability, that some of these statements will need revision in the near future.

ACTION OF ACIDS IN CHEESE-RIPENING

The necessity of the presence of some acid in milk and in cheese-curd during the process of making cheddar cheese seems to have been well established, since cheese made without acid fails to ripen satisfactorily. In the absence of acid, little or no brine-soluble protein or water-soluble substance is formed, even after long periods of time. The work of acid, whatever may be the way in which its specific influence is exerted in cheese-ripening, is something like this: Lactic acid is formed by the action of micro-organisms upon milk-sugar during the process of cheese-making; and its formation continues not only during the time the curd is in the cheese-vat but also in the curd as it is put in the press and later. Under normal conditions, the acid continues to be formed so long as any milk-sugar remains in the cheese. Just how long that is, varies according to conditions of manufacture and especially with the temperature at which the cheese is kept during the ripening. Under ordinary conditions, all sugar in cheese disappears within two weeks. Roughly speaking, there is between 1 and 2 per cent of milk-sugar in cheese when put in the press. How rapidly this undergoes change can be seen from the following illustrations, in which three different cheeses are represented:

MILK-SUGAR IN CHEESE

	No. 1	No. 2	No. 3
	Per cent	Per cent	Per cent
When put in press.....................	1.70	0.77	1.52
3 hours after being in press..........	1.05	0.68	0.64
6 hours after being in press..........	0.68	0.44	...
12 hours after being in press..........	0.68	...	0.80
15 hours after being in press..........	0.58	...	...
2 days after being in press.............	0.58	0.10	0.36
4 days after being in press.............	0.50	0.04	0.32
1 week after being in press............	0.10	0.03	0.22
2 weeks after being in press...........	0.07	0.00	trace

These figures illustrate well the great variation in detail that may occur in the disappearance of milk-sugar in cheese, which means, of course, the formation of lactic acid.

At no stage of the process of making cheddar cheese, and in no cheese, do we find, under normal conditions, uncombined lactic acid *as such,* or what we call free lactic acid. What then becomes of the lactic acid known to be formed? There exist in the milk substances which are ready to combine with lactic acid as fast as it is formed and to change the acid from the active condition of a free acid to that of a neutral salt.   These substances are chiefly lime compounds or compounds containing calcium as a base.   Over one-half and, probably, about three-fourths, of the calcium compounds in milk are in such form as enable them to combine with lactic acid.   A considerable part of the calcium in milk is in combination with phosphoric acid in the form of insoluble compounds, probably dicalcium phosphate in large part, which is held in suspension in the form of very minute, solid particles.   Some believe that the calcium phosphate is in direct combination with casein in milk.   The action that probably takes place can be represented as follows:

Lactic acid + *insoluble* calcium phosphate = calcium lactate + *soluble* calcium phosphate (mono or acid-calcium phosphate).   Now, mono-calcium phosphate is an *acid* salt; it neutralizes alkalis and tastes sour.   Therefore, when we talk about lactic acid in cheese-making, we really mean the products formed by the action of lactic acid—calcium lactate and calcium acid phosphate.

The first effect of the formation of these soluble lime salts is to promote the coagulating effect of rennet; and the particular thing accomplished by ripening milk for cheese-making is the formation in small, but sufficient, quantities of calcium lactate and soluble calcium phosphate.   The succeeding changes in curd, the formation of a superficial film on each small piece of curd, the shrinking with the simultaneous expulsion of whey, the stringing on a hot iron, the change in texture of curd to the softer, velvety form, resembling the meat of a chicken's breast, the plastic condition—these changes all appear to be associated with the continued formation of lactic acid, resulting in larger amounts of calcium lactate and acid phosphate. To what extent temperature and action of rennet-enzym share in producing these changes cannot be definitely stated now. It has been pretty satisfactorily established that in cheddar cheese-making there is, contrary to what was believed at one time, no combination of any kind between the lactic acid and the protein of the cheese-curd, but that the acid formed is practically all used by the lime salts of the curd in the formation of the calcium compounds mentioned.

During the cheese-making process, the cheese-curd or paracasein undergoes some very marked changes, as we have just noticed above. We have a simple means of measuring the extent of these changes, depending on the behavior of the curd when treated with warm (123° to 132° F.), dilute brine (a 5 per cent solution of common salt in water) (p. 330). The changes taking place and thus measured can be illustrated as follows, using the results of a special experiment, taken from the records of the New York experiment station:

	Per cent of protein soluble in brine solution	Per cent of protein soluble in water
When curd was cut................	3.13	...
When whey was removed..........	4.50	...
When curd was put in press	30.15	3.77
2 hours after curd was put in press	46.46	4.25
9½ hours after curd was put in press	96.06	6.48

It is seen that the increase of the brine-soluble protein is very rapid between the time when the whey was removed and the curd was put in press. The peculiar behavior of the curd during the cheddaring process is probably due to the formation of the brine-soluble substance; and the formation of this substance appears to be associated, at least in considerable measure, with the formation of soluble lime salts resulting from the action of lactic acid. From some work done at the New York experiment station, it seems that when this brine-soluble compound is not formed, we do not get water-soluble substances, and this means that we get no cheese-ripening. In other words, the formation of the brine-soluble substance appears to be prerequisite to further ripening changes.

Reviewing briefly the action of acid in cheese-making and cheese-ripening, its chief work appears to be combination with the insoluble lime salts of the milk, producing calcium lactate and calcium acid phosphate. These compounds, in conjunction with the degree of heat used and, perhaps, also in association with the action of rennet-enzym, produce marked changes in the curd in respect to body, texture and solubility in brine solution. In the cheese-making process, the insoluble portion of the curd begins to change into a form that is soluble in warm, 5 per cent brine, this change taking place rapidly during the cheddaring operation and continuing until all the protein of the curd is in this form; the change appears to be complete 9 or 10 hours after the curd is put in press. Then this brine-soluble curd begins to change into an insoluble form, this reverse change going on very rapidly for a few hours and then more gradually for many months. From this insoluble form appear to come the water-soluble proteins and protein derivatives that are found in cheese. Much work yet remains to be done before all the details of the action of acid in cheese-making are fully understood.

ACTION OF RENNET-ENZYM IN CHEESE-RIPENING

For a long time, there was doubt as to whether rennet-extract had anything to do with cheese-ripening. It may be now regarded as definitely settled that rennet-extract contains a peptic ferment which has a curd-dissolving power. This fact has nothing necessarily to do with the question as to whether the peptic enzym is the same as the coagulating enzym, or whether two different enzyms, each with a different function, are present. The action of rennet in cheese-ripening is quite similar to that of a pepsin digestion. There is one important condition for the peptic action of the rennet-enzym—the presence of an amount of acid or acid salts, corresponding to about 0.3 per cent of lactic acid. The acid produced in cheese-curd and cheese furnishes the needed conditions. Whether this is the chief function of acid in connection with the formation of water-soluble proteins and derived proteins in cheese-ripening, or whether the salts formed by lactic acid exercise some influence apart from rennet action, may not be regarded as satisfactorily determined at the present time.

In order to study the effect of rennet-enzym in dissolving the insoluble protein of cheese-curd, it is necessary to destroy the enzyms and micro-organisms present in milk. This is done by heating the milk to a temperature of 185° to 208° F., after which the milk is cooled and, in order to prevent bacterial action, treated with chloroform before being made into cheese. The heating of the milk to the stated temperature diminishes the readiness and completeness with which the rennet-extract coagulates milk-casein; but the power of prompt coagulation by rennet can be restored by addition of calcium chlorid or carbon dioxid gas or any ordinary acid or acid salt. In thus eliminating other factors of cheese-ripening than rennet-enzym, we necessarily produce conditions that do not exist in normal cheese-making, such as (1) heated milk, (2) absence of milk-enzyms, (3) absence of enzym-forming or acid-producing micro-organisms, and (4) the addition of calcium chlorid or carbon dioxid or lactic acid. Several experiments were carried on at the New York experiment station under the foregoing conditions and, in the table following, we give some of the results of this work. Lactic acid, when used, was added to form 0.2 per cent of the milk.

PEPTIC ACTION OF RENNET IN CHEESE WITH AND WITHOUT ACID

Age of cheese when analyzed	Cheese made with or without acid	Percentage of nitrogen in form of:			
		Water-soluble proteins and derived compounds	Brine-soluble proteins	Paranuclein, caseoses and peptones	Amino acids
Fresh	Without	6.07	3.75	5.46	0.81
Fresh	With	4.55	26.80	3.78	0.77
12 months	Without	8.47	3.36	4.51	3.96
12 months	With	25.10	11.59	20.87	4.98

In studying this table, we can readily observe the following indications:

(1) When no acid, or acid salt, is present in the cheese-making process, practically no changes take place in the protein of the green cheese, even in the course of a year; the different classes of compounds remain about the same in amount at the end of a year as in the fresh cheese. Rennet-enzym, in the absence of acid or acid salts, has practically no dissolving effect on the protein of green cheese and, therefore, does little or no work in the formation of water-soluble protein in the process of cheese-ripening.

(2) When lactic acid was added to milk at the rate of 0.2 per cent, the results were in marked contrast with those given when no acid was used. Thus, we have (a) a considerable amount of brine-soluble protein in the fresh cheese, and (b) a large increase of water-soluble nitrogen compounds at the end of 12 months. It is noticeable that the increase in these water-soluble compounds is largely confined to the paranuclein, caseoses and peptones; the amount of amino acids remains small as compared with a normal cheese of the same age.

That rennet-enzym acts like pepsin in dissolving the protein of fresh cheese-curd has been shown by experimental work. Heated milk (100 cubic centimeters), treated with chloroform to prevent bacterial action, was put into sterilized bottles; 0.22 cubic centimeter of Hansen's fresh rennet-extract was added to some bottles, and to others 0.06 gram of aseptic scale-pepsin for each 7 grams of protein in milk. In the case of one-half of the bottles, 0.5 cubic centimeter of pure lactic acid was added. The bottles were kept at 60° F. The germ content was shown to be insignificant. In one set of experiments milk was used and in another, cheese. The results obtained with rennet-extract and commercial pepsin in the case of milk are given below.

COMPARISON OF DIGESTING ACTION OF RENNET-EXTRACT AND COMMERCIAL PEPSIN

Kind of enzym material used	With or without lactic acid	Age of milk when analyzed	Percentage of total nitrogen in form of:		
			Water-soluble proteins and derivatives	Caseoses and peptones	Amino acids
		Months			
. . . .	. . . . . .	Fresh	9.98	. . . .	. . . .
Rennet ..	Without	1	11.96	5.50	6.47
Pepsin...	Without	1	8.91	2.22	6.69
Rennet...	With	1	27.52	20.39	7.13
Pepsin...	With	1	33.51	25.93	7.58
Rennet...	Without	3	16.44	8.06	8.37
Pepsin...	Without	3	11.42	2.42	9.00
Rennet...	With	3	39.17	29.01	10.16
Pepsin...	With	3	44.47	34.22	10.25
Rennet...	Without	6	15.95	12.74	3.21
Pepsin...	Without	6	10.34	6.60	3.74
Rennet...	With	6	44.00	38.46	5.54
Pepsin...	With	6	48.76	44.74	4.02
Rennet...	Without	9	18.00	12.90	5.13
Pepsin...	Without	9	10.08	6.51	3.57
Rennet...	With	9	50.77	42.66	8.11
Pepsin...	With	9	56.96	48.05	8.91

An examination of this table shows that there is a very fair parallel in the digesting action of rennet-extract and commercial pepsin. Thus, the action increases when acid is added; the increase of soluble proteins is largely confined to caseoses and peptones; the amount of amino acids remains practically unchanged; no ammonia is formed. The results indicate that the action of pepsin was able to account for all the changes observed in the case of rennet-extract *in the presence of acid*. But an interesting difference is observable in connection with the results when no acid was present. We notice that, in the absence of acid, there is a gradual increase of soluble compounds in the case of rennet-extract from 9.98 to 18.00 at the end of 9 months, but no such increase is seen with the commercial pepsin. This difference suggests that the rennet-extract contained, in addition to the peptic ferment proper, a digesting enzym not contained in the commercial pepsin; this enzym shows the ability to dissolve insoluble protein even in the absence of acid. This observation has been confirmed by the work of others.

The effect of commercial pepsin in increasing in cheese the amount of water-soluble proteins, when

EFFECT OF COMMERCIAL PEPSIN IN CHEESE-RIPENING

No. of experiment	Age of cheese when analyzed	Form of Enzyms added	Nitrogen, expressed as percentage of nitrogen in cheese, in form of:				
			Water-soluble proteins and derivatives	Brine-soluble	Para-nuclein, caseoses and peptones	Amino acids	Ammonia
			Per cent	Per cent	Per cent	Per ct.	Per ct.
1	Fresh	Rennet-extract	4.76	65.45	2.41	2.36	.0
1	6 months		28.37	17.14	15.87	6.35	2.00
2	Fresh	Rennet and 1 gm. pepsin	6.97	36.76	4.11	2.86	.0
2	6 months		29.80	17.04	16.47	7.10	1.91
3	Fresh	Rennet & 15 gm. pepsin	25.00	59.53	22.80	2.20	.0
3	3 months		46.67	11.61	41.00	5.68	0.49

used in increasing amounts, is shown by the results given on page 365, which were obtained in an experiment in which the cheese was made in an entirely normal way, except that hydrochloric acid was used in place of lactic acid or a "starter."

The following tables are taken from the records of the Wisconsin experiment station:

DIGESTING ACTION OF DIFFERENT AMOUNTS OF RENNET-EXTRACT IN CHEESE

Amount of rennet-extract used	Age of cheese when analyzed	Percentage of nitrogen in form of:		
		Water soluble proteins and derivatives	Caseoses and peptones	Amino acids
Ounces	Months			
3	1	13.80	10.18	3.62
12	1	18.85	15.17	3.68
24	1	24.83	21.06	3.77
3	3	23.33	11.77	11.56
12	3	31.93	20.18	11.75
24	3	34.54	22.80	11.74

DIGESTING ACTION OF RENNET-EXTRACT AND PEPSIN IN CHEESE

Cheese made with large amount of rennet and with rennet plus pepsin	Age of cheese when analyzed	Percentage of nitrogen in form of:		
		Water-soluble proteins and derivatives	Caseoses and peptones	Amino acids
Normal cheese	70 days	26.67	14.57	12.10
Normal cheese and pepsin..	70 days	37.47	25.07	12.40

We may summarize as follows the results established by investigation regarding the relation of rennet-extract to the cheese-ripening process:

(1) Rennet-extract contains an enzym which has the power of digesting or dissolving the insoluble protein in cheese.

(2) Such digesting action by rennet-extract does not take place in cheese which has been made without any acid or acid salt in the milk and curd.

(3) The digestive action of the enzym contained in rennet-extract exerts its digesting power only in the presence of acids or acid salts. In the case of normal cheese, the acid formed in the cheese-making process is lactic acid, which, however, does not act as free acid, since it reacts with calcium salts, forming neutral calcium lactate and calcium acid phosphate and, probably, citrate. The acid salts enable the rennet-enzym to exert its digesting power. The same general result may be accomplished by adding a free acid or an acid salt to milk during the cheese-making process.

(4) The extent to which the digesting enzym of rennet-extract can act depends largely upon the degree of acidity developed in the cheese-making process. It is probable that no action begins until the equivalent of 0.30 per cent of lactic acid has been formed.

(5) The products formed by rennet digestion of cheese proteins are largely confined to the bodies known as caseoses and peptones, only small amounts of amino acids being formed and little or no ammonia.

(6) Increased use of rennet-extract in cheese-making results in a more rapid formation of water-soluble protein compounds. This is not due, as some formerly thought, to an increased amount of water in cheese, which was supposed to be a necessary result

of using larger amounts of rennet-extract. Increased amounts of whey in cheese may, if not too excessive, favor more rapid action of the peptic ferment in rennet, because increase of whey in cheese means increase of milk-sugar and this means more lactic acid.

(7) Commercial pepsin, when used in milk and cheese, behaves in a manner closely resembling rennet-extract; since it acts only in the presence of some acid or acid salt and forms relatively small amounts of amino acids as compared with caseoses and peptones.

(8) Rennet-extract, therefore, contains an enzym which has the power of performing the same kind and amount of digesting work in cheese-ripening as pepsin.

(9) Rennet-extract appears to contain, in addition to the peptic ferment, another ferment which has the power to digest milk-casein to some extent in the absence of acids or acid salts.

ACTION OF GALACTASE IN CHEESE-RIPENING

The main characteristics of the milk-enzym, galactase, have been discussed already (p. 297). It has been shown that galactase prepared from separator-slime in the manner described by Babcock and Russell contains, at least, two other enzyms. But we are not particularly interested to know in this discussion whether galactase is one or two or more enzyms; the point of importance here is that milk contains a substance which has the power under certain conditions of converting milk-casein and the paracasein of cheese-curd into soluble forms of proteins and protein derivatives. The fact, first discovered by Babcock and Russell, that there is such an enzym has been abundantly confirmed by work done at the New York experiment station and elsewhere. The work done by the discoverers in studying the properties of galactase led them to regard as one of the distinguishing characteristics of this enzym its ability to convert casein and paracasein into simpler proteins and protein derivatives, finally forming ammonia. On the basis of this property, the conclusion was reached by them that galactase is the chief agent in the ripening of cheddar cheese. Work done at the New York experiment station failed to confirm the conclusion that galactase could form ammonia in the case of either milk or cheese. In carrying on the work in New York, cheese was made from milk to which chloroform had been added and the cheese was kept in an atmosphere of chloroform, in order to prevent the action of micro-organisms. The only ripening agents present were, therefore, galactase and the enzym or enzyms of rennet. Cheese, thus made and kept, has developed no ammonia, or possibly slight traces only, even after 24 months. The data on the next page illustrate this fact.

Stated in a general way, these results show that (1) in cheese made and ripened in the presence of chloroform, the amount of caseoses and peptones is largely in excess of the amount of amino acids; (2) the reverse is true in normal cheese; (3) that ammonia appears in normal cheese much earlier and in larger amounts than in chloroformed cheese, appearing in the latter only after 12 months. About as much ammonia appeared in the normal cheese in 1 month as appeared in the chloroformed cheese in 2 years. The amount of amino acids formed in the chloroformed cheese in 2 years was about equal to the amount formed in the normal cheese at 5½ months.

From these results, it is seen that, in a normal cheese, the amino acids continuously increase, while

DIFFERENCE IN CHARACTER OF CHEMICAL CHANGES IN NORMAL AND IN CHLOROFORMED CHEESE

Character of cheese	Age	Percentage of nitrogen in form of:				
		Water-soluble proteins and derivatives	Caseoses and peptones	Amino acids	Ratio of (1) to (2)	Ammonia
	Months		(1)	(2)		
Normal cheese	1	16.70	2.95	5.42	1:1.80	0.86
Chloroform "	1	8.73	3.71	0.86	1:0.23	.00
Normal "	1½	20.30	2.51	8.49	1:3.40	1.29
Chloroform "	1½	12.00	7.31	1.82	1:0.25	0.00
Normal "	3½	29.80	5.37	12.60	1:2.40	2.51
Chloroform "	3½	17.50	10.20	3.22	1:0.31	0.00
Normal "	5½	34.60	4.97	18.50	1:3.70	3.38
Chloroform "	5½	22.30	12.40	4.73	1:0.39	0.00
Normal "	7	36.10	3.08	20.10	1:6.50	4.42
Chloroform "	7	24.00	10.90	8.11	1:0.74	0.00
Normal "	9	37.85	2.70	23.50	1:8.70	4.87
Chloroform "	9	29.50	12.52	11.60	1:0.93	0.00
Normal "	12	42.30	3.03	24.87	1:8.22	5.69
Chloroform "	12	34.70	11.89	15.77	1:1.33	0.35
Normal "	15	45.10	4.47	27.43	1:6.14	6.04
Chloroform "	15	37.40	15.68	14.41	1:0.92	0.98
Normal "	18	46.07	2.44	30.97	1:1.27	5.45
Chloroform "	18	37.05	10.60	21.06	1:2.00	...
Chloroform "	24	40.26	21.82	18.45	1:0.84	1.04

the caseoses and peptones increase for some months and then decrease. In a chloroformed cheese, the different classes of compounds under discussion all increase continuously from the beginning for two years and more. In normal cheese, traces of ammonia appear at an early stage of ripening, while, in chloroformed cheese, the first traces usually appear

only after the lapse of about one year, and the increase
is so very slow, that even after two years, only minute
amounts are present.   From these results, it appears
that while galactase performs important work in the
ripening of cheese, it cannot be the chief factor in this
process, because its action produces amino acids only
very slowly, and ammonia practically not at all within
the normal lifetime of cheddar cheese.

One of the properties of galactase is its sensitive-
ness to acids.   In milk containing 0.15 per cent of
hydrochloric acid, the galactase is much less active
than in milk containing less acid.   In the work done
at the New York experiment station, the addition of
as much as 0.2 per cent of acid materially increased
the amount of soluble protein compounds in cheese.
Thus, cheese made with no acid had not ripened at all
in 3 months, while cheese made with acid under conditions otherwise the same, contained 32.37 per cent
of its nitrogen in soluble form in 3 months.   This fact
also is not consistent with the belief that galactase
is the chief agency in the process of cheese-ripening.

ACTION OF MICRO-ORGANISMS IN CHEESE-RIPENING

We come now to a consideration of the fourth and
last agency which has been assigned as one of the
causes of the chemical changes in the ripening of cheddar cheese, *micro-organisms*.   Although we discuss
this subject last, it was, in point of time, the first to
be studied.   When the subject of cheese-ripening was
first taken up for serious study, it was thought that
the whole process was due to the action of bacteria,
and all efforts were confined to this single line of

investigation for years, to the neglect of all other possibilities. The general statement of this theory is that the changes observed in proteins during the cheese-ripening process are caused by the direct action of micro-organisms. This has appeared in many different forms according to the particular kind of micro-organisms to which the work was attributed. Of the different micro-organisms assigned as the cause of cheese-ripening, we can mention only one, the lactic acid organisms. Freudenreich has been the most prominent champion of this explanation of the changes in cheese-ripening, and he devoted years of investigation to the lactic acid organisms. In favor of this particular theory, we have the following facts: (1) The lactic acid species of bacteria are abundant from the start and increase in numbers enormously for some time, suppressing the growth of those bacteria that are known to have the power of transforming milk-casein and the paracasein of cheese-curd into soluble products. (2) There is a coincidence in time between the early marked advance in the formation of soluble proteins and the period of bacterial increase. Against this theory we have the following facts: (1) The lactic acid bacteria that are most useful in cheese-making have not been satisfactorily shown to have the power of changing milk-casein or paracasein into soluble products. (2) Ammonia is found at an early stage of cheese-ripening, but it has not been proved that lactic acid organisms produce ammonia. (3) A large proportion of the chemical changes in cheese proteins appear after the lactic acid bacteria have greatly decreased in number. This has been explained by saying that the bacteria secrete an enzym which digests cheese proteins, and this continues the work long after the bacteria themselves disappear. The existence of such enzyms from such a source has not been satisfactorily proved yet. The weight of evidence up to the present time appears to indicate that the chief, if not the only, work of the lactic acid bacteria is completed when milk-sugar has been changed into lactic acid.

We may ask here, What justification have we for the germ theory in general? (1) It has been shown that various germs found in cheese have the power to cause in milk-casein and paracasein changes much like those observed in cheese. (2) Cheese-curd, treated with germicides, fails to ripen. (3) Milk, sterilized and made into sterile cheese, does not ripen. Apparently, there is no ripening, at least nothing like complete ripening, when there are no micro-organisms in cheese. The relations of certain micro-organisms to certain kinds of cheese, especially of the soft type, have been satisfactorily worked out, but the relations to hard types of cheese, like the cheddar, are far from being satisfactorily known.

In going over the results of investigations that bear on the subject of cheddar cheese-ripening, we have seen (1) that lactic acid bacteria do an important and necessary work in changing milk-sugar into lactic acid, which reacts with calcium salts in the milk, forming neutral calcium lactate and acid calcium phosphate. (2) We have seen that, in the presence of the acid medium thus furnished by the action of lactic acid bacteria, the peptic enzym contained in rennet is able to bring about quite extensive chemical changes in the protein of the curd or green cheese, forming such compounds as paranuclein, caseoses and peptones and much smaller proportions of amino acids and little or no ammonia. (3) Galactase is able to perform chemical work similar in character to that of rennet-pepsin, but how much insoluble protein it can render soluble in a given period of time, we do not know. (4) None of the three agencies previously mentioned has the power of forming ammonia, as found in normal cheese-ripening. It, therefore, appears that bacteria alone must be responsible for the production of ammonia and of a large proportion of the amino acids.

It is obvious that the process of cheese-ripening is not as simple as was once believed, but, on the contrary, is exceedingly complex. We cannot say yet just what part each agent plays nor to what extent each is independent of, or dependent upon, the others. For example, the digesting action of rennet is clearly dependent upon acidity. Does the action of rennet have anything to do with the changing of the insoluble curd into a brine-soluble substance and back again into a substance insoluble in brine? Or are these changes immediately dependent upon acid-forming bacteria? Does the rennet have any digesting effect until the brine-insoluble form of protein appears? What forms of cheese proteins can galactase or other milk enzyms attack and under what conditions of acidity, temperature, etc.? When do the bacteria begin their work in rendering soluble the insoluble cheese proteins? Or do they act only upon the products formed by rennet or galactase? Is the bacterial work confined to one specific micro-organism, or is the work associative?

We thus see that there are many details still unsettled; but, in view of what we think we know now, we are justified in believing that the chemical changes of cheese-ripening are the result of several different kinds of fermentative agents, the precise relations of each of which to the details of the ripening process have not been satisfactorily worked out yet.

CHEESE FLAVORS

In connection with the ripening of cheese, the question of cheese flavor is, of course, one of paramount importance. What do we know about the origin of cheese flavor, the particular substance or compound that the flavor comes from, and the method of its formation? Very little, in detail. When we speak or think of flavors in cheese, we too commonly view them in a vague, misty and mysterious way. As a matter of fact, flavors are realities, and sometimes very striking ones, and they come from real things. Every flavor represents one or more specific chemical compounds. Some one chemical compound, or, it may be, some mixture of two or more definite chemical compounds, is entirely responsible for each and every flavor found in cheese, or, for that matter, anywhere else, whether pleasant or otherwise.

The study of the problem of cheese flavors has received less attention than that of the chemical changes in cheese proteins, though the two questions are probably closely related. The questions that present themselves in connection with the normal flavors of American cheddar cheese are: (1) What are they? (2) Where do they come from? (3) What produces them or what is the manner of their formation?

The following facts have some bearing on these questions:

(1) Newly made cheese has no real cheese flavor.

(2) Some days or weeks must pass before real cheese flavor begins to appear.

(3) The breaking down of the proteins contained in the cheese-curd and green cheese, resulting in the formation of water-soluble protein derivatives, precedes, to some extent, the appearance of flavor in cheese.

(4) Cheese flavors are produced by some chemical change in some compound or compounds present in green cheese.

(5) In experiments where bacterial action is prevented, we do not find cheese flavor.

(6) Neither galactase nor rennet nor pepsin appears to be able to produce compounds that have any flavor at all.

(7) Flavor develops more quickly at higher than at lower temperatures.

(8) Flavor develops more rapidly in a moist than in a dry cheese.

(9) Many of the abnormal flavors of cheese can be traced directly to specific micro-organisms. For example, the offensive odor, usually characterized as "taint," is traced to a gas-producing organism closely related to *Bacillus coli communis,* a species of bacteria commonly found in the intestinal tract.

(10) Bitter flavor in cheese has been identified as a compound formed from acetaldehyd (produced by the alcoholic fermentation of milk-sugar) and ammonia, the product of bacterial action.

(11) The flavoring substance, whatever it is, is present in extremely small amounts

(12) A cheesy flavor often develops in butter that is not kept at sufficiently low temperature. A distinct cheesy flavor-is common in kumiss, when it is one or two weeks old.

What suggestions can we derive from the preceding statements?

(1) It is quite possible that the particular compounds which furnish cheese flavor are certain protein derivatives that are formed only after the lapse of some time and are much simpler than the principal protein found in the green cheese. This suggestion is supported by certain facts. (a) Cheese flavors do not appear until these simpler compounds begin to be formed. (b) Such compounds are known to be capable of furnishing flavors. (c) Extremely minute quantities of such substances go a long way in providing flavor. Owing to the extremely minute quantities of such compounds present, the problem of isolating and identifying them is one of great difficulty.

(2) We find that, in cheese cured at low temperatures, we have, in general, about the same kinds of compounds as in cheese cured at higher temperatures, but the chemical changes have not gone quite so fast and we have smaller quantities of these compounds formed that produce flavor. This is in full agreement with the characteristic mild flavor of cold-ripened cheese.

(3) In old cheese, characterized by very strong flavor, especially a pungent odor and biting taste, ammonia is always present in large quantities as com-

pared with mild-flavored cheese. The pungent flavors are due to ammonia compounds.

(4) As to the material source of flavoring compounds in cheese, it is quite probable that they come from the changing of paracasein into simpler compounds, especially such compounds as amino acids and ammonia.

(5) Fat was formerly regarded as the sole source of flavor in cheese, and in butter also. It is true that when fat in cheese decomposes, it may form a variety of flavoring substances, such, for example, as butyric acid, the characteristic flavor of rancid cheese and butter; but such flavors are offensive. Fat in cheddar cheese does not appear to undergo any appreciable change in the early stages of cheese-ripening, especially when cheese is ripened under proper conditions of temperature. The decomposition of fat which gives rise to the small white specks sometimes observed in cheese ripened at low temperature does not affect the flavor in any way.

(6) What is the probable cause of formation of cheese-flavoring compounds? It is well-known that the action of certain bacteria is responsible for many of the bad flavors of cheese. Up to the present time, we are unable to find any satisfactory cause other than micro-organisms for the real, desirable cheese flavor; because, in the absence of living organisms or of the enzyms secreted by them, we get no flavor.

CHAPTER XXVI

Commercial Relations of Cheese-Ripening

In the three chapters preceding, we have considered cheese-ripening in relation to (1) the conditions that affect the loss of weight during the ripening process, (2) the chemical changes taking place, and (3) the causes of the changes that occur in the process. Incidentally, we have touched upon some of the practical relations of the results, but have reserved for a separate chapter a more detailed discussion of the commercial aspects of cheese-ripening. We propose now to take up for more extended treatment some of the practical applications of the results of investigation and shall consider the following subjects: (1) Extent of ripening losses at cheese-factories, (2) value of water in cheese to dairymen, (3) moisture in cheese in relation to commercial quality, (4) the proper percentage of moisture in cheese, (5) value of water in cheese to consumers, (6) the reduction of ripening losses in commercial investigations, (7) the relation of conditions of ripening to the quality of cheese, (8) the effects of freezing on quality of cheese, (9) financial application of results of cheese-ripening investigations.

FACTORY LOSSES IN RIPENING

From inquiries made among cheese-makers several years ago, we found quite a variation in respect to the loss of moisture experienced by them in ripening cheese. One of the most complete records, covering an entire season, furnished by a cheese-maker and factory owner who has better than average conditions in his curing-rooms, made the average loss of weight during 30 days amount to about 5 pounds per 100 pounds of cheese. Others reported an average loss for the first 30 days as high as 10 pounds per 100 pounds of cheese. The average loss was somewhere between these two extremes, probably not far from 7 pounds per 100 pounds of cheese. In many factories, conditions have not improved since the inquiry was made.

VALUE OF WATER IN CHEESE TO DAIRY-MEN

To the cheese-maker and producer of milk, water in cheese is money *when put there in the right way and in the proper proportions*. It is essential, in the process of manufacture, to incorporate water in cheese in quantities best suited to the requirement of the market for which the cheese is intended, and then it is equally essential that the water be kept there with the least possible loss. From the dairymen's standpoint, it is desirable to sell as much water in cheese as will suit the consumer. In preventing excessive loss of moisture, there is more water to sell at cheese prices, and at the same time a resulting product that suits the consumer better. In the conditions prevailing in many factories, high temperatures which cause increased loss of moisture also cause loss of fat by exudation from the surface of the cheese. At 75° F. and above, this *loss becomes considerable*. It has been shown that the loss of moisture in curing-rooms can be reduced to 4 pounds per 100 pounds of cheese under conditions practicable at factories. Using this figure as a basis for calculation, we find that, for every 100 pounds of cheese, an average of 3 pounds of water could be saved to sell at cheese prices. This would mean an average increase of 30 cents, received for every 100 pounds of cheese. This would mean an average saving of $300 a season for a factory with a total season's output of 100,000 pounds of cheese. One cheese-maker reports that he calculated one season's loss from shrinkage and found it over $600. While such losses may not be regarded as large in comparison with the total receipts, they constitute a noticeable percentage when viewed as unnecessary decrease of profits, and are well worth saving.

MOISTURE IN CHEESE IN RELATION TO COMMERCIAL QUALITY

We have just called attention to increased receipts coming from cheese, as a result of preventing excessive loss of moisture. Such saving of moisture not only increases the amount of cheese to be sold but also increases the value of the cheese from the standpoint of commercial quality.

The relations existing between moisture and flavor are known only in a very general way. But we know something of the general relation between moisture and texture. Excessive moisture produces a degree of softness, which is undesirable, from a commercial standpoint, and at ordinary temperatures favors the formation of holes, a serious fault in the texture of cheddar cheese intended for export trade. On the other hand, deficient moisture favors the production of a crumbly, dry, mealy body, which is an undesirable condition. High temperatures cause excessive loss of moisture and result in the production of a crumbly body. This condition injures the commercial quality of cheese and results in lower prices for such cheese. The following table illustrates, in a practical way, the effect of different temperatures upon texture and moisture:

EFFECT OF TEMPERATURE OF CURING ON TEXTURE AND MOISTURE OF CHEESE

Temperature of curing-room	Texture of cheese (Perfect texture is 25)	Moisture lost by 100 pounds of cheese
		Lbs.
55°F.	24.6	8.5
60°F.	24.4	9.0
65°F.	23.6	9.2
70°F.	22.0	10.2
75°F.	21.4	10.7
80°F.	20.6	13.1

WHAT PERCENTAGE OF MOISTURE SHOULD CHEESE HAVE?

Much of the cheese made in New York contains, in the fresh state, from 36 to 37.5 per cent of water. The home-trade cheese, much of which is made in the fall, contains 38 to 40 per cent of water. For the average consumer, it is safe to say, the amount of moisture in cheese should be not less than 33 to 35 per cent at the time of consumption. Taking everything into consideration, it is reasonable to expect better results in reference to quality by holding a moderate amount of moisture in the green cheese and so ripening as to lose only a small amount of water, than by holding an excessive amount of moisture in the green cheese and so ripening as to lose a larger amount of moisture. Some cheese-makers expect that they must lose 10 pounds of weight per 100 pounds of cheese in ripening, and they attempt to meet this loss by retaining 40 per cent or more of moisture in the cheese. Such a practice cannot lead to good results from any point of view.

A fact that should not be lost sight of in this connection is this: Cheese ripened at such low temperatures as are favorable to diminishing the loss of moisture can carry larger amounts of moisture from the start without impairing the quality

VALUE OF WATER IN CHEESE TO CONSUMERS

In the first place, cheese that has not lost too much of its moisture is more pleasing to the taste of the average consumer. In the next place, the more completely a cheese dries out, the harder and thicker is the rind and the greater the loss to the consumer. Most people have become accustomed to such a waste, but much of it is unnecessary. In a carefully ripened cheese, the rind is comparatively moist and only a very thin portion need be lost, and even this can be used in cooking.

REDUCTION OF RIPENING LOSSES IN COMMERCIAL INVESTIGATIONS

In 1902-3 an investigation, on a commercial scale, was undertaken by the Dairy Division of the Bureau of Animal Industry, United States Department of

Agriculture, in co-operation with the experiment stations of Wisconsin and New York, in which cheese was ripened at 40°, 50° and 60° F., some being covered with paraffin.   In 1903-4 the Dairy Division

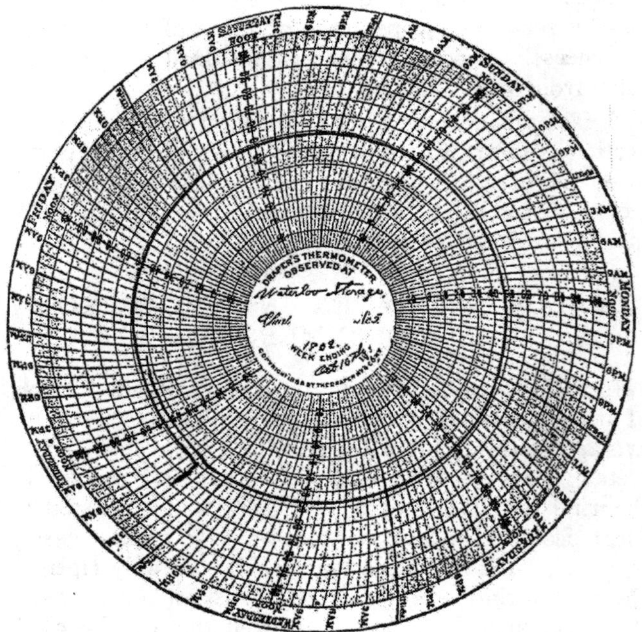

FIG. 47—A WEEK'S TEMPERATURE RECORD OF A CURING-ROOM
HELD AT 50°F

repeated the work, but used a lower range of temperatures, 28°, 34° and 40° F., and, in one case, 5° F.   The object of these investigations was to study on a commercial scale, under commercial conditions, (1) the influence which different temperatures have upon (a) the loss of weight in cheese, and

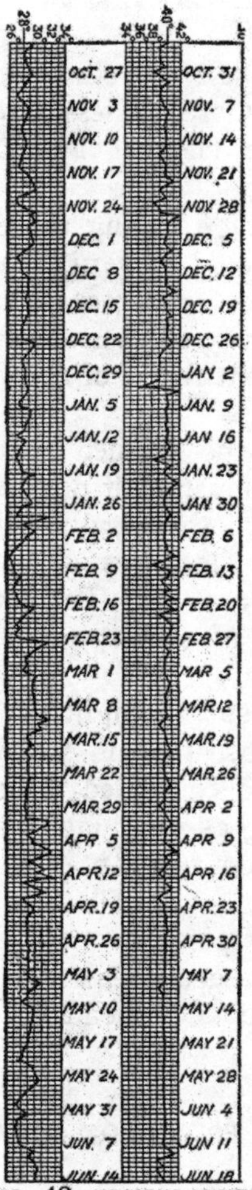

FIG. 48--TEMPERATURE RECORD COVERING SEVERAL MONTHS IN CASE OF CURING - ROOMS HELD AT 28° AND 40° F.

(b) the commercial qualities of the cheese; and (2) the influence of covering cheese with paraffin upon (a) the loss of weight in cheese, and (b) the commercial qualities of the cheese, when kept at different temperatures.

In the different sets of experiments, the cheeses used were of the following sizes: (1) Cheddars, 65-70 pounds; (2) Cheddars, 40-45 pounds; (3) Flats or Twins, 30-35 pounds; (4) Daisies, 20 pounds; (5) Young Americas, 10 to 12½ pounds; (6) Prints, 10 pounds.

The experiments were begun in October and extended through periods of time lasting 20 to 35 weeks. The cheeses were obtained direct from factories in New York, Pennsylvania, Ohio, Michigan, Illinois, Wisconsin and Iowa. They were 10 to 15 days old when placed in storage. In most cases they represented the cheddar type manufactured for export trade, close-textured, firm-bodied and long-keeping. In some cases the Michigan type was used, which is characterized as soft-bodied, of high water content, more or less porous and poor in keeping quality. Another type represented was the sweet-curd, more or less intermediate in qualities between the cheddar and the Michigan home-trade types.

The cheeses were placed in storage during the experiments where the temperature could be very closely kept under control. Various devices and records are in use for ascertaining the uniformity of the temperature from day to day. Two different forms of records are given in Figs. 47 and 48.

It is not practicable to present the detailed results of the different experiments; we must limit our consideration to a general summary of the results. We shall present the results relating to the losses of ripening under the following subdivisions: (1) Temperature, (2) size of cheese, (3) type of cheese, and (4) coating with paraffin.

Influence of temperature on loss of weight.—The results of the various investigations agree in the following respects: (1) The cheese continued to lose weight in nearly every case as long as weighings were made (about 250 days), this being true at all temperatures employed (28°-60° F.). (2) The loss of weight was least at the lowest temperature (28° F.) and increased with rise of temperature. This can be illustrated in case of the 65-70-pound cheddars, as follows:

POUNDS OF WEIGHT LOST FOR 100 POUNDS OF CHEESE
STORED AT

	28°F.	34°F.	40°F.	50°F.	60°F.
27 weeks	1.81	4.18	4.68	6.00	9.90
35 weeks	2.88	5.12	5.87	...	...

At the end of 27 weeks, the loss of weight was more than 3 times as great at 40° F. as at 28° F., and about 5 times as great at 60° F. as at 28° F. At the end of 35 weeks, the loss at 40° F. was just twice as great as at 28° F.

Influence of size of cheese in loss of weight.— Small-sized cheeses, other conditions being the same, lost a larger amount of moisture than large cheeses. This tendency is shown at different temperatures by the following tabulated statement:

WEIGHT LOST PER 100 POUNDS OF CHEESE IN 20 WEEKS

Average weight of cheese	At 40°F.	At 50°F.	At 60°F.
Pounds	Pounds	Pounds	Pounds
70	2.5	2.4	4.2
45	2.7	3.7	5.1
35	3.9	5.9	8.5
12½	4.6	8.1	12.0

The variation in loss between different sizes is much less at lower than at higher temperature.

Influence of type of cheese on loss of weight.— Firm-bodied, close-textured cheese loses water less rapidly than soft-bodied, open-textured cheese (p. 324).

Influence of paraffin coating on loss of weight.— Cheese covered with paraffin loses less weight than cheese not so coated. By covering cheese with paraffin, a saving in loss of weight can be effected amounting to 5 or 6 pounds per 100 pounds of cheese at 60° F.; and at 50° F. or below the total loss of weight can be reduced to 1 or 2 pounds per 100 pounds of cheese in the ordinary period of ripening. At 40° F., the loss in case of the large-sized cheddar was reduced about one-half, as compared with cheese not coated; at 34° F., nearly three-fourths of the loss was prevented; at 28° F., the losses were very slight, only a little over ½ pound in 27 weeks. The use of paraffin coating makes a greater proportionate saving in small cheeses than in large ones. In the case of the Young America cheeses, the loss at 40° F. was reduced to about one-fourth of what it was when the cheese was uncoated

RELATIONS OF CONDITIONS OF RIPENING TO QUALITY OF CHEESE

In all the experiments mentioned, carefully selected experts judged the cheese from a commercial standpoint and scored them. These examinations were made at regular intervals during the continuation of the experiments. The results will be considered with reference to the effect of (1) temperature, (2) coating with paraffin.

Influence of temperature on quality.—Below 40° F., and down to 28° F., the temperature does not appear to have any marked effect upon the commercial quality of cheese. Cheese ripened at 40° was superior, almost without exception, to cheese ripened at higher temperatures. The following figures show the average scores at different temperatures:

Temperature	Score
40°F.	95.7
50°F.	94.2
60°F.	91.7

There was more marked deterioration in quality between 50° and 60° F. than between 40° and 50° F. In general, the higher the temperature, the greater is the relative deterioration of cheese in quality for each degree of temperature.

The following figures demonstrate that the difference in quality falls mostly on the flavor (50, perfect), and to a less extent on texture and body (25, perfect):

Qualities	At 40°F.	At 50°F.	At 60°F.
Flavor....................	47.4	46.4	44.8
Body and texture..........	23.4	23.0	22.2

At any given time, the cheese ripened at 40° F. was usually better in quality than that at 50° F., and that at 50° F. was better than that at 60° F. The longer the time of ripening, the greater was the difference in favor of the lower temperatures, as illustrated in the following table:

Age of cheese	Score at 40°F.	Score at 50°F.	Score at 60°F.
Weeks			
10	96.3	94.7	92.
20	93.8	91.5	89.7
28	94.2	91.9	...
35	95.3	...	...

The cheese cured at 60° F. showed such deterioration of quality in 20 weeks that it was sold in order to prevent complete loss.

Influence of paraffin coating on quality.—The effect of covering cheese with paraffin was, in several cases, to improve the quality of the cheese so covered. The difference was more marked at 60° F. than at lower temperatures. The cheese coated with paraffin and ripened at 40° gave its highest score at the end of 35 weeks. In no case did the cheese coated with paraffin show any depreciation in quality as compared with cheese not so covered. These results are in harmony with what one might reasonably predict. Any condition which maintains in the cheese the uniformity of the moisture, when not in excess, favors the normal ripening changes.

The finish of cheese was greatly improved by a coating of paraffin, since the growth of molds is prevented. In every case cheeses covered with paraffin were entirely clean, while the others were more or less heavily coated with molds.

FIG. 49—SECTION OF FROZEN CHEDDAR CHEESE AFTER STORAGE 5½ MONTHS AT 5° F.

THE EFFECTS OF FREEZING ON QUALITY OF CHEESE

Cheese placed in a room kept at 5° F. was immediately frozen hard. After a time the ends and sides appeared to be lumpy, due to the expansion of the frozen water in the cheese. After being 6 months in a frozen condition, the cheese was slowly thawed and examined. When freshly cut, the appearance was normal, but the surface dried out more rapidly than in normal cheddar cheese. The body was crumbly, as in the case of a cheese deficient in water. Little or no ripening had taken place and such insipid flavor as there was did not resemble anything normal. The frozen cheese also showed a mottled appearance, not shown by any other cheese ripened at 28° F. or above. Fig. 49 shows the appearance of a cheese after being kept at 5° F. for several months.

FINANCIAL APPLICATION OF RESULTS OF CHEESE-RIPENING INVESTIGATIONS

Any reduction in loss of weight or any improvement in quality in cheese-ripening means an increase of money that can be realized in the sale of cheese. We have seen that the curing of cheese at temperatures as low as 40° F. has the effect of (1) preventing loss of moisture and (2) increasing the value of the cheese. Therefore, we not only have more cheese to sell but can sell it at a higher price. Taking cheese 20 weeks old as a basis for comparison, we know how much weight is lost at different temperatures and also the difference in price. From these figures the following tabulated statement is given:

MONEY RETURNS AT SEVERAL TEMPERATURES

Temperature of curing	Cured cheese equivalent to 100 pounds of green cheese	Market price of 1 pound of cheese	Receipts from cheese
Degrees F.	Pounds	Cents	Dollars
40	96.2	13.275	12.77
50	95.2	13.050	12.42
60	92.2	12.675	11.69

These figures indicate that from 100 pounds of green cheese put into the curing-room we were able to realize from that cured at 40° F., 35 cents more than from cheese cured at 50° F., and $1.08 more than from that cured at 60° F. From the cheese cured at 50° F., we received 73 cents more for 100 pounds than from that cured at 60° F.

If we compare our results obtained with cheese covered with paraffin with those given by cheese not so covered, we have the following tabulated statement:

COMPARATIVE VALUE OF PARAFFINED AND UNPARAFFINED CHEESE

Temperature of curing-room	Cured cheese equivalent to 100 pounds of green cheese		Value of 1 pound of cheese		Receipts from cheese	
	Paraffined	Not paraffined	Paraffined	Not paraffined	Paraffined	Not paraffined
Deg. F.	Pounds	Pounds	Cents	Cents	Dollars	Dollars
40	99.7	96.2	14.25	14.25	14.21	13.70
50	99.5	95.2	14.25	14.25	14.19	13.56
60	98.6	92.2	13.75	13.50	13.56	12.45

At 40° F. the difference in favor of the paraffined cheese is 51 cents for 100 pounds of cheese originally placed in the curing-room; at 50° F. the difference is 63 cents, and at 60° F., $1.11. Covering cheese with paraffin results in greater saving at higher temperatures than at lower temperatures.

Comparing paraffined cheese cured at 40° F. with unparaffined cheese cured at 60° F., we find a difference of $1.76 for 100 pounds of cheese in favor of the paraffined cheese and the lower temperature.

These experiments demonstrate that, by curing cheese at lower temperatures than those that have been commonly in use, it is possible to obtain a perfect, edible quality of cheddar cheese, which means cheese of clean, mild, delicate flavor, somewhat lasting, but not so sharp as to bite the tongue; and body such that a piece of cheese on the tongue dissolves completely, leaving only a sensation of smoothness and richness, with no trace of harshness or grittiness. Such cheese can be eaten without the disagreeable effect of long after-tasting, which imperfectly cured cheese produces. The consumption of cheese can be greatly stimulated by making the cheese right and then ripening it under proper conditions of temperature and moisture.

METHODS OF PROVIDING PROPER CONDITIONS FOR CHEESE-RIPENING

There are three ways in which the evils resulting from improper conditions of ripening can be overcome: (1) Immediate sale and removal of cheese, (2) providing proper conditions in cheese-factory and (3) central curing-stations. We will briefly consider each.

Immediate sale and removal.—In factories which are provided with no adequate facilities for ripening cheese, it has in many cases come to be a custom to sell the cheese before it has had a chance to deteriorate. So far as the cheese-factory is concerned, this system relieves it of responsibility for the cheese after its manufacture; but the factory patrons lose such advantage as would come from providing good curing-rooms and holding the cheese. The buyer has an opportunity for any increased profit that comes from ripening the cheese properly; but too often he has no equipment for ripening and hastens to dispose of the cheese as quickly as possible. In such cases the cheese is put before consumers when it is still so green as to do injustice to the reputation of the cheese-maker and the cheese-factory. The most extensive cheese buyers usually have cold-storage plants and hold the cheese.

Providing proper conditions in cheese-factory.— In many cases, probably in the majority of factories, the best interests of the factory will be conserved by providing a curing-room as a part of the factory equipment, such as is described on page 103. This is practicable, efficient and economical from every point of view.

Central curing-stations.—In Wisconsin and Canada the problem of cheese-curing has been solved, to some extent, by providing buildings, centrally located with reference to a number of cheese-factories, where the cheese are taken as soon as practicable and stored until sold. Such curing-stations are provided with a modern cold-storage equipment and are able perfectly to control conditions of temperature and humidity. The cost of ripening cheese in this way is more than repaid by the increase of price received for the cured cheese.

Part IV

Methods of Making Different Varieties of Cheese:

Stilton.
English Sage.
Cottage.
Pasteurized Neufchatel
Cream.
Club.
Edam.
Gouda.

CHAPTER XXVII

Methods of Making Different Varieties of Cheese

While the original purpose of the authors was to confine the matter of the book to the subject of cheddar cheese, it has seemed desirable to devote one chapter to a brief description of the methods of making some other varieties of cheese. We have chosen for the most part those varieties which can be made with simple equipment. Such varieties as Swiss cheese, for example, can not be properly treated in a limited way.

STILTON CHEESE

In England Stilton cheese is the most popular of all blue-mold varieties. In Canada, only a small quantity of Stilton cheese is manufactured and, in the United States, a still smaller quantity.

First stages of cheese-making process.—The method of making modern Stilton cheese does not vary greatly in the early stages from that of cheddar cheese-making. Up to the time of salting, the process is practically the same in both cases. The main characteristic in Stilton cheese is that it should contain a uniform growth of blue mold distributed through its interior mass.

Starting mold-formation.—The salt before being applied should be mixed with a small amount of

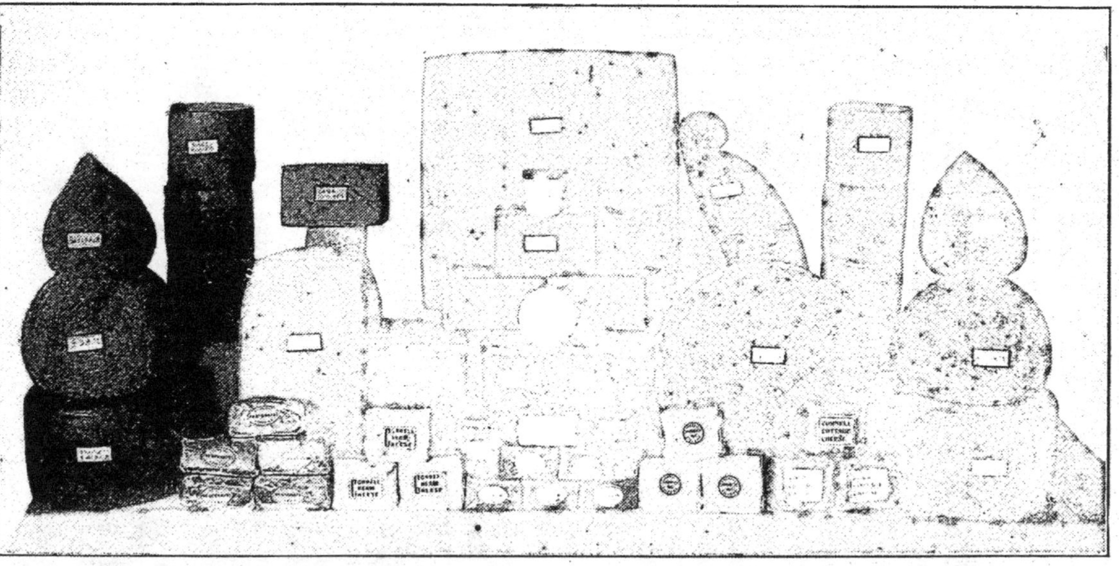

VARIETIES OF FANCY CHEESES

mold growth. As a result of this even distribution of salt through the curd, the mold becomes uniformly distributed over the surface of each piece of curd.

Pressing cheese.—The cheese is made in ordinary Young-America hoops and should weigh about 12 pounds each. The pressure should be light but continuous for at least 48 hours.

Ripening process.—To have Stilton cheese ripen into the best condition it should be kept in a damp, moldy cellar, where the temperature does not go above 65° F. Here the cheese soon becomes coated with blue mold, which influences the ripening process.

Stilton cheese should not be consumed before it is at least 2 months old.

ENGLISH SAGE CHEESE

Early stages of process.—Up to the time of milling, the process is similar to that of cheddar cheese. The method usually followed is to divide the milk, placing about one-fourth in a small vat, to which is added green vegetable coloring-matter at the rate of 12 ounces for 1,000 pounds of milk. The balance of the milk is handled without being colored. When the whey is removed, the colored curd is evenly mixed with the uncolored to produce the desired mottled appearance. (This result can also be accomplished without dividing the milk by treating the curd with the coloring-matter just before salting.) Before pressing, sage flavoring-extract is sprayed over the curd. When finished, the cheese should present a uniformly green mottled appearance.

Pressing cheese.—The regular-sized English sage cheese weighs about 5 pounds, but in America all sizes are found, weighing from 2 to 80 pounds. The pressure in hoops should be continuous for 24 to 48 hours.

Ripening process.—Sage cheese can be ripened in an ordinary cellar or cool room where the temperature does not go above 60° F. It should be held until it has developed the pronounced flavor that is characteristic of the cheese.

COTTAGE-CHEESE

Cottage-cheese is manufactured and consumed extensively in the United States. The original Dutch cottage-cheese is the product made by allowing milk to stand until it coagulates by the ordinary process of souring. The curd is put into cotton bags to drain, and, after all free whey has escaped, the curd is salted. It is then pressed into the form of balls and is ready for immediate consumption.

The modern method of cottage-cheese-making differs somewhat from the above and gives a more uniform quality of cheese.

Material to use.—Skim-milk should be used, as whole-milk loses too much of its fat in the manufacturing process.

Preparation and use of starter.—In making cottage-cheese on a large scale, time can be saved and quality improved by hastening the souring of the milk through the use of a starter prepared in the manner already described (p. 18). The character of the starter is of much importance, since the flavor of the cheese almost entirely depends upon it. Impure starters may cause slimy fermentation, and from such curd the whey will not separate easily.

1. **Method of making cottage-cheese without starter.**—Milk is kept at a temperature of 70° to 75° F. until well curdled, which will usually require about 48 hours. The curdled mass is then broken by hand or cut by a curd-knife into large pieces, which should be as uniform as possible. The temperature is raised to 90° F., where it is kept till the whey appears clear. Heating should not be done too rapidly, as it injures the texture of the cheese. From 30 to 40 minutes should be required for this. About 15 minutes after completion of the heating, or when the whey has become well separated from the curd, the whey is removed and the curd placed in muslin bags or on racks, where it is allowed to drain.

The curd is then salted at the rate of 1 pound for 100 pounds of curd, or according to taste, then shaped into pound or half-pound balls, and finally wrapped in oiled paper. For the finest quality of cheese, the curd, before being made into balls, should be mixed with thick, ripened cream at the rate of 1 ounce of cream for 1 pound of cheese.

2. **Method of making cottage-cheese with use of starter.**—As soon as the skim-milk is placed in the manufacturing vat, from 2 to 3 per cent of good commercial starter is added and thoroughly mixed through the entire mass. The subsequent steps are similar to those given in preceding paragraph.

3. **Method of making cottage-cheese with use of starter and rennet.**—The starter is added as previously described. About 8 hours later rennet-extract is added at the rate of 1 ounce for each 1,000 pounds of milk. The rennet should be well diluted with cold water to prevent too rapid coagulation. The balance of the process is similar to that already described. When rennet is used, the coagulation can be secured with a smaller percentage of acid development. About 0.4 per cent acid in the whey at the time of its removal makes the best flavor and texture.

4. **Method of making cottage-cheese from skim-milk and buttermilk.**—This process is now becoming popular with manufacturers of cottage-cheese, since it affords a way of utilizing milk that might otherwise be wasted. The buttermilk and skim-milk are mixed in various proportions. The temperature for heating the milk depends on the amount of buttermilk and the amount of acidity. The lower the temperature used consistent with a good coagulation, the smoother will be the texture of the cheese. In making cottage-cheese by any of these methods the quality can generally be improved and greater uniformity secured by the use of a small amount of rennet.

5. **Method of making cottage-cheese by direct addition of hydrochloric acid.**—Have the milk at 70° to 80° F. Measure out pure hydrochloric acid, of specific gravity 1.20, at the rate of 10 ounces for 100 pounds of milk. Dilute with ten times its weight of cold water and add to milk gradually, stirring the milk constantly while the acid is being

added.   Continue the stirring until the curd separates completely, leaving a clear whey entirely
free from milkiness.   The whey is then removed from
the curd and the operation completed as before.   In
order to get the proper flavor, it will be necessary to
mix with the curd some sour, thick milk or cream.
This method does not give as satisfactory results as
the others described.

Qualities of cottage-cheese.—Flavor and texture
are the most important qualities in cottage-cheese.
The flavor should be that of mildly-soured milk
or well-ripened cream.   There should be an entire
absence of all objectionable flavor, such as bitter
taste, stable flavor, etc.   If the cheese tastes too sour
it is usually due to keeping too much whey in the
curd.   The use of a starter is apt to insure the right
kind of flavor.   The texture of cottage-cheese is
largely dependent on the amount of moisture in the
cheese.   When the percentage of moisture is much
below 70, the cheese is harsh, dry and sawdust-like.
The right texture of cottage-cheese is smooth and
free from grittiness.   Difficulty is often experienced
in securing a uniform quality at all seasons of the
year.   The trouble is generally caused by too sudden changes in the temperature of the curd or in
the development of lactic acid.   Cottage-cheese
should be kept in a cool place.   It usually sells for
5 to 10 cents per pound.

Yield of cottage-cheese.—From 100 pounds of
milk one should obtain from 20 to 22 pounds of cheese.
Variation in moisture makes much variation in
yield.

Composition of cottage-cheese.—Cottage-cheese of the best texture contains 70 to 75 per cent of moisture. Curdling milk at too high a temperature and heating the curd too high or too long will make the cheese too dry. Cottage-cheese contains about 3.5 to 4 per cent of milk sugar and 2 to 2.5 per cent of nitrogen.

PASTEURIZED NEUFCHATEL CHEESE

This type of soft cheese is one of the most palatable of the kind. It is mild in flavor and easily digested.

Method of making.—Place 30 pounds of clean, sweet, whole-milk in an ordinary, plain shotgun can. The milk should then be heated to 165° F. for 20 minutes by placing the can in hot water. After reaching this temperature it should be immediately cooled to 72° F. When cool, 1.0 cubic centimeter of clean, commercial starter is added, diluted in 100 cc. of cold water. When the starter has been evenly stirred through the milk, rennet is added at the rate of 0.4 cc. to 30 pounds of milk. The rennet should be diluted with cold water, at the rate of 1 cc. of rennet to 99 cc. of water. Enough rennet should be used to give a firm coagulation in 12 hours. As soon as the milk has become firmly coagulated, it should be poured from the can onto a strainer-rack where the whey is allowed to drain from it. At this time, the whey dripping from the curd should have from 0.30 to 0.32 per cent acidity. High acidity spoils the characteristic flavor and taste. While the curd is drying, it should have the portions on the outside of the strainer stirred into the more moist portion in the center. This is to prevent hard particles forming from excessive drying. Some pressure may be used to aid in expelling the whey. The draining of whey should be so regulated that, at the time of salting, it will not have more than 0.40 per cent of acidity. When all free whey has escaped, salt is applied at the rate of 1½ pounds to 100 pounds of cheese. The cheese is shaped by small cylindrical molds and then wrapped in parchment paper and tin-foil. After being kept for 24 hours in a cool place, the cheese is then ready for eating.

CREAM CHEESE

The manufacture of cream cheese is very similar to that of pasteurized Neufchatel cheese, with the exception that the milk is not usually pasteurized. Milk is modified so that it tests about 10 per cent of milk-fat. At the time of adding rennet, the acidity should not be more than 0.15 per cent.

The cheese is shaped by square molds and each weighs usually about ¼ pound.

Sometimes cream cheese is made by adding cream to the curd of pasteurized Neufchatel cheese just before salt is applied. This method makes a cheese of very fine quality.

CLUB-CHEESE

Club-cheese is one of the most extensively used varieties of cheese. Practically every hotel and restaurant in every country uses more or less of it.

The manufacturing process is simple enough, and yet the desired quality is hard to obtain. The value of the cheese depends entirely upon the quality of the constituents used.

Method of making.—One grinds 8 pounds of well-ripened cheddar cheese of finest quality in an ordinary meat-grinding machine. After the cheese has been through the machine once, one pound of butter of the best quality is mixed with it and the whole mass again run through the machine. The mixture is then stirred and worked with the hands till free from all lumps. It is then packed in jars of some form and must be kept in a cool place. It is well to smear the inside walls of the jar with melted butter before packing the cheese in it and then put a thin layer of melted butter over the top of the packed cheese before putting on cover. Finest club-cheese usually sells for about 40 cents a pound.

EDAM CHEESE

Edam cheese is a sweet-curd cheese, made from partially skimmed milk. It comes to the market in the form of round, red balls, each weighing from 3½ to 4 pounds when cured. They are largely manufactured in Northern Holland and derive their name from a town which is famous as a market for this kind of cheese

Kind of milk used.—Milk from which one-fourth to one-third of the fat has been removed is used. Too great pains cannot be taken in regard to the condition of the milk. It should be fresh, free from every trace of taint; in brief, it should be in as perfect condition as it is possible to have milk.

Treatment of milk before adding rennet.—The temperature of the milk should be brought up to a point not below 85° F. nor much above 88° F. When the desired temperature has become constant, then the coloring-matter should be added to the milk and thoroughly incorporated by stirring before the rennet is added.

Addition of rennet to milk.—When the temperature reaches the desired point 85° to 88° F. and remains there stationary, the rennet-extract is added, 4½ to 5½ ounces being taken for 1,000 pounds of milk, or enough to coagulate the milk in the desired time, at the actual temperature used. The milk should be completely coagulated, ready for cutting, in about 12 to 18 minutes from the time the rennet is added.   The same precautions observed in making cheddar cheese should be followed in making Edam cheese with reference to care in adding the rennet, such as careful, accurate measurement, dilution with pure water before addition to milk, etc.

Cutting the curd.—When the curd breaks clean across the finger, it should be cut; the curd is cut a very little softer than in the cheddar process as ordinarily practiced.   First, a vertical knife is used and the curd is cut lengthwise, after which it is allowed to stand until the slices of curd begin to show the separation of whey.   Then the vertical knife is used in cutting crosswise, after which the horizontal knife is at once used. Any curd adhering to the bottom and sides of the vat is carefully removed by the hand, after which the curd-knife is again passed through the mass of curd lengthwise and crosswise, continuing the cutting until the curd has been cut as uniformly as possible into very small pieces.

Treatment of curd after cutting.—When the cutting is completed, then one commences at once to heat the curd up to the temperature of 93° to 96° F. The heating is done as quickly as possible. While the heating is in progress, the curd is kept constantly agitated to prevent settling and consequent overheating. As soon as the curd shows signs of hardening, which the experience of the worker will enable him to determine, the whey is drawn off until the upper surface of the curd appears, when one should commence to fill the press-molds.

Filling molds, pressing and dressing cheese.— The molds, which are described later in detail, are well soaked in warm water previous to use, in order to prevent too sudden chilling of curd and consequent checking of separation of whey. As soon as the whey is drawn off, as indicated above, one commences to fill the pressing-molds. The filling should be done as rapidly as possible to prevent too great cooling of curd. When the curd has been put into the molds, its temperature should not be below 88° F. Unless care is taken to keep the curd covered, the portion that is last put into the molds may become too much cooled. In making Edam cheese on a small scale, it is a good plan to squeeze the moisture out by the hands as much as possible and then break it up again before putting in the molds, when the curd should be pressed into the mold by the hands as firmly as possible. The molds should be filled as nearly alike as possible. The cheese should weigh from 5 to 5¼ pounds each when ready for the press. When the filling of molds is completed, they are put under continual pressure of 20 to 25 pounds for about 25 or 30 minutes. While the cheese is being pressed, some sweet whey is heated to a temperature of 125° or 130° F. and this whey should not be allowed to go below 120° F. at any time while it is being used. When the cheeses are taken from their molds, each is put into the warm whey for two minutes, then removed and dressed. For dressing Edam cheese the ordinary cheese-bandage cloth is used. This is cut into strips which should be long enough to reach entirely around the cheese and overlap an inch or so, and which should be wide enough to cover all but a small portion of the ends of the cheese when put in place. Before putting on the bandage, all rough projections should be carefully pared from the cheese. In putting on the bandage, the cheese is held in one hand and the bandage is wrapped carefully around the cheese, so that the whole cheese is covered, except a small portion on the upper and lower surface of the cheese. These bare spots are covered by small pieces of bandage cloth of a size sufficient to cover the bare surface. The bandage is kept wet with the warm, sweet whey, thus facilitating the process of dressing. After each cheese is dressed, it should be replaced in the pressing-mold, care being taken that the bandage remains in place and leaves no portion of the surface of the cheese uncovered and in direct contact with the mold. The cheese is then put under continual pressure of 60 to 120 pounds and kept under this continual pressure for 6 to 12 hours.

Salting and curing.—There are two methods which may be employed in salting, *dry-salting and wet-salting.* In *dry-salting,* when the cheese is finally taken from the press, it is removed from the press-mold, its bandage is removed completely and the cheese placed in another mold, quite similar, known as the salting-mold. Each cheese is placed in a salting-mold with a coating of fine salt completely surrounding it. The cheese is salted in this way once each day for 5 or 6 days. Each day the cheese should be turned when it is replaced in the mold, so that it will not be rounded on one end more than another. This is for the purpose of making both ends uniform in shape, giving each the proper rounding peculiar to the shape of the cheese. In the method of wet-salting, the cheese is placed in a tank of salt brine, made by dissolving common salt in water in the proportion of about one pound of salt to 2½ quarts of water. Each cheese is turned once a day and should be left in the brine 7 or 8 days. When the cheese is taken from the salting-mold or salt bath it is placed in warm water and is given a vigorous, thorough brushing in order to remove all slimy or greasy substances that may have accumulated on the outer surface of the cheese. When the surface of the cheese is well cleansed, it is carefully wiped dry with a linen towel and placed upon a shelf in the curing-room. In being placed on the shelves, the cheeses should be placed in contact so as to support one another. until they have flattened out at both ends so much that they can stand upright alone. Then they are placed far enough apart to allow a little air space between them. Another method of securing the flattened ends is to support each cheese on opposite sides by wedge-shaped pieces of wood. After they are placed on the shelves in the curing-room, they are turned once a day and rubbed with the bare hand during the first month, twice a week during the second month, and once a week after that. When any slimy substance appears on the surface of the cheese, it should be washed off at once with warm water or sweet whey. The special conditions of the curing-room will be noticed in detail below. When the cheeses are about two months old, they can be prepared for market, which is done in the following manner: They are first made smooth on the surface by being turned in a lathe or in some other manner, after which the surface is colored. For coloring, some carmine is dissolved in alcohol or ammonia to get the proper shade, and in this color-bath the cheeses are placed for about one minute, when they are removed and allowed to drain, and as soon as they are dry the outside of each cheese is rubbed with boiled linseed oil, in order to prevent checking. They are then wrapped in tinfoil, which is done very much like the bandaging. Care must be taken to put the tin-foil on so that it presents a smooth, neat appearance. The cheeses are finally packed in boxes, each box containing 12 cheeses, arranged in two layers of six each, with a separate partition for each cheese.

Curing-room.—Much more attention must be given to the conditions of the curing-room as regards moisture and temperature than in the case of cheddar cheese. The curing-room should be well ventilated, should be quite moist and its temperature should be kept between 50° and 65° F. These conditions are best secured in some form of cellar.

Utensils employed in making Edam cheese.—Aside from the molds, continual press and salting-vat, the same apparatus that is used in making

FIG. 50—EDAM PRESS-MOLD AND COVER

cheddar cheese can be used in making Edam cheese. The pressing-mold is turned preferably from white wood or, in any case, from wood that will not taint. Each mold consists of two parts; the lower part constitutes the main part of the mold, the upper portion is simply a cover. The lower portion or body of the mold has several holes in the bottom, from which the whey flows when the cheese is pressed. Care must be taken to prevent these holes being stopped up by curd. This portion of the mold is about 6 inches deep and 6 inches in diameter across the top. The salting-mold has no cover and the bottom is provided with only one hole for the outflow of whey; in other respects it is much like the pressing-mold.

Fig. 50 shows the external appearance of the press-mold with cover in position, the inner surface of the cover, and the inside appearance of the press-mold.   Fig. 51 shows the press-mold and cover in

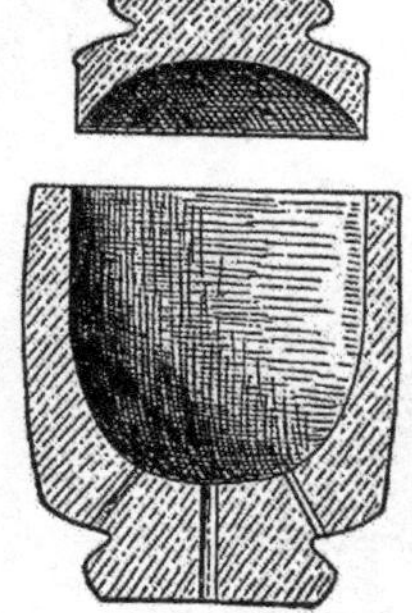

FIG. 51—CROSS-SEC-
TION OF EDAM
PRESS-MOLD AND
COVER

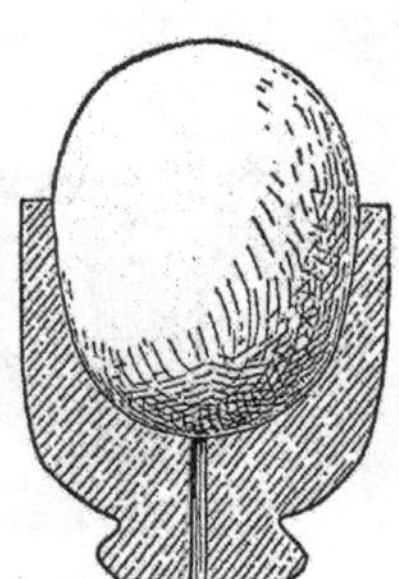

FIG. 52—EDAM SALT-
ING-MOLD IN CROSS-
SECTION

cross-section. Fig. 53 shows the salting-mold in external and internal appearance and Fig. 52 shows cross-section of the same.

Qualities of Edam cheese.—The *flavor* of a perfect Edam cheese is difficult to describe. It is mild, clean and pleasantly saline. In imperfect Edams the flavor is more or less sour and offensive.

In *body*, a perfect Edam cheese is solid, rather dry and mealy or crumbly. This condition is secured by the use of partially skimmed milk, together with the special conditions of manufacture employed.

In *texture,* the perfect Edam cheese should be close and free from pores.

Some general remarks.—There are a few points which may be best brought to our attention by contrasting some of the conditions used in the manufacture of Edam cheese with those employed in the manufacture of our American cheddar cheese.

(1) One is made from partially skimmed milk; the other, when at its best, is made from whole milk.

FIG. 53—SALTING-MOLD, INSIDE AND
OUTSIDE APPEARANCE

(2) While it is very important in making cheddar cheese to have the milk in perfect condition, it is absolutely essential in making Edam cheese.

(3) In making cheddar cheese, the removal of moisture is largely effected in the vat by the use of a higher temperature in heating the curd. In making Edam cheese, the removal of moisture depends more upon the fineness of cutting the curd and subsequent pressing. The latter process is much less economical as regards loss of milk constituents.

(4) In making cheddar cheese, more or less lactic acid is formed according to special conditions; in making Edam cheese, every effort is made

to hasten the process at every stage and prevent the formation of lactic acid. In one case, we work to produce an acid curd; in the other, a curd as free as possible from acid.

(5) The details of salting and curing differ radically in the two methods. In general, the manufacture of Edam cheese requires labor and care in giving attention to many more details than the manufacture of cheddar cheese, however much the latter should have for best success.

(6) Edam cheese sells for two or three times as much per pound as the best American cheddar.

GOUDA CHEESE

Gouda cheese is a sweet-curd cheese made from whole-milk. In shape, the Gouda cheese is somewhat like a cheddar with the sharp edges rounded off and sloping toward the outer circumference at the middle from the end faces. They usually weigh 10 or 12 pounds each, though they vary in weight from 8 to 16 pounds. They are largely manufactured in southern Holland, and derive their name from the town of the same name.

Kind of milk used.—Fresh, sweet milk that has been produced and cared for in the best possible manner.

Temperature of milk before adding rennet.—The temperature of the milk should be brought up to a point not below 88° F. nor much above 90° F. When the desired temperature has been reached and has become constant, then the coloring-matter is added and thoroughly incorporated by stirring before the rennet is added.

Addition of rennet to milk.—The rennet should not be added until the milk has reached the desired temperature (88° to 90° F.) and this temperature has become constant. Then one adds 4 to 5 ounces of fresh rennet-extract for 1,000 pounds of milk. The milk should be completely coagulated, ready for cutting, in 15 or 20 minutes. The same precautions should be used in adding rennet as those previously mentioned in connection with the manufacture of Edam cheese.

Cutting the curd.—The curd should be cut when it is of about the hardness generally observed for cutting in the cheddar process. The cutting is done exactly as in the cheddar process except that the curd is cut a little finer in the Gouda cheese. Curd should be about the size of peas or wheat kernels when ready for press and as uniform in size as possible.

Treatment of curd after cutting.—When the cutting is completed, one commences at once to heat the curd and to stir carefully. The heating and constant stirring are continued until the curd reaches a temperature of 104° F., which should require from 30 to 40 minutes. When the curd becomes rubber-like in feeling and makes a squeaking sound when chewed, the whey should be run off. The whey should be entirely sweet when it is removed.

Pressing and dressing cheese.—After the whey is run off, the curd is put in the molds at once without salting. Pains should be taken in this process to keep the temperature of the curd as near 100° F. as possible. Each cheese is placed under continual pressure amounting to 10 or 20 times its own weight and kept for about half an hour. The first bandage is put on in very much the same manner as the bandage in Edam cheese-making. The cheese is then put in press again for about one hour. The first bandage is then taken off and a second one like the first one put on with great care, taking pains to make the bandage smooth, capping the ends as before. The cheese is then put in press again and left 12 hours or more.

Salting and curing.—When the cheese is taken from the press the bandage is removed and it is placed for 24 hours in a curing-room like that used in curing Edam cheese, as previously described (p. 412). Each cheese is then rubbed all over with dry salt until the salt begins to dissolve, and this same treatment is continued twice a day for ten days. At the end of that time, each cheese is carefully and thoroughly washed in warm water and dried with a clean linen towel. The cheeses are then placed on the shelves of the curing-room, turned once a day and rubbed like cheddars. The temperature and moisture are controlled as described in the curing process of Edam cheese. If the outer surface of the cheese gets slimy at any time, they are carefully washed in warm water and dried with clean towels. Under these conditions, the cheese ripens in 2 or 3 months.

Utensils employed in making Gouda cheese.—The molds, continual press and curing-room are the only things needed in the making of Gouda cheese that differ from the utensils employed in making cheddar cheese. The mold used for Gouda cheese consists of two parts, which are shown separate in Fig. 54, while in Fig. 55 the two parts are shown united, ready for pressing. These molds were made of heavy pressed tin. The inside diameter at the middle is about 10 inches. The diameter of the ends is about 6½ inches. The height of the mold (as seen in Fig. 55) is about 5½ inches, and this represents the thickness of the cheese, but by pushing the upper down into the lower portion, the

FIG. 54—TWO PARTS OF GOUDA MOLD, SHOWN SEPARATE

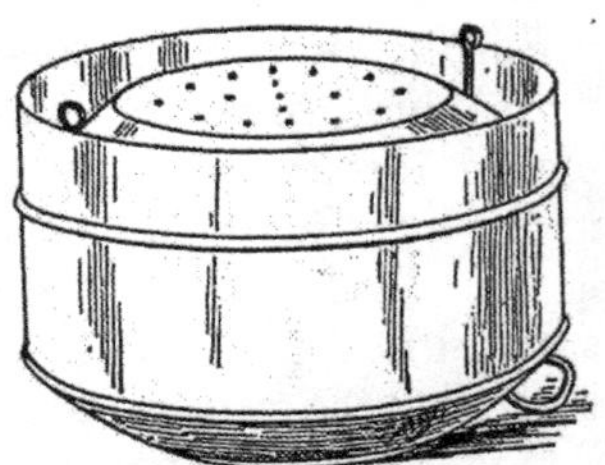

FIG. 55—TWO PARTS OF GOUDA MOLD, UNITED

thickness can be decreased as desired. A simple way to make a Gouda mold is to take two rounded wash basins made of pressed tin, cut them down so that they will be about 1½ inches deep. Then on one portion is soldered a rim of tin about 3 inches wide (see Fig. 54 A, or Fig. 55, lower portion of mold). On the second wash basin is soldered another rim of tin 3 inches wide, about ½ inch of which projects beyond the open side of the wash basin, the rest projecting on the other side (see Fig. 54 B and Fig. 55, upper portion). This upper part, or B, should be made of such diameter that it will just fit into the inside of the other portion, as shown in Fig. 55.   The upper portion is provided with two rings soldered on and the lower portion with two handles to facilitate handling. In the ends of the molds or the portions made from wash basins there are 18 or 20 perforations about ⅛ inch in diameter, made for the purpose of letting the whey run out.

Part V

Methods of Testing
Cheese-Factory Organization
Literature of Cheese-Making

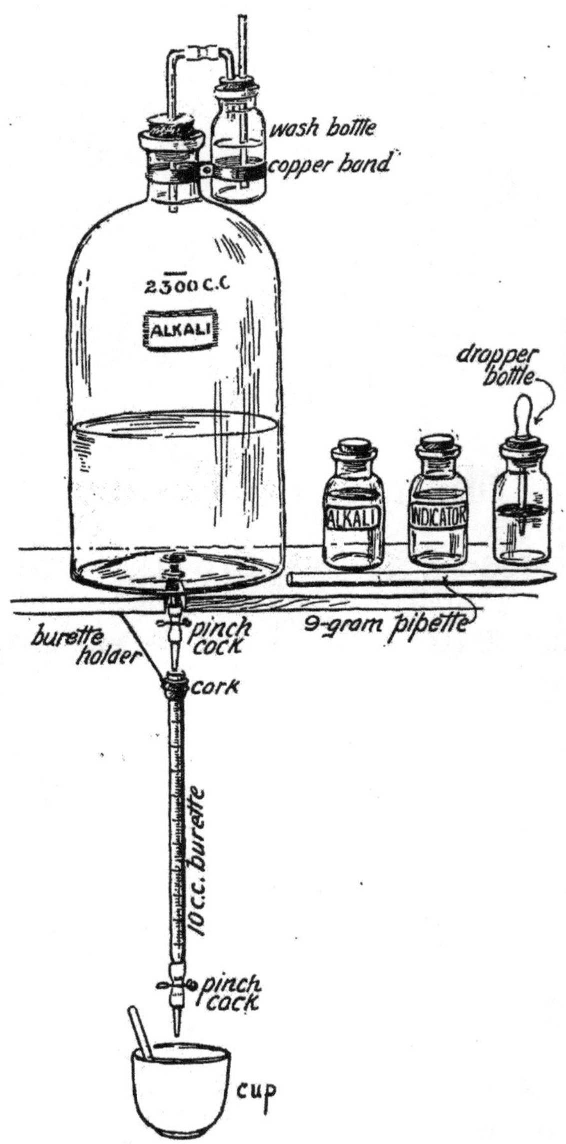

PUBLOW'S APPARATUS FOR MEASURING ACIDITY

CHAPTER XXVIII

Methods of Testing Used in Cheese-Making

It is our purpose in this chapter to give, for the most part, only an outline of the methods of testing* used in connection with cheese-making, since the full details would occupy too much space. The methods to be considered cover the following substances:

1. Fat in (1) milk, (2) whey, (3) curd, and (4) cheese.
2. Acidity in (1) milk, (2) whey, (3) curd, and (4) cheese.
3. Strength of rennet-extracts.
4. Dirt and ferments in milk.
5. Specific gravity.
6. Hot-iron test.
7. Casein in milk.

THE BABCOCK TEST FOR FAT

This is a method for determining the amount of fat in milk and its products. The test is based (1) on the action of strong sulphuric acid upon the solids of milk other than fat, by which the milk-fat is released from the restraining influence of other compounds and so is free to collect in one separate mass, and (2) on the use of centrifugal force, which is employed to complete separation of the fat. The Bab-

*For a full description of all the details of most of these methods, see "Modern Methods of Testing Milk and Milk Products," published by the Orange Judd Company.

cock test finds occasion for use in connection with cheese-making in the following ways: (1) Testing milk of individual patrons when dividends are made on the basis of the milk-fat; (2) testing milk to ascertain if its fat content has been seriously affected by skimming; (3) testing milk to use as a basis for estimating the yield of cheese and regulating the amount of salt used (p. 38); (4) testing whey and press-drippings to ascertain if the loss of fat is excessive, and (5) testing cheese for percentage of fat.

Apparatus and materials used.—The following list includes the apparatus and materials used in making this test: (1) Test-bottles, graduated from 0 to 10 per cent, so that each smallest division represents 0.20 per cent when 17.5 cubic centimeters (18 grams) of milk are used; (2) pipette for measuring milk, holding 17.6 cubic centimeters to mark; (3) measure for acid, holding 17.5 cubic centimeters to mark; (4) centrifugal machine, having a wheel 12 to 20 inches in diameter, easily capable of being run at a speed of 700 to 1,200 revolutions a minute; and (5) commercial sulphuric acid having a specific gravity between 1.82 and 1.83, preferably just 1.825 (Testing Milk, etc., pp. 32-52).

Sampling milk for testing.—Milk that has curdled, or on the surface of which cream has risen and dried, or milk the fat of which has partially churned, is difficult to sample. These difficulties should not be common in cheese-factory work, but, when they arise, careful attention should be given to the details prescribed for such cases (Testing Milk, etc., pp. 22-24). The samples to be tested must be thoroughly mixed.

Composite samples.—In order to avoid testing milk daily, composite samples may be prepared and tested at intervals of a week or ten days. Much care must be used in preparing and keeping composite samples (Testing Milk, etc., pp. 24-31).

Method of operating the test.—(Testing Milk etc., pp. 53-66). In brief outline, the different steps are given as follows:

(1) Mix thoroughly sample of milk, which is at 60° to 70° F.

(2) Quickly fill pipette to mark with milk.

(3) Run milk into test-bottle.

(4) Fill acid-measure to mark with acid and pour into test-bottle.

(5) (a) Mix milk and acid thoroughly by rotary motion; (b) let stand 2 to 5 minutes; and (c) mix again.

(6) Put test-bottles in tester (centrifuge) and whirl 4 or 5 minutes at proper speed.

(7) (a) Add fairly hot water up to neck of bottles; (b) whirl one minute; (c) add hot water to 8 or 9 per cent mark; and (d) whirl one minute.

(8) Read results at temperature of about 130° F.

Special precautions.—The following statements give an outline of the particular points to be observed in making the test in order to insure accuracy:

(1) Always make tests in duplicate.

(2) Make sure that the sample is a representative one.

(3) Have the temperature of the milk and acid at 60° to 70° F. before putting in test-bottle.

(4) Use only acid of right strength.

(5)   Mix milk and acid thoroughly as soon as acid is added.

(6)   Mix a second time after a short interval.

(7)   Make sure that the tester runs at the right speed and does not jar.

(8)   Use only clean, soft water in filling bottles.

(9)   Read bottles before they cool and at about 130° F.

(10)   To guard against mistakes, read each test twice.

Testing whey for fat.—The test is conducted in the usual way, except that special bottles having small necks for more accurate reading are used and less acid is generally sufficient (Testing Milk, etc., pp. 81-83).

Testing curd and cheese.—Care must be taken in sampling. The weighed sample (8 to 10 grams) is treated in the test-bottle with about 10 cc. of water (65°-70° F.), after which the acid (17.6 cc.) is added and the test completed in the usual way (Testing Milk, etc., pp. 83-85). The acid should be added carefully, about 1 cc. at a time, mixing the acid and water by shaking after each addition. After all the acid has been thus added, shake the whole vigorously until the cheese is completely disintegrated.

TEST FOR ACIDITY

Fresh milk contains substances (casein and acid phosphates) which neutralize alkali and in this respect behave like acids. The amount of this acidity is approximately equivalent to 0.10 per cent. Amounts of acid above this figure are usually due to the action of lactic acid that has been formed by the bacterial decomposition of the sugar in the milk. It is the amount of acid thus formed which we usually desire to determine.

The method of ascertaining the acidity of milk is based upon the chemical action taking place between acids and alkalis. Acids and alkalis neutralize each other and form compounds called salts, which are neutral (neither acid nor alkaline). A substance used in showing whether a solution is acid, alkaline or neutral is called an *indicator*. The one in most common use is a compound called phenolphthalein, which turns pink in alkali solutions and colorless in acid or neutral solutions. Only a few drops need be used in making one test. There are several different methods for testing acidity, but all are alike in principle.

Publow's acid test.—(1) *The apparatus* (p. 422) consists of (1) a plain 5-pint bottle with an opening in the bottom, through which a brass pipe is connected so securely as to prevent leakage. (2) A small 2-ounce wash-bottle, fastened to the neck of the large bottle by a copper band and connected by means of rubber corks and glass tubing. (3) A plain 10 cc. burette graduated in tenths and a simple wire burette-holder. (4) A straight, non-bulbous, 9-gram pipette, which can be easily cleaned. (5) A simple rubber-stoppered dropping-bottle. (6) A plain white cup and stirring-rod. (7) A small bottle containing 50 cc. of a solution of caustic soda (equal to 9.2 grams of purest caustic soda), which, when added to 2,250 cc. of water, makes 2,300 cc. of a tenth-normal alkali solution. The large bottle is marked to show the level of 2,300 cc. in order to save time in measuring. (8) A small bottle of phenolphthalein indicator.

(2) **Preparing alkali solution.**—As the most accurate, convenient and economical method of prepar-

ing a tenth-normal alkali solution, a concentrated solution of caustic soda is advised, of which 50 cc. is sufficient to make 2,300 cc. of a tenth-normal solution. This solution retains its strength indefinitely when tightly corked. The tenth-normal solution is prepared by adding the contents of the small bottle of alkali to the large bottle without any loss, rinsing the small bottle several times and each time pouring the rinsings into the large bottle. Soft water is then added to the large bottle until it reaches the level of the mark (2,300 cc.) filed on the bottle. In order to keep this alkali solution without loss of strength, the small wash-bottle referred to above (2) is attached to the neck of the larger one in the manner indicated, after being half filled with the tenth-normal alkali solution.

(3) **Method of use.**—The liquid to be tested (milk, whey, cream or starter) is measured by means of the 9-gram pipette and run into the white cup. Two drops of phenolphthalein solution are added, after which the alkali, a drop at a time, is run into the cup from the burette (arranged in the manner indicated on p. 422), until the solution in the cup, which must be constantly stirred, shows a very faint pink color that does not disappear for 15 seconds or longer. Each tenth cc. of alkali used represents .01 per cent of acid.

Manns' acid test.—For details see Testing Milk, etc., pp. 101-103.

Farrington's alkaline tablet test.—In this form of test, the alkali and indicator are mixed together in the form of tablets. Five tablets are dissolved so as to make 97 cubic centimeters of solution, which is added, in small portions, from a graduated cylinder to 17.5 cubic centimeters of milk until the pink color remains. Each cubic centimeter of alkali solution used stands for 0.01 per cent of acidity equivalent to lactic test (Testing Milk, etc., pp. 103-105).

Testing acidity of whey.—Whey is tested in the same manner as milk. The sample of whey tested should be free from all curd particles, since curd has some power to neutralize alkali (Testing Milk, etc., pp. 109-110).

Testing acidity of cheese.—An extract of a weighed amount of cheese is made and this extract is tested for acidity in the usual way (Testing Milk, etc., p. 110).

Special precautions in making acidity tests.— In carrying out tests for acidity, certain points of the operation must be kept carefully in mind.

(1)   The material tested must be thoroughly mixed before taking a sample.

(2)   The water used in preparing the alkali solution should be neutral, soft and clean.   Distilled water is best.

(3)   Alkaline tablets must be kept dry.

(4)   The alkali solution, whichever form is used, must be kept from contact with air as much as possible to prevent change of strength.

(5)   Prepare fresh solution of alkaline tablets for best results.

(6)   Make tests only in a good light.

QUICK TEST FOR ACIDITY OF MILK

It is often desirable to ascertain quickly whether milk or cream contains more or less than 0.2 or 0.3 per cent of acid.   This can be done by the following method: An alkali solution is prepared by dissolving in an 8-ounce bottle 2 alkali tablets for each ounce of water used. A No. 10 brass cartridge shell, on which a wire handle is soldered, is used for measuring the sample to be tested and also the alkali. A cartridgeful of milk is placed in a teacup and then a cartridgeful of the alkali solution is added. The contents of the cup are mixed by a rotary motion. If the sample tested remains white, it contains over 0.2 per cent of acidity; if a pink color remains, the acidity is less than 0.2 per cent. The intensity of the pink color indicates the relative amount of acid present, since the color will be more intense in proportion as there is less acid. Any other measure may be used in place of the brass cartridge-shell, but in every case care must be taken to use equal amounts of milk and of alkali solution.

This test can be used at the weigh-can in case of milks that are suspected of containing 0.2 per cent or more of acid.

THE MARSCHALL TEST

In this test the same general procedure is followed as in the Monrad test, but the rate of coagulation is observed in a different way. The following pieces of apparatus are used: (a) A testing cup or basin, of about a pint capacity, for holding the milk to be tested. On the inside wall of this cup there are graduated spaces beginning with zero at the top and going by half-divisions to 7 near the bottom of the cup, while in the bottom of the cup is a glass tube with a very small bore. (b) An ounce bottle with a mark on it to indicate 20 cc. (c) A spatula for stirring the milk. (d) A 1 cc. pipette.

The operation of conducting this test is as follows: Measure with the pipette 1 cc. of the rennet-extract used and empty it into the ounce bottle, previously half filled with clean, cold water. Rinse the pipette two or three times by drawing water into it from the bottle and allowing it to run back into the bottle. Mix well by shaking. Then place the milk to be tested in the test-cup, setting it in a level position and allowing the milk to run out at the bottom. Taking the bottle of diluted rennet in one hand and the spatula in the other, watch the level of the milk in the cup. The moment the upper surface of the milk drops to the zero mark, pour the diluted rennet into the milk and stir well. Then leave it alone. When the milk coagulates, it stops running through the glass tube. From the graduated scale, read the number of spaces uncovered on the inside of the cup, showing how many divisions of milk have run out. The more slowly the milk coagulates, the larger the amount that runs out; the more quickly the milk coagulates, the smaller the amount that runs out and the fewer spaces there are uncovered. When about 2½ spaces are uncovered, the milk is ready for addition of rennet. The temperature must be watched, being tested at the start and finish, especially in a cold room.

Some objectionable features of the Marschall test should be noticed. A difference in the size of the bore of the glass tube in the bottom of the cup obviously makes a difference in the results. It is found that the size of the bore of the glass tubing varies in different cups. Therefore, the results given by one cup can not be compared with those of another, unless they are tested on the same milk and found to agree. Special pains must be taken to keep the tube open, since a little dirt quickly stops it. The Marschall test is convenient for ordinary work, but is not capable of as great delicacy as is the Monrad test. Results obtained by different workers can be compared by the Monrad test, but not by the Marschall test

THE MONRAD TEST

This test is based upon the amount of time required for a definite quantity of milk at a given temperature to become coagulated by a fixed quantity of rennet.

The pieces of apparatus required are the following: (1) A tin cylinder for measuring milk, holding, when full, 160 cc., (2) a 5 cc. pipette, (3) a 50 cc. glass flask, (4) a thermometer, and (5) a half-pint tin basin.

In testing the ripeness of milk by means of rennet-extract, one first prepares a dilute solution of the rennet, as follows: One measures with the small pipette 5 cc. of rennet-extract into the 50 cc. flask. The pipette is then rinsed twice with water by sucking it full of cold, clean water to the mark, the rinsings also being run into the 50 cc. flask. The flask is then filled with water to the 50 cc. mark, and the contents are well mixed by shaking. The next step is to fill the tin cylinder with the well-mixed milk to be tested and this is emptied into the half-pint basin. The milk must be at the temperature at which one adds the rennet in cheese-making, which is generally about 84° to 86° F. To the milk at the desired temperature, one adds 5 cc. of the diluted rennet solution, mixes it through the milk quickly, using the thermometer as a stirrer. The exact time when the rennet-extract is added to the milk is noted by the second hand of a watch, and then again when the milk has coagulated; the number of seconds required to coagulate the milk is recorded. The exact point of coagulation can be seen more sharply by scattering a few particles of charcoal (as the blackened end of a partly burned match) on the surface of the milk, and then with the thermometer starting the surface into motion around the dish. The black particles stop the instant the milk coagulates. By using a stop-watch great accuracy and delicacy can be attained. Care should be taken to keep the temperature of the milk at the one desired point, testing frequently with the thermometer; and in case the temperature drops, it can be raised by placing the basin of milk in warm water. In ordinary cheddar cheese-making, milk is ready for the addition of rennet when it coagulates in 30 to 60 seconds under the foregoing conditions.

METHOD OF TESTING RENNET-EXTRACTS

Different brands of rennet-extract vary somewhat in their strength, that is, the rapidity and completeness with which they coagulate milk when used in the same amount. It is therefore important to have a means of testing their strength, in order that their value may be definitely known and that cheese-makers may be able to know in advance of using how much they must use for the best results. The Monrad and Marschall tests are available for this purpose.

In order to test the comparative strength of different rennet-extracts, one treats different portions of the same milk with the different extracts to be tested.

In all other respects, the details of the methods previously given are followed. All conditions must be kept alike in the different tests. The strength of the rennet-extracts is shown by the rapidity with which the milk is coagulated; the stronger the rennet, the less the time of coagulation.

METHOD OF TESTING PEPSIN

Pepsin is beginning to be used in cheese-making as a substitute for rennet-extract. Vivian has worked out the important details. The scale-pepsin, of strength known as 1-3000, prepared from stomachs of sheep, is recommended. It may be used at the rate of 5 grams for 1,000 pounds of milk. In testing scale-pepsin by the rennet-test, one can dissolve the scale-pepsin at the rate of 5 grams in 4 ounces of water and use this solution exactly like a rennet-extract with milk. It should be tested in comparison with a sample of rennet-extract whose use in cheese-making has been tested, the test being made on different portions of the same milk.

TESTS FOR FERMENTS AND INSOLUBLE DIRT IN MILK

Those forms of micro-organisms or ferments that make trouble in cheese-making are not readily perceptible to the senses when milk is delivered at the cheese-factory, but the results of their work develop later either during the cheese-making process or later in ripening cheese. When such ferments appear, it is desirable to locate them in some particular herd or herds with a view to removal of the causes of trouble. It is also desirable to get an idea of the amount of suspended dirt in milk, as this may often be an indication of the general bacterial condition of the milk, since bacteria generally keep company with dirt. We have tests for accomplishing these objects.

TEST FOR DIRT IN MILK ·

The following is a quick, simple, practicable method for indicating in a rough way how much suspended dirt milk contains: Provide several granite-iron funnels 2½ or 3 inches in diameter. Place in these some clean absorbent cotton, making the upper surface as smooth and flat as practicable and somewhat compact. Have these near the weighing-can so that one can be attached on inside of can. When milk is dumped in can and thoroughly mixed, take a pint and pour on cotton in funnel. Any suspended dirt quickly shows. The method might be improved by laying a circular piece of white muslin on top of the cotton. The test performed under the eyes of a patron would be convincing. Milk should contain *no visible dirt in suspension.*

THE FERMENTATION OR WISCONSIN CURD-TEST

Milk frequently contains objectionable forms of organisms or ferments that are not made perceptible by ordinary methods of observation. The condition arises particularly in milk used for cheese-making and may result in serious injury to the quality of the cheese. The Wisconsin experiment station (Wisconsin experiment station 12th and 15th annual reports, 1895 and 1898) has applied certain principles to the development of a test that enables one to identify milk containing certain forms of undesirable ferments likely to do serious injury. This method is based, in general, upon the plan of making conditions favorable for the rapid development of the ferments present in milk.

Apparatus.—The apparatus consists of the following parts: (1) Pint glass jars or tin cans with covers, (2) a well-insulated tank to hold the jars, (3) rennet-extract, (4) a thermometer, (5) a case-knife or similar instrument for cutting curd, and (6) a small pipette for measuring rennet-extract.

Operation of test.—The test is conducted as follows: The jars, including covers, just previous to use, are sterilized with live steam, scalding water or dry heat (212° F.). Each jar or can is filled about two-thirds full with the milk to be tested and the sterilized cover put on at once. The jars are then placed in the tank which is filled with water at 100° to 102° F. up to the upper surface of the milk in the jars. The temperature of the water should be kept at 100° to 102° F. during the whole operation. To hasten the warming of the milk, the jars are taken out and shaken occasionally. The temperature of the milk is observed with a sterile thermometer, and when the milk has reached 98° F., one adds 10 drops of rennet-extract to each jar and mixes thoroughly by giving the contents of the jar a rotary motion. When the milk has coagulated, it is allowed to stand until it is firm, usually about 20 minutes. To enable the whey to separate more readily, the curd is then cut fine with a thin knife, which must be carefully rinsed with hot water after finishing each jar and before using it in another, in order to avoid carrying contamination from one milk to another and spoiling the test. The curd is allowed to settle completely. When the whey has been separating half an hour, thé samples are examined for flavor by smelling, after which the whey is carefully poured out of the jars and this is repeated at intervals of 30 to 40 minutes for 8 hours or more. Under the favorable conditions of temperature, similar to those employed in cheese-making, the organisms present develop readily and reveal their presence in different characteristic ways. The jars are finally opened, any whey present is drained off, and the following tests are applied: (1) The curd is cut into two pieces. The curd will be solid and free from holes on the cut surfaces, if the milk is not tainted. If it is spongy and full of holes, it contains those undesirable organisms that produce gases in the curd and injure it for cheese-making, showing in the form of "floating curds" and "huffy" cheese. The holes are usually small, their common name being "pin-holes." (2) The curd is examined with reference to any marked disagreeable odors that may be present. Some undesirable organisms reveal their presence by smell without making spongy curd. This may, perhaps, be best perceived by smelling of a freshly cut surface of the curd. Offensive odors are, of course, an undesirable indication. Special apparatus for performing the test is furnished by dairy-supply houses, but pint fruit-jars and other home-made appliances will answer satisfactorily.

By this method one can learn what particular lot of milk among several is responsible for undesirable fermentations. Moreover, having traced the source of contamination to a single herd of cows, it is easily possible, by applying the test to single cows, to ascertain which individual or individuals may be the source of trouble.

Precautions.—Two points must be carefully observed in carrying out this test: (1) The temperature must be kept as near 98° F. as possible, in order that the bacteria may develop as desired. This can be done by keeping the temperature of the water surrounding the jars at 100° to 102° F. The temperature must be watched. (2) The thermometer and the knife used should be made not only clean but sterile each time after using in one sample before placing them in another.

TEST FOR SPECIFIC GRAVITY AND SOLIDS OF MILK

(Milk Testing, etc., pp. 127-132)

Process of using Quevenne lactometer.—The sample of milk to be tested for specific gravity is brought to a temperature between 50° and 70° F. For convenience the milk is placed in a cylinder, which is nearly filled. The lactometer is carefully lowered into the milk until it floats and is allowed to remain half a minute or more. Then one reads and records (1) the point at which the lactometer scale comes in contact with the upper surface of the milk; and (2) the temperature. The lactometer reading is then corrected, if the temperature is above or below 60° F. For example, the lactometer settles in milk, which is at a temperature of 65° F., to the point marked 29. Adding to the reading for correction 0.1 for each degree above 60° F., which in this case is 0.5, the reading becomes 29.5. This means that the specific gravity is 1.0295. If the temperature of the milk were 55° F., the correction is subtracted and the reading becomes 28.5, equal to specific gravity 1.0285.

Babcock's formulas for solids and solids-not-fat.— The following formulas were devised by Dr. Babcock:

(1) *Formula for determining solids-not-fat.—*Solids-not-fat=¼L+0.2f, in which L is the reading of the Quevenne lactometer and f is the per cent of fat in the milk.

(2) *Formula for determining solids in milk.—* Total solids=¼L+1.2f.

These formulas can be expressed in the form of rules as follows:

Rule 1.—To find the per cent of solids-not-fat in milk, divide the reading of the Quevenne lactometer by 4, and to the result add the number giving the per cent of fat in the milk multiplied by 0.2.

Rule 2.—To find the per cent of solids in milk, divide the Quevenne lactometer reading by 4, and to the result add the number giving the per cent of fat multiplied by 1.2.

THE HOT-IRON TEST

This test is used for the purpose of ascertaining when to remove whey from curd and when to mill curd. An iron of convenient size and length for holding, as a half-inch gas-pipe, is heated fairly hot at one end. The iron is carefully wiped with a cloth until it is clean and smooth. A handful of curd is then taken and placed in dry cloth and squeezed by the hand, until the surface has been well dried. The curd is then gently pressed against the portion of the iron where it is hot enough to make the curd stick to the iron but not hot enough to scorch it. The curd is then carefully drawn away from the iron and, if in proper condition, produces fine, silky threads, the length of which depends upon the amount of acidity of the curd.

VOLUMETRIC TEST FOR CASEIN

A new test for casein has been recently worked out at the New York experiment station by Van Slyke and Bosworth (Technical Bulletin No. 10, Sept., 1909). In outline the method is as follows: Into a 200 cc. flask one measures 17.5 cc. (18 grams) of milk, adds about 80 cc. of water and 1 cc. of phenolphthalein, after which a solution of sodium hydroxid (caustic soda) is added until the mixture is neutral. Standardized acetic acid is then added until the casein is completely precipitated, the volume of the mixture is made up to 200 cc. by addition of water and then filtered. Into 100 cc. of the clear filtrate, a standardized solution of sodium hydroxid is run until neutral. The solutions are so standardized that 1 cc. is equivalent to 1 per cent of casein in the milk examined. Therefore, the number of cc. of standard acid used, divided by 2, less the amount of standard alkali used in the final titration gives the percentage of casein in the milk. The operation usually requires 12 to 15 minutes when apparatus and solutions are at hand in convenient form ready for use; several determinations can be carried on at the same time with much relative economy of time.

Apparatus.—(1) Two 50 *cc. burettes,* accurately graduated to one-twentieth cc. Automatic burette fillers save much time in making many determinations.

(2) *Flasks,* so-called volumetric, holding 200 cc. and accurately marked. Flasks having necks 4½ to 5 inches long and ¾-inch inside diameter are desirable for greatest convenience.

(3) *Pipette* (Babcock test form), accurately graduated to deliver 17.5 cc. (18 grams) of milk.

(4) *Pipette* graduated to deliver 100 cc.

(5) *Pipette* graduated to deliver about 1 cc. and provided with a rubber bulb (so-called dropper).

(6) *Cups,* plain white, holding 200 cc. or more.

(7) *Funnels,* glass or granite-ironware, 3 to 4 inches in diameter.

(8) *Filter-papers* cut round, 6 to 7 inches in diameter; or fine linen filters cut to proper size and shape, which can be washed after use and used repeatedly.

(9) *Measuring-cylinders,* accurately graduated and holding 1,000 cc.

Solutions.—(1) *Sodium hydroxid* (caustic soda). This solution may be made most conveniently by preparing a regular tenth-normal solution in the manner recommended by Publow (p. 427), and then diluting 795 cc. of this to one liter (or one may directly dilute the 50 cc. of concentrated alkali to 2,900 cc.). In such a solution 1 cc. corresponds to 0.09 gram of casein (or 1 per cent). In making standard solutions, pure distilled water should be used if possible, or else as pure rain-water as can be obtained. Alkali solutions must be kept in tightly-stoppered bottles to prevent loss of strength. "Alkaline tablets" cannot be used for the casein test.

(2) *Acetic acid.*—This solution is so made that a given amount of it will exactly neutralize the same amount of the standard alkali solution of the strength above indicated. The simplest way of preparing this solution is to purchase a *normal* solution and dilute 100 cc. of this to 1,260 cc. To prevent fermentation of dilute acetic acid and consequent change of strength on long standing, it is desirable to add a small amount of pure mercuric chlorid (corrosive sublimate) and to keep the solution in tightly-stoppered bottles.

(3) *Phenolphthalein solution.*—This is made by dissolving one gram of the dry, powdered compound in 100 cc. of 50 per cent alcohol and adding to the prepared solution one or more drops of dilute alkali until the solution is very slightly pinkish in color.

Performing the test.—(1) *Measuring and diluting sample of milk.* The milk to be tested is well mixed and a 17.6 cc. pipette filled to the mark and the milk run into a 200 cc. flask. Then add about 80 cc. of pure, soft water (preferably, distilled).

(2) *Neutralizing the milk.*—Add 1 cc. of phenolphthalein solution to the dilute milk and then run into it the alkali solution from a burette, in small portions, shaking vigorously after each addition of alkali, until a faintly, but distinctly, pinkish shade of color remains even after considerable agitation. Marked excess of alkali must be avoided.

(a) Preparation of a color-standard.—More satisfactory results in neutralizing can be obtained by preparing a color-standard for comparison. This can be prepared as follows: About 20 cc. of fresh skim-milk and 80 cc. of water are put into a 200 cc. flask and a very small amount of pure corrosive sublimate added to prevent souring. A few drops of ordinary carmine ink are considerably diluted with water and this ,is carefully added, a few drops at a time, to the diluted skim-milk until a faint but distinct pinkish coloration appears. This can be more readily perceived by placing beside the flask another flask half full of uncolored diluted skim-milk. The coloration must be as slight as possible and yet be appreciably distinct when compared with uncolored milk. After the color-standard has been prepared, the flask is stoppered. It is well to keep this standard in a dark place when not in use. With some carmine colors, the pinkish shade in the milk deepens on standing, especially when exposed to light, and with others it may fade. If any deepening of color is observed at any time, addition of dilute skim-milk will reproduce the proper shade; in case of fading, the addition of one or more drops of carmine ,ink is called for. Skim-milk is used because, in case of normal milk, the fat separates on standing, adheres to the sides of the flask, and obscures the color.

(b) Use of color-standard.—In neutralizing a sample of milk, the color-standard is placed beside the sample under examination for constant comparison after each addition of alkali. The flasks should be placed on a white surface and in a good light. In fresh milks, it is usually found that 3 or 4 cc. of alkali is sufficient to neutralize the milk. One can add 2 or 3 cc. of alkali at the start and then add it in smaller portions, until the milk begins to show signs of neutrality, after which the alkali is added drop by drop.

(3) *Precipitation of casein.*—(a) Addition of acid. Into the neutralized sample of diluted milk, which should be at a temperature of 65° to 75° F., one now runs from a . burette some of the standardized acetic acid, adding the acid approximately in 5 cc. portions

and shaking vigorously for a few seconds after each addition. It is usually safe to add about 25 cc. of acid before examining the milk to see if the casein separates in the form of white flakes. After adding 20 to 25 cc. and shaking, the mixture is allowed to stand still. If enough acid has been added, the casein separates promptly in large, white flakes, and on standing a short time the liquid above the settled casein appears clear and not at all milky. If the addition of 25 cc. of acid is insufficient, add 1 cc. more of acid and shake; continue the addition of acid 1 cc. at a time, until the casein is observed to separate promptly and completely on standing at rest for a short time. The number of cc. of acid used to effect precipitation is noted and this result is recorded as A.

(b) Influence of temperature.—For convenience of work and uniformity of results, the temperature of the mixture at the time of the addition of acid may be between 65° and 75° F. Under these conditions, many milks give satisfactory results with just 30 cc. of acid. In case of milks containing 3.5 to 4 per cent of casein, one may need to use as much as 35 to 40 cc. of acid. Rarely has it been found that 25 cc. of acid is excessive. The amount of acid may be 2 or 3 cc. in excess of that required to effect complete precipitation without seriously affecting the accuracy of the results, provided the temperature of the mixture is below 75° F. At temperatures above 75° F., good results are attainable, but care must be taken not to use much excess of acid; and, of course, the higher the temperature, the less will be the amount of acid required. In working at temperatures under 65° F., the casein separates more slowly or requires more acid to separate promptly. When working with milk that is much below 65° F., it is well to use for dilution water that is at a temperature of about 80° F.

(4) *Filtration of casein.*—After the casein is completely precipitated, one adds pure, soft (preferably, distilled) water to the flask until the 200 cc. mark is reached. The flask is then vigorously shaken 10 or 15 seconds, in order to distribute the acid through the mixture as uniformly as possible. The contents of the flask are then poured on a clean, dry filter, and the filtrate caught in a cup. The funnels, filter and cups used to catch filtrate should all be dry before being used. It is well, generally, to allow the filtration to continue until practically all of the liquid has run into the cup.

(a) Rapidity of filtration.—The usual time of filtration should not exceed 3 to 5 minutes. The rapidity depends upon the temperature of precipitation and the completeness of the separation of casein. In general, the higher the temperature of the mixture when precipitated with acid, the more rapid should be filtration, other conditions being uniform. In case of insufficient acid, the filtration is slower.

(b) Appearance of filtrate.—The filtrate should be quite clear, though this is not always a sure indication that the right amount of acid has been used. Sometimes the filtrate may be clear when not quite enough acid has been used, in which case the filtration is apt to be slow. In case of milk rich in fat, a slight turbidity may appear, due to fat-globules in the filtrate. The filtrate should be free from all marked signs of turbidity or anything like milkiness. If such a filtrate appears, a new sample of milk should be taken and the operation repeated from the beginning, more acid being used than before. With a little experience, especially under proper instruction, no difficulty should be found in recognizing quickly when the casein is separated so as to give satisfactory results.

(5) *Titration with alkali.*—After filtration is completed, one measures 100 cc. of the filtrate with the pipette into a cup and then runs into this from the burette the standard alkali until a faint but distinct pink color remains clearly marked throughout the solution for half a minute or longer before beginning to fade. The number of cc. of alkali used is noted and this result is recorded as B.

The last portions of the alkali must be added carefully, a drop at a time, agitating the mixture well after each addition. The exact neutral point is not perfectly sharp on account of the presence of phosphates, and the appearance of the desired coloration is, therefore, not as sudden and pronounced as might be desired. With experience one should have no difficulty in getting within one drop of the correct amount of alkali. The chief precaution to be observed is to have the same shade and duration of color every time. Thus, one should not in one titration add alkali until a deep pink coloration appears, lasting for some minutes, and in another a coloration that disappears within 5 seconds. In the case of milk rich in phosphates, the solution usually grows quite turbid as the neutral point is approached, making it necessary to use more care in observing the color of the end-point of the reaction.

If one desires to make a second titration of the same filtrate, one can use 50 cc. of the remaining portion, multiplying the result by 2 and recording this as B.

(6) *Calculation of results.*—The calculation of the percentage of casein from (1) the amount of acid used (A) in precipitating casein and (2) the amount

of alkali used (B) in neutralizing 100 cc. of filtrate is very simple. *Divide A by 2 and from the result subtract B;* or, expressed as a formula,

$$\frac{A}{2}-B=\text{per cent of casein in milk.}$$

Example: One used 30 cc. (A) of acid in precipitating casein and 11.95 cc. (B) of alkali in neutralizing 100 cc. of filtrate (one-half of filtrate from the casein precipitate corresponding to 9 grams of milk). Substituting 30 for A and 11.95 for B in the formula, we have

$$\frac{30}{2}-11.95 \quad (=15-11.95)=3.05 \quad \text{(the percentage of casein in milk).}$$

(7) *Use of preservatives.*—In making a casein determination by this method, it is desirable, when possible, to use milk not more than 24 hours old, which has been kept in a cool place. Milk which is sour or which coagulates on heating cannot be used with satisfactory results. However, by adding to fresh milk pure, powdered mercuric chlorid (corrosive sublimate) in the approximate proportion of 1 part to 1,000 or 1,500 parts of milk, and then keeping mixture at a temperature of 50° or lower, one can obtain satisfactory results with milk that has been kept two or three weeks. Milk thus treated should be shaken often enough to keep the fat well incorporated in the body of the milk. The desired amount of mercuric chlorid may be approximately measured by taking for one quart of milk the amount of mercuric chlorid that will lie easily on the surface of a silver dime, or, more conveniently, the amount held by a 0.22-inch pistol cartridge-shell, one-half inch long, when loosely filled. Commercial

mercuric chlorid tablets containing coloring-matter cannot be used.

(8) *Summary of precautions.*—Assuming that the graduated glassware is accurate and the standardized solutions of correct strength, the following special points are to be observed with care in making test.

(a) Preliminary neutralization.—In neutralizing the sample of milk, excess of alkali must be avoided, which can be controlled by the use of a properly prepared color-standard.

(b) Conditions of precipitation.—Before precipitating with acid, have the dilute, neutralized milk at a temperature between 65° and 75° F. Add enough acid to cause the casein to separate promptly in large flakes, leaving the supernatant liquid clear. Shake the mixture vigorously at intervals during the addition of acid; also after complete precipitation and again after dilution to 200 cc. mark.

(c) Filtration.—Allow most of the liquid to run through the filter before making the final titration with alkali.

(d) Titration with alkali.—In titrating the filtrate with alkali, avoid an excess of alkali. Add the alkali solution cautiously until, after thorough agitation, a faint but distinct pink color remains through the solution half a minute or longer. The same uniform shade and duration of pink color should be obtained as nearly as possible in all cases.

(e) Acid milk.—Milk that is sour or that coagulates on heating should not be used.

(f) Use of preservatives.—Milk treated, when fresh, with a small amount of pure powdered mercuric chlorid (corrosive sublimate) and then kept in a cool place gives good results for two or three weeks.

CENTRIFUGAL TEST FOR CASEIN

The following centrifugal method has been worked
out at the Wisconsin station by Hart:

Apparatus and reagents.—(1) Testing-tube, with
neck so graduated that each division represents 0.20
per cent when one uses 5 cc. of milk. (2) Centrifuge,
of special form, run by hand, having a wheel 15 inches
in diameter and geared to give a speed of 2,000 revolutions a minute. (3) Pipette for measuring 5 cc. of
milk. (4) Cylinder for measuring 2 cc. of chloroform.
(5) Dilute acetic acid containing 0.25 per cent of
acetic acid, prepared by diluting 10 cc. of glacial acetic
acid (99.5 per cent) to 100 cc. with water, and then
diluting 25 cc. of this solution to one liter. (6) Chloroform of the best quality.

Method of operating test.—In a testing-tube one
puts 2 cc. of chloroform, then on top of this 20 cc.
of the dilute (0.25 per cent) acetic acid. One then
runs in 5 cc. of milk (65° to 75° F.), after which the
thumb is placed over the opening of the tube and the
tube inverted to bring the mixture into the barrel-
shaped portion of the tube; then the whole is shaken
with a fair degree of vigor for 15 or 20 seconds, accurately timed with watch before one. In the shaking
process, the chloroform takes up most of the fat and
the acid precipitates the casein in fine particles. The
sample is then ready for the centrifuge and should be
whirled within 30 minutes. The centrifuge is closed
before whirling and is brought to a speed of 2,000
revolutions a minute, after which it is run at this rate
7½ to 8 minutes. This must be done with such precision that it is important to use a metronome during
the operation. After whirling, the testing-tubes are

removed and placed in a rack in an upright position and then read after 10 minutes or more. The chloroform and fat should be at the bottom and on top of this a white, cylindrical mass of casein. The end surfaces of this casein cylinder, which should be flat, are read on the scale directly, the result being the per cent of casein in the milk, if the test is successful. While fresh milk is desirable for best results, it is said that seven-day composite samples may be used by taking one-ounce samples of milk each day in a brown or amber-colored glass receptacle, adding on the first day and again on the third day one-fourth of an ordinary potassium bichromate tablet (equal to 1½ or 2 grains). The mixture is gently agitated daily by a rotary motion, and kept well stoppered in a dark, cool place.

Conditions affecting accuracy of results.—(1) Use of sour milk. (2) Use of milk containing preservatives, except bichromate. (3) Too strong or too dilute solution of acetic acid. (4) Poor quality of chloroform. (5) Temperature of acid and milk below 65° or above 75° F. (6) Shaking mixture of acid, chloroform and milk too short or too long a time, too hard or not hard enough. (7) Allowing shaken mixture to stand too long before whirling. (8) Running centrifuge too slow or too fast, or for a longer or shorter time than 7½ or 8 minutes. (9) The use of a revolving wheel greater or less than 15 inches without a corresponding change in the number of revolutions. (10) Reading the results in less than 10 minutes after whirling. (11) Any condition which disturbs the distinct flatness of the upper or lower surface of the cylindrical column of compacted casein.

CHAPTER XXIX

Cheese-Factory Management

STATEMENT FOR PATRONS

Whenever a dividend is made, each patron should receive with the dividend a statement containing all necessary items, which will enable each patron to calculate the dividend and satisfy himself that no errors have been made. It is convenient to use a printed blank form for making such statements to patrons. The form given below is suggested as covering all important points, but one much simpler may usually answer the purpose. It is also highly desirable that a general statement be issued at the close of the season, giving a summary of the whole season's work.

Statement of..........................Cheese-Factory.

1. Name of patron ....
2. Statement for month of (or whatever the period of time is)..............19....
3. Sales include dates from...........................to...
4. Number of pounds of cheese in sale (or sales).......................................
5. Number of pounds of milk represented in sale (or sales)........................
6. Amount of money received....................................$..............................
7. Price received per pound for cheese (at each sale, and average if more than one)...cents
8. Expenses deducted...$..............................
9. Balance for dividends ....$..............................
10. Net value of one pound of milk (*weight-of-milk basis*)....................cents
11. Number of pounds of milk delivered by you...
12. Value of milk delivered by you ....$..............................
13. Total number of pounds of milk-fat represented in sale (when fat basis is used)...
14. Average per cent of milk-fat in milk ....per cent
15. Net value of one pound of milk-fat...cents

16 Average per cent of milk fat in milk delivered by you............................
17. Number of pounds of milk fat delivered by you................................
18. Value of milk-fat delivered by you...
19. Debtor by....................pounds of cheese at................cents per pound........
20. Money due you...
21. Number of pounds of cheese made from 100 pounds of milk.....................
22. Number of pounds of milk required to make one pound of cheese............
23. Number of pounds of cheese made for one pound of fat in milk................

BUSINESS MANAGEMENT OR ORGANIZA-
TION OF A CHEESE-FACTORY

The business management of a cheese-factory is generally carried on according to one of two systems; in one case the ownership of the factory is private, while, in the other, it is vested in a stock company.

In the case of private ownership of the cheese-factory, the owner receives a certain price per pound for making the cheese and is responsible for all expenses connected with the operations of cheese-making. The milk and cheese are regarded as the property of the patrons and they have some organized arrangement for selling the cheese and distributing the money. In some cases where the ownership of the factory is private, the milk is contracted for at a certain price and then the patrons have nothing to do with the business management.

When a cheese-factory is owned by a stock-company, the patrons are the stockholders. They form a definite organization and through chosen officers carry on the entire business management from the hiring of a cheese-maker to the sale of the cheese.

Preliminary steps in establishing a co-operative cheese-factory.—When a community is considering the question of organizing a stock-company for the purpose of building and running a cheese-factory, the first point to be ascertained is the number of cows which can be utilized as a source of milk supply. This information can be gained only by a careful personal canvass. In general, it may be said that no attempt should be made to establish a factory unless at least 150 cows within a radius of 3 or 4 miles can be relied upon to furnish milk. Dairymen should be on their guard against so-called factory "sharks," a name applied to representatives of supply houses who make a business of promoting co-operative factories and creameries. The promoter makes exaggerated representations of the profits of cheese-making for dairymen without reference to the number of available cows. When he is successful in persuading farmers to organize a company, he attends to the building and equipment, turning over the plant to the farmers at a price which nets him one to two thousand dollars. Before erecting a cheese-factory, inquiry for plans and cost should be made of the state department of agriculture or of the nearest agricultural college. In general, it will be found safe and profitable to have nothing whatever to do with any traveling agents.

Formation of a cheese-factory company or association.—After a successful canvass has been made and there have been obtained signed agreements to furnish milk from a certain number of cows, on the part of those who intend to join the association, a meeting should be called for organization. The money may be raised either by individual pledges to purchase a certain number of shares of stock at a certain price; or an elected board of directors may be authorized to borrow the amount of money needed, the debt being discharged by taking a fixed proportion from the dividends of the association members.

Articles of agreement or constitution and by-laws.—When it has been decided to form a cheese-factory association, it is necessary to prepare an agreement to be signed by all the members; this agreement embodies the details of organization, usually in the form of a constitution and by-laws. Different conditions will call for differences in the details of such an agreement. Suggestions can be given here, but they will need modification and adaptation to suit the conditions peculiar to each association.

(1) *Name and object.*—This association shall be known as the.....................Cheese-Factory Co-operative Company; its object is to manufacture cheese from normal (whole) milk. The undersigned agree to become members of said company.

(2) *Capital stock.*—The capital stock of the company shall be $..........., divided into............ shares of $...:.....each.

(3) *Officers.*—The officers of the company shall be a president, a secretary and a treasurer, and these, with three other members of the company, shall constitute a board of directors. These officers shall be elected by ballot at the annual meeting and shall hold office one year or until their successors have been elected and qualified. Vacancies in the board may be filled by the directors

for the time ensuing until the next annual election.

(4) *Duties of officers.*—(1) The president shall preside at all meetings of the company and of the board; in his absence, some other member of the board shall preside. He shall perform such other duties as may be indicated. All documents, drafts, etc., involving the interests of the company, shall be signed by the president. He shall call special meetings when necessary. (2) The secretary shall keep an accurate record of all proceedings of the meetings of the company and of the board. He shall issue notices of meetings, appointments on committees, statements to patrons, etc.; he shall sign all papers, carry on the correspondence, etc. (3) The treasurer shall receive and disburse the money of the company. He shall give receipt for all money belonging to the association. He shall make out dividends, etc. He shall pay out money only upon orders signed by the president and secretary. He shall keep a correct financial account between the company and its members. He shall keep a proper set of books, which shall be open for inspection to members of the company. He shall give bonds for $.........
(4) The board of directors shall elect one of their number as general business manager of the company, who shall be responsible for the conduct of the business details of the company. The board shall appoint any needed agents, manage the company's investments, audit all accounts and fix compensation for services in all cases. They shall make regulations and enforce them. They shall arrange for the keeping of a record of all necessary details;

such as weights of milk delivered daily by each member, fat-test of the same, the amounts of cheese made day by day, the sales of cheese, current expenses, etc. They shall distribute monthly among the members or patrons the money due them. They shall make a complete statement at the annual meeting covering for the year all' matters relating to the business of the company. Meetings of the board may be called by the president or by any two of its members.

(5) *Meetings.*—The regular annual meetings of the company shall be held on the first Tuesday of the month of........................ Special meetings may be called by the president or on written request of ten members of the company. Written notices for all special meetings must be sent to each member of the company three days in advance of such meeting. In addition to the election of officers and presentation of reports, the members shall decide by majority vote at the annual meeting in what manner the dividends shall be made (weight-of-milk, fat-basis, etc.).

(6) *Regulations.*—The following are samples of what regulations may be made: (a) The price for making cheese shall be..............cents a pound. (b) Members shall be held responsible for furnishing milk from the number of cows promised. (c) The cheese-maker may reject such milk as is tainted or of too high acidity or is any way unsuited to make high-grade cheese. (d) Milk must not be received unless it has been properly strained and delivered at the factory at a temperature not above...........degrees F. (e) The milk of each

patrons shall be tested for its percentage of fat not less often than once in 10 days. (f) A testing-committee consisting of the secretary or treasurer, one other director and one member not an officer shall assist the cheese-maker in testing the milk. (g) A patron's prēmises may be inspected by order of the board to ascertain the suitability of the conditions for producing and caring for clean milk. The board may order samples of milk taken at patron's farm when desired. (h) No patron shall, in any manner, adulterate milk to be taken to the factory, as by watering, skimming, addition of preservative, etc. No patron shall take more than......pounds of whey for 100 pounds of milk delivered.

(7) *Voting power.*—Members may, at all meetings of the company, be entitled to one vote for each 1,000 pounds of milk furnished by him during the preceding season or during the preceding portion of the current season, as shown by the records; or each may have one vote for each share of stock owned by him.

(8) *Amendments.*—Any changes or amendments to the constitution or by-laws may be made in writing and posted conspicuously in the cheese-factory one month previous to action upon them. Two-thirds vote of the stockholders is required to make such changes.

CHAPTER XXX

The Literature of Cheese-Making

It is desirable to give references to the literature of cheese-making for the benefit of those who wish to go to original sources of information. In preparing the list given below, the aim is mainly to cover the ground represented in the subject-matter of the book. A selection has been made of what may be regarded as the most useful material for this purpose, no attempt being made to present an exhaustive list of everything written on the subject.

In order to render the material most readily available for reference, the following plan is adopted: There is first given a continuously numbered list of the publications referred to; the arrangement is, first, by institutions and then under each the individual articles are given in chronological order. Then follows an index of the subjects treated in this list of publications. It is believed that this plan will prove the most useful in enabling anyone to consult the literature.

PUBLICATIONS RELATING TO CHEESE-MAKING

Cornell University Experiment Station, Ithaca, N. Y.

1   1st Ann. Rept. (1879-80). Experiments upon the curing of cheese (pp. 9-27). *Babcock.*

2   Bul. 85 (March, 1895). Whey-butter. *Wing.*

3   Bul. 158 (Jan., 1899). Sources of gas and taint-producing bacteria. *Moore and Ward.*

4   Bul. 178 (Jan., 1900). The invasion of the udder by bacteria. *Ward.*

5   Bul. 203 (July, 1902). The care and handling of milk. *Hunziker.*

Iowa Agricultural College Experiment Station, Ames, Iowa

6 Bul. 21 (1893). Investigations in cheese-making (pp. 751-767). *Wallace.*

7 Bul. 24 (1894). Changes during cheese-ripening (pp. 969-984). *Patrick.*

8 Bul. 57 (1901). Experiments in curing cheese. *McKay.*

Michigan State Agricultural College Experiment Station, East Lansing, Mich.

9 Special Bul. 16 (June, 1902). Aeration of milk. *Marshall.*

10 Special Bul. 21 (Sept., 1903). Cheese problems: (a) Relation of yield of cheese and per cent of fat in milk. (b) Paraffining cheese. (c) Cheddar vs. stirred curd. (d) Cheese-ripening as affected by temperature and moisture. (e) Sage cheese. (f) Gassy milk. *Michels.*

11 Special Bul. 23 (Jan., 1904). A preliminary note on the associative action of bacteria in the souring of milk and in other milk fermentations. *Marshall.*

12 Special Bul. 29 (May, 1904). Additional work upon the associative action of bacteria in the souring of milk and in other milk fermentations. *Marshall.*

13 Special Bul. 33 (June, 1905). Extended studies of the associative action of bacteria in the souring of milk. *Marshall.*

14 Special Bul. 42 (March, 1908). Bacterial associations in the souring of milk. *Marshall.*

15 Bul. 183 (June, 1900). Gassy curd and cheese. *Marshall.*

16 Bul. 201 (June, 1902). Aeration of milk. *Marshall.*

Minnesota Agricultural Experiment Station, St. Anthony Park, Minnesota

17 Bul. 19 (Jan., 1892). Experiments in cheese-making. Incorporating cream into cheese (pp. 20-25). *Snyder.*

18 Bul. 27 (Feb., 1893). Losses of milk-solids in cheese-making (pp. 57-62). *Snyder.*

19 Bul. 35 (Oct., 1894). Manufacture of sweet-curd cheese. *Haecker.*

New York Agricultural Experiment Station, Geneva, N. Y.

20 Bul. 37 (Nov., 1891) and 10th Ann. Rept. (pp. 220-299). Investigation of cheese: (a) Experiments in the manufacture of cheese. (b) Influence of composition of milk on composition and yield of cheese. (c) A study of the process of ripening of cheese. *Van Slyke.*

21 Bul. 43 (June, 1892). Experiments in the manufacture of cheese during May. *Van Slyke.*
22 Bul. 45 (Aug., 1892). Experiments in the manufacture of cheese during June. *Van Slyke.*
23 Bul. 46 (Sept., 1892). Experiments in the manufacture of cheese during July and August. *Van Slyke.*
24 Bul. 47 (Nov., 1892). Experiments in the manufacture of cheese during September and October. *Van Slyke.*
25 Bul. 50 (Jan.; 1893) and 11th Ann. Rept. (pp. 299-
467). Summary of the results of experiments made in the
manufacture of cheese during the season of 1892. *Van Slyke.*
26 Bul. 54 (May, 1893) and 12th Ann. Rept. (pp. 276-
319). Experiments in the manufacture of cheese: Part I
Manufacture of cheese from normal milk rich in fat. Part II,
Study of cheese-ripening process. *Van Slyke.*
27 Bul. 56 (May, 1893) and 12th Ann. Rept. (pp. 244-
275). Experiments in the manufacture of cheese: Part I,
The manufacture of Edam cheese. Part II, The manufacture
of Gouda cheese. *Van Slyke.*
28 Bul. 60 (Oct., 1893). Investigation relating to the
manufacture of cheese. Part I, Results of work done in the
No. 1 factory of E. L. Stone at Mannsville, Jefferson Co.,
during the season of 1893. *Van Slyke.*
29 Bul. 61 (Nov., 1893). Investigation relating to the
manufacture of cheese. Part II, Results of work done in the
factory of G. Merry at Verona, Oneida Co., N. Y., during the
season of 1893. *Van Slyke.*
30 Bul. 62 (Dec., 1893). Investigation relating to the
manufacture of cheese. Part III, Results of Work done
during the season of 1893 in 48 different factories, located
in 8 different counties. *Van Slyke.*
31 Bul. 65 (Jan., 1894) and 12th Ann. Rept. (pp. 319-
486). Investigation relating to the manufacture of cheese.
Part IV, Summary of the results of work done in cheese-
factories during the seasons of 1892-3. *Van Slyke.*
32 Bul. 68 (March, 1894). Investigation relating to
the manufacture of cheese. Part V, Fat in milk as a practical
basis for determining the value of milk for cheese-making.
Van Slyke.
33 Bul. 71 (May, 1894). Some reasons why there
should be a legal standard for cheese in New York state.
Van Slyke.
34 Bul. 79 (Nov., 1894) and 13th Ann. Rept. (pp. 351-
379). Comparison of different breeds of cattle. The cost of
cheese production. *Van Slyke.*

35 Bul. 82 (Dec., 1894) and 13th Ann. Rept. (pp. 452-522). Results of investigation relating to the manufacture of cheese for the season of 1894. *Van Slyke.*

36 Bul. 105 (Aug., 1896) and 15th Ann. Rept. (pp. 37-65). Effects of drouth upon milk and cheese production. *Van Slyke.*

37 Bul. 110 (Oct., 1896) and 15th Ann. Rept. (pp. 66-106). Milk-fat and cheese yield. *Van Slyke.*

38 Bul. 183 (Dec., 1900) and 19th Ann. Rept. (pp. 29-51). Notes on some dairy troubles: (*a*) Flavor in milk and its products. (*b*) Fishy flavor in milk. (*c*) Bitter flavor in Neufchatel cheese. (*d*) Sweet flavor in cheddar cheese. (*e*) Rusty spot in cheddar cheese. *Harding, Rogers and Smith.*

39 Bul. 184 (Dec., 1900) and 19th Ann. Rept. (pp. 251-260). The influence of the temperature of curing upon the commercial quality of cheese. *Smith.*

40 Bul. 203 (Dec., 1901) and 20th Ann. Rept. (pp. 165-193). A study of enzyms in cheese. *Van Slyke, Harding and Hart.*

41 Bul. 207 (Dec., 1901) and 20th Ann. Rept. (pp. 194-219). Conditions affecting weight lost by cheese in curing. *Van Slyke.*

42 Bul. 225 (Dec., 1902) and 21st Ann. Rept. (pp. 27-53). Control of rusty spot in cheese-factories. *Harding and Smith.*

43 Bul. 231 (Feb., 1903) and 22d Ann. Rept. (pp. 165-187). The relation of carbon dioxid to proteolysis in the ripening of cheddar cheese. *Van Slyke and Hart.*

44 Bul. 233 (June, 1903) and 22d Ann. Rept. (pp. 188-217). Rennet enzym as a factor in cheese-ripening. *Van Slyke, Harding and Hart.*

45 Bul. 234 (July, 1903) and 22d Ann. Rept. (pp. 218-242). Experiments in curing cheese at different temperatures. *Van Slyke, Smith and Hart.*

46 Bul. 236 (July, 1903) and 22d Ann. Rept. (pp. 243-273). Conditions affecting chemical changes in cheese-ripening. *Van Slyke and Hart.*

47 Bul. 261 (Jan., 1905) and 24th Ann. Rept. (pp. 238-271). Some of the relations of casein and paracasein to bases and acids and their application to cheddar cheese. *Van Slyke and Hart.*

48 Technical Bul. 3 (Dec., 1906) and 25th Ann. Rept. (pp. 203-286). I, The action of dilute acids upon casein when no soluble compounds are formed. II, The hydrolysis of the sodium salts of casein. *Van Slyke (L. L.) and Van Slyke (D. D.).*

49 Technical Bul. 4 (April, 1907). I, Some of the first chemical changes in cheddar cheese. II, The acidity of the water-extract of cheddar cheese. *Van Slyke and Bosworth.*
50 Technical Bul. 6 (Dec., 1907). Chloroform as an aid in the study of milk-enzyms. *Harding and Van Slyke.*

Oregon Agricultural Experiment Station, Cornwallis, Ore.

51 Bul. 78 (March, 1904). Canning cheese. *Pernot.*

U. S. Department of Agriculture, Bureau of Animal Industry, Dairy Division, Washington, D. C.

52 Bul. 11 (Nov., 1895) and 55 (Feb., 1903). Statistics of the dairy. *Alvord.*
53 Bul. 15 (Oct., 1896). The cheese industry of the state of New York. *Gilbert.*
54 Bul. 17 (Nov., 1896). Dairy schools. *Pearson.*
55 Bul. 49 (June, 1903). The cold-curing of cheese. Report upon experiments conducted under the auspices of the U. S. Department of Agriculture, Bureau of Animal Industry, Dairy Division, in co-operation with the Wisconsin Agricultural Experiment Station and the New York Agricultural Experiment Station. *Alvord.*
56 Bul. 62 (July, 1904). The relation of bacteria to the flavors of cheddar cheese. *Rogers.*
57 Bul. 75 (Sept., 1905). Records of dairy cows in the United States. *Lane.*
58 Bul. 83 (March, 1906). The cold storage of cheese. *Lane.*
59 Bul. 85 (May, 1906). The cold-curing of American cheese. *Doane.*
60 Bul. 105 (Jan., 1908). Varieties of cheese: descriptions and analyses. *Doane and Lawson.*
61 Bul. 110 (Nov. 1908). Development of lactic acid in cheddar cheese-making. *Doane.*

Utah Agricultural Experiment Station, Logan, Utah

62 Bul. 73 (Aug., 1901). Experiments in cheese-making (pp. 41-54). *Linfield.*
63 Bul. 96 (March, 1906). Canning cheese. Paraffining cheese (pp. 128-132). *Clark and Crockett.*

Vermont Agricultural Experiment Station, Burlington, Vt.

64 5th Ann. Rept. (1891). (*a*) Making cheese from different qualities of milk (pp. 88-95). (*b*) Losses in cheese-making (pp. 95-100). *Cooke and Hills.*

Wisconsin Agricultural Experiment Station, Madison, Wis.

65 8th Ann. Rept. (1891).   The feeding value of whey (pp. 38-48). *Henry.*

66 11th Ann. Rept. (1894). (*a*) Influence of fat upon yield of cheese (pp. 131-134). (*b*) Influence of fat on quality of cheese (pp. 134-137). (*c*) Yield of cheese in factories from different qualities of milk and at different seasons (pp. 137-144). (*d*) Loss in curing cheese (pp. 145-146). (*e*) Cleaning milk with a centrifugal cream-separator for cheese production (pp. 146-149). *Babcock.*

(*f*) Sources of bacterial contamination of milk (pp. 150-165). *Russell.*

(*g*) Effect of salt upon cheese (pp. 220-222). *Decker.*

67 12th Ann. Rept. (1895). (*a*) The centrifugal separation of casein and insoluble phosphates from milk (pp. 93-99). (*b*) Relation between yields of milk-solids and cheese (pp. 100-120). (*c*) Relation between specific gravity and solids of milk (pp. 120-126). (*d*) Hot iron test (pp. 133-134). (*e*) Albumen cheese (pp. 134-136). *Babcock.*

(*f*) Effect of aeration on flavor of tainted curds in cheese-making (pp. 127-129). (*g*) Gas-producing bacteria and their relation to cheese (pp. 139-150). *Russell.*

(*h*) Influence of acid on texture of cheese (pp. 129-133). *Russell and Decker.*

(*i*) Ripening milk before setting (pp. 136-138). *Decker.*

68 13th Ann. Rept. (1896). (*a*) Rise and fall of bacteria in cheddar cheese (pp. 95-111). (*b*) Pure lactic acid cultures in cheese-making (pp. 112-126). *Russell.*

(*c*) Moisture supply in cheese-curing rooms (pp. 156-163). *Decker.*

69 14th Ann. Rept. (1897). (*a*) Unorganized ferments of milk: a new factor in the ripening of cheese (pp. 161-193). (*b*) Influence of temperature on the ripening of cheese (pp. 194-210). *Babcock and Russell.*

70 Bul. 60 (May, 1897). The cheese industry: its development and possibilities in Wisconsin. *Babcock and Russell.*

71 Bul. 61 (Sept., 1897). The constitution of milk with especial reference to cheese-production. *Babcock.*

72 Bul. 62 (Sept., 1897). Tainted or defective milks. Their causes and methods of prevention. *Russell.*

73 15th Ann. Rept. (1898). (*a*) Effect of varying strengths of rennet in curdling milk (pp. 31-34). (*b*) Action of rennet in watered milk (pp. 35-36). (*c*) Action of common salt on rennet action (pp. 37-41). (*d*) Methods of handling sour milk in making cheese (pp. 42-44). *Decker* (*e*) Improved curd test for detection of tainted milks (pp. 45-53). *Babcock, Russell and Decker.*

(*f*) Properties of galactase, a digestive ferment of milk (pp. 77-87). (*g*) Distribution of galactase in cow's milk (pp. 87-92). *Babcock, Russell and Vivian.*

(*h*) Relative absorption of odors in warm and cold milk (pp. 104-109). *Russell.*

74 16th Ann. Rept. (1899). (*a*) Coating cheese with paraffin (pp. 153-155). *Decker.*

(*b*) Action of proteolytic ferments on milk with special reference to galactase, the cheese-ripening enzym (pp. 155-174). *Babcock, Russell and Vivian.*

(*c*) Effect of digesting bacteria on cheese-solids (pp. 187-193). *Russell and Bassett.*

75 17th Ann. Rept. (1900). Influence of rennet on cheese-ripening (pp. 102-122). *Babcock, Russell and Vivian.*

76 18th Ann. Rept. (1901). (*a*) Print cheese (pp. 132-135). *Farrington.*

(*b*) Influence of cold-curing on quality of cheese (pp. 136-161). *Babcock, Russell, Vivian and Baer.*

(*c*) Influence of sugar on nature of fermentation in milk and cheese (pp. 162-176). *Babcock, Russell, Vivian and Hastings.*

77 19th Ann. Rept. (1902). (*a*) Influence of cold-curing on quality of cheddar cheese (pp. 150-164). (*b*) Influence of temperature approaching 60°F. on development of flavor in cold-cured cheese (pp. 165-173). (*c*) Influence of varying quantities of rennet on cold-cured cheese (pp. 174-179). (*d*) Conditions affecting development of white specks in cold-cured cheese (180-184). *Babcock, Russell, Vivian and Baer.*

78 Bul. 94 (Aug., 1902). Curing of cheddar cheese with reference to cold-curing. Consolidated cheese-curing stations. *Babcock and Russell.*

79 Bul. 101 (July, 1903). Shrinkage of cold-cured cheese during ripening. Experiments in paraffining cheese. *Babcock, Russell and Baer.*

80 21st Ann. Rept. (1904). (*a*) Relation of flavor development in cold-cured cheddar cheese to bacterial life in same (pp. 155-163). *Russell and Hastings.*

81 Bul. 115 (Sept., 1904). The quality of cheese as affected by rape and other green forage plants fed to dairy cows. *Baer and Carlyle.*

82 22d Ann. Rept. (1905). (*a*) The Swiss cheese industry of Wisconsin; whey butter-making (pp. 157-180). *Farrington.*

(*b*) Lactose-fermenting yeasts, the cause of abnormal fermentation in Swiss cheese (pp. 207-221). *Hastings.*

83 Bul. 128 (Sept., 1905). A Swiss cheese trouble caused by a gas-forming yeast. *Russell and Hastings.*

84 Bul. 132 (Dec., 1905). The manufacture of whey-butter at cheese-factories. *Farrington.*

85 23d Ann. Rept. (1906). (*a*) Development of factory dairying in Wisconsin (pp. 100-106). *Russell and Baer.*

(*b*) Distribution of lactose-fermenting yeasts in dairy products (pp. 107-115). *Hastings.*

86 24th Ann. Rept. (1907). (*a*) Influence of metals on the action of rennet (pp. 134-159). *Olson.*

(*b*) Analyses of old cheese, skim-milk cheese, etc. (pp. 160-170). *Woll and Olson.*

87 Bul. 162 (April, 1908). Rusty cans and their effect upon milk for cheese-making. *Olson.*

Dominion of Canada Dairy Commission, Department of Agriculture, Ottawa, Can.

88 2d Ann. Rept. (1891-2). Experimental cheese-making (pp. 146-153). *Robertson and Ruddick.*

89 3d Ann. Rept. (1892-3). Experiments in cheese-making (pp. 214-219). *Robertson and Ruddick.*

90 Rept. Conference Dairy Instructors and Experts (1903). The cool-curing of cheese (pp. 96-110). *Ruddick.*

91 Rept. of Dairy Com'r (1906). (*a*) Cool-cured cheese (pp. 8-9). (*b*) Management of a cool curing-room (pp. 13-14). (*c*) Coating cheese with paraffin (pp. 14-15). *Ruddick.*

92 Rept. of Dairy Com'r (1907). (a) The cheese industry (pp. 8-17). (*b*) Cool-cured cheese (pp. 17-18). *Ruddick.*

Ontario Agricultural College, Guelph, Ontario, Canada

93 Buls. 95 and 96 (1894) and 20th Ann. Rept. (1894). (*a*) The composition of milk, whey and cheese in relation to one another (pp. 20-33). *Shuttleworth.*

(*b*) Experiments in cheese-making (pp. 134-141). *Dean.*

94 Bul. 102 (May, 1896) and 22d Ann. Rept. (1896), (pp. 41-56). Experiments in cheese-making. *Dean.*

95 23d Ann. Rept. (1897). (*a*) Experiments in cheese-making (pp. 41-59). *Dean.*

(*b*) Bad flavor in cheese caused by undesirable bacteria in water used in factory (pp. 141-144). *Harrison.*

96 24th Ann. Rept. (1898). Experiments in cheese-making (pp. 40-64). *Dean.*

97 25th Ann. Rept (1899) Experiments in cheese-making (pp. 54-65). *Dean.*

98 26th Ann. Rept. (1900). Experiments in cheese-making (pp. 37-44). *Dean.*

99 27th Ann. Rept. (1901). Experiments in cheese-making (pp. 44-55). *Dean.*

100 28th Ann. Rept. (1902). (*a*) Experiments in cheese-making (pp. 64-68). *Dean.*

(*b*) Investigations regarding the ripening of cheese (pp. 40-41). *Harcourt.*

101 Bul. 120 (May, 1902). Bitter milk and cheese. *Harrison.*

102 Bul. 121 (June, 1902). Ripening of cheese in cold storage compared with ripening in ordinary curing-rooms. *Dean, Harrison and Harcourt.*

103 29th Ann. Rept. (1903). Experiments in cheese-making (pp. 60-76). *Dean.*

104 Bul. 130 (Dec., 1903). Bacterial contents of cheese cured at different temperatures. *Harrison and Connell.*

105 Bul. 131 (Dec., 1903). Ripening of cheese in cold-storage versus ordinary curing-rooms. *Dean and Harcourt.*

106 30th Ann. Rept. (1904). Experiments in cheese-making (pp. 74-81). *Dean.*

107 31st Ann. Rept. (1905). Experiments in cheese-making (pp. 115-126). *Dean.*

108 Bul. 141 (April, 1905). Gas-producing bacteria and their effect on milk and its products. *Harrison.*

109 32d Ann. Rept. (1906). Experiments in cheese-making (pp. 108-119). *Dean.*

Index to Literature of Cheese-Making

The reference numbers below indicate the serial numbers (in heavy type) in the preceding list of publications, which go from 1 to 109.

Index

STANDARD BOOKS

PUBLISHED BY

ORANGE JUDD COMPANY

NEW YORK	CHICAGO
439-441 Lafayette Street	*Marquette Building*

---

*B*OOKS *sent to all parts of the world for catalog price. Discounts for large quantities on application. Correspondence invited. Brief descriptive catalog free. Large illustrated catalog, six cents.*

Soils

By CHARLES WILLIAM BURKETT, Director Kansas Agricultural Experiment Station. The most complete and popular work of the kind ever published. As a rule, a book of this sort is dry and uninteresting, but in this case it reads like a novel. The author has put into it his individuality. The story of the properties of the soils, their improvement and management, as well as a discussion of the problems of crop growing and crop feeding, make this book equally valuable to the farmer, student and teacher.

There are many illustrations of a practical character, each one suggesting some fundamental principle in soil management. 303 pages. 5½ x 8 inches. Cloth. . . . . . $1.25.

Insects Injurious to Vegetables

By Dr. F. H. CHITTENDEN, of the United States Department of Agriculture. A complete, practical work giving descriptions of the more important insects attacking vegetables of all kinds with simple and inexpensive remedies to check and destroy them, together with timely suggestions to prevent their recurrence. A ready reference book for truckers, market-gardeners, farmers as well as others who grow vegetables in a small way for home use; a valuable guide for college and experiment station workers, school-teachers and others interested in entomology of nature study. Profusely illustrated. 5½ x 8 inches. 300 pages. Cloth. $1.50

The Cereals in America

By Thomas F. Hunt, M.S., D.Agri., Professor of Agronomy, Cornell University. If you raise five acres of any kind of grain you cannot afford to be without this book. It is in every way the best book on the subject that has ever been written. It treats of the cultivation and improvement of every grain crop raised in America in a thoroughly practical and accurate manner. The subject-matter includes a comprehensive and succinct treatise of wheat, maize, oats, barley, rye, rice, sorghum (kafir corn) and buckwheat, as related particularly to American conditions. First-hand knowledge has been the policy of the author in his work, and every crop treated is presented in the light of individual study of the plant. If you have this book you have the latest and best that has been written upon the subject. Illustrated. 450 pages. 5½ x 8 inches. Cloth. $1.75

The Forage and Fiber Crops in America

By Thomas F. Hunt. This book is exactly what its title indicates. It is indispensable to the farmer, student and teacher who wishes all the latest and most important information on the subject of forage and fiber crops. Like its famous companion, "The Cereals in America," by the same author, it treats of the cultivation and improvement of every one of the forage and fiber crops. With this book in hand, you have the latest and most up-to-date information available. Illustrated. 428 pages. 5½ x 8 inches. Cloth. $1.75

The Book of Alfalfa

History, Cultivation and Merits. Its Uses as a Forage and Fertilizer. The appearance of the Hon. F. D. Coburn's little book on Alfalfa a few years ago has been a profit revelation to thousands of farmers throughout the country, and the increasing demand for still more information on the subject has induced the author to prepare the present volume, which is by far the most authoritative, complete and valuable work on this forage crop published anywhere. It is printed on fine paper and illustrated with many full-page photographs that were taken with the especial view of their relation to the text. 336 pages. 6½ x 9 inches. Bound in cloth, with gold stamping. It is unquestionably the handsomest agricultural reference book that has ever been issued. Price, postpaid . . . $2.00

Clean Milk

By S. D. Belcher, M.D. In this book the author sets forth practical methods for the exclusion of bacteria from milk, and how to prevent contamination of milk from the stable to the consumer. Illustrated. 5 x 7 inches. 146 pages. Cloth. $1.00

Feeding Farm Animals

By Professor THOMAS SHAW. This book is intended alike
for the student and the farmer. The author has succeeded in
giving in regular and orderly sequence, and in language so
simple that a child can understand it, the principles that govern
the science and practice of feeding farm animals. Professor
Shaw is certainly to be congratulated on the successful manner
in which he has accomplished a most difficult task. His book
is unquestionably the most practical work which has appeared
on the subject of feeding farm animals. Illustrated. 5½ x 8
inches. Upward of 500 pages. Cloth. $2.00

Profitable Dairying

By C. L. Peck. A practical guide to successful dairy management. The treatment of the entire subject is thoroughly
practical, being principally a description of the methods practiced by the author. A specially valuable part of this book
consists of a minute description of the far-famed model dairy
farm of Rev. J. D. Detrich, near Philadelphia, Pa. On this
farm of fifteen acres, which twenty years ago could not maintain one horse and two cows, there are now kept twenty-seven
dairy cattle, in addition to two horses. All the roughage,
litter, bedding, etc., necessary for these animals are grown on
these fifteen acres, more than most farmers could accomplish
on one hundred acres. Illustrated. 5 x 7 inches. 200 pages.
Cloth. $0.75

Practical Dairy Bacteriology

By Dr. H. W. CONN, of Wesleyan University. A complete
exposition of important facts concerning the relation of bacteria
to various problems related to milk. A book for the classroom, laboratory, factory and farm. Equally useful to the
teacher, student, factory man and practical dairyman. Fully
illustrated with 83 original pictures. 340 pages. Cloth.
5½ x 8 inches. $1.25

Modern Methods of Testing Milk and Milk Products

By L. L. VANSLYKE. This is a clear and concise discussion
of the approved methods of testing milk and milk products.
All the questions involved in the various methods of testing
milk and cream are handled with rare skill and yet in so plain
a manner that they can be fully understood by all. The book
should be in the hands of every dairyman, teacher or student.
Illustrated. 214 pages. 5 x 7 inches. $0.75

Animal Breeding

By THOMAS SHAW. This book is the most complete and comprehensive work ever published on the subject of which it treats. It is the first book which has systematized the subject of animal breeding. The leading laws which govern this most intricate question the author has boldly defined and authoritatively arranged. The chapters which he has written on the more involved features of the subject, as sex and the relative influence of parents, should go far toward setting at rest the wildly speculative views cherished with reference to these questions. The striking originality in the treatment of the subject is no less conspicuous than the superb order and regular sequence of thought from the beginning to the end of the book. The book is intended to meet the needs of all persons interested in the breeding and rearing of live stock. Illustrated. 405 pages. 5 x 7 inches. Cloth. . . $1.50

Forage Crops Other Than Grasses

By THOMAS SHAW. How to cultivate, harvest and use them. Indian corn, sorghum, clover, leguminous plants, crops of the brassica genus, the cereals, millet, field roots, etc. Intensely practical and reliable. Illustrated. 287 pages. 5 x 7 inches. Cloth. $1.00

Soiling Crops and the Silo

By THOMAS SHAW. The growing and feeding of all kinds of soiling crops, conditions to which they are adapted, their plan in the rotation, etc. Not a line is repeated from the Forage Crops book. Best methods of building the silo, filling it and feeding ensilage. Illustrated. 364 pages. 5 x 7 inches. Cloth. $1.50

The Study of Breeds

By THOMAS SHAW. Origin, history, distribution, characteristics, adaptability, uses, and standards of excellence of all pedigreed breeds of cattle, sheep and swine in America. The accepted text book in colleges, and the authority for farmers and breeders. Illustrated. 371 pages. 5 x 7 inches. Cloth. $1.50

Clovers and How to Grow Them

By THOMAS SHAW. This is the first book published which treats on the growth, cultivation and treatment of clovers as applicable to all parts of the United States and Canada, and which takes up the entire subject in a systematic way and consecutive sequence. The importance of clover in the economy of the farm is so great that an exhaustive work on this subject will no doubt be welcomed by students in agriculture, as well as by all who are interested in the tilling of the soil. Illustrated. 5 x 7 inches. 337 pages. Cloth. Net . . .$1.00

The New Egg Farm

By H. H. STODDARD. A practical, reliable manual on producing eggs and poultry for market as a profitable business enterprise, either by itself or connected with other branches of agriculture. It tells all about how to feed and manage, how to breed and select, incubators and brooders, its labor-saving devices, etc., etc. Illustrated. 331 pages. 5 x 7 inches. Cloth. $1.00

Poultry Feeding and Fattening

Compiled by G. B. FISKE. A handbook for poultry keepers on the standard and improved methods of feeding and marketing all kinds of poultry. The subject of feeding and fattening poultry is prepared largely from the side of the best practice and experience here and abroad, although the underlying science of feeding is explained as fully as needful. The subject covers all branches, including chickens, broilers, capons, turkeys and waterfowl; how to feed under various conditions and for different purposes. The whole subject of capons and caponizing is treated in detail. A great mass of practical information and experience not readily obtainable elsewhere is given with full and explicit directions for fattening and preparing for market. This book will meet the needs of amateurs as well as commercial poultry raisers. Profusely illustrated. 160 pages. 5 x 7 1-2 inches. Cloth. . $0.50

Poultry Architecture

Compiled by G. B. FISKE. A treatise on poultry buildings of all grades, styles and classes, and their proper location, coops, additions and special construction; all practical in design, and reasonable in cost. Over 100 illustrations. 125 pages. 5 x 7 inches. Cloth. $0.50

Poultry Appliances and Handicraft

Compiled by G. B. FISKE. Illustrated descriptions of a great variety and styles of the best homemade nests, roosts, windows, ventilators, incubators and brooders, feeding and watering appliances, etc., etc. Over 100 illustrations. Over 125 pages. 5 x 7 inches. Cloth. $0.50

Turkeys and How to Grow Them

Edited by HERBERT MYRICK. A treatise on the natural history and origin of the name of turkeys; the various breeds, the best methods to insure success in the business of turkey growing. With essays from practical turkey growers in different parts of the United States and Canada. Copiously illustrated. 154 pages. 5 x 7 inches. Cloth . . . $1.00

Bean Culture

By GLENN C. SEVEY, B.S. A practical treatise on the production and marketing of beans. It includes the manner of growth, soils and fertilizers adapted, best varieties, seed selection and breeding, planting, harvesting, insects and fungous pests, composition and feeding value; with a special chapter on markets by Albert W. Fulton. A practical book for the grower and student alike. Illustrated. 144 pages. 5 x 7 inches. Cloth. $0.50

Celery Culture

By W. R. BEATTIE. A practical guide for beginners and a standard reference of great interest to persons already engaged in celery growing. It contains many illustrations giving a clear conception of the practical side of celery culture. The work is complete in every detail, from sowing a few seeds in a window-box in the house for early plants, to the handling and marketing of celery in carload lots. Fully illustrated. 150 pages. 5 x 7 inches. Cloth. $0.50

Tomato Culture

By WILL W. TRACY. The author has rounded up in this book the most complete account of tomato culture in all its phases that has ever been gotten together. It is no second-hand work of reference, but a complete story of the practical experiences of the best posted expert on tomatoes in the world. No gardener or farmer can afford to be without the book. Whether grown for home use or commercial purposes, the reader has here suggestions and information nowhere else available. Illustrated. 150 pages. 5 x 7 inches. Cloth. $0.50

The Potato

By SAMUEL FRASER. This book is destined to rank as a standard work upon Potato Culture. While the practical side has been emphasized, the scientific part has not been neglected, and the information given is of value, both to the grower and the student. Taken all in all, it is the most complete, reliable and authoritative book on the potato ever published in America. Illustrated. 200 pages. 5 x 7 inches. Cloth. $0.75

Dwarf Fruit Trees

By F. A. WAUGH. This interesting book describes in detail the several varieties of dwarf fruit trees, their propagation, planting, pruning, care and general management. Where there is a limited amount of ground to be devoted to orchard purposes, and where quick results are desired, this book will meet with a warm welcome. Illustrated. 112 pages. 5 x 7 inches. Cloth. $0.50

Farm Grasses of the United States of America

By WILLIAM JASPER SPILLMAN. A practical treatise on the grass crop, seeding and management of meadows and pastures, description of the best varieties, the seed and its impurities, grasses · for special conditions, lawns and lawn grasses, etc., etc. In preparing this volume the author's object has been to present, in connected form, the main facts concerning the grasses grown on American farms. Every phase of the subject is viewed from the farmer's standpoint. Illustrated. 248 pages. 5 x 7 inches. Cloth. . . . $1.00

The Book of Corn

By HERBERT MYRICK, assisted by A. D. SHAMEL, E. A. BURNETT, ALBERT W. FULTON, B. W. SNOW, and other most capable specialists. A complete treatise on the culture, marketing and uses of maize in America and elsewhere, for farmers, dealers and others. Illustrated. 372 pages. 5 x 7 inches. Cloth. $1.50

The Hop — Its Culture and Care, Marketing and Manufacture

By HERBERT MYRICK. A practical handbook on the most approved methods in growing, harvesting, curing and selling hops, and on the use and manufacture of hops. The result of years of research and observation, it is a volume destined to be an authority on this crop for many years to come. It takes up every detail from preparing the soil and laying out the yard, to curing and selling the crop. Every line represents the ripest judgment and experience of experts. Size, 5 x 8; pages, 300; illustrations, nearly 150; bound in cloth and gold; price, postpaid, ... $1.50

Tobacco Leaf

By J. B. KILLEBREW and HERBERT MYRICK. Its Culture and Cure, Marketing and Manufacture. A practical handbook on the most approved methods in growing, harvesting, curing, packing and selling tobacco, with an account of the operations in every department of tobacco manufacture. The contents of this book are based on actual experiments in field, curing barn, packing house, factory and laboratory. It is the only work of the kind in existence, and is destined to be the standard practical and scientific authority on the whole subject of tobacco for many years. 506 pages and 150 original engravings. 5 x 7 inches. Cloth. $2.00

Farmer's Cyclopedia of Agriculture

*A Compendium of Agricultural Science and Practice
on Farm, Orchard and Garden Crops, and the
Feeding and Diseases of Farm Animals* : : : :

By EARLEY VERNON WILCOX, Ph.D.
and CLARENCE BEAMAN SMITH, M.S

*Associate Editors in the Office of Experiment Stations, United States
Department of Agriculture*

THIS is a new, practical, and complete presentation of the whole subject of agriculture in its broadest sense. It is designed for the use of agriculturists who desire up-to-date, reliable information on all matters pertaining to crops and stock, but more particularly for the actual farmer. The volume contains

Detailed directions for the culture of every

important field, orchard, and garden crop

grown in America, together with descriptions of their chief insect pests and fungous diseases, and remedies for their control. It contains an account of modern methods in feeding and handling all farm stock, including poultry. The diseases which affect different farm animals and poultry are described, and the most recent remedies suggested for controlling them.

Every bit of this vast mass of new and useful information is authoritative, practical, and easily found, and no effort has been spared to include all desirable details. There are between 6,000 and 7,000 topics covered in these references, and it contains 700 royal 8vo pages and nearly 500 suberb half-tone and other original illustrations, making the most perfect Cyclopedia of Agriculture ever attempted.

*Handsomely bound in cloth, $3.50; half morocco
(very sumptuous), $4.50, postpaid*

Printed in the USA
CPSIA information can be obtained
at www.ICGtesting.com
LVHW042155281024
795074LV00034B/216